OVERKILL
OR
UNDER-KILL

OVERKILL
OR
UNDER-KILL

A review of Anglo/Iraqi Relations 1961–91

Anthony Paice

The Book Guild Ltd

First published in Great Britain in 2023 by
The Book Guild Ltd
Unit E2 Airfield Business Park,
Harrison Road, Market Harborough,
Leicestershire. LE16 7UL
Tel: 0116 2792299
www.bookguild.co.uk
Email: info@bookguild.co.uk
Twitter: @bookguild

Typeset in 11pt Adobe Jenson Pro

Printed and bound by CPI Group (UK) Ltd, Croydon, CR0 4YY

ISBN 978 1915352 439

British Library Cataloguing in Publication Data.
A catalogue record for this book is available from the British Library.

MIX
Paper | Supporting responsible forestry
FSC® C013604
FSC
www.fsc.org

To all those who suffered from Saddam's cruelty, particularly the Kuwaiti hostages who were abandoned by the world and others who received no compensation for their suffering.

Anthony Paice

CONTENTS

ACKNOWLEDGEMENTS

It is not possible for me to list all those friends and colleagues who have supported and trusted in me for well over thirty years. During this time I have had to endure false and misplaced allegations against my conduct in August 1990. These caused both anger and depression which my family had to tolerate. First thanks, therefore, go to my late wife, Chris, who bore the brunt of my sometimes difficult behaviour.

This book, however, would never have been completed but for the sterling support of my present wife, Anne, who having heard accounts of the Iraqi invasion of Kuwait, chose to believe me and to insist that the truth deserved to be told. There are also several colleagues who have helped me greatly during the preparation of *Overkill or Under-kill*. With absolutely no wish to undervalue their encouragement, but out of respect for their personal security, I will not name them; they know who they are. Nevertheless, I can express my appreciation for the proof-reading undertaken by another special lady, Mary Bentley.

I consider that I should single out Sir Harold (Hooky) Walker, British ambassador in Baghdad in 1990, who took pains to go through my draft text line by line and whose comments helped enormously.

In the last year or so, I have also received the backing of those who suffered the plight of just being passengers and crew on board BA149. Of those, I would like to mention Clive Earthy, chief purser on the flight who saw first-hand what was going on. I must then add my good friend, Stephen Davis, who like many others in the media, got the wrong end of the stick, but unlike others, tracked the truth to its lair and exposed a long-running cover-up.

I am also grateful to my indexer, Rob Gibson, for his timely and most helpful assistance.

Anthony Paice
December 2022

FOREWORD

My first encounter with Tony Paice began with a complaint. It was an inauspicious start to what would later become a treasured friendship.

I was writing a book, Operation Trojan Horse, about a planeload of passengers and crew on a British Airways flight which landed in Kuwait as Saddam Hussein's Iraqi army invaded in August 1990. There was a mystery about why the flight had landed and in the course of investigating the story for three decades I had written and broadcast stories which featured one Anthony Paice of the Foreign Office.

Tony, I stated, had been based at the British embassy in Kuwait in August 1990 and had briefed British Airways that it was safe to fly to Kuwait, despite the fact that an Iraqi army was gathered on the border and that Saddam had threatened for months to invade. The passengers and crew of BA149 were captured and used as human shields. Many suffered terribly.

It seemed as if Tony had got it wrong and as I had a sworn affidavit from British Airways staff stating he said it was safe to fly, I was confident that my report was accurate.

Through a mutual acquaintance, Tony reached out to Clive Earthy, the Flight 149 chief purser and a meeting was arranged at a pub near Clive's home in Winchester, Hampshire.

Tony, who was about to get married, told Earthy he was writing this book and that 'the shit was about to hit the fan.'

Tony said his role in the affair had been misrepresented and that what I had previously reported – that he had advised British Airways that it was safe to fly – was wrong. He was angry about the way he had been blamed and he intended to get the truth out. Then he stunned Earthy by talking about a secret mission involving BA149 that the British government had denied for three decades.

Clive Earthy made the introductions and Tony and I started a correspondence, which began like this:

Dear Stephen Davis,

From the little I know, it [my reporting] would appear to be a little wide of the mark, certainly as far as my role/action and my embassy's part in the matter were concerned. I have had to put up with repeated inaccurate allegations, lies and halftruths for over thirty years now and firmly believe that it is high time that history was owed the facts. As Clive Earthy may have told you, I have a completed book ready for publication which not only vindicates me and my embassy colleagues, but points the finger away from my old employers and shows that there were assessment failures in London and Washington, but no intelligence failure on the ground. I make it clear why Flight 149 flew that night and that the Kuwait embassy— – not least myself – were totally unaware of the so-called deniable special operation involved. My book is now being vetted and I have an important meeting on 25 August to discuss the way forward. There are circles in London that will be found with egg on their faces when my account comes out. I am happy to talk after the meeting, but am not interested in a further half-baked rendition of what happened on 1/2 August 1990. On the contrary, I will have some tough questions.

I replied saying I welcomed tough questions and was happy to correct any mistakes.

A few exchanges later, Tony replied:

Many thanks. For your information, my exact words to O'Toole [the British Airways manager] early evening on 1 August 1990 were: 'If you have a plane going through at midnight, that will probably get through. But any Iraqi invasion will be in the early hours, so don't bank on anything same time tomorrow.' I don't think anyone could have given a closer steer. My ambassador said something similar. What O'Toole did with our advice, I am unable to say, but he went home; I did not.
Apologies accepted!

Kind regards,
Anthony Paice

That generosity was typical of the man I later got to know.

Tony had retired after a long and successful career. He read history and war studies at King's College, London, before working for the Liberal Party and on a BBC series, then joining the Foreign and Commonwealth Office, where he had held a number of key roles and developed considerable expertise in the history and politics of the Middle East.

After further research, I realised his complaint was justified. He had stayed behind after the invasion; he and the ambassador, Michael Weston, had shown a great deal of courage in holding the fort. Tony did not leave until he had helped get a large convoy of Westerners out of Kuwait and into Jordan via Iraq.

He was clearly a man who felt, with much justification, that his actions had been misrepresented by history.

We continued to talk and in August 2021, he attended a press conference of the human shields in London alongside me as I launched my book.

He challenged the official version of events and raised serious questions about the misuse of intelligence in the lead-up to the Gulf War.

For a man who had spent a career working for Her Majesty's Government, and who had signed the Official Secrets Act, it was an act of extraordinary courage.

He did it out of a desire to correct the historical record and out of empathy for the suffering of the human shields.

These are qualities he brings to this important book. Here is a man who was a true insider, an eye witness to some of the most important events in the Middle East, with an historian's rigour and an outsider's willingness to challenge conventional wisdom.

As an investigator reporter, I have always believed in the famous quote that the best journalism is the first rough draft of history.

Tony has written a book that is not just a rough draft but history written by a man who was there.

Stephen Davis
2022

One

A DISTANT OMEN

Police Lieutenant Yusuf Al-Khorafi deployed his platoon and supporting water bearers amongst the tents and awnings hastily thrown up as makeshift protection from the merciless midday sun. Flaps drawn back revealed small groups of red-faced Tommies, some with exposed and sun-burnt torsos; several too exhausted to move and waiting to be stretchered away to hospital. As the Kuwaiti policemen passed among the British casualties to nature's extreme, they received murmurs of thanks from parched throats and groans of appreciation as bared heads and bodies were tended with salve-soaked cloths. Outside, medics brought in more victims from the hurriedly prepared dug-outs forming a defensive line in the sand along the northern border with Iraq.

It was Monday 3 July 1961 and the men of 24 Infantry Brigade under the command of Brigadier DGT Horsford[1] had landed only hours before from the light aircraft carrier HMS *Bulwark* that had departed from Karachi the previous Thursday. The urgency of the troops' deployment had been underlined by their commanding officer's remark to the press that he believed an Iraqi invasion of the Kuwaiti Emirate was to be expected. One more end of Empire scrap in which Tommy Atkins was at hazard, at least in the eyes of many sitting on the opposition benches at Westminster.

Why the emergency? It was a question increasingly asked in political circles at the time, even though there was a natural wish to help the underdog and, of course, to support British forces in the field. After all, the first six months of 1961 had produced peaceful portents. Following months of tension, in April Iran and Iraq had settled their differences over navigation rights in the Shatt al-Arab waterway, crucial to tanker-borne oil supplies to the West. Then, on 11 May, the charismatic American president, John F Kennedy, addressed the other major sore in the Middle East: he wrote to principal players in the region – Nasser of Egypt, Chehab of Lebanon, King Saud of Saudi Arabia and Brigadier Abd al-Karim Qassim of Iraq – offering his good offices in helping to eliminate Arab/Israeli tensions. After amicable negotiations, too, the UK had agreed to end Kuwait's status as a British-protected state;[2] the Emirate's full sovereignty was confirmed in an exchange of letters on 19 June between the two countries.

Before any international crisis, however sudden, there are always straws in the wind. Baghdad was already flexing its muscles early in the year by referring to the traditionally named Persian Gulf as the Gulf of Arabia. As a usurper only three years in power, Brigadier Qassim was facing mounting problems at home. The Kurds were once again rebelling in the north, his former allies the Moscow-backed Communist Party of Iraq had gone into conspiratorial opposition and, from March, the right-wing and intensely Arab Nationalist Ba'athist Party had taken to the streets. Behind these developments lay one word – oil. Kuwait, Saudi Arabia, Iran and Iraq were respectively the world's fourth, fifth, sixth and seventh largest producers. As forces of nationalism burgeoned in Iraq, so the government in Baghdad moved inexorably towards a takeover of production from the two major foreign companies, British Petroleum and American Oil. Although talks between the companies and the government resumed on 2 April, they soon broke down. Four days later, the Iraqi government issued a decree which banned Anglo/American interests from expanding their drilling operations. In striking contrast, on 7 June, the old imperial power and its 'protectorate' agreed to the setting-up of a petro-chemical industry in Kuwait. Not for the last time, there were accusations in Baghdad coffee shops and nationalist clubs alike against Kuwaiti lackeys of imperialism.

Under stress on the domestic front, the now totally military government in Baghdad[3] looked to ingratiate itself with the people by seeking chauvinist solutions. Having welcomed the end of British protection in the northern Gulf, Qassim studiously avoided congratulation of his fellow Arab neighbour's achievement of independence. Six days later, on 25 July, he declared Iraq's sovereignty over Kuwait. He claimed that the Emirate was part of Basra *wilayah* (province) and announced the Emir's status as *Qa'imqam* (district leader) under the provincial governor (*mutasarrif*). In so doing, he was hardly departing from the stand evinced by Nuri Sa'id, the Anglophile chief minister under the Iraqi monarchy deposed in 1958. He was merely following the Ottoman imperial precedent, pointing out that Kuwait – all land abutting onto Saudi Arabia's northern border – had always been an integral part of the nineteenth province of the Turkish Empire, certainly until its collapse in 1918. With the withdrawal from the theatre of the former British mandatory power appointed in the post-First World War settlement, it was time for a return to historical ownership, however tenuous that might have been. Significantly, and not fully understood by contemporary commentators, Qassim also said that he would not use force to impose his claim to sovereignty. He was not really in a position to do so, since the bulk of his army was heavily engaged with the Kurds. Nevertheless, perhaps peeved at the deteriorating relations over oil, the British government chose to act precipitately, to check any cross-border threat. Behind the scenes, too, there was concern that long-standing intelligence assets in Iraq had been compromised by the Soviet spy George Blake, arrested in April.[4] Was Whitehall blind to the nuances or reassurances that well-placed agents might have provided?

Still buoyed by the landslide Tory victory of October 1959 and the accolade 'Super-Mac', Prime Minister Harold Macmillan reported on Monday 3 July to the House of Commons that British troops had landed two days before in Kuwait. They had been sent in following a request for military assistance lodged on 30 June by the Kuwaiti Emir. Macmillan claimed that Iraqi forces had been reported mustering around Basra; the UK had a clear obligation to assist the newly independent Emirate, he averred. The Wykehamist leader of the opposition, Hugh Gaitskell, immediately backed the government, but pointed out that there were those who would think the action was being taken because of Iraqi moves to nationalise the oil industry. The Prime Minister responded: he did not want a long campaign or the heavy financial burden that would impose, but he added somewhat plaintively, Iraq had appeared to recognise Kuwait's independence only two weeks before. This might suggest that embassy and other reports had been rather more reassuring than subsequent events justified.

In marked contrast to huffing and puffing from the right-wing Conservative John Biggs-Davison that the United Nations should not be allowed to meddle in Kuwaiti affairs, the more cerebral leader of the Liberal Party, Jo Grimond, posed three perceptive questions. Would British troops be under joint or Kuwaiti command? What exactly was happening on the frontier? Had there been consultations with Arab neighbours? Macmillan assured the House that there were already promises of support from Saudi Arabia and confirmed that British troops would be under the command of Air Marshal Sir Charles Elworthy[5] who could expect close cooperation from the Kuwaitis. He was less certain about what was happening on the ground since the whole area was masked by a heavy sandstorm. Nonetheless, he believed that the Iraqis posed a serious threat to forces 'under our command'.

Even at this early stage concern was voiced about the severe conditions British troops faced. Knowing that soldiers were 'living under well-nigh impossible conditions', Sir Arthur Vere-Harvey[6] called for everything to be done to provide them with 'reasonable amenities'. Vere-Harvey knew a thing or two: as a former senior Royal Air Force officer, he was already in touch with friends in the Air Ministry who were receiving initial reports of conditions in the desert. His intervention was intuitive since, at a press conference on 5 July, Brigadier Horsford did not mince his words. Describing what his troops had to face as 'cruel', he continued: "They are living, working, digging in the red-hot wind – burning, hot, stinging sand. In a temperature of 115 degrees it drains all one's energies. The morale is terrific, but there's a limit. Chaps are passing out quite a lot from heat exhaustion." This from a man who had experienced the privations of Kohima, over months, not just one or two days.

Under pressure from his own backbench, the Prime Minister made it clear that his Service ministers had been 'told that everything should be done for the comfort of the men', whom he congratulated and 'the spirit of all those concerned'. Indeed, everything was going rather well. The troops, he added, were 'quite prepared and ready to do their duty in the way that the British would expect'. Satisfied, at least for the moment, the opposition benches changed tack, albeit it was the feisty pacifist Emrys Hughes, devoid of the Labour Whip, who led off. Was it the 'wealthy, fabulous Ruler of Kuwait or the British taxpayer' who would foot the bill? The next day, the maverick Tory MP Gerald Nabarro (Kidderminster) played a variation on the theme. What contribution did Kuwait oil supplies make to the UK balance of payments? The hapless Chancellor of the Exchequer, Selwyn Lloyd, who would be the senior-most Tory cabinet minister to be dismissed in the celebrated 'Night of the Long Knives' a year later, did not know, but offered instead Kuwait's oil production figures for 1960 – eighty million tons of crude. All the more reason, Hughes and Manny Shinwell, Labour's former minister of defence, weighed in that the Emir should pay.

During the weeks that followed, a small group of opposition MPs harried the government on questions of funding, of early handover to others more acceptable to world opinion and quite what the emergency had been all about. On the last point, had the Iraqi leader not denied threatening troop movements?[7] Their persistence was met with bland assurances laced with exasperation at the criticism of what, to ministers at least, was essentially a difficult but entirely necessary military operation. As time went by, the government was able to give satisfaction on all counts – bar one. The one gripe that would not go away was the accusation that troops had been insufficiently prepared for a desert campaign in the middle of a Kuwait summer. Repeatedly, and somewhat loftily, the Secretary of State for War, John (Jack) Profumo, batted away a series of allegations. He sent his Under Secretary of State, James Ramsden, on a two-day (12/13 July) fact-finding mission to Kuwait. Ramsden returned to confirm to the House of Commons that all really was well. There had been some casualties, not many, and they had all been looked after. The chaps had plenty of beer, soft drinks and ice. One man, more than any other, did not believe the assurances coming from the government front bench.

Colonel George Wigg[8] was a complex character. He did not really belong to the 'officer class'. Born in 1900, he came from Basingstoke in Hampshire and won a scholarship to the recently opened Queen Mary's School, which was to specialise as a technical centre of instruction, regarded as one down from the elitist grammar schools in surrounding towns. Family poverty obliged him to leave formal education early and, in 1919, he joined up, enlisting in the Royal Tank Regiment. He served as a 'tankee' until 1937, during which time he came to appreciate the role of armour in warfare, not least how formidable tanks could be in a swift-moving situation and, conversely, how vulnerable they could be in open country without air cover. At the outbreak of the Second World War, he signed up again and was commissioned into the Army Education Corps. He spent a lengthy period in Iraq and knew the desert well. In 1961, he was well aware that the Iraqi Army was equipped with Soviet tanks and that the air force could deploy MIG 19s that could outstrip the Hunter squadron sent as air cover for British ground forces. He was assiduous in maintaining and developing contacts amongst soldiers still in service and with officials at the War Office. Alerted by Brigadier Horsford's press conference, Wigg behaved like a terrier and kept up an almost one-man campaign against what he considered was War Office negligence over the lack of preparation and acclimatisation of the troops sent into Kuwait. If, he reasoned, the War Office, indeed the Ministry of Defence as a whole, could assert that it had prepared at length for the eventuality of an Iraqi military threat to Kuwait after independence and had placed forces ready for intervention, how was it that the squaddies had gone to war without sufficient protection against the sun and briefing as to how to combat heat exhaustion?

His colleague Tom Driberg, the colourful and unapologetically homosexual MP for Barking, had set the ball rolling. Since the Burma campaign during the Second World War, he had championed soldiers serving at the front and monitored the conditions to which they were exposed. In a written question to the Secretary of State for War on 6 July, he asked to what extent troops serving in Kuwait had been 'conditioned to a tropical climate and instructed in the elementary techniques of avoiding heat exhaustion'. Profumo answered: "Most of the troops serving in Kuwait are already acclimatised, having been moved from other tropical stations. All soldiers receive instruction in the elementary techniques of avoiding heat exhaustion as part of their recruit training." He added the assurance that 'special instructions had been sent to the Persian Gulf'. The woodenness of his reply was emphasised when Driberg called for beer to be supplied immediately to the troops. Apparently oblivious of the de-hydrating effects of alcohol, Profumo walked into the trap: he was 'glad to be able to inform the Honourable Member that an adequate supply of beer had arrived in Kuwait' and that there would be a continuous supply from now on.

This cut no ice with Wigg. He pointed out, on 11 July, that until the second week of August at least temperatures would continue to rise; the worst was yet to come. Having undoubtedly checked, he asked whether the War Office had consulted Professor Woodruff, the Army's consultant on tropical medicine. Had Dr Cuthbertson, the Army's consultant on physiology and nutrition, been approached? Was the War Office talking to Professor Maegraith, who had conducted research on the spot into the effects of extreme heat in Kuwait?[9] As a Parthian shot, he lobbed in the bean-counter story originating from Brigadier Horsford, that the War Office had refused him daily expenditure of £250 on soft drinks. Harold Watkinson, Secretary of State for Defence and, since, better known as the Schweppes magnate,[10] was unmoved: he thought everything was 'reasonably adequately covered'. If it were not so, the Under Secretary for War would report to the House after his forthcoming inspection visit to Kuwait. Unsatisfied, Wigg tabled more questions the same day concerning the number of men admitted daily to hospital, on what special dietary arrangements had been made to prevent hyperexia and whether the Air Officer commanding British troops had secured the advice of those well-qualified in its prevention and treatment. Watkinson merely referred him back to blandishments given earlier in the day to Labour's senior frontbencher George Brown. Wigg, of course, knew the answers; the War Office had done little or nothing.

Despite continued stonewalling, the opposition pressed on, to little avail. When the moderate Labour MP Christopher Mayhew, representing the garrison constituency of Woolwich East, asked the next day for a statement on the welfare and accommodation of the troops in Kuwait, Profumo referred him back to Watkinson's perfunctory response to Wigg. Profumo continued to stall when Shinwell and Driberg put supplementary questions. For a few days, further discussion on the subject abated, but on Monday 17 July, Watkinson promised to consider the report he now had from Under Secretary James Ramsden, 'with a view to making improvements necessary for the well-being of the forces' in Kuwait. Rather than stifle debate, this provoked a reaction from his own benches: Colonel John Cordeaux[11] wanted to know what incidence of heat exhaustion had occurred among marine commandos, among the first units to have come ashore on 1 July. Having clearly read a *Daily Mirror* report alleging that one commando had been withdrawn because a third of its complement was suffering from heat exhaustion, he observed that Royal Marines did not normally fall out or collapse in extremes of weather when on active service. Immediately, Wigg jumped in: had the Secretary of State for War consulted the experts he had named – or not? Answering for his superior, Ramsden, fresh from Kuwait, dismissed the angry question. "The problems associated with tropical medicine, physiology and nutrition affecting our troops in Kuwait," he insisted, were understood and 'it was not necessary to seek special advice on this occasion'. Wigg had scored an obvious hit: why then, he retorted, did the government maintain a panel of most distinguished advisers, if they were not to be consulted? Cornered, Ramsden could only stammer that, "From what I saw... they [British forces] are settled down to the drill and routine appropriate to the hot weather – everything is satisfactory." This produced a chorus of shouts of 'Cassandra' from the Tory benches aimed at Wigg. At this, the doughty colonel riposted: "I think the government have used their public relations services to prevent the public from knowing the truth." He was accusing the War Minister of a cover-up.

Profumo could not leave it there. Shortly afterwards, he rose to remind the House, somewhat sanctimoniously, of his and its duty to keep British troops in Kuwait as long as the Emir considered it necessary and the Commander-in-Chief felt there was uncertainty over the future. He then turned on George Wigg and took 'this opportunity of refuting' what he had said. "I believe," he continued, "that this is not a public relations exercise, but that it has been highly successful and creditable to the Army." An exasperated Wigg objected and, before the Speaker could close down further debate, accused Profumo of sending in troops without anti-aircraft cover, with ineffective anti-tank weapons, with no ground strike force and more. "If that satisfied him [Profumo]," he exploded, "well, God help us if he had been disappointed." From that point on, the differences between one opposition spokesman and the Secretary of State for War had become personal. It would have far-reaching consequences.

Arguments over government shortcomings during the Kuwait campaign continued for the rest of the month, but a clearly annoyed and frustrated Wigg conserved his powder. Then, on 1 August, as rumblings of a crisis in Berlin began to crescendo, the Commons debated defence policy. In recognition of his contributions hitherto and expertise, Wigg was chosen to lead for the opposition. His first priority was Kuwait, not Berlin. After protesting against accusations that he had been disloyal, he described the Kuwait campaign as a venture little different from the discredited Suez operation in 1956 when essential equipment – landing craft – had then also been missing. Similarly, during the subsequent intervention in Jordan when troops had only been sustained by American transport aircraft. But now, he asked, why in the first place was the Kuwait operation launched? He cited the *Daily Telegraph* correspondent Ian Colvin, who had reported from Basra on 22 July that for twenty miles at least from the border, there was no sign of armour or motorised troops. Roads and all approaches to the frontier were bare and open. No one had seen any tank transporters for months. Wigg then listed a number of what he considered to be curious coincidences, implying that the whole operation had been a put-up job. "These are fortuitous happenings," he alleged, "which, on investigation, do not stand up." After a further attack on the campaign's shortcomings, he declared it 'a wash-out'. The Americans knew this, so did the Russians, and British prestige in the Middle East had fallen. He then attested his personal credentials for the stand he was taking. "I spent three summers there, a year in Basra and two years in

Baghdad. I happen to know the area fairly well." As a peroration before at last moving on to events in Central Europe, he mentioned his discussion with the distinguished nutritionist Professor Yudkin,[12] who had told him nobody needed to suffer from hyperexia; it was known how it could be prevented. Wigg's speech produced a laconic intervention from Jo Grimond. Curiously, he had received a courteous cable on 5 July inviting him to Baghdad. "I dare say," he mocked, "that if I had gone, I would have learned a good deal about the operation." He, too, was unconvinced by the government record. Emrys Hughes went further: the operation had been 'the most wonderful military excursion since the days of the Grand Old Duke of York'. On the government benches there was fury at Wigg's allegations and apparent negativity: Ramsden called it 'mischievous', a particularly serious charge.

What the aftermath might have been, had there been an inquiry into the conduct of the Kuwait campaign, is difficult to assess. There was no White Paper and the Defence Review published the following February made only a passing, self-congratulatory reference. In one respect, the government was fortunate: it was saved from further inquisition by attention necessarily re-focussing on the events that August which produced the Berlin Wall and NATO/Warsaw Pact tanks facing each other at Checkpoint Charlie. As a would-be entrant to university in the autumn, I came down each morning to scan the press for any hint that my dream of studying for a history degree would be shattered by a military call-up. To a large degree, however, events in the Gulf had turned out well. Most, if not all, troops were withdrawn by the end of September, replaced by an Arab League force policing the border. Kuwait, too, bore the lion's share of the cost. Not a shot had been fired in anger and there were no British deaths,[13] bar one accidental fatality. Kuwait's independence was accepted worldwide and the Emirate entered the United Nations as well as becoming a member of the Arab League.

Nevertheless, George Wigg was not going to forget how unnecessary – in his view – the operation had been, nor what he regarded as a cover-up by government ministers, particularly over its failure to protect soldiers from heatstroke. The political cartoonists' depiction of the old colonel with elephantine ears was apposite. Refusing to forgive and forget, Wigg determined to keep a close eye on the elegant War Minister, but it was to be many months before he discovered what 'Jack' Profumo had really been up to, even as the troops for whom he had shamelessly protested his responsibility in the Commons, were enduring the blazing Kuwait sun. For the moment, however, Profumo could enjoy basking under the reputation of having led a military task to a satisfactory conclusion. When Macmillan drew up his list of those to be dismissed during the 1962 'Night of the Long Knives', Profumo's name was not included, unlike that of his senior colleague Harold Watkinson. Had the press revealed what was becoming increasingly rumoured in London nightlife, the War Minister would surely have been a timely political casualty.

It is, of course, well recorded that George Wigg played a crucial role in bringing about Profumo's downfall in June 1963. That he had little respect for the War Minister's integrity is clear enough; he knew that Profumo had been economical with the truth in July 1961. More than that, he despised the tall, polished frontbencher opposite as – in the words of Harold Wilson – a representative of the 'effete society'. His ears were, therefore, all the more sensitive to his contacts in Fleet Street and in murkier parts of Soho, who had long known Profumo to be a serial philanderer not above using the excuse of late-night sittings in the Commons as cover for his several affairs. More cover-up. What Wigg does not appear to have known at the time – or surely, he would have made hay with it – was that, just a few days after British troops landed in Kuwait, Profumo was frolicking in a swimming pool with what he later described as 'a very pretty and sweet' girl and a Soviet embassy naval attaché identified as a GRU intelligence officer. At least one source considered reliable by the Security Service was convinced that Profumo had already eyed up Christine Keeler at Murray's cabaret club, where she had worked as a hostess. Having signed off papers in the War Office and asked his Under Secretary to go out to Kuwait to report conditions on the ground, Profumo thought nothing of taking himself and his beautiful actress wife, Valerie Hobson, away from London for a weekend break at the Astor family's Thames-side mansion of Cliveden. It is not difficult to imagine what a sun-burnt Royal Marine commando would have made of that. Another participant in the fun and games at Cliveden was Dr Stephen Ward, who was in touch with the Security Service and reported the GRU officer Yevgeniy Ivanov's presence. Unaware of this, Profumo continued to develop a sexual relationship with Keeler. The 'hot potato', however, was soon reported to Downing Street and, on 9 August, Sir Norman Brook, the cabinet secretary, took the minister aside and warned him to be more careful in his private life.

All might have been swept under the carpet and Profumo's peccadillos dismissed as a hot-Italian-blooded aristocrat's noblesse oblige. *Queen* magazine hinted in July 1962 at a triangular relationship between Profumo, Keeler and Ivanov, but the story did not catch on in Fleet Street. Then, on 14 December the same year, one of Keeler's former boyfriends, Gordon Edgecombe, fired a gun when Dr Ward refused him entry to his flat in Wimpole Mews. The police were called and Edgecombe was charged. The incident unsettled Keeler, who started to talk about her various relationships and began to explore the possibility of selling her story to the press. Despite the fact that she handed over a love letter she had received from Profumo, the two papers approached backed down from publication after heavy pressure from both Ward and Profumo. The latter continued to have the support of Harold Macmillan. One of Keeler's interlocutors, however, knew exactly who would be interested. A former Labour MP, John Lewis,[14] who hated Ward, passed all that he had been told to George Wigg. Nevertheless, the only people to really worry about the escalating gossip were in GRU headquarters; Ivanov was recalled to Moscow on 22 January 1963. The Shadow Foreign Secretary, Harold Wilson, who valued Wigg, refused to take up the matter, even after his election as leader of the Labour Party on 14 February.

Edgecombe was brought to trial at the Old Bailey on 14 March. Consternation then broke out when the key Crown witness, Keeler herself, went missing. Westminster came alive. The ostensible concern was over the freedom of the press after two journalists, Reginald Foster of the *Daily Sketch* and Brendan Mulholland of the *Daily Mail*, had been sent to prison for contempt of court. During the tribunal investigating the Vassall spy scandal, they had refused to answer questions about their sources and were sent down by the presiding judge, Lord Radcliffe. Their plight was raised by the Conservative MP for Gravesend, Peter Kirk, who belonged to the same branch of the National Union of Journalists and claimed close friendship with Foster and Mulholland. The debate started just before nine o'clock on the evening of 21 March. It was not until almost two hours later that Wigg rose to comment on press freedom and its interface with national security. Like other members of the opposition, he feared that newspapers were hamstrung by owners ready to spike stories at government bidding and journalists fearing they might find themselves on the wrong side of the law. Wigg was well into his speech when he dropped the bombshell; he did not mince his words. There was not an honourable member in the House, nor a journalist in the press gallery, nor anyone in the public gallery, who, in the last few days, had not heard rumour upon rumour involving 'a member of the government front bench'. The press, he continued, had got as near as it could – 'it had shown itself willing to wound, but afraid to strike'. After blaming the press lords for not having 'the guts to discharge the duty' that they were claiming for themselves, he challenged the Home Secretary to bring the senior member of the government concerned to the dispatch box, where he might deny the truth of the rumours surrounding Edgecombe, Keeler and her friend Mandy Rice-Davies. Alternatively, a select committee might be set up to question those involved.

Wigg received strong support from two other members of the National Union of Journalists, Dick Crossman (Coventry East) and Barbara Castle (Blackburn). Both were heavy-hitters on the opposition benches. Mrs Castle's words were particularly telling. "We hear a lot about the distortions that appear in the press, the power of distortion in the press. I suggest that that power is nowhere near as great as the power to withhold the truth that lies in the hands of the government." She provoked Tory anger when she accused the unnamed government front-bencher of failing to do his duty in not informing the police where Keeler was. At this Wigg leapt in again and accused the Secretary of State for War of attempting to bludgeon the Commonwealth Relations Secretary into revealing information he had received from serving officers. 'To his great honour', the latter had 'told him to go to hell'.[15]

Profumo was not in the chamber but he was hurriedly summoned and went into a huddle with lawyers who prepared a personal statement for him to deliver the next day in the Commons. He started the statement with an immediate inaccuracy; he referred wrongly to the comments under protection of Parliamentary privilege the night before being made during the Consolidated Fund Bill. He glossed over his relationships with Keeler (first met at Cliveden in July 1961 and last seen the following December), Ward (known only slightly) and Ivanov (only met twice). There was 'no impropriety whatsoever' in his brief relationship with Keeler and he had no idea where she was. He ended the statement by threatening to sue for libel and slander if the allegations were repeated outside the House. Wigg watched from the opposition benches and is said to have left the House 'with black rage' in his heart because he knew what the facts were; as in July 1961, he 'knew the truth'.[16]

For a few weeks, Profumo might have thought he had got away with it again. Wilson, however, passed the thick dossier he had from Wigg to Macmillan, who ordered Lord Dilhorne to investigate whether there might have been any breaches of security. Profumo and his wife left for a Whit weekend in Venice only to be called back to London. At this point, he lost his nerve and confessed to his wife before repeating his confession to Macmillan's private secretary. He resigned the next day – 4 June 1963. Lord Denning was then appointed to conduct an inquiry in which he concluded that there had been no security leaks and that the former Secretary of State for War was 'guilty of an indiscretion, but no one could doubt his loyalty'.[17] The report was branded a 'whitewash' by some, albeit Denning did not shrink from calling Profumo a liar. Sadly, his remit did not require him to enquire into Profumo's record in 1961 when the War Minister might have been severely criticised for negligence. Within a month of the report's publication, the Prime Minister had resigned, in large part, it is thought, because he feared he was seriously ill. Thirteen years later, the man who had done more than anyone to bring Profumo down, found himself under arrest, allegedly for kerb-crawling.

This was in sharp contrast to the disgraced minister who managed to save his marriage and moved into the East End of London to do penance as a charity worker.

The lurid aspects of the Profumo affair so over-shadowed events that little was remembered of the first Iraqi attempt to take over Kuwait. They eclipsed Iraq's very claim to sovereignty over the Emirate. It was a dispute, however, that was never likely to go away; it would eventually claim thousands of lives both sides of the border and throw many more out of their livelihoods while causing enormous infrastructural damage in the Gulf. The issue was totally obscured by the events that summer in Berlin, a priority concern that swept away any critical appraisal of the Kuwait operation and the implications that arose from it. A dreadful irony emerged. While cooler heads prevailed in Europe and the outbreak of conventional warfare never again threatened in Europe, for all the hiatus of the Cuba Missile Crisis in 1962 and Kremlin paranoia subsequently, the Kuwait accident waiting to happen remained. Rarely could two parallel international issues have led to such contrasting and unanticipated outcomes. While Germany was united and Eastern Europe liberated with all the political, economic and social benefits that accrued from this, the Iraqi claim to Kuwait was allowed to fester, flaring up at intervals and leading to an endemic and burning instability in the Middle East, laced with the rise of international terrorism promoted by radical Islam. Operation Vantage, the somewhat unfortunate codename for the 1961 Kuwait operation, was only the beginning of a very long saga which has yet to end and may never do so.

Two

A HISTORY OF AN IMPERIAL BRITISH-PROTECTED STATE

For the British government, the Kuwait crisis of 1961 was largely predicated on the belief that it had a specific duty to defend the newly independent Emirate. Oil was, of course, an important consideration, but the need to protect the sovereignty of a candidate member of the United Nations was the proclaimed justification for precipitate action.[18] By the time of the threat of an Iraqi invasion there was an element of false premise in the constitutional basis for the decision. The fact that both the UK and Kuwait had undergone negotiations for 'independence' leading to a treaty of 'mutual cooperation and friendship' appears to have rested on British interpretation of the 23 January 1899 agreement with Sheikh Mubarak al-Sabah as having created some form of protectorate status. It was an outdated interpretation. The late-Victorian exchange of identical and signed texts with side letters certainly contained the notion that Kuwait was under the protection of British imperial authority if threatened by any number of third countries at the time. Nevertheless, it was primarily an agreement, negotiated by a middle-ranking official of the Indian Raj, which gave Britain sole trading agency rights and bound the Kuwaiti ruler not 'to cede, sell, lease, mortgage, or give for occupation or for any other purpose, any of *his territory* to the government or subjects of any other power without the previous consent of Her Majesty's Government'. It was not so different from the clutch of bilateral imperial trading agreements arising from a Britain anxious to exclude Germany,

Russia and France from the Gulf; it was not drawing a line with the Turkish Empire which was then still an ally. A man like Sheikh Mubarak would have been reluctant to shed sovereignty to any greater extent – or at all and, indeed, jibbed when his own foreign policy adventurism was restrained during the years leading up to the First World War. Sixty years later, moreover, the Raj was a fading memory and Britain's role East of Suez was already subject to serious question.

With the collapse of the German, Russian and Turkish Empires and partition, with the French, of Middle Eastern spheres of influence, the 1899 agreement – it never was a treaty – lost its relevance and became a shred of imperialism, no more. Although the Iraqi state, thanks entirely to the post-1918 British mandate, could rightly claim to have inherited a large portion of the Turkish Sultan's domain, at no time did this entitle Baghdad to claim sovereignty over Kuwait. In any case, at no time in history had the Turks ever been able to exert and consolidate control over the Emirate. The border issue was always in the background, if clouded by the sands of the desert, but it invariably cropped up as the century progressed when an Iraqi leader was in need of a bout of chauvinism to protect his position at home. Saddam Hussein's invasion of Kuwait in August 1990 is just such a case in point. Iraqis and Kuwaitis are and always have been as different as chalk from cheese, however much they have on occasion sworn fealty to one another within the Arab brotherhood. A potted history of the peoples of the Emirate will bear this out.

Three hundred years ago, the Persian or Arabian Gulf – depending on which shore you stood – would have teemed with fish. Out in a small boat in 1989 with a senior Kuwaiti companion, I asked after the ecological health of the waters off the Emirate's coast. My friend looked rueful; he replied that the fish population had halved over the previous thirty years. Looking over the gunwale, there still seemed to me to be plenty of life below, although by no means all edible. Three hours later, we sat down to dine off two tasty Ehrenberg's snappers, an attractive species with translucent yellow fins and mottled stripes along its body. It is also recognisable for its black spot about a third along from the dorsal fin. Whoever were the first settlers in what would become coastal Kuwait, they would surely have been casting their nets around the islets two or three miles out to sea for a rich and seemingly ever-replaceable harvest. Six or seven species are still listed as good to eat. Fishing went right back into the mists of pre-history and the origins of the fishermen were distinct from other neighbouring Arabs. Geographically, north of present-day Saudi Arabia, the Emirate can still boast offshore islands, inlets and the shelter of the bay of Kuwait itself.

Since well before antiquity, however, this coastal people sought another and more valuable resource from the sea – pearls. Writing in the second century AD, Athenaeus of Naucratis in ancient Egypt, repeated the description of pearl fishing made by Isidore of Charax (a settlement on the edge of the Shatt al-Arab waterway) towards the end of the first century BC. The locals, therefore, had always enjoyed an easily gathered commodity with which they could trade. Long before the advent of the Prophet Mohammed (died 632) and the rise of Islam, the peoples of the northern Gulf had bartered, intermingled and usually collaborated. It is doubtful whether the great Islamic schism after the battle of Karbala in 680 had much effect on the fish sellers and pearl merchants of the day. While dynasties, Sunni and Shi, rose and fell over the centuries, these peoples remained largely in blissful ignorance, on the very edge of bitter religious and political rivalries. I once heard a senior Kuwaiti official rail: "We never had any dispute between the Sunnis and Shi'a until the [1979] Iranian Revolution."

Not until the late eighteenth century did the Ottoman Turks consolidate their hold on Basra at the top of the Gulf and, even then, it became a provincial capital in little more than name only. In 1911, the population of the city was mostly Jews and Christians engaged in trade, the only Turks being officials serving at the very extremes of empire. On the eve of the First World War, therefore, Turkey's hold on the north-east of the Arabian Peninsula was tenuous, bordering on non-existent. Kuwait, on the other hand, was already an entity in its own right, if not regarded by all as a fully independent state. The word 'Kuwait', or little fort, first appears in a map dated 1765 and drawn up by the German mathematician, cartographer and astronomer Karsten Niebuhr. He had joined a Danish expedition in 1761 that travelled throughout the Gulf region for six years. During the summer of 1765, Niebuhr, who had survived the deaths of several of his companions, arrived at 'Charedsch' (Charax) and neighbouring Basra. There he witnessed the confusingly triangular hostilities between the local Turkish commander, Karim Khan, Persian forces and an Arab Shaikh named Suleiman. The fighting attracted naval units sent by the British Indian authorities in Bombay and the intervention of the local but unnamed 'English' political agent. The Dutch, who had built a trading post at Basra decades before, together with Danish and German explorers, might have had their own narrow interests, but the British, jealous for the security of their routes to India, could never afford to ignore local rivalries.

In August 1765, Niebuhr left Basra and travelled down the desert coast before crossing the Arabian Peninsula to Aleppo in Syria. Early on in this progress, he came across 'many Arab tribes, all regarding their areas of settlement as independent'.[19] What Niebuhr was observing first-hand was a cultural divide between expansionist empires, Turkish and Persian, and particularistic desert peoples, together with the British, not for the last time, seeing the advantages in supporting the underdogs who might harry their potential rivals in the region.

By the early eighteenth century, the British East India Company was already well aware of the importance of the northern Gulf. It offered an alternative to the long sea voyage round the Cape of Good Hope for mail to be sent back to Whitehall. Ships took dispatches up the Gulf to Basra or Kuwait, from whence couriers joined camel trains across to Aleppo in northern Syria; thence, through Europe, to England. Moreover, there was already a thriving export of manufactured goods and foodstuffs from Bombay to Basra, where English merchants enjoyed much lower tariffs than their European rivals. The one-time Bombay councillor Francis Warden considered that a town existed at Kuwait as early as 1716.[20] Long before Warden's account, however, the Dutch East India Company had produced a chart in the seventeenth century showing 'Grane' as the name for the earliest recorded settlement. The term means little hill and it is here that Barrak, Sheikh of the Bani Khalid tribe, rulers of Eastern

Arabia at the time, built a small fortress. Its construction has been dated to 1680.[21] From then on, if not before, Grane became more than a quiet haven for fishermen and pearl divers.

Sheikh Barrak's Bani Khalid tribe belonged to the Adnani confederation of northern Arabs, as distinct from the Al-Qahtani, or southern Arabs. The Adnani claimed ancestry from Adnan, a descendant of Ishmael, the patriarch Abraham's eldest son by his wife Sarai's servant, Hagar, an Egyptian.[22] Sheikh Barrak had established his tribe's supremacy over Eastern Arabia by the late seventeenth century and had expelled the Turks from the prestigious and fertile oasis of Al-Hasa in eastern Arabia in 1670.[23] The building of the Kuwait fort should be seen in this context. The Bani Khalid were considered successful in husbandry, in their trade with Persia and India and, in general, exerted a peaceful influence in the northern Gulf. They were quite distinct from the Turks or any of the peoples of Mesopotamia. Under their rule, the port at Kuwait flourished during the first half of the eighteenth century and developed as a terminus for caravans traversing Arabia to the Mediterranean.

During the last years of the seventeenth and into the early decades of the eighteenth centuries, Kuwait received a wave of migrants. Lasting drought in Central Arabia and unrest around Basra under the Turks, pushed people respectively east and south into still-peaceful and prosperous Bani Khalid territory. The migration brought in the al-Utub from Umm Qasr in southern Iraq, whom the Turks had expelled because of their predatory attacks on shipping and caravans, together with – and crucially for the port of Kuwait – the al-Sabah from the Arabian interior. The Bani Khalid Sheikhs indulged both groups who, remarkably, settled down together peacefully. The ruler at the time, Sa'dun bin Muhammad bin Ghurair al-Hamid, used the talents of the immigrants wisely. The al-Sabah proved to be good administrators. They had lived in the Najd or Central Arabia for centuries and could trace their origins well before the advent of Islam. Indeed, many had been Christians. They could not claim descent from the Prophet. Neither were they known to live by the sword, a trait which would have made them more than acceptable to the Bani Khalid. During the first half of the eighteenth century and, even after

Sheikh Sa'dun's death in 1722, they helped instead to keep the rougher al-Utub under control through an agreed division of responsibilities. The latter eventually migrated south to Bahrain, leaving the al-Sabah in pole position. Helped by a lack of ostentation and greed, the al-Sabah earned the respect of the indigenous inhabitants in the town. At some point in the 1750s, after the death of the Bani Khalid Sheikh Suleiman al-Hamid (in 1752) and the distraction of Bani Khalid tribesmen to face the fiercely expansionist and their bitter enemies, the al-Wahhabi, the Kuwaiti townsfolk chose Sabah al-Sabah as their Sheikh; he was to administer justice and the affairs of a thriving commercial centre.

Apart from their practicality in administrative matters, the Sabah were also known for a lack of ostentation and greed. We have a glimpse of Sheikh Sabah's conduct and authority in 1758 from an account by Dr Edward Ives, a naval surgeon, who had sailed out to India four years earlier by sea. For his return to England, he chose the less well-trodden overland route across Persia to the Gulf. He then called in at what is now known as Kharg Island, about twenty miles off the north Persian coast, at the time a recently opened Dutch trading post under the command of Baron Tiddo van Kniphausen. When asked for advice as to the best onward route to Aleppo, the baron sent a *felucca*, a one or two lateen-sailed boat, over to Kuwait to fetch Sabah. The suggestion was that the Sheikh should accompany Dr Ives and his party in a caravan which would take up to thirty days to reach the northern Syrian terminus, thus saving between two and four weeks by not going via Basra and Baghdad. The plan demonstrated Sabah's knowledge of his neighbours in the northern Gulf and of the conditions of travel over the vast Arabian interior. It showed, too, that he retained good relations with tribes across the desert. But there was a price to pay – two thousand piastres.[24] This was too much for Baron Kniphausen, who offered only half, much to Sabah's aggrieved disappointment; he had expected more understanding from a fellow merchant. After all, the planned caravan would have consisted of five thousand camels and one thousand men. So, Dr Ives was obliged to take the route via Basra.[25] The episode also reveals another characteristic apparent centuries later. The Sabah were of hard-headed desert stock and, not for nothing, did they come to be known as 'the Jews of the northern Gulf'.

In the years that followed, Kuwait prospered as the eastern terminus for desert caravans. In addition, Niebuhr estimated that the sheikhdom was a haven to over eight hundred small merchant and fishing vessels.[26] The latter plied as far south as Bahrain where pearls were most plentiful. Meanwhile, the al-Sabah established themselves in the central quarter (*Wasat*) of the town. Under the Bani Khalid, a defensive wall had not been considered necessary, but by the 1770s the East India Company records were documenting a mud construction, easily damaged by heavy rainfall.[27] It remained largely intact, however, well into the twentieth century. Behind its wall, Kuwait developed into a mercantile centre, as well as a fishing port, and increasingly, an Arab rival to and a refuge from the Persians encroaching into Basra. The Turks did not figure at the time.

The al-Sabah preserved their leading position in Kuwait by extensive consultation with other tribal groupings. Disputes were put to a separate judiciary headed by a judge (*qadi*) supported by a group of recognised wise men (*ulama*). In 1764, Sheikh Sabah I was succeeded by the youngest of his five sons, Abdullah, who was apparently chosen for his bravery, wisdom and generosity.[28] Abdullah also provided longevity to al-Sabah tenure since he did not die until February 1815. During the early years of his reign, a closely related tribe, the al-Khalifa, disappointed at not being chosen for rulership instead, migrated to Bahrain, where they set up their own dynasty which remains in power today. Over a fifty-year reign and with no other claimants, the al-Sabah became a permanent fixture in the political leadership of Kuwait.

To complete this early picture, it is necessary to look at the wider context of European intrusion. The Portuguese were the first to penetrate the Gulf at the very end of the fifteenth century, when they sought trading opportunities. By 1602, however, they had been expelled from their main base, Bahrain, and during the following century, their influence was almost totally eclipsed by the British and Dutch working closely together. The French formed an East India Company in 1664 but were never to rival the British and Dutch in the Gulf, both jealous for the security of their logistical communications to India and the Far East respectively. By the end of the eighteenth century, it was the British that had become the dominant European power in the Gulf. At the outset, it was Basra, Bahrain and Bandar Abbas (in the southern Gulf) that were regarded by the British as of greatest importance, but as Kuwait increased in prosperity during the stability of Sheikh Abdullah's rule, so priorities began to change. The advantages of safer travel and mail dispatch overland were soon recognised by the Indian Raj. Tribes in the Arabian interior, with whom the al-Sabah retained good relations and who were easily seduced by gifts and subsidies, afforded a more reliable and shorter passage than long voyages round the Cape, always vulnerable to a lurking French warship, piracy and storms.

The Persian siege of Basra in 1775 increased British motivation to send dispatches overland – via Kuwait. A letter of 11 June 1776 from the consul at Aleppo to his opposite number in Basra, Mr Latouche, illustrates the increasing importance of Kuwait to British trading and other interests. "If the town of Grain is suffered to remain neuter, caravans may be made no doubt to and from thence to this place, for as long war will probably be caused by the loss of Bussora [Basra], that city will be deserted unless merchants can find some method of carrying on trade near it. Grain [Kuwait] seems to be well situated to serve as a substitute to Zebere [Zubara in Qatar]." That, he argued, was only possible provided the town did not fall into Persian hands. Despite the shortcomings of his syntax, the Aleppo consul was pointing up an embryonic political dimension growing in the relationship between Britain and Kuwait. That said, the use of desert routes via Kuwait did not happen immediately. It was a gradual process and, for trading purposes at least, did not favour a tedious cross-desert journey. A string of camels loaded with merchandise was still too tempting for marauders in the interior. Diplomatic and other sensitive mail, however, was less of a hostage to fortune and its comparatively swift and safe delivery to Europe via Aleppo, before the opening of the Suez Canal in 1869, had an obvious attraction. Given Britain's sometimes troubled relations with the Ottoman and Persian Empires, a diplomatic bag was better lost or stolen in Arabia. Relations between Bombay and Sheikh Abdullah, moreover, remained good.

The rise of the strictly Islamist Wahhabi tribe in Eastern Arabia also had a strong bearing on Kuwait's political development. By the end of the eighteenth century, the Wahhabi had broken the Bani Khalid comprehensively and ruled over the fertile Al-Hasa oasis to the south. That they did not easily go on to take over Kuwait remains somewhat of a mystery. True, there were Shi-ite rivals on the coast that distracted the Wahhabis and prevented them from obtaining a trading monopoly. A major factor, however, was the continuing presence of the British. For a short time in the 1790s, they even transferred their trading base from Persian-occupied Basra to Kuwait and opened a factory there under the supervision of a political agent. With the outbreak of Anglo-French hostilities in 1793, too, they had been able to persuade Sheikh Abdullah to their cause and obtained Kuwaiti connivance in the interception of French shipping and dispatches.

The presence of the Royal Navy was not enough to persuade the Wahhabi to leave well alone. Indeed, even with a British agent in residence, Kuwait suffered a series of Wahhabi raids down to the end of the century. Despite losing casualties in skirmishes outside the walls, however, the town was not overrun. Kuwait had one telling military advantage: a strong fleet which could menace Wahhabi trading in retaliation, deterring them from more decisive action. The Kuwaitis also managed to acquire superior weaponry from other potentially more powerful neighbours. The Ottomans, too, were concerned at the rise of Wahhabism, especially when it started to penetrate southern Iraq. This culminated in a punitive expedition in 1796 launched at Al-Hasa – by land and sea. Two hundred Kuwaiti vessels were hired by the Ottoman commander, Ali Pasha.[29] There were other occasions when British power was used instead to blunt Wahhabi attacks on Kuwait. In 1805, a force of four thousand Wahhabis mounted two men apiece on two thousand camels attacked the town and were driven off by cannon brought ashore from British warships and by Indian sepoy guards at 'John' Company's factory. There would have been other instances of discreet British intervention, albeit these were never recorded since Bombay policy was to remain neutral. From then on, however, the Wahhabis had to face challenges from enemies elsewhere in Arabia, tribal forces that did not appreciate austere Islam. Thus, as the nineteenth century wore on, Kuwait was able to preserve its independence under a wise, respected and long-lived ruler. There is no evidence either that Kuwait felt it necessary to buy off the Wahhabis, as many neighbouring tribes were obliged to do.

In the wake of Napoleon's thrust into Egypt in July 1798 and increased French efforts to sever trading routes to India, the British began to formalise political ties with Gulf Arab rulers. The first agreement was a treaty with the Sultan of Muscat, signed only three months later on 2 October. A further treaty, signed in 1800, strengthened British facilities for control over the Straits of Hormuz, the gateway to the Gulf and for increased measures to be taken against piracy. There might also, at the time, have been a promising naval cooperation agreement between Britain and Kuwait. This would have envisaged the use of Kuwaiti pilots, instead of Omanis, for navigation of the treacherous waters at the top of the Gulf. In 1809, this ostensibly attractive proposition was put by the Kuwaitis to Captain John Wainwright, the commodore of the squadron deployed by the Admiralty to flush out piracy in the Gulf. Sadly, he was under strict instructions to do nothing that would annoy the Wahhabis and, reluctantly, had to turn down the offer. Not the last time an appeasement policy was to be pursued with Kuwait's enemies,[30] but it indicated the limits of British imperial expansionism.

During much of the first half of the nineteenth century, Kuwait was left very much to its own devices. The Wahhabis by-passed it, the Turks never occupied it or took it under their wing, and the British had no great motivation to get involved once the French threat had been removed. The Kuwaitis shunned both piracy and slavery, unlike other Arabs, so there was no reason for London or Bombay 'crusaders' to become involved. In 1821, however, the British agent in Basra chose to remove his factory and other trading facilities to Kuwait once more. During a Turkish internecine dispute, his insistence on remaining neutral had not been accepted and the Basra agency was besieged in March. Despite the availability of several other alternative havens, the agent chose the Kuwaiti offshore island of Failaka for his retreat. The move reinforced the view that Kuwait was an independent entity, not least thanks to its competent fleet which had earned the respect of the Royal Navy and the government in Bombay. It did not, however, take long for the Turks to realise the economic losses sustained after the British withdrawal. Profuse apologies and assurances for the future were made; the Basra factory re-opened two years later.

Another power entered the eastern Arabian power struggle during the late 1830s. In 1801, the Ottomans had sent a middle-ranking but highly efficient tax-collector to Egypt, supported by troops, to help clear up the mess left by the brief French occupation and their expulsion by Vice-Admiral Nelson and General Abercrombie. Mehmet Ali Pasha, to give him his Ottoman title, was an Albanian, open to European ideas.[31] He is credited with widespread reforms in Egypt while suppressing the Mamluks, the warrior slave caste that had dominated much of the eastern Mediterranean since the thirteenth century. He promoted the role of women in Muslim society and gave assurances to the Coptic Christians that their beliefs would be tolerated. His great ambition, however, was set down in a statement he was reported to have made in about 1811: "I am well aware that the Ottoman Empire is heading by the day to destruction... On its ruins I will build a vast kingdom... up to the Euphrates and the Tigris." Without wishing to supplant the Sultan, he endeavoured to rebuild a secular caliphate not so different from that which had once ruled from Baghdad. After taking over the Hejaz in 1812 and subsequently crushing the al-Saud in the Najd region, he continued to increase his military and naval strength. Finally, in 1836, he launched an attack on eastern Arabia and southern Iraq, where, without breaking with the Sultan, he came up against Ottoman commanders of similar standing.

For three years Ottoman took on Ottoman, with the Egyptian wing advancing as far as the Al-Hasa oasis and the Gulf coast. In what became a stand-off, Kuwait was left untouched and independent. The only – and slight – dent in the Emirate's sovereignty was Mehmet Ali's appointment of a resident agent, Kurshid Pasha, not only to organise the re-supply of his forces but to collect intelligence on his rivals in the theatre – Arab, Persian and Ottoman. The rapid Egyptian takeover of most of Arabia alarmed the great powers in Europe and, on 15 July 1840, the London Convention was signed by Britain, Austria-Hungary, Prussia and Russia on the one hand and the Ottoman Sultan on the other. Mehmet Ali was forced to pare down his naval and military forces and to withdraw from many of his conquests. His dream of a caliphate was shattered. Even before this international action, the British Resident in Bushire,[32] Captain Samuel Hennell, had repeatedly warned Mehmet Ali's commander in Eastern Arabia not to advance beyond Al-Hasa. He used Kuwait's ruler, Sheikh Jabir I, as his intermediary with Khurshid Pasha. Thus, for the purposes of this account, Kuwait was left unscathed, while once again its strategic importance was enhanced. During this period, British, Iraqi and Egyptian intelligence agents eyed up one another and competed for the latest information, in pursuit of their respective national interests. For a short while – and foreshadowing a later relationship in the decades before the 1990 invasion of Kuwait – the Egyptian representative attending the Sheikh's *majlis* (audience) was placed on the right of the ruler, a sign of honour and respect but not of suzerainty.[33] The canny Sheikh Jabir threw his benevolent neutrality in favour of Cairo, rather than the ultimately more menacing Baghdad. Once again, the predecessors of modern Iraq were not in a position to compromise Kuwait's sovereignty. Anger, too, was expressed in Baghdad and Basra at Kuwaiti ships being used to transport supplies from Bushire to Al-Hasa and at the defection of an Ottoman battalion to the Emirate.

British relations with Sheikh Jabir I (1815–59) were usually friendly, but one amusing incident in October 1839 illustrates the sensitivities required in balancing one large neighbouring power against another. At the end of that month, Hennell's assistant Lieutenant Edmunds arrived at Kuwait on a special mission to prospect for a secure route for mail across to the Mediterranean. His naval vessel fired the usual salute in honour of the ruler but received no reciprocal salvo. Edmunds had to wait three days at anchor before he could talk to Sheikh Jabir. It emerged subsequently that the Kuwaitis merely wished to mislead the Egyptian agent as to the real nature of Anglo/Kuwait relations. Fortunately, Hennell and Edmunds were able to distinguish between what might have been interpreted as a gratuitous insult and shrewd diplomacy.

Contemporary accounts of the Emirate under Sheikh Jabir and his successor, Sabah II (1859–66) are almost exclusively through European travellers' eyes. In 1818, James Silk Buckingham, the Devon-born sailor and journalist, considered Kuwait to be a great seaport with a sizeable population. He painted a picture of the mud-walled settlement with the desert sand-dunes 'creeping up upon it'. The people were 'brave and freedom-loving' and, unlike neighbouring towns and peoples, had always kept their independence.[34] In 1831, Joachim Hayward Stocqueler, of Portuguese extraction, travelled from Bombay to Kuwait by sea. Originally, he was destined for Basra, but the Kuwaiti *baghlah* (buggala) in which he sailed was too deep in draught for navigation into the Ottoman port: further evidence of Kuwait's superior facilities.[35] Consequently, he had to stay in Kuwait several days in early April to await a smaller vessel to take him on to Basra. He went ashore and, after a mid-morning repast of coffee, milk, bread and *halwa*, strolled through the town and has left us with the following contemporary description: "Koete, or Grane as it is called in the maps, is in extent about a mile long and a quarter of a mile broad. It consists of houses built of mud and stone, occasionally faced with coarse *chunam* [a plaster made from shell lime and sand] and it may contain four thousand inhabitants. The houses being for the most part square in form, with a courtyard in the centre (having windows looking into the yard)... a very bare and uniform exterior... the streets of Kuwait are wider than those of Muscat and Bushire, with a gutter running down the centre." The town wall facing into the desert was more for show than protection 'as it is not a foot thick'. It had three gates 'and two honey-combed pieces of ordnance' protecting each of them. There were no plantations, he added, 'within or outside the wall' and the water was 'far from sweet'. 'Most singular', for this traveller, 'was the exact uniformity of costume among all ranks and ages and the fact that there being no natives of any other country resident in the place'.

Three decades later, Colonel Lewis Pelly, the East India Company's Chief Political Resident in the Gulf (1862–72), paid his first visit to

Kuwait.[36] His reports were collated later and published in 1874 in Calcutta; he left little doubt where his preference lay. "I confess," he wrote in 1865, "that during my recent journey to Kuwait I was much impressed by the Arab character." Ten years later, he built the case for closer British interest in the Emirate. In contrast to what this account has identified hitherto, Pelly claimed, misleadingly, that Kuwait recognised Turkish suzerainty, but he accepted, 'it was practically independent'. In this, he may have been over-compensating for Turkey, still seen as an ally Britain needed to prop up against Russian encroachment in south-eastern Europe and her inching towards a warm sea outlet. Pelly, nevertheless, regarded the Emirate as illustrative of 'what may be done in the Gulf by common sense' in the creation of trade. "Here," he continued, "is a clean active town with a broad and open main bazaar and numerous solid stone dwelling-houses standing along this strand and containing some twenty thousand inhabitants, attracting Arab and Persian merchants from all quarters." Clearly, the population had burgeoned since Stocqueler's day, thanks to the port's prosperity.

Pelly then summarised Kuwait's successful economic performance. It imported two hundred thousand rupees of goods, chiefly from Malabar and Bombay – long (white) cloths, rice, planks and spices. Against this, exports totalled four hundred thousand rupees, including eight hundred horses at three hundred rupees each to supply the British and Indian armies, sixty thousand rupees' worth of dates and forty thousand of wool. Trade was carried by 'highly reputed' sailors, even if the vessels were built in Muscat. Some thirty merchantmen plied annually to and from Bombay, each vessel loaded with an average of one hundred tons. On the landward side of the town, the desert Bedouin sold their goods at the two gates and were not allowed entry if armed. Kuwait could boast six thousand 'fighting men', but they were for the maintenance of 'peaceful relations'. The Emirate paid no tributes, punishment was rare and the government had adopted a non-interventionist approach. People were expected to get along.

In Pelly's view, Kuwait was potentially more attractive than Bushire, where his Political Residency was still based: as a terminus 'for our sea-going steamers, as a coaling and telegraph station'. Moreover, Kuwait's climate was comparatively good and, although the water was brackish, 'fever was unknown'. He had noted, too, how the Sheikhs were surprisingly well-informed; they read the *Oriental Paris Gazette*,[37] admired the British attitude towards the Turks but wondered why they did not do more for the Christian Greeks. Strikingly, Pelly described 'the Chief Sheikh' (Sabah II) as 'a remarkable man, his eyes undimmed by eighty years'. He also provided a colourful portrait of the ruler at a time when photos were rare. Sheikh Sabah never wore shoes 'and his feet seem to have been the original of the Hercules [statue] at Florence. He has a voice like a trumpet, stopping every now and again with a loud "Hah", something between that of the patriarch of the flock and the sudden blast and pause in a favourite polka'. His speech 'recalls the large utterance of the early gods'.

Pelly was also able to shed light on how the ruler's benevolence promoted the success of Kuwait society. Sabah had told him that 'among the heirlooms of his family was an injunction still daily, religiously observed, to relieve the stranger; a large dinner[38] in an allotted hall, is prepared every evening for all wanderers and strangers who may wish to share it' – the sole restriction being that weapons 'must be left at the gate'. This policy accounted for 'much of the peace, goodwill and neighbourhood and mercantile prosperity of this town'. Lastly, Pelly threw an interesting slant on Kuwait's apparent recognition of Turkish suzerainty. Sabah himself had admitted as much but in the same breath had explained that Turkish-flagged vessels paid customs in Bombay at much lower rates than other merchantmen. "Kuwait, shrinking from this foreign pressure, turned to her Sultan, and suddenly changed colour. Truly, trade is sensitive as women's modesty." A basis, alas, for Iraqi claims on the Emirate a hundred years' later, but more a comment on Kuwaiti mercantile opportunism. Nevertheless, equable and respected behaviour by Sheikhs Jabir I and Sabah II ensured that what disagreements there were did not impair relations with the Egyptians in Najd and Al-Hasa or undermine the association with the British.

There were, however, persistent issues with the Ottomans and tribes in southern Iraq. To the north-west of Kuwait lay lands inhabited by the al-Zubair, many of whom were related to Kuwaitis. Less peaceful, the al-Zubair evaded payment of duties to Basra and raided the city's territory intermittently. To the north of the al-Zubair lived the al-Muntafiq and the two tribes shared age-old blood feuds. At times of dispute over tribal leadership, the loser invariably sought refuge in Kuwait. The Emirate demonstrated similar hospitality to Wahhabi and Saudi refugees alike down to the end of Sabah II's rule. In 1866, he was succeeded by Abdullah ibn Sabah bin Jabir, at a time when the feud between the Saudi brothers, Abdullah and Su'ud bin Faisal, was causing increasing instability in Najd. Under the watchful, if worried, eye of the British, Baghdad launched an expedition to Al-Hasa in 1871, preparatory to an attempt to gain control of central Arabia.

Despite Anglo-French efforts during the mid-century Crimean War, Russian reduction of Ottoman sway over the Slavic Balkans had continued. Smarting from this, Istanbul sought compensation from easier pickings in the Muslim areas of Arabia. The situation in Najd provided the opportunity, especially after the chosen ruler, Abdullah ibn Faisal, was defeated in battle by his brother, Su'ud, leading the Bedouin against settled areas. Very generally speaking, it was a conflict as much between peoples following the traditional desert way of life and those developing an embryonic urban community. Abdullah appealed to the Sultan in Istanbul, as his historical overlord. The latter was content to leave the response to his newly appointed (1869) governor in Baghdad, the highly regarded Medhat Pasha. He was delegated to lead an expedition to Najd which would restore Abdullah as *Qa'immaqam*, a title of more honorary than administrative importance. It had been given to Abdullah in 1865 as a mark of imperial favour. Watching from across the water in Bushire, the British became anxious at the perceived danger of an Ottoman presence on the eastern Arabian coast that would threaten Royal Naval dominance of the Gulf. Since the early years of the century, successive treaties had been negotiated which had secured trading preferences and entry through the Straits of Hormuz. This process had culminated in 1861 with an all-embracing maritime agreement struck in Bahrain which attracted the signatures of many of the small sheikhdoms in the Gulf. One important signature was missing: the Kuwaiti Emir, with one eye on his Ottoman neighbour, remained doggedly neutral.

British concern deepened when the Kuwaiti fleet, commanded by Sheikh Abdullah II, transported Turkish soldiers in April 1871 from Basra to the Al-Hasa coast and assisted the Ottoman attack on ports to the south of Kuwait. Cannon-fire from Kuwaiti ships was crucial in procuring the early surrender of several towns, ending with al-Dammam on 5 June. Ottoman forces on land, however, did not fare so well. The privations of long desert marches and disease reduced their ranks considerably. Seeing the balance tipping in favour of Su'ud al-Faisal, Sheikh Abdullah travelled to Doha in Qatar to persuade the local ruler to join the Ottoman thrust towards Riyahd. He was unsuccessful and after three more years of desultory struggle, the Medhat Pasha expedition fizzled out,[39] albeit the Ottomans were able to hold on tenuously to Al-Hasa. In examining Sheikh Abdullah's motivation, it seems clear that he was shrewd enough to appreciate what might have happened, however successful, or not, Medhat Pasha had been. If Riyadh had been entered and Najd brought to heel, Baghdad could have claimed the whole of Arabia. Falling short of that, the Ottoman temptation would have been to cut losses by holding on to Al-Hasa and also taking a grip on the land above – Kuwait. That did not happen, thanks to Kuwait's care to avoid treaty obligations. Annoyed though they might have been, the British had no cause to complain about Kuwaiti involvement in the campaign, while at the same time Sheikh Abdullah earned the Sultan's gratitude, rather than retribution. Indeed, Sheikh Abdullah was even offered the prestige title of *Qa'immaqam* of Oman and the governorship of Al-Hasa, in return for the collection of taxes to be paid to Constantinople. Again, not wishing to antagonise the British or act as an Ottoman satrap, the Kuwaiti ruler rejected both offers. He held to his neutrality – as far as he could. It is a trait that continued far into the twentieth century and infuriated the Americans during the Cold War.

Sheikh Abdullah II maintained this neutrality and Ottoman favour until his death in 1892. He was succeeded by his brother, Muhammad, a rather less impressive figure. Honest, pious and scholarly though he was, he was considered indecisive. He was also obliged to share power with two of his surviving brothers, Jarrah and Mubarak. This led to dissension. In 1896, the dominant Mubarak, commanding Kuwaiti forces, had both of his brothers assassinated. It is necessary to go into the detail of what happened, since the murders were unique in Kuwait's history and brought about a sea change in her relations with neighbours and, most important, with the British.

Waiting for Sheikh Muhammad's son, Sabah, to go out to *Salat al Fajr* (dawn prayers) one morning in May, Mubarak left his two sons, Jabir and Salim, to keep watch and went up to the roof of the palace[40] where the ruler was still sleeping. In cold blood, Mubarak shot him. According to son Jabir's account, the sound of the shot was the signal for him to find Jarrah and kill him too. In Jabir's own words: "I went up to the roof, heading for Jarrah's quarters. I noticed a small door. It was shut. I pushed it open, and there was Jarrah sitting on the bed, and his wife standing nearby. I raised my gun and fired. I pulled the trigger. It did not go off, so I stepped back, ordering my servants to finish the job. As Jarrah fell, he cried, 'fear Allah for the murder of your uncle.'"[41] Who was behind these dastardly acts? Constantinople was convinced that the British had instigated the assassinations. After all, Mubarak had, it was alleged, just previously spent a month visiting the British Resident in the Gulf at Bushire. That said, there has been no detailed account, in published official papers, or elsewhere, of the visit or any proof of British involvement. One would surely have expected the Resident to have written up any discussion with a leading Arab figure. Perhaps he did and the account was censored, but given subsequent events it is most unlikely.

What is certainly true is that there was disagreement between Government of India officials in Calcutta and the Foreign Office in London. The former were urging their Political Resident to assume a more aggressive diplomacy with the aim of promoting a British-sponsored Arab confederation. The Foreign Office, however, thought otherwise and, concerned not to irritate a Turkey now coming under the covetous eye of the German Empire, considered ill-advisedly that the British government 'has no concern with Kuwait which is under Turkish sovereignty'.[42] These words would come back to haunt Whitehall. In fact, at the time that Mubarak murdered his brother, Britain was still more concerned about Russian predations in the Balkans than she was about any threat from the Ottomans in the Gulf. The strongest sea power in the world had nothing to fear from a land-based Turkey and oil had yet to be discovered in the Middle East and certainly not in Kuwait – for over another twenty years.

Nevertheless, Mubarak's coming to power ended Kuwait's benevolent neutrality towards the Sultan and his governor in Baghdad. It irritated Baghdad that the Kuwaitis continued to shelter refugees from the desert interior, notably members of the Saudi family whom Medhat Pasha had ousted from Riyadh. The violence of Sheikh Muhammad's overthrow, moreover, was not to be forgotten. His sons were bent on vengeance and found support from tribes across the Gulf around Bushire. They were subvented, too, by Yusuf ibn Abdullah al-Ibrahim, a rich Kuwaiti merchant who had been party to Mubarak's earlier exclusion from the town. After the murders he removed himself to Basra, where the Turkish *wali* (governor), the expansionist Hamdi Pasha, was only too happy to receive him. This line-up provided the Ottomans with an opportunity to extend their authority into the Emirate, where they had never been before. In the face of a mounting threat to his position, Mubarak turned to the British. He met with increasing sympathy from successive Political Residents and their staff who, as India rather than Whitehall-based officials, saw advantage in improving access to the harbourage, coaling and telegraphic facilities Kuwait had to offer.

It took some time before Whitehall was convinced. One incident illustrates London's reserve when those on the ground were more than ready to progress towards closer relations with Kuwait. On 19 September 1895 while the Turcophile Muhammad was still in power, the British Indian *baghlah, Haripasa,* was attacked in Kuwaiti territorial waters close to the mouth of the Shatt al-Arab by pirates and four of its crew were killed. Rogue elements close to Sheikh Mubarak were suspected. For eighteen months or more, telegrams flew between Whitehall, both the Foreign and Indian Offices, and Constantinople, Baghdad and Bushire. There was much agonising over whether indemnity could be exacted from

Turkey in recognition of her ultimate responsibility for Kuwait. There were differences between London and the Gulf as to whether Turkey could really justify an historic claim on Kuwait's sovereignty. Political officers in Bushire considered that Kuwait was entirely independent, for all that maps showed it to be part of the Ottoman Empire.[43] The India Office, however, was concerned that the Turkish flag was seen flying over the Emir's palace in August 1896 by the commander of HMS *Sphinx*. During this naval visit, Sheikh Mubarak had also refused to come aboard and the *Sphinx* had been obliged to ride at anchor until a meeting could be arranged. Weighing up all the argumentation, Lord Salisbury sent instructions on 2 April 1897 to Sir Philip Currie, ambassador at Constantinople (1893–98): he did not think much should be made out of the *Haripasa* incident. Satisfactory arrangements could be negotiated with the Turks over measures to be taken for the protection of British vessels without causing offence or raising the question of sovereignty. The Foreign Secretary thought it undesirable to hold the Sublime Porte responsible.

Instead, the Gulf Resident was to use his next meeting with Sheikh Mubarak to issue a serious warning that there should be no recurrence.[44] In implicitly recognising that the Sheikh was the authority on the spot, this would have had the effect of underlining, rather than diluting Kuwait's claim to independence. In the event, an offer from Mubarak made in Bushire during the previous month wrong-footed any admonition; the Emir wanted the British to protect him, not so much from the Turks, but from the several other enemies around him. While this was being considered, Mubarak continued to be menaced by his enemies; Sir Philip Currie reported on 16 July that the Kuwaitis had repulsed an attack by Persians. In his reply the next day, Salisbury was not to be moved: there was to be no intervention unless British subjects were affected or Arab chiefs, further down the Gulf with whom Britain was already engaged, became involved. In a separate telegram the same day, the Foreign Secretary advised his ambassador that the British government had never admitted that Kuwait was under the protection of the Turks, but 'since it is practically under Turkish influence', it was doubtful whether it could be denied.[45] Currie, however, raised the temperature: he reported the presence of a Turkish corvette at Bushire awaiting instructions to go to Kuwait and that five hundred al-Zubairi were praying for Mubarak's removal. Further, the late Sheikh Muhammed's son was asking for British support should his family be restored to power.

Calcutta began to show concern for the threats to Kuwait. On 20 October, it reported to the India Office that the Turkish gunboat had left Bushire for the Arab coast, intending to pay particular attention to Kuwait. Seven days later, the Government of India forwarded reports from its Resident in Bushire that Yusuf al-Ibrahim and the Qatari Sheikh Jasim al-Thani were intent on attacking Kuwait – in the Turkish interest. It sought agreement for a British warship to be despatched to watch events. This was approved, but with the India Office rider that the ship should not get involved unless British interests were menaced. At that point in time there were no British residents in Kuwait. Meanwhile, in September, an assistant political officer from Bushire had visited the Emirate and had held two meetings with Mubarak. The Sheikh had protested his innocence in the *Haripasa* affair; the pirates, he claimed, were based on the other side of the Gulf and he had no control over them. They had attacked Kuwaiti vessels, too, and he was willing to supply intelligence on them. He also explained his reticence in not going on board a British warship; he did not want to give cause for Turkish offence by showing any ostensible favour towards the Royal Navy. Mubarak repeated his proposal for some kind of protectorate status, but he had also spent time and money in the hope of the Sultan restraining more aggressive Ottoman elements. His courting of both sides is a measure of the Sheikh's still insecure hold on Kuwait at the time, not a readiness to yield sovereignty.

In forwarding the account to the India Office, the incoming Political Resident, Major, later Lieutenant Colonel, MJ Meade, argued in favour of the ruler's offer. Kuwait had a good harbour and could become the terminus for a railway from Port Said, at the Mediterranean mouth of the Suez Canal, a scheme long in imagination but short in implementation. Meade had also noticed that Mubarak was disillusioned by Ottoman support for his opponents, despite his outlay of considerable sums in the

Court at Constantinople. To him the Turks were grasping and unreliable, and they were out to absorb his Emirate.[46] This argumentation continued to cut little ice with Salisbury,[47] but then at the end of the year, Currie sent a disturbing report to the Foreign Secretary. His vice-consul at Bushire had reported the appointment of a hawkish general, Mohsin Pasha, in Kirkuk who was sending troops to the Gulf. The ambassador's consul-general in Baghdad had also sent collateral to Calcutta; a force of six thousand Ottomans was being mustered for an attack on Kuwait, supported by the late Sheikh Muhammad's sons, Yusuf al-Ibrahim and the Qataris. At the end of March 1898, Meade appealed for a defensive arrangement to thwart this threat, but as the year wore on, no Turkish invasion transpired and Salisbury turned to other priorities. Mubarak's friend, Sheikh Isa al-Khalifa, the Bahraini ruler, had already intervened some months previously and had persuaded his Qatari neighbour to withdraw his support for Yusuf al-Ibrahim, who withdrew his forces. There are shades of 1961 in this particular episode.

It was not, therefore, a perceived need to defend Kuwait that precipitated a more positive approach to Mubarak. Towards the end of 1898, however, Salisbury's position shifted. The Permanent Under Secretary at the Foreign Office, Sir Thomas Sanderson, wrote to Calcutta that he believed his political master would accept an accommodation with Mubarak, if the Government of India were to take responsibility for it.[48] Lord George Hamilton at the India Office repeated this view. What had changed the Foreign Secretary's mind? In short, the European power game had intruded into the Middle East: Britain's old enemy, Russia, was showing a strong interest in building a railway from Tripoli in Syria to Kuwait and wanted to seek concessions in the Emirate. This was a fresh angle on the long-held Russian design to gain access to a southern warm-water port and, ironically, had implications for her intervention in Syria in the twenty-first century. The Russian interest rang alarm bells. Suddenly, there was a requirement to obtain the Kuwaiti ruler's assurances that he would not cede, lease or mortgage land to other governments or their agents. And there would be sums of money available to underpin any such undertaking. It was a major buy-out – or bribe – that Britain would offer, to keep others out.

Action moved to the India Office after Calcutta agreed that immediate steps should be taken, 'with utmost secrecy', to obtain Mubarak's concurrence. On 18 January 1899, Lord George instructed Meade to go to Kuwait to make an offer of three thousand rupees (approximately £320,000 today) annually in return for his promise not to provide facilities to other powers.[49] On 12 February, Calcutta was able to advise the India Office that the deal had been done: "of his own free will and desire [Mubarak] does hereby pledge and bind himself, his heirs… not to receive any agent or representative of any other government." The ruler's two brothers, however, refused to sign because the British had failed to accord full protectorate status. Mubarak dismissed their refusal; he did not need their approval. If the Foreign Secretary retained any reservations, he was to receive further assurances, this time from the Royal Navy. On 15 February, the Commander-in-Chief of the East Indies station, Rear Admiral Sir Archibald Douglas, confirmed that his ships could defend Kuwait without the support of ground troops.[50]

Meade's long account[51] recording his arrival in Kuwait on 21 January, only three days after receipt of Lord George's instructions, and subsequent negotiations, enclosed a bond signed with Mubarak dated two days later. The Gulf Resident referred to the ruler's concern about what retaliation the Turks might exert over his six thousand pounds' worth of property he held in Iraq. Mubarak expected that Britain would help him counter any move against his possessions. There was no mention in the bond of what Britain would do in this event, let alone if the Turks were to move militarily against the Emirate. Reading between the lines, Mubarak seems to have taken in good faith that effective British action would be forthcoming. Very little, however, was left to him in writing, apart from Meade's personal note to the Sheikh, assuring him of 'the good offices of the British government towards you, your heirs and successors as long as you, your heirs and successors scrupulously and faithfully observe the conditions of the said bond'. This generalised formula, however, had been used in previous agreements down the Gulf, notably with the Sultan of Oman. Arguably, the latter was more defensible than Sheikh Mubarak in Kuwait.

Within two months, nonetheless, a suspicious Salisbury wanted to know why the Navy had been deployed in the Gulf and had to be placated by reports sent to him of Turkish troop deployment around Bushire. In September, his newly arrived ambassador at Constantinople, Sir Nicholas O'Connor,[52] was able to demonstrate that, with the assurances he had received, Mubarak was more than able to stand on his own two feet. The Emir had blocked a Turkish attempt to secure the appointment of a harbour-master at Kuwait and had appointed one of his own people. O'Connor could also report that the Sultan had accepted a *fait accompli* and had even refused to countenance the *Wali* of Bushire's plan to invade the Emirate. From now on, too, Mubarak kept his word. In January 1900, three Germans arrived in Kuwait with a Turkish escort, intent on seeking concessions for the construction of a terminus for a spur or continuation of the Berlin-Baghdad railway. The Sultan had agreed to the visit without consulting Mubarak. Rightly concerned that the Turks were using the German initiative for their own ends, the Emir was careful to provide a full account of the visit to his new British allies. No terminus was ever established and Kuwait remains without a railway to this day.

Mubarak was far less successful in pursuit of his ambitions for the Arab interior, for which he received scant support from his new ally. Although he had neutralised the menace from across the Gulf, thanks to the Royal Navy, he still faced rivals in central Arabia, particularly the old horse-trader Abd al-Aziz al-Rashid (ibn Rashid), Emir of Jabal Shammar in northern Najd; he had grown rich from the export of his herds through Kuwait port. Ibn Rashid supported Ottoman suzerainty over Arabia and attracted in Yusuf al-Ibrahim, together with the sons of the murdered Sheikh Muhammad, whom he sought to restore to power. A Kuwaiti port controlled by a favourable regime and the Ottomans would have improved ibn Rashid's trading potential and profit. Parallel to this, however, the al-Saud family remained in the hunt for control of Najd and a return to Riyadh. It was a mix of these two factors – and with his coastline secured – that prompted Mubarak in December 1900 to lead a large force of townsmen and loyal Bedouin to Riyadh. He succeeded in re-establishing Abd al-Rahman al-Saud as ruler at Riyadh, but when he sought to bring northern Najd under Saudi control, he was heavily defeated at the battle of al-Sarif[53] on 17 March 1901. Ibn Rashid's superior force overwhelmed the Kuwaitis, killing some eight hundred of Mubarak's followers. The disaster destroyed any hope that the Kuwaiti Sheikh had of creating 'a great state in Arabia'.[54] The al-Saud and Mubarak fled and reached Kuwait on 31 March.

This serious weakening of his military position drove Mubarak all the more into the arms of British – practically, if not legally inscribed – protection. Kuwait, in truth, was just another maritime sheikhdom, like the others Britain had gathered in down the Arabian coast. Another marine incident the following year underlined this situation. Egged on by the Ottomans, whose few officials in Arabia simply stepped aside, Ibn Rashid launched a series of largely unsuccessful raids against Bedouin outside Kuwait town who remained loyal to Mubarak. This sequence culminated in a planned night raid on Kuwait town itself, in collaboration with Yusuf al-Ibrahim. Aided by the sons of the late Sheikh Muhammad, Yusuf arranged for two large boatloads of armed men to enter the port after dark, thus surprising Mubarak's diminished forces. Fortunately for Mubarak, his British allies spotted the two vessels and got word to Mubarak. Having lost the element of surprise, the vessels withdrew towards al-Fao island. A few nights later, on 5 September, they were discovered by HMS *Lapwing*[55] off Bushire. Her crew forced the two vessels onto the muddy shore and routed some 250 armed men aboard them. One British crewman was killed and two wounded in the fighting, the first but by no means the last casualties Britain would suffer in defence of Kuwait. It was, however, Yusuf al-Ibrahim's last throw and he died, after seeking refuge with a similarly chastened Ibn Rashid, in 1906.

The Anglo-Kuwaiti agreement of January 1899 was one of the shortest 'secret' arrangements in history. In seeking to blunt German railway interest in the northern Gulf, Sir Nicholas O'Connor called on the Ottoman minister of external affairs during the same year to underline the British view that all should respect the status quo in the Gulf. He followed up by meeting the German ambassador and disclosed to him the agreement with Mubarak, thus demonstrating that Kuwait, at least, was not likely to be a fruitful target for the railway engineers of other countries. The German ambassador accepted this plain-speaking and exploratory visits to the Emirate ceased.

In the years that followed, Britain consolidated her relationship with Kuwait by negotiating a series of other specific agreements with Mubarak. The first, on 24 May 1900, secured the Emir's promise to play a full part in controlling the smuggling of arms to Afghanistan, an endemic commercial activity down the Gulf. He accepted that British – and Persian – warships had the right to search merchant vessels, in case they were carrying contraband. Nearly four years later, on 28 February 1904, Mubarak agreed to the establishment of a British Post Office at Kuwait. The same day, a detailed lease (updated in 1907) was signed by Mubarak and the future first Political Resident in the Emirate, Major S G Knox. Land at Bander Schwaik, later to be known as Schuwaik port, was handed over to British control for the establishment of a coaling station and other marine facilities. In future, British goods would not be subject to duty in excess of 'four per cent per invoice'. In the event of any requirement for an increase in this rate, 'the consent of the precious Imperial English Government' would be sought first.[56] The British rental for taking over and developing Kuwait's only deep-sea port at the time was sixty thousand rupees paid annually in advance, approximately £6,145,000 in today's money. Britain had put the final peg in place for complete naval domination of the Gulf.

The arrival of a political agent in the Emirate on 6 August 1904, to the exclusion of all others, strengthened Britain's hold, not only on the commercial aspects of the relationship but also gave her immediate influence on the political life of the Emirate. More agreements followed: on 29 June 1911, the political agent Captain WHI Shakespear obtained Mubarak's signature to the exclusion of foreign sponge and pearl divers so that the Kuwaiti sheikhs and their people should not lose out.[57] More importantly, on 26 July 1912, Lieutenant Colonel Sir Percy Cox, the Political Resident in the Gulf, wrote to the Emir to advise him that Captain Shakespear would shortly be delivering details of the 'High and Imperial Government's… desire', with Kuwaiti cooperation anticipated, for a wireless telegraph installation in the Emirate.[58] On the eve of the First World War, the first intimations of the discovery of oil appeared. On 27 October 1913, Cox sought Mubarak's agreement to the visit of Rear Admiral Slade[59] who wished to make an assessment of the bitumen deposits at Burgan in the 'hope of obtaining oil therefrom'. The Emir welcomed the visit and detailed one of his sons to escort the admiral into the desert. He concluded: "We shall never give a concession in this matter to anyone except a person appointed by the British government."[60] The great bribe was proving to be an excellent investment.

There was one further – and vital – ingredient in the run-up to the First World War which would prove a hostage to future fortune. Stemming from British concern over the possible extension of the German-financed Baghdad railway and, with it, unwelcome influence, London had sent a memorandum to Istanbul on 29 July 1911 which was to lead to negotiations on the status of Kuwait. Plagued by movements for autonomy in her eastern provinces and, having lost any real naval power in the Gulf, the Ottomans wanted to reach some sort of accommodation with the British over relations in the northern Gulf. Turkey also hoped that a better understanding with Britain would help her against the predations of other major European powers. Britain, after all, had been the traditional friend of the 'Sick Man' for much of the previous century. On Whitehall's part, there was a growing concern over Germany becoming ever more engaged in Asia Minor and the Levant.

On 6 May 1913, Britain and the Ottoman Empire initialled an agreement – signed on 29 July – which was more distinctive for its ambiguity than its clarity. This was, in part, due to a difference of interpretation of such terms as 'sovereignty' and 'suzerainty'. Altogether, the draft convention comprised ten articles concerning the status of Kuwait and its territorial boundaries; it dealt also with relations over the sheikhdoms down the Gulf. It attempted to define Kuwait as two zones – red and green – with differing degrees of autonomy. Essentially, the red area covered a semi-circle against the coast with Kuwait town at its centre and outposts, north and south, at Khawr al-Zubayr and al-

Qurrayin respectively. It also included the offshore islands of Warba and Bubiyan where the British had considered the Turkish military outposts to be a threat. The green zone defined territory beyond where the Emir of Kuwait would be expected to exercise the administrative rights and duties of an Ottoman *kaymakam* (district administrator) but would have to collect tributes on the Empire's behalf.

The provisions were, however, contradictory. Britain was required to acknowledge Kuwait as an autonomous provincial sub-district (*kaza*) of the Ottoman Empire, in return for Istanbul accepting the validity of the series of bilateral agreements over the previous decade between the British and Sheikh Mubarak. The latter understanding, however, only extended over the red zone. Out of respect for Kuwait's autonomous status, Istanbul agreed not to interfere in her affairs, notably in questions of rulership succession. It would also not lay claim to any administrative responsibility or occupy the Emirate militarily. Touchingly, any Ottoman flag flown over the Emirate was permitted to have the title 'Kuwait' inscribed upon it. In return, Britain agreed to declare that she would not declare Kuwait to be a protectorate. As matters stood in the agreement, alas, the status of the Kuwaiti Emir was left ambiguous in that he was beholden to both London and Istanbul as, respectively, an 1899 treaty partner and an imperial official. Perhaps fortunately, the convention was never ratified and the outbreak of war the following year rendered it a dead letter. The fact that the negotiations had demonstrated British readiness to sign away Kuwait's potential protectorate status would come back to haunt successive Emirs.

Nevertheless, when war broke out in August 1914, the India Office and Admiralty could take comfort from the fact that the Gulf was a British lake where the Royal Navy could quickly overcome any Turkish vessels and coal up under Ottoman noses with little risk of counteraction. Indeed, the War Office planners could regard southern Iraq as a soft under-belly to be exploited should hostilities last beyond Christmas. The First World War, however, would confirm the wisdom of the nineteenth-century strategists in Whitehall, if not the Government of India, that no matter how strong the Royal Navy was at sea, for British land forces to be committed to the Ottoman mainland would be a hazardous and costly venture. Nonetheless, the political pundit in 1914 or late 1918 could not have envisaged that one day the Emirate would become an oil-rich prize and that a monster would seek to swallow it up.

Three

ANCIENT PATH TO A FEARSOME DICTATORSHIP

What produced the ogre? The lands that constitute modern Iraq were not always infamous. Biblical Eden has been placed at the head of the Gulf, in the 'land between two rivers'. More reliably, there is evidence of an early civilisation that settled the lower Tigris and Euphrates basin, a peaceable people who lived off the verdant riverside pastures and fish-rich waters. Strife was apparently unknown to them: an ancient 'good life'. What happened to them is unclear, but they have a part resemblance in the Marsh Arabs, who have survived – just – the countless vicissitudes of the twentieth and early twenty-first centuries. Sadly, the cradle of civilisation, a source of pride for many Iraqis, was warped by millennia of political evil and disease. This culminated in a state headed by a man every bit as wicked as Hitler or Stalin, with the paraphernalia of protective organisations as bad, or worse, than the Gestapo or the NKVD. Affording me the protection of his diplomatic car in August 1990, as we drove from his residence to the embassy, 'Hooky' Walker[61] mused: "One really has no idea of how repressive society is here, unless they actually *live* here." Looking back on the second half of the twentieth century, it is surprising that Saddam was indulged for so long, but then one remembers the many apologists for Nazism and Soviet Communism, not to mention Chairman Mao.

The grotesque figure of Saddam obscures the glories of Iraq down through the ages which he adulterated for his own purposes. Only a few months before he invaded Kuwait in August 1990, a magnificent pageant was staged in the spacious grounds of the Regency hotel standing on the Emirate's coast, just south of the city. Handsome men and beautiful women depicted the place of ancient Iraq through flamboyant costume and choreography against colourful backdrops and fountain displays. It was quite a night and a major triumph for those who wished to promote a less dour image of a country that had only recently been so long at war. The timing was immaculate and the propaganda exercise – not to belittle it – was based on authoritative history. Any Iraqi that night, performer or member of the audience, had good reason for self-congratulation. Sadly, it told only one side, an impressive side, of the story. Some might have recognised it at the time as a dose of cultural imperialism; Kuwait, certainly, had nothing like it to offer in return. A perceptive onlooker might have seen the writing on the wall.

Ancient Iraq had all the advantages for development. Climate and natural fertility facilitated one of the earliest known centres of animal domestication and agriculture near Kirkuk, ironically a city now on the fault line between Arab and Kurd. At Jarmo, just to the east of the city, archaeologists in the 1950s discovered evidence of small but permanent settlements of up to 150 thriving on herds of pigs, sheep and goats and a diet that included wheat, emmer (early barley), pulses and pistachios. These early farming communities dated to the seventh millennium BC. Three millennia later, their descendants had mastered irrigation further down the valleys of the twin-river system and had formed thirteen city states from Baghdad down to the shores of the Gulf. This still non-aggressive early Bronze Age civilisation, known as Sumerian for its colonisation of the land between the Tigris and Euphrates, corresponded to similar advances along the Nile and the Indus. The Sumerians worshipped a variety of gods, essentially for the purpose of preserving and enhancing fertility. They were subdued during the period 2400–2200 BC by a Semitic[62] people originating from the Caucasus, known as the Akkadians, named after their legendary capital Akkad, the site of which has never been established. From their ranks arose the first known despot, Sargon the Great (2334–2279 BC), who ruled over the 'fertile crescent' stretching from the Persian Gulf, interestingly through Kuwait, Iraq, Jordan, Syria, parts of Asia Minor, even to Cyprus. His descendants entrenched the empire and fought off challenges from the Egyptians and the ancient Greeks, among others. They dominated the known world. Saddam was well aware of this early flowering of what he regarded as an Iraq-centric civilisation, existing at a time when Europeans were mostly little more than tribal and the Americas quite unknown. Under Saddam, young boys in particular waxed precociously proud from the tuition they received in early Mesopotamian history.

In contrast to the warrior Sargon, however, the Akkadians' most famous and far-reaching personality was the Patriarch Abraham. He is recorded in Genesis as emigrating from Ur on the Euphrates in southern Iraq to Canaan.[63] Abraham was appointed to lead 'God's chosen people' away from Mesopotamia towards Palestine. It should not be forgotten that Iraq and Israel have never signed a peace treaty – since the re-creation of the state of Israel in 1948 – and that Iraq still does not recognise the Jewish state, whose original founding fathers might be regarded as ancient renegades. Perhaps the longest feud in history.

While the Jews introduced the world's first monotheistic religion, Saddam would have underlined the major contributions to civilisation from Mesopotamia: language, measurement and in 1751 BC – in the time of Abraham – the Hammurabi code of law. All great empires, however, come to an end, and early Babylon was no exception. It was sacked by the Hittites in 1550 BC[64] and then conquered three hundred years later by the Assyrians.[65] All this had happened long before a kingship was established in Israel, with the ascent of King Saul in 1028 BC and the foundation, under King David, of the city of Jerusalem in 1000 BC. The great temple there, moreover, was not begun until 961 BC, during the reign of King Solomon. Meanwhile, the Assyrians had created a centralised system of government in which the ruler's strong arm ensured an efficient, if ruthless, administration, quite the opposite of the Yahweh-fearing Israelites. Saddam, who knew his ancient history, was only prepared to put on a public show of religiosity for political purposes and chose ancient Assyrian methods for organising his state.

Saddam's own city – Tikrit[66] – of which he was immensely proud, is first mentioned in history during the ninth century BC, during the reign of the Assyrian king Tukulti-Ninnurta;[67] it is at about this time that Assyrian chronological history begins. Saddam's Iraq was, therefore, no longer 'pre-history', something that could not be said for most of Europe or the Americas. In the Iraqi dictator's mind, however, there was another cause for disdain. In 722 BC, a second Sargon advanced towards the Mediterranean, captured Samaria and took away all the able-bodied people from the vulnerable northern half of the Jewish kingdom[68] to Nineveh. Although itself destroyed by the neo-Babylonian Chaldeans in 612 BC, the city was restored by the fabulous Nebuchadnezzar who is credited with the construction of the 'hanging gardens of Babylon', one of the seven wonders of the ancient world. Saddam, as Simon Henderson points out,[69] was fascinated by Nebuchadnezzar; he named one of his elite armoured divisions after him. It was, after all, Nebuchadnezzar's army that destroyed the temple in Jerusalem in 597 BC and then took the Jews from Judah back to Babylon (587–86 BC). There the large bulk of the Jewish nation languished until, in 538 BC, Cyrus the Great, king of the Persians, captured a Babylon weakened by war and rebellion. This event created another bogey in Saddam's mind which he tried to neutralise in his nearly eight years' struggle with Iran from 1980.

The Mesopotamian golden age was never to be revived: during the fourth century BC, Alexander the Great conquered Babylon. It was not just a military occupation; it was culture-changing. The Greeks pursued trade and commerce, not agriculture and irrigation. More importantly, it was during their supremacy that Aramaic replaced the old Sumerian language. Saddam's beloved Mesopotamia disappeared. For the Iraqi dictator, as a child, the post-First World War British mandate and maintenance of an imported monarchy at Baghdad, were as bad as the ancient Persian and Greek occupations. To add insult to injury, Jews left behind in Babylon had compiled an important version of the Talmud, the rabbinical religious law, and while Israel was able, under Judah Maccabee, to throw off the Hellenist yolk (167–60 BC), Saddam's forbears stagnated. The above is but a crude run-down of millennia, which could easily be elaborated by historians of the ancient world. The point is that, seen through Saddam's eyes, the oppressors and heroes alike of Mesopotamia were writ large in his mind and fuelled his paranoia.

Now we come to the Christian era. Thanks to the early converts in Damascus, of whom Ananias[70] is mentioned in the New Testament as having baptised Saul (subsequently St Paul), the new faith spread eastwards. According to the apocryphal Acts of the Holy Apostle Thomas,[71] a reluctant Thomas, also known as Judas, 'doubting' Thomas and Didymus (twin), was persuaded to leave Damascus for India where the disciples had decided he should spread the Gospel. The story goes that a certain merchant, Abbanes, sent to the city by King Gundaphoros who ruled over a part of present-day Kurdistan, bought him as a slave on the orders of Jesus appearing in a vision. Thomas and Abbanes left Damascus together on their way to meet Gundaphoros. The gate pointing north-east out of Damascus still stands and is known as Baba Thoma. Gundaphoros, who is sometimes thought to be identical with – or the son of – one of the three Magi, Caspar, welcomed Thomas, was converted by him and helped him on his way to India.[72] It is accepted that the apostle reached Mylapore on the Malabar Coast, near Madras. There he attracted converts until his martyrdom in AD72. His legacy was a thriving Christian community which survives to the present day and uses the Syriac rite. Travellers reporting to the court of Alfred the Great in late ninth-century Wessex attested to its existence and Portuguese explorers found the apostle's tomb in 1522. The legend of Thomas's evangelical exploits does not provide any detail of his conversions en route, but the eastern Aramaic-speaking Assyrians descended from communities around Nineveh are thought to have been converted by him. They are one of the oldest Christian groups in the world.

Another fascinating Christian figure associated with Iraq is that of St George, ironically, of course, patron saint of England. Although better known for slaying dragons and thought to have been a member of the Roman emperor's praetorian guard before his conversion, he has been venerated in the Eastern Orthodox Church since Byzantine times. The Anglican church in Baghdad is dedicated to St George. A much older church dedicated to the legendary saint is at Ankawa, a suburb of Irbil in Kurdistan. It is thought to have been rebuilt in AD816, but parts of it date back to the fourth century, not long after George's martyrdom. Ankawa has the reputation of being one of the oldest inhabited cities in the world. Another traditionally strong Christian centre was the city of Mosul in north-west Iraq. It was a prime target for conquest by ISIL during the summer of 2014 and the inhabitants, especially Christians, were treated savagely. Yet they were 'people of the Book' and owed their traditional beliefs to the Patriarchs of the Old Testament (Torah) from Abraham to the great prophets. One of the major prophets, Ezekiel, is thought to have been buried at Al-Kiff in southern Iraq and his tomb was incorporated into the Al-Nukhailah mosque there. Given the persecution Judaeo-Christians have suffered over nearly fourteen hundred years, it is a wonder so many have survived through to modern Iraq – some 1.5 million in 2003, or just over six per cent of the total population. Their position in the country has not been helped by inaccurate quotations from the prophets, Jeremiah and Isaiah, concerning the fate of Babylon and 'great slaughter in Bozrah [Basra]' which appeared in the British tabloid press during the lead-up to the liberation of Kuwait in March 1991.[73]

By the time the Prophet Mohammed received his first revelation in 610, calling on him to restore the monotheistic religion of Adam and Abraham, the Christian world had largely forsaken its Christ-given commission to champion the poor. The Emperor Constantine might have made Christianity the official religion of Rome and thus saved it from persecution, but it lost its spiritual edge as a result. While its evangelistic efforts had made substantial progress in northern Europe, thanks to the patronage of successive Popes and the monastic movement, the more secular portion of the Empire lapsed into complacency. The advent of Islam in the seventh century was in large part to fill the spiritual gap left by Christian decadence. The new religion's potential adversaries, the Byzantines and the Sassanian Persians, were also at odds with one another: in 627, three years before Mohammed took Mecca and destroyed the polytheistic idols at Ka'ba, the eastern Emperor Heraclius crushed the Persians at Nineveh. Ten years later, the Islamically inspired Arabs defeated the Persians at the battle of Qadisiyya. Saddam Hussein was to use the 1,360th anniversary of this victory to raise national morale as Iraqi troops became bogged down in the early months of his war with Iran.

Muslim conquests followed thick and fast: Jerusalem was taken in 638 and Alexandria five years later. In between, Persia was conquered. All might have gone even faster but for the great Sunni/Shia schism triggered by the battle of Karbala deep in present-day Iraqi territory. It took place on 10 October 680 and ended with the massacre of the house of Ali, the fourth in succession to the messenger of God who held the caliphate from 656 to his assassination five years later. It was the culmination of a dynastic struggle that had begun in 644 with the death of Umar bin al-Khattab, the second caliph and close companion of Mohammed, who had boasted the title of commander of the faithful (*amir al-mu'minin*). Ali, the son of the Prophet's uncle Talib, had then contended for the succession but had been rejected by the six-man committee that elected Uthman bin Affar instead. Twelve years later, Ali arranged for the assassination of his rival and was elected caliph. During the next five years, he vanquished or assassinated the last of the Prophet's old companions and family. While celebrating another victory in 661, Ali was himself assassinated and was succeeded by his son, Hassan. By the end of the same year, Hassan had been ousted by Mu'awiya, the governor of Syria, a former opponent of Mohammed and a supporter of Uthman. Hassan's younger brother, Husain, sought to wrest the caliphate back from Mu'awiya, but he and his remaining brother, Abbas, were killed at Karbala. For a religion that claims, at its best, to support peaceful means for settling disputes, Islam had a bloody beginning, a complete antithesis to the behaviour of the early Christians. Might, it appears, was right.

The blood feud, for such it was, came out of the desert. A society which even today is prepared to sanction the amputation of a thief's limb would have had as little tolerance for a perceived renegade or rival as for a poisoner of wells. Early Mohammedan austerity, too, was induced as much by the demands of desert conditions for survival as any religiosity. Only an unwise person drinks alcohol under the hot sun and disrespect of the necessities for mutual hospitality is considered unpardonable. Nevertheless, in the late seventh century, the tough Arab desert-dwellers, fired up by religion, were usually unbeatable on the battlefield. Only the great divide between those claiming to follow the teachings and sayings (the *Sunna*) of Mohammed, also claiming his blessing, and those supporting Ali and his sons who claimed sponsorship through close family ties, prejudiced more overwhelming success against the Byzantines. Without the schism, Constantinople might have been conquered over seven hundred years earlier. The Muslims certainly tried, but failed, in 718. Instead the caliphate had to fall back on Damascus, where Mu'awiya had founded the Umayyad dynasty, so named after the clan of the Al-Quraysh, Mohammed's own tribe. He passed the caliphate to his son Yazid, the victor at Karbala. Mu'awiya and his successors ruled from Damascus until the middle of the eighth century, but the city remained a polyglot of cultures and not completely dominated by the new religion. It would become as much a rival to Baghdad as Tehran in Persia.

Although the expansion of Islam had been spectacular in the West, the consolidation of the new religion's hold on people's minds was more impressive in the East. It was helped by a period of economic prosperity in the lands between the Tigris and Euphrates which attracted in migrants and willing converts from neighbouring empires. New cities sprang up, including at Karbala and Najaf where the martyr Husain and his father, Ali, were respectively enshrined. While the Umayyads continued their expansion along the north coast of Africa and into the Iberian Peninsula, their lines of communication and supply became over-extended. The surge ran out of steam and was blunted by Charles Martel, the Hammer, at the battle of Tours in 732. In the years that followed, Damascus suffered from further dynastic quarrels which broke out in the face of successive failures. They led to a rebellion by supporters of the descendants of another of the Prophet's uncles, Abbas. For the most part, allegiance was transferred to the Abbasids, whose first caliph, Abu'l Abbas al-Saffah (749–54), chose Baghdad as his capital. He was succeeded by Caliph Mansur, who rebuilt the city (762–66), one of whose major (and prosperous) districts would become Al-Mansuriyya. He also built the fortress at Tikrit, Saddam

Hussein's birthplace. Mansur (754–75) was succeeded in due course by another powerful personality, Harun al-Rashid (786–809), and this continuity of leadership produced another golden age. It was not to last. On Harun's death, civil war broke out and the Caliph Mu'tasim (833–42) even had to transfer his capital temporarily to Samarra, a new city lying to the north on the Tigris.

A caliph could never forget that he was appointed to act as the interpreter of what the Prophet had learnt from divine revelation. He was not simply a secular ruler, no matter how splendid his court might become. As his dominions widened, he needed to use the glue of spirituality to hold the caliphate together. There is a parallel in ninth-century Wessex when Alfred the Great was able to defend his kingdom in the face of the dire threat from the Vikings, with the aid of an already developed parish structure and monastic scholarship. His successors were then able to roll back Danish settlements and culture and unite all England. Alfred had the Bible which he had translated into the vernacular. For their part, the Abbasids also sought to underpin their rule in religious (Islamic) terms and governed in accordance with the Qur'an. The exact date of its formularisation is in dispute, but by the beginning of the dynasty, it was certainly a recognised and regarded as unchangeable text. Further, the caliphs claimed their legitimacy through descent from the Prophet's family. From the Qur'an, the law – *sharia* – was derived. The Abbasids delegated interpretation of it and mediation to a new professional class, the judges (*qadis*) who were appointed in all urban centres. Complementary to them was the development of academies for the study of Islam and encouragement of scholarship. With the Caliphate based at Baghdad, Islamic structure was particularly strong in the lands between the two great rivers.

There was another important dimension of Islam with huge significance for today. The adherents to Ali (*Shi'atu Aliy*)[74] did not disappear after the battle of Karbala. Their claim to legitimacy through Ali, the Prophet's first cousin and, as generally accepted by both sides of the Muslim divide, first convert, was stronger than that posed by the Abbasid caliphs. The Shia also believed that Mohammed had declared Ali – his son-in-law through marriage to his daughter, Fatima – to be the *Imam* (leader) of the faithful by divine right. Even after Karbala, the Imamate succession was maintained. During the Abbasid period, however, many Shia accepted the caliphate in the cause of peace and reconciliation while preserving their religious identity through the founding of schools and academies throughout the Mesopotamian region. The Abbasids encouraged a parallel development in scholarship: in 830, Harun al-Rashid founded the Bayt al-Hikmah (House of Wisdom) in Baghdad. It was, as such, a library or archive of manuscripts and artefacts but was lost with all its contents during the 1258 siege of Baghdad. In its time, it was a centre for the translation of Greek into Arabic and spawned other centres up and down the caliphate. This cultural spread helped to preserve Islamic society even after the Abbasids were finally broken by Hulagu the Mongol and Baghdad, along with most of Tikrit, was destroyed that year. It was a date writ large in Saddam's mind. Sunni and Shia, however, continued to rub along together in the wider world. That all changed in 1979 when a new regime in Iran took control of both secular and spiritual power as an exclusively Shia regime and one ready to expand internationally. It produced another bogeyman in Saddam's mind which he would use ruthlessly to suppress the Shi-ite minority in Iraq. He had plenty of support; a young Sunni associate speaking some years later professed to hate the Shia more than he did the Americans.

Another section of the population deserves special mention. We have already noted the acute enmity between the ancient Mesopotamians and the Hebrews and the enslavement of the Judaeans in Babylon. Not all Jews, by any means, went back to Israel before the birth of Christ; indeed, a substantial population remained behind and were much in evidence during the early medieval period. True to their tradition they were engaged in finance and commerce and helped provide an impetus to the economy. As so often since in many parts of the world, this won them no favours; their strict adherence to Judaism and distinctive social behaviour caused them to be set aside by the caliphate authorities. During the ninth century, they were heavily taxed and forced to live in ghettoes, long before the creation of similar enclaves in England, such as Jewry Street in Winchester and Old Jewry in the City of London. More sinisterly, the Baghdadi Jews were the first to be 'decorated' – by the Caliphate – with yellow patches on their clothing to mark them out from the rest of the community. Given the subsequent close interest post-1871 Germany took in Asia Minor and Iraq in the run-up to the First World War, it is not surprising that the Nazis should have taken note and insisted on the German Jews wearing the same stigma after coming to power in 1933. The caliphs, like many a medieval ruler, exploited Jewish wealth and financial acumen, but they did not persecute. Rather, using the Jews as bankers, they were able to skirt round Islamic rules on usury. Jew and Arab, therefore, were able for the most part[75] to coexist and the Jewish community remained a strong and reasonably content part of Iraqi society down to 1914.

The Sunni Abbasids lost control in 945 when the Shi-ite Buwayhids, a nomadic group from the Caspian shores in northern Persia, founded their own dynasty in Baghdad. Just over one hundred years later, the Buwayhids were replaced by another nomadic force, the Sunni Saljuq Turks emerging from the Asian interior. Neither of these usurpers had strong commercial interests and they failed to revitalise an economy already in decline. During the eleventh and twelfth centuries, irrigation and drainage systems were neglected and swamps and marshes re-appeared in the delta; further north the landscape became increasingly more arid. In parallel, urban centres deteriorated as society became progressively more nomadic, yet still aggressive. In 1075, the Saljuq Turks captured Jerusalem, sparking the Crusades, the first of which was launched in 1099, when Godfrey of Bouillon re-took the Holy City. In 1138, one of Saddam's great heroes was born at his native Tikrit. Saladin, of Kurdish descent, rallied the Islamic forces and, in 1187, destroyed the Latin kingdom of Jerusalem. Despite the best efforts of Richard I of England and Philip Augustus of France during the Third Crusade of the early 1190s, Jerusalem was lost to Western Christianity for all time, save for a few dedicated religious orders caring for holy places under sufferance and often at loggerheads with one another. Islam regained its self-respect and, at about the same time, the Mesopotamian economy recovered. The city of Karbala was rebuilt on the proceeds of the increasing numbers of pilgrims visiting Imam Husain's shrine at the turn of the twelfth and thirteenth centuries. Ironically, a Christian monastery survived in Tikrit and became famous for its production of woollen fabrics. In a strange way, the inter-communal tolerance that once persisted in the Middle East, in the face of occasional outrages, was already in existence during the Middle Ages, for all the savagery of the Crusades.

So far, we have looked at the chronological events that built up the prosperity of the Mesopotamian basin with Baghdad at its centre. There had been inevitable economic ups and downs, but until the middle of the thirteenth century, the indices were generally on the rise. Then came the cataclysmic year of 1258, during which Baghdad lost its pre-eminence amongst the great Arab centres of culture and political power. Non-Muslim Mongols from the steppes of inner Asia supported by Turkish tribesmen swept through Iran and Iraq, destroying most of the city and laying waste its fertile hinterland. The Mongols sought to advance westwards but were stopped in Syria by the Mamluks, the military slave caste that had taken over in Egypt only a few years before and would control the holy cities in western Arabia for nearly three hundred years. The Abbasid caliphate in Baghdad finally came to an end and with it the whole politico-religious system that had dominated society in Mesopotamia and beyond. While Islamic philosophers and scholars continued to yearn for its return, this was never to be. Indeed, no political force sought to re-instate it – and then, only with a travesty – until ISIS in the early years of the twenty-first century. Baghdad-centred Iraq was not to rise again for centuries. The sacking of Baghdad decimated a population numbering one and a half million in the late tenth century; it reversed the prosperity produced by trade passing through from the Baltic to China. Nevertheless, economically, within a few decades the city had recovered. In 1321, the Venetian traveller Marino Sanuto reported that most valuable goods such as spikenard, cloves, nutmeg and mace passed through Baghdad and Tabriz on their way to the Mediterranean and the developing kingdoms in Europe. There is something very impressive about Iraqi resilience which goes back centuries and that Saddam was able to exploit.

Despite Signor Sanato's optimistic picture, Baghdad's medieval woes were not over. The Ottoman Turks were now looming around Byzantium and had crushed the Christian Serbs at Kosovo in 1389. The potential threat they posed was masked by another fearful threat from the north-east. In 1394, Mongol Timur[76] caused a pyramid of skulls to be erected at Tikrit to mark the number of local people his troops had massacred. Saddam repeated the idea in 1989 when he opened the Sword of Victory arch on the approach to central Baghdad, complete with five thousand Iranian helmets captured during the Iran/Iraq War. Timur was not finished with Iraq: in 1401, his forces devastated Baghdad and, although other invasive Tartar and Turcoman dynasties were set up in the aftermath to bring back some semblance of recovery, the city could not return to its former glory and leadership. Without its former economic and social dynamism, its hinterland became increasingly provincial and urban life declined into misery. Without their own leader to re-establish cohesion, the Mesopotamians fell inevitably under the influence of neighbouring Persia.

In 1453, the Western world was rocked by the conquest of Byzantium by the Ottoman Turks. Once entrenched securely in the old eastern half of the former Roman Empire, the Ottomans spread out into Iraq where they came up against the Safavid Shahs of Persia. Following the decisive battle of Chaldiran in 1514, they were able to annex eastern Anatolia and northern Iraq. Two years later, after defeating the Mamluks in Egypt, the Ottomans laid claim to the title of Caliph. Selim I, their Sultan from 1512 to 1520, was the first to enjoy the status which granted him both religious and secular authority over most of the Islamic world. His son and successor, Suleiman the Magnificent, secure in the knowledge that the east posed no immediate threat to him, took on the Christian powers in the Mediterranean and Eastern Europe. In 1522, he took Rhodes and, four years later, he destroyed Hungarian hopes of independence. He went on to besiege Vienna in 1529. Frustrated by the Austrian Hapsburgs, he turned his eyes eastwards again. By the mid-1530s, he had completed the conquest of Iraq and was able to re-open the old trade routes from Baghdad to the Mediterranean. The Ottomans promoted Sunni Islam and, to begin with at least, tolerated the Shia living in the south. Their continuing struggle with Shi-ite Persia, however, meant that southern Iraqis were increasingly regarded with suspicion. The religious divide in Iraq continued to deepen with the Ottomans relying more on Sunni populations in the cities. Suleiman died in 1566, but his great achievement in bringing about law and order within the Ottoman Caliphate continued to have a beneficial effect on Mesopotamian prosperity. During the late sixteenth century, European explorers reported Baghdad as a thriving centre of merchandise once more. In 1583, Ralph Fitch[77] was one of the first Englishmen to travel overland to India, using the route stretching from Aleppo on the Syrian coast, via Fallujah in Al Anbar province and Baghdad, to Basra. Within a few years, an important dimension to this story was added: in 1600, the British East India Company was founded in London, introducing a whole new strategic element to Westminster's foreign, military and maritime policy.

Ottoman dominance did not last. Its naval power was destroyed at the 1571 battle of Lepanto by Don John of Austria and a combination of unfavourable commercial conditions led to a general decline in the economy. Turkish rule in Baghdad was weakened by incursions from Kurdish tribes in the north. This was another thorn in the side that would survive to the present day. In the south, Basra's improved situation as a trade centre at the head of the Gulf loosened political ties with Baghdad. In addition, the adjacent strategically important Shatt al-Arab waterway came under the control of an independent Arab tribe, the al-K'ab. At the same time, the al-Muntafiq tribal confederation, led by the Sa'dun of Mecca, spread into southern Iraq, further diluting the authority of the former Caliphate. No realistic constitutional assessment of the political state of play at the beginning of the seventeenth century could have awarded Baghdad or Constantinople any suzerainty over the northern Gulf or any part of Arabia.

The see-sawing of Mesopotamian misery continued throughout the seventeenth century. Baghdad experienced a tragic famine in 1621, a disastrous flood in 1633 and a widespread visitation of the plague in 1635. The politico-religious struggle with Persia did not cease and, in 1623, hundreds of Sunnis were massacred there. Thousands of southern Mesopotamians, too, were sold into slavery. Such events placed the hideous behaviour of the Spanish Inquisition into relative, if still obnoxious, insignificance. They were stamped, too, on the minds of young Iraqi (Sunni) nationalists in the twentieth century. Tragedy continued. Even the resurgence of the Ottomans under Sultan Murad from 1638 onwards and the accompanying slaughter of fifty thousand (mostly) Persians could not prevent further serious flooding of Baghdad in 1656 and the dreadful double affliction of famine and plague in 1689, the same year that England finally brought the resentments of its Civil War to an end with the Glorious Revolution. Meanwhile, tribal migration from Arabia spread northwards, causing sporadic conflict in the search for potable water. By the last years of the century, civilisation had broken down in Mesopotamia.

In the face of this situation, the Ottoman rulers in Constantinople were forced to abandon direct rule over Iraq and, in 1704, Hassan Pasha, a Mamluk, was accepted as governor of Baghdad. He was able to extend his over-lordship as far as Basra, into Kurdish areas and along the borderlands adjacent to Persia. During his rule revenues were allowed to remain in Iraq and were used for investment in local economic improvement, rather than disappear into the central Caliphate coffers. Hassan was succeeded by his son, Ahmed, in 1723, but he was unable to prevent one hundred thousand dying of starvation during the Persian siege of Baghdad ten years later.

Indirect rule continued under the Pashas into the eighteenth century, disrupted by further natural disasters, family strife and assassinations. The government in Baghdad was certainly incapable still of exercising any sway over the Gulf region where, in 1756, the al-Sabah were establishing an autonomous sheikhdom at Kuwait. In parallel, British interest in the area was enhanced by concern in both London and Bombay for the maintenance of trade and travel routes to India and for the perceived need to bolster the Sublime Porte against an expanding Russian Empire. The latter's intent on finding a warm sea outlet, either through the sub-continent into the Indian Ocean, or along the length of the Black Sea and into the Mediterranean, continued unabated. Thus, in 1764, the British were prepared to indulge the Baghdadi Pasha's vessels flying the red ensign as they plied between the Gulf and Bombay. In the wake, too, of Basra's success as a trading post, the East India Company established a residency there two years later. Anglo/Turkish collaboration deepened despite civil strife in and around Baghdad and further natural disasters in the following decades. Encouraged by the benign Sultan Suleiman the Great (1780–1802),[78] by the end of the eighteenth century the Pasha in Baghdad was content to share the formulation of administrative policy with 'John' Company's local representative. This cooperation extended to acceptance of the Company's deployment of a gunboat flotilla, permitted to patrol up and down the Tigris and the Euphrates in joint action against smugglers, gun-runners and other undesirable elements. In the year 1808, the new British resident, James Rich, represented the best kind of British colonial contribution and behaviour. Subsequently, described as the second most important (to the Pasha) individual in Iraq,[79] he had mastered several languages, including Farsi, Turkish and Arabic, and, thus, was able to understand local customs, religious philosophy and legal systems. He was able to pass himself off as a Mamluk during his extensive travels and started the long line of politically astute British residents and representatives in Baghdad who appreciated the value of secret intelligence. His legacy would extend down through the following centuries, brought to an end only by the First World War and Turkey's decision to support the Central Powers.

Although the French were given an occasional opportunity to build a relationship,[80] British influence in Iraq increased exponentially throughout the nineteenth century. British traders won major concessions: in 1833, they paid only 5.5 per cent tariffs on their goods, compared with the twenty per cent charged to local merchants. The 1838 Battal Limani Anglo/Ottoman Treaty reduced this margin but allowed for a major increase in British exports to the region. British equipment was introduced for a wide range of service industries, from the new steamer routes running the length of the twin rivers to Oman in 1859,[81] the introduction of printing (1860) and a postal system (1874) to the starting up of the electric telegraph (1861). Caught between the two colossi, the industrially advanced Britain and the resources rich Indian Sub-Continent, Iraq was ripe for entrepreneurial exploitation using external investment that ran rings round traditional Islamic financial thinking. Against the background of repeated conflict over land reform – or the lack of it – and repeated natural disasters that killed thousands at a time, the Iraqi economy passed more and more 'into the hands of strangers'.[82] Like the old 'India hands' of the mid-twentieth century, it would produce a cadre of Iraqi-philes whose sentimentality would later see merit in preserving good relations with Baghdad despite the worst of atrocities of its government.

Beneath the soil, meanwhile, British explorers discovered two further major reasons for extending interest in Mesopotamia. In 1841, the distinguished archaeologist Sir Austen Layard visited Iraq for the first time, his travels being helped by a newly opened steamer service along the Tigris. Six years later, he started his programme of excavation of Babylon. Other Western archaeologists weighed in subsequently and, indeed, it was a Frenchman who discovered the Hammurabi Code in 1901 and took the stone tablets to the Louvre. Far more significant, however, was the discovery during the 1870s of oil at Baku on the Caspian Sea coast which prompted further exploration in southern Iran and Ottoman territory. The Persians encouraged this activity; the Ottomans did not, despite the fact that oil seepages had long been noted in the Mosul and Kirkuk areas. With a further major strike in Persia's Khorramshahr in 1908, the Turkish Petroleum Company was founded four years later by Gulbenkian with British financiers anxious to prevent the Americans muscling in. We have already noted the timely purchase of control of the Anglo-Persian Oil Company and exploration of Kuwait's potential on the eve of the First World War. While there were many middle-class Iraqis who valued the British connection, increasingly, there were many more frustrated by missed opportunities and resentful of the imperial connection. This growing element in the population would fuel the intense nationalism that swept Saddam into power.

For all its social instability and natural calamities, the Iraqi economy was prospering at the end of the century. Instead of having to import vast quantities to keep the population from starving, Iraq was exporting one hundred thousand metric tonnes of grain annually. In 1914, Iraqi trade volume was up fifteen-fold on levels recorded in the 1870s. The wealth produced had a knock-on effect for social progress amongst the upper classes: secular education was introduced along with the Western ideas that went with it; the first state schools were opened in 1869. Intermediate level, technical and secondary schools followed to feed the developing administrative services and a small officer corps for the now conscripted armed forces. At the same time, the first newspapers appeared in Baghdad, followed shortly afterwards by socialist-influenced Egyptian journals. Disputation would be further promoted by the founding in 1908 of the Baghdad College of Law, which ran a three-year course, sufficiently respectable for its graduates to find scholastic and professional places in Britain. Three years later it was also turning out civil servants as well as lawyers. On the eve of the First World War, improved literacy and educational facilities were largely responsible for the sending of a hundred officer cadets annually to Istanbul Military College and for the publication of eighty-nine newspapers and journals within Iraq. In 1915, however, Mesopotamia's 160 schools were nearly all devoted to primary education. There were still only four secondary institutions.

At the top of society, therefore, huge strides had been made which benefited the officer classes and intelligentsia, but little had been done for the vast swathes of landless labourers and artisans who populated the city suburbs and the still impoverished areas between the two great rivers. There was little to reflect the glories of previous millennia. Potentially rich for exploitation by outsiders, it did not have the political infrastructure to represent or voice the widespread dissatisfaction of large sections of the population. At the outset of the Great War, Iraq remained a large but neglected part of the Turkish Empire and ripe for implosion and instability once Istanbul lost control of the military situation. By 1917, when the British took Baghdad, Iraqi infrastructure was in ruins. Unlike 2003, however, Britain was able to benefit from a singular mandate and the resources and experience of the Indian Raj, from which to make a promising stab at reversing the ills that had accumulated in Iraq over the centuries.

Four

BRITAIN BECOMES HEAVILY ENGAGED IN THE COLLAPSING TURKISH EMPIRE (1914-19)

When Britain declared war on the Central Powers – Germany and Austria-Hungary – on 4 August 1914, her interests in the Middle East were confined to Egypt and the Sudan, principally as a means for protecting navigation of the Suez Canal, and the shorter passage to the Indian Sub-Continent. A lesser priority, an offshoot of the first, was maintenance of freedom of the seas from piracy, including trade into the Gulf. The latter did not require any substantial military presence and was almost entirely left to the Royal Navy, which for much of the nineteenth century had benefited from agreements with individual sheikhdoms and emirates along the Gulf shores. During the opening years of the twentieth century the Navy's role was still a minor one and never required a presence of more than the occasional port visit by a sloop of war of barely a thousand tons. No capital ship went anywhere near the Middle East, not least since the Admiralty's strategy was to concentrate major units in the North Sea and along the English Channel in case the burgeoning German *Kriegsmarine* should come out to fight. The great naval construction race of the thirty years or so before the First World War had left Britain with but a slender margin of superiority, always at hazard to Germany's development of the submarine. Neither the Turkish nor Austria-Hungarian fleets presented a threat to the Royal Navy. Coaling stations, an indication of further-flung strategic interests, existed only at Bombay, Goa (with licence from Portugal), Trincomalee and Aden; a naval base in Bahrain, HMS *Jufair*, was not opened until 1935. Although coaling facilities had been agreed at Kuwait, they were no more than local. Any naval activity in the theatre was as much a concern to the Viceroy in Delhi as to the Admiralty in Whitehall. There was no infrastructure in place for a major campaign. Strongly supported by the Indian Viceroy, Lord Hardinge, the Colonial and Foreign Offices were reluctant to provoke a major military confrontation with the Ottomans, lest it arouse calls for *jihad* amongst the large Muslim population within the Raj. After all, the Sultan in Constantinople was also the Caliph.

When war came, the expectation was that the military trial of strength would take place along the Franco/Belgian/German frontiers. Within weeks, however, both sides were literally bogged down in trenches facing one another across a no-man's land that would change little for nearly four years. As Britain and France were increasingly bled white, minds in Whitehall searched desperately for an alternative strategy, one which might also use imperial resources and the good offices of local allies. This was the essence of Winston Churchill's vision as First Lord of the Admiralty which materialised into the ill-conducted and abortive Gallipoli campaign. Churchill had previously taken another vital decision shortly after he took office in October 1911; from then on, all newly constructed warships were to be fuelled by oil, not coal. This was only three years after the founding of the Anglo-Persian Oil Company which was quickly brought under British commercial control. Even the non-interventionist Lord Hardinge in Delhi could accept that British-owned or financed oil installations at Abadan and elsewhere along the Persian west coast required protection. Long before the first British and Anzac forces landed on the Gallipoli peninsula, therefore, some five thousand British Indian troops were diverted to the Gulf to protect British interests there. The contingent had embarked in one of the first troop convoys to bring reinforcements for the Western Front from the Raj. It sailed from Bombay on 16 October 1914 at a point when Turkey was still neutral. Whitehall, too, had recognised the necessity for prophylactic action before the almost foregone conclusion of Constantinople throwing in its lot with Berlin. Discretion, however, remained the better part of valour and, thus, it was not until the convoy was in the middle of the Indian Ocean that Brigadier Walter Delamain, commander of 16 Indian Brigade (listed as part of 6 [Poona] Division of the Indian Army), was permitted to open the sealed orders which required him to detach from the convoy the four ships containing his formation and to proceed up the Gulf to Bahrain. To proceed further – to Basra – would have been too provocative. Nevertheless, over the next four years, this small force would multiply inexorably into an army comprised of three corps – at one time or another amounting to eight divisions – and supported by thousands of locally recruited auxiliaries. It would end its major operations with the capture of Baghdad.

Delamain's troops were composed of the best and most loyal sepoys of the Indian Raj – Pathans, Punjabis, Sikhs and Dogras. They were steeled further by a British battalion – the Dorsets. Their commander, too, was much experienced in the brush fire wars of the pre-1914 British Empire. Despite these positive factors, it all started badly. Accustomed only to seeing the occasional Royal Naval sloop, Bahrain was totally unprepared for the reception of several troopships and escorts. Yes, Sir Percy Cox was on hand to reassure the brigadier about the political context: he told Delamain, ambiguously and presumptuously, that the Emirate was 'a quasi-British protectorate'. This did not prevent Bahrain from soon running out of food and potable drink, forcing the soldiers to remain on their transports, thirsting in unseasonably late October hot weather and eating 'disgraceful' food.[83] Not for the last time in this story, British forces were being deployed without adequate protection from the relentless Gulf sun. It was only going to get worse. Few of those enduring the harsh conditions knew why they were there and it was only early the next month that morale rose on the news that Turkey was entering the war. This coincided with the brigade's move north, ostensibly to protect oil installations further up the Persian coast but also to shield Sheikh Mubarak of Kuwait, considered Britain's most reliable ally in the Gulf. By 6 November, five hundred of Delamain's force had landed on Turkish territory – at Fao on the mouth of the Shatt al-Arab – and the 1,070-ton sloop HMS *Odin* had knocked out the Turkish artillery in the nearby ancient fort. The landings proved a farce with many soldiers, unused to manoeuvring small boats, being swept back out to sea, or onto Persian soil, as the always treacherous tide turned. Fortunately, the Turks had fled.

The Turkish troops facing the Indian brigade initially were less than impressive. They were starved of supplies which had to be sent across a Mesopotamia without railheads, flood-free roads or sufficient river transportation. Moreover, following the immediately pre-war purges in the wake of the Turkish military disasters in the Balkans (1912–13), there were few experienced officers. With more resolution, self-confidence and cohesion, the thirteen thousand-strong Turkish force should have been sufficient to push Delamain's brigade back into the sea before it had the opportunity to build a bridgehead. Instead, they withdrew north, leaving Basra to the invaders, who were quick to turn the port into a strategic supply base. Supported by shellfire from a strong naval flotilla, the Indian and British soldiers alike were able to withstand the quagmire caused by torrential rain and could claim early skirmishing victories on the coast as the Turks fell back. But the warnings of what was likely to come the further British forces pressed inland were there. In this, the serious shortage of river transports able to ply amidst the vagaries of the river system, was a crucial factor in re-supply and re-deployment operations up the Tigris. One illicit diary entry says it all: after a violent storm as darkness fell on 17 November, Major WC Spackman, a medical officer of the 48th (Pioneers) Bengal Infantry on board a supply dhow, recorded the 'loss of my sleeping bag of camel's wool, two blankets, my toilet things, much of my khaki including my great coat and all available underclothes and pyjamas… all went to the bottom of the river'.[84] Doubtless, Tommies on the Western Front lost as much of their personal possessions, but they were the more easily supplied from across the English Channel and by many voluntary support organisations.

Far from finding themselves in the legendary cradle of civilisation – Mesopotamia, the land between two rivers – British and Indian troops alike encountered a mixture of desert and swamp and a sparse local population with little or no administrative infrastructure. From May to

September, often longer, the daytime temperatures soared to over fifty degrees centigrade and, at night, they could fall to near freezing. The landscape, which has changed little to the present day, was described graphically by Robert Byron (1905–41) in his travelogue *The Road to Oxiana* (1937): "Mesopotamia has remained a land of mud deprived of mud's only possible advantage, vegetable fertility. It is a mud plain, so flat that a single heron reposing on one leg beside some rare trickle of water in a ditch, looks as tall as a wireless aerial. From this plain rise villages of mud and cities of mud. The rivers flow with liquid mud. The air is composed of mud refined into a gas. The people are mud-coloured; they wear mud-coloured clothes and their national hat is nothing more than a formalised mud-pie."[85] Byron was writing decades before Saddam sought to drain the marshlands in the south of Iraq, threatening the very existence of a civilisation going back into the mists of time.

At the outset, the *élan* of the Indian crack troops was sufficient to break third-rate enemy formations fearful of a bayonet charge. Commentaries at the time suggest that officers, at least, were cock-a-hoop, as if they were still chasing bandits on the North-West Frontier. The casualties had yet to mount up on the British side and the huge problem of caring for the wounded in such a bleak terrain had still to manifest itself. Basra fell almost without a shot being fired, other than to restore some degree of control over the looters who had run riot after the withdrawal of the Turkish garrison. The *Daily Mail* crowed after the fall of the city on 23 November in typical gung-ho terms: 'Another Red Patch on the Map.' If it had ever been, however, Basra was not the fabled seaport of Sinbad the Sailor. Rather, it was 'a maze of tortuous lanes... ankle-deep in filth, offal and litter', with a 'total absence of any sanitary system... and numerous disease-ridden brothels.' Not then, an ideal centre for hospitals, convalescence, rest and recuperation.

It is not easy to be precise about deaths from enemy action or from illness. It is safe to say, however, that far more died from the latter during the Mesopotamian campaign. One assessment puts the figures at eighty-five thousand battle casualties and 170,000 dying from disease. These overall figures have been broken down as follows: 11,008 killed outright, 5,288 died of wounds, 2,341 missing, 12,879 captured and 53,697 wounded; 16,712 died of disease and 154,343 evacuated sick. The last figure is quite extraordinary since it represents over a sixth of the total number of combatants deployed in theatre by the Allies. Many sent out from Britain were totally unused to climatic extremes; my grandmother's brother left Liverpool on 4 June 1915 on board the RMS *Tunisian* with replacements for the 1st/4th battalion of the Royal Hampshire Regiment. He died of pneumonia 11 July 1916, having contracted 'influenza' in the Tigris valley and was buried near Kut. He saw no action on the battlefield. The Hampshires had lost nine of its eleven officers and 180 of its 240 other ranks engaged in the battles around Amara in January 1915. In a country where there was nothing to forage or purchase, poor diet added to the generally discomforting conditions. Indian troops were worst affected. The commander of 3 Division, General Hugh Keary recorded in May 1916 that 'sickness [was] excessive' with 'cholera, bowel diseases of all sorts as well as jaundice and other things'. By mid-July, one unit – the 82nd Punjabis – was suffering from an 'appalling' rate of sickness; as a result of a lack of green food, 119 men were sent to hospital in nineteen days.[86] During the same period the equivalent of three divisions, up to forty-five thousand men, were evacuated from Basra to India. At the other end of the casualty spectrum were the lead-swingers. Private, subsequently Lance-Corporal, Edward Roe, a veteran of the retreat from Mons, wrote of the imaginative excuses dreamt up for men to remain under convalescence in Basra. One 'malingerer', he wrote, successful already in prolonging his stay for seven months, complained to a new, yet 'fearless' medical officer, of unidentifiable pains in his chest. He was sent out on light duty but returned the next day, complaining that his false teeth had been taken off overnight by a jackal. He was despatched to the dentist with a broad grin on his face, since he knew this would eke out his stay in Basra for another six months.[87]

In one way or another, British forces suffered severely in Mesopotamia, more so than their opponents. Turkish forces during the campaign numbered just over half the nearly nine hundred thousand British-Indian forces' strength. While losing 13,069 soldiers on the battlefield and many more – some fifty-six thousand – were wounded or died of their wounds, their efforts tied down a numerically far superior force. For all those engaged it was a hellish struggle and, as in the European trenches, the combatants might have complained in their illicit diaries, but they did not have the opportunity for the wider and more public criticism their descendants were able to voice ninety years later. The campaign has not, until recent times, received the critical analysis that the Western Front and the Allenby/Lawrence of Arabia saga have attracted.

Beyond the landings and initial military successes, including an apparently brilliant victory at Kut al-Amara in September 1915 – even so, almost a year on from the start of the campaign – political anomalies continued to dog progress. The Foreign Office remained anxious that the old ambitions of the Raj should not get out of hand. This concern grew as the British generals in the field, inevitably, had to put military considerations first. They were egged on by Sir Percy Cox who argued that the Arabs would never come out against the Central Powers unless the Turks were pushed out of Mesopotamia. Moreover, it was clear to the men on the ground in Basra, military and civilian, that 'no remnant of Turkish administration now remains in the region'. In its place 'the British flag has been established'. Indeed, the Basra Declaration after occupation of the city, drafted by Cox, spoke of annexation, a far cry from the comparatively minor task given to Delamain only a few weeks before. When Delhi assumed that the government of Iraq would fall to the Government of India, because of its 'intimate connection with the Gulf', alarms bells rang in Whitehall. There were, after all, the competing concerns of the French and Russian allies to be considered, not to mention conduct of the principal theatre of operations in Flanders. Additionally, from April 1915, there was the debilitating struggle on the Gallipoli beaches. London, therefore, made it quite clear that, in accordance with Allied agreement for any occupation of enemy territory to be regarded as only temporary until the war, there was to be no attempt to alter the existing provincial administration in Mesopotamia. Indeed, there were those in Whitehall, the First Lord of the Admiralty among them, who argued for a complete withdrawal.[88]

Cox thought differently. It was still the cool season and there were rumours of Arab rebellion against the Turks around the holy city of Najaf, less than 150 miles south of Baghdad. In the face of strong misgivings in Whitehall, he urged a determined advance on the Iraqi capital which, given uncertain Arab loyalty to the Turkish Empire, the disarray of enemy forces and pressure being exerted elsewhere by the Russians in Armenia, he considered would fall easily. The more determined the thrust north, the greater likelihood of local support. Despite continuing reservation in both London and Delhi, the Military Secretary in the India Office, Sir Edmund Barrow,[89] favoured an immediate advance on Qurna, thirty miles north of Basra and occupying a key position at the confluence of the Tigris and Euphrates. It is also one of the supposed sites of the Garden of Eden. Out of purely military considerations, Barrow, among others, stressed that soldiers could not simply hang around in Basra or wait for worsening conditions as summer approached; they had to be given something to do. Fooled by the welcome the urban middle classes gave him in Basra, he totally underestimated the latent Arab ill-will and suspicions in the Gulf as to British intentions.

He reckoned, too, without the ungovernability of the area beyond Basra. Here, respect was reserved for the religious leadership – the *mujtahids* accepted as authority in Shi-ite Islamic law – that held spiritual power in the great cities of Lower Mesopotamia: Najaf, Karbala and Khadimain. When Constantinople, urged on cynically by German advisers, called for *jihad* against the *kafirs* (infidels or unbelievers), many Shia clerics were more than ready to inflame the streets, a harbinger of events ninety years later. By January 1915, holy war had been preached in every mosque in Mesopotamia.[90] As Sheikh Ajaimi al-Mansur of the Al-Muntafiq tribal confederation put it a year or so later: "...what greater loyalty is there than this, that I should carry out faithfully what God ordered me in regard to *Jihad* against non-believers, the enemies of God and our religion." Although in Cairo, the British Arab Bureau was using imagination in winning over the Sunni Arabs in Western Arabia, three hundred years of rule in India managing Muslim/Hindu coexistence had not prepared British officials or generals for this intensity of religious fervour. At this distance, it is quite extraordinary that such a revered luminary as Gertrude Bell could see the 'task of controlling the tribes of the desert [as not] one of the most difficult problems of Mesopotamian administration'.[91] This contempt for a formidable politico-religious force expressed at the heart of British Intelligence in the Middle East was hardly helpful in bringing objectivity to expanding military operations. Foreign Office Arabists made similar misjudgements in 1990 when concluding that Saddam would not attack Kuwait.

Even in Basra, government had evaporated. Again, foreshadowing the mistakes of the early twenty-first century, British officials sought to fill the power vacuum with a system that conformed with British standards of efficiency. It might have worked in India; Iraq was quite another story. Recruitment of local police proved impossible; cadres from the Punjab and Aden had to be brought in as a result. Efforts at introducing education were stymied by existing tuition emanating from the mosques being restricted to close study of the Quran and Arabic. Faced with hostility, a plague of theft and disorder, the only immediate measure available was the punishment detail which only deepened resentment and inflamed a bad situation further. Neither could it be ruthless or extensive enough to cow the population. Yet, nothing grieved British soldiers more than to see the bodies of their dead comrades exhumed in the night by thieves only interested in making off with their shrouds. Such behaviour, repeated in North Africa during the Second World War, only convinced the ordinary British soldier that Arabs were a 'filthy' race and of a lower order. Ironically, Westerners today are referred to in some Arab quarters as 'the filth'. Apart from individuals like Shakespear at Kuwait, Bell and Lawrence, first-hand knowledge of Arab culture and society was a rarity. When a comparatively well-intentioned Iraqi, Nuri al-Sa'id, offered his services to Cox, with suggestions as to how Arab officers in the Turkish Army might be suborned, he was deported to India for having consorted with elements whose potential loyalty was regarded as doubtful.

With the advance on Qurna early in December 1914, troubles really began. All those involved in planning the operation were woefully ignorant of the Mesopotamian interior's terrain; there had never been the call for a pre-war staff exercise. There was no cavalry deployed for early reconnaissance and the infantry had to cross ground that afforded little or no cover. When it came to crossing rivers as much as two or three hundred yards wide, there was all but no appropriate transport vessels; charts for accurate navigation were non-existent. It was little consolation that the Turks were almost equally blind. Despite this, the Qurna garrison surrendered on 9 December. It was no Garden of Eden, merely 'a collection of filthy lanes, and mud and reed hovels, with a few brick houses, barracks and custom house'. It was not a satisfactory base from which to progress further or to garrison troops. As the New Year wore on, the land around Qurna became inundated and defences against flooding became a greater priority than deployment to the north. Troops wilted under unseasonable heat and the ever-present threat of malaria.

After a good deal of prevarication in Delhi and London, British forces were made up to Corps size with two divisions, under the command of Lieutenant General Sir John Nixon, an infanteer turned cavalry officer, with the reputation of being 'a thruster'. Despite worsening conditions as the cooler season came to an end, he pushed his forces to Shaiba en route to Kut al-Amara. This afforded him an early enough victory in March which only encouraged him in his conviction that the capture of Baghdad was a realistic goal, even without waiting for reinforcements. The further this son of the Raj marched his forces north, the more the campaign became a Government of India affair, with London slow to commit further resources to a theatre it still regarded as subsidiary to Europe and the Eastern Mediterranean. For Nixon, however, nothing succeeded like success and, as inferior Turkish forces fell back before his troops, he insisted that the advance should become a hot pursuit. On 28 September, the Turks abandoned Kut and now, some nearly ninety miles distant from Basra and supplies, the British column occupied the town. So far, casualties had been light – only ninety-four dead – compared with Turkish losses of some four thousand, of which nearly a third had been taken prisoner. If one ignored the numbers that had fallen out through sickness or were needed to guard re-supply columns and prisoners, it looked like a comprehensive and strategic victory.

The term 'mission creep' was first used during the Vietnam War when the American military advisory role was transformed almost overnight into the full-scale defence of a country. The expression, however, is particularly apt when applied to the 1915 campaign pursued by Nixon and Cox. There were those, too, in the popular press and from commerce, who agitated for a continuous advance on Baghdad, citing the ease with which the Turkish Army had so far been sent packing. With Gallipoli threatening to become a major disaster, Whitehall was also coming around to the view that the capture of Baghdad would compensate as an easier target. Mission creep without unanimity of purpose is a recipe for calamity. So it was with the occupation of Kut al-Amara. The War Office recognised the dangers in a further advance on Baghdad,[92] considering that the Turks were still able to mass forces before the city, forces that would far outnumber troops at Nixon's immediate disposal or the reinforcements that might, or might not, be afforded. There was certainly a conflict between Delhi and London as to where to find the additional strength needed to capture and, more importantly, to hold Baghdad.

The road to defeat started with increasingly determined fifth column raids on British positions concentrating around Aziziyeh, some sixty miles – 102 by river – above Kut. Locally successful Arab inroads into defensive lines betrayed not only the reduced strengths of individual units but also their exhaustion and low morale, especially among the Indian sepoys. All the bolstering British battalions were down to half-strength. Additionally, the problems of re-supply had multiplied after a sudden drop in river levels had stranded many of the transports. Against the increasing qualms of his senior officers, but apparently still intent on taking Baghdad, Nixon ordered his divisional commander, General Townshend,[93] to advance against a Turkish column located at El Kutuniya, twelve miles upriver from Aziziyeh. The move forward was to start on 14 November and the first objective was to root out the Turks dug in at Salman Pak, close to the site of the ancient battle of Ctesiphon,[94] where the ruined palace of the Sassanian king Chosroes may still be seen. What would not have been fully understood at the time is that Salman Pak is believed to be where the Prophet Mohammed's barber was buried.

More importantly, British commanders did not appreciate that, by 17 November, the bulk of a new crack Turkish division, commanded by the eminent German military theorist General Colmar von der Goltz had arrived at Ctesiphon. Previously second-rate enemy units prone to panic and flight were now steeled by 'rugged' Anatolian peasants who filled the ranks of the new formation. They now outnumbered the inadequately supplied, worn out and depleted British. Additionally, Nixon had pushed his forces well beyond the range of supporting naval artillery.

Over two days, the outcome of the second battle of Ctesiphon was uncertain, but on 24 November, the Turkish Army withdrew towards Baghdad, having suffered severely, losing some six thousand casualties and three thousand deserters. The British were left controlling the field but with the formidable task of moving 3,500 wounded by carts on iron-rimmed wheels to the nearest river vessels available. "Ten miles over rough desert or sun-baked ploughland, all intersected by a mass of ditches and several deep nullahs."[95] Contemporary accounts of what the Tommies and Indian sepoys suffered before any medic was able to attend to their injuries paint scenes as bad, if not worse, as any on the Western Front.

Fearing a Turkish counterattack with fresh reinforcements, Townshend chose to fall back on Kut. Reluctantly, after having learnt how weak his remaining and immediately available strength actually was, Nixon agreed. After an impressive fighting retreat which testified to Townshend's qualities as a commander, his division was able to consolidate behind defensive lines around Kut. The town had few, if any, strong points. There, British and Indian troops alike waited for a promised relief that never came. They were soon cut off and, after repeated unsuccessful attempts to come to their rescue and nearly five months of resistance, in appalling conditions, Townshend was obliged to surrender unconditionally on 29 April 1916. In what has been assessed as the worst Allied defeat of the First World War, the entire Kut garrison passed into a cruel enemy's hands. Over thirteen thousand British and Indian prisoners were dispersed; the officers were sent to Baghdad, the other ranks marched to Aleppo hundreds of miles away.

The fall of Kut was not the first major defeat the Allies had suffered at the hands of the Turks in the Middle East theatre. It came less than four months after the final evacuation of Gallipoli. Although still licking its wounds, however, the British Army now had one less drain on its resources and both men and supplies could be diverted to Mesopotamia. Moreover, while Arab irregulars had repeatedly harassed Townshend's retreat and potential relief columns along the Tigris and Euphrates, Sharif Hussein of Mecca was about to lead the great Arab revolt with attacks on isolated Turkish garrisons and railways; he declared war on 5 June. Ironically, too, on the same day that Kut surrendered, a secret agreement between Britain and France was concluded on the post-war carve-up of the Turkish Empire. Leaving Sharif Hussein in complete ignorance and taking little account of the military situation on the ground, the Sykes-Picot agreement divided 'Turkish Arabia' into spheres of influence.[96] After a Turkish defeat, France would take over Syria and Britain would get Iraq. Whatever past misgivings and lack of military success hitherto, Baghdad had now to be taken.

Throughout the fierce heat of the 1916 summer, the British Army in Mesopotamia was brought back up to strength and prepared for a renewed offensive once the cooler weather had set in. It had a new commander, 'thruster' Nixon having been replaced, first by a stand-in, Sir Percy Lake, and then by Frederick Stanley Maude, the youngest of the divisional commanders in theatre.[97] Maude had a reputation as a master of detail and had impressed at the Dardanelles by reconstituting a shattered 13th Division into a fighting formation 'second to none'. He, too, was offensive-minded and instructed his subordinate commanders to act aggressively as soon as each new 'jumping-off' position had been established. Nevertheless, unlike Nixon, he took care to consolidate his supply lines as each objective was taken. Not unlike Montgomery after his less successful predecessors in the Western Desert during the Second World War, Maude was given what he asked for. By December 1916, British effective combat strength in Mesopotamia had risen to one hundred thousand. In contrast, Turkish forces had been drained by pressure on other fronts, notably in the Caucasus.

Maude's offensive began in earnest in mid-December and, after, as he put it, 'very strenuous fighting' and some heavy casualties, by mid-February 1917, the Turks were in full retreat. With much improved support from naval units along the rivers, the enemy was turned into 'a disorganised rabble'. Kut was re-taken on 23 February and seven thousand prisoners captured with vast quantities of stores and equipment. Maude pushed his forces on to Aziziyeh and then, having waited for re-supply, continued the march on Baghdad. After all the privations and heavy casualties suffered by the British-Indian forces since October 1914, the capture of Baghdad was achieved on 10 March. It was a truly amazing feat of arms and military leadership. That said, it was to be the beginning of a long and rock-strewn road that would lead eventually to the chaos Iraq poses for the world today. Almost as an ill omen, Maude died of cholera in November 1917 when directing operations around Ramadi and Tikrit. Saddam would have known that.

Five

THE BRITISH MANDATE

After General Allenby's final defeat of the Turkish Army at Megiddo in Palestine in September 1918, he permitted Prince Faisal al-Hussein to enter Damascus with 'Lawrence of Arabia' at his side. Istanbul's control of its empire collapsed. Even in major urban centres the lights went out and the ruthless Australian general waited until the population was desperate before he sent in his engineers and medics to restore some semblance of social order. Ninety-five years later, US/British forces would be faced with a similar situation after the collapse of Saddam's Iraq. By November 1918, however, most of Iraq had come under British military administration; only a Turkish detachment held out in Mosul in north-east Iraq. The Kurdish highlands in the north and the old Shi-ite cities of Karbala and Najaf had long been beyond Turkish administrative control. Any hope of renewing some form of influence over Basra or Kuwait had long since disappeared. The Turkish empire had ceased to exist; chaos reigned in many areas.

Into this vast power vacuum stepped the old surviving colonial powers, Britain and France, both exhausted from four years of trench warfare, the German U-boat blockade and a vicious influenza pandemic. Despite all this, both London and Paris seemed intent on retaining, even expanding their influence in the Middle East. The better placed were the British, whose army of six hundred thousand in Mesopotamia had already taken Baghdad on 11 March 1917 and within six months had gained a degree of control in central Iraq. To the West, British and Arab forces had seized the Levant. Within weeks of the November 1918 Armistice, British troops, including my paternal grandfather serving with the Royal Hampshires, were occupying Istanbul and controlling the Bosporus. With few troops on the ground, but determined to exact reparations, the French laid claim to the German holdings in Turkish Petroleum. In April 1919, Britain and France reached agreement on their percentage holdings in the company; oil had already become a major factor behind post-war diplomatic calculation. At the end of the negotiations for peace, dragging out over a series of conferences for four or five years, both powers emerged with an international licence to dominate the development of large tracts of the former Turkish empire, under which the black gold awaited exploitation. At the San Remo conference in April 1920, Britain was accorded mandates from the freshly fledged League of Nations which gave her control over Iraq and Transjordan. At the same time, France received the mandate for the new state of Lebanon and, to the north and east, the territory that would form modern Syria. The League expected both powers to foster the development of their charges towards independence and eventual full membership of the new world order.

With a colonial infrastructure dating back centuries, the British were in a better position to restore law and order. As before the War, Gulf affairs fell within the remit of the India Office which now put its stamp on the government of Iraq. The Ottoman administrative system was dismantled and by the end of 1918, the country was being ruled increasingly as part of the Raj. The Anglo/Indian legal code came to replace Turkish law, the Indian rupee was introduced as the currency and British officers from the sub-continent were drafted in to organise the civil and military services. By 1920, the number of British administrative officials had risen to 1022. From July 1918 onwards, British regulations were being applied to endemic tribal disputes, even if they had limited effect outside major urban centres. Semi-independent groupings such as the Kurds and major Iraqi tribes were left to rule themselves, provided they did not cross swords with the occupying power. As a result, although British troops had penetrated the Iraqi interior to not far short of Mosul by late 1918, the Kurdish highlands and large tracts of the Shi-ite south between Karbala and Najaf were never pacified. This was to leave running sores for Baghdad-based future governments.

At one end of the old Turkish imperial spectrum, the August 1920 Treaty of Sevres provided for an independent Kurdistan which it was envisaged would also enter the League of Nations. This, of course, never happened and the Kurdistan population stretching over Iranian, Iraqi, Syrian and Turkish territory, to this day, has been unable to take its place in the world, despite its unique characteristics and achievements. At the other end, Kuwait remained firmly outside the Iraqi orbit, although the British did not consider it as a candidate for statehood. Was it not, after all, merely a petty tribal emirate and useful trading post? There seemed to be no pressing reason to change the pre-war position, as was the case with the other sheikhdoms down the Gulf.

Despite their dominant military power, it was not all plain sailing for the old colonial powers. In order to initiate their mandate over Syria, the French had first to fight off Prince Faisal and local Syrian militias on 24 July 1920 at Maisalum just outside Damascus. Seven weeks earlier in Iraq, Sunni and Shi-ite tribes united in revolt at Rumaythah, after a local sheikh had been imprisoned for not paying agricultural debts. The operation to suppress the rising cost four hundred British dead and £40 million, the equivalent of £1.2 billion today. Large expanses of territory in the mid-Euphrates region south of Diwaniyyah and Muntafiq remained outside British control. This situation did not improve even after the treaty of Sevres had finally and formally broken up the former Ottoman empire. Nevertheless, the settlement allowed the Arabic-speaking Sir Percy Cox to arrive at Basra on 1 October 1920 as Britain's first High Commissioner to Iraq and to start the civilianisation of the mandatory administration in earnest. This was the man tasked to prepare Iraq to become an independent Arab state. His brief included the drawing up of an international boundary with Kuwait.

Cox was a servant of empire. Born in 1864, the son of a cricketer, he was educated at Churchill's subsequent alma mater, Harrow, and from his earliest days showed an interest in natural history, geography and travel – a colonial official in embryo. As a third son, he went to Sandhurst and then joined the Cameronians on station in India. Three years later, in 1889, he was promoted to the Bengal Staff Corps, having been singled out for his planning skills. In the same year, he married his life-time partner, Louisa, the youngest daughter of the Irish-born surgeon-general, John Butler Hamilton. His early career progressed through the last years of the nineteenth century in British Somaliland and Muscat. During this period, he was engaged in activities as wide-ranging as leading successful expeditions against pirates in the Gulf, through to appointment as the Viceroy's representative with the Maharajah of Baroda. In October 1899, the incoming Viceroy, Lord Curzon, chose Cox as Political Agent and Consul at Muscat, where he succeeded in blunting French encroachment. From 1904, he was the first British Political Resident in the Gulf and Consul-General for several provinces in Persia, residing at Bushire. There he struck up a close relationship with his subordinate, Captain Shakespear, the agent at Kuwait. Like him, he got on well with Emir Mubarak but was, at the same time, in favour of conciliation with the Ottomans in order to promote trade and oil exploration by the Anglo-Persian Oil Company. He also played a large part in ensuring that the Ibn Saud did not align with the Turks in 1914. During the war, he occupied a series of senior military/intelligence posts alongside the British military thrust through Mesopotamia to Baghdad. By the second half of 1918, he had become a figure of central importance to the government there. Too old to volunteer for the trenches – and too valuable an operative – he survived the carnage of the First World War, unlike many a good young administrator from the Raj.

Cox knew the Gulf and its littoral states like the back of his hand and he was quick to make important Iraqi friends, not least the former Ottoman officer and Basra-based nationalist, Nuri Pasha as-Sa'id. Like perhaps better-known historical figures such as TE Lawrence and Gertrude Bell, Cox recognised that the promotion of Arab nationalism was the better solution for settling the Middle East than old-style colonialism. He was, therefore, exactly the right man to be put in charge of Britain's mission to develop Iraq into a nation-state. He is to be credited with the early and impressive achievements towards that goal, albeit starting from a low base. Iraq had remained a primitive agricultural economy with minimal irrigation facilities – only 143 pumps serving seventy-five square miles.

As he was quick to recognise, an increasingly effective central control was required in Baghdad, reinforced by professional police and intelligence services. He encouraged an Arabised civil service with British advisors aided by the prospect of growing resources and promoted prosperity with the advantage of increasing engagement in oil exploration. Within this context, Cox had sufficient self-confidence to place and maintain a nationalist government in power. And he had known many of its top personalities for years. They shared, after all, a decided unity of purpose in achieving the ultimate goal.

The new High Commissioner also appreciated that Britain's financial situation after four years of total war necessitated a drawing in of administrative horns overseas. Growing unrest in the sub-continent was threatening to stretch British resources dangerously. Having stabilised government under his trusted colleague, the *Naqib* of Baghdad, Abd Al-Rahman al-Gaylani,[98] Cox was able to attend the March 1921 Cairo Conference called by the then Colonial Secretary of State, Winston Churchill. There Cox tabled proposals for the reduction of troops from Mesopotamia with a resulting welcome decrease in expenditure. His second objective was to choose a ruler for Iraq. In this, he was a strong proponent of the third son of Sharif Husain of Mecca, Prince Faisal. The latter had collaborated closely with TE Lawrence during the advance through the Levant to Damascus and, besides having proven military skills, was considered to be a good political operator. On 11 July, he was duly elected Faisal I by the Iraqi Council of State. After his passing military failure before Damascus the previous year and disappointment in the post-war settlement of the Middle East, this long-standing friend of Britain was receiving due compensation, largely thanks to Cox's shrewd judgement. It was a choice, nevertheless, that irked many an Iraqi nationalist who regarded Faisal as a failed interloper. The new king's reputation was hardly enhanced by his father's expulsion from Mecca in 1924 by the Ibn Saud. For the young Saddam, indeed, the imposition of Faisal was a grievous insult. At the time, however, Britain's stock remained high: at a royal durbar held on 31 July 1921 on the bank of the Euphrates, the influential sheikhs of the Sunni Dulaim and Anizah tribal confederations swore allegiance 'to you because you are acceptable to the British government'.[99] Further significant political progress was made four weeks later when a constitutional monarchy was inaugurated with Gaylani as Prime Minister.

The following year, Cox completed the demarcation of Iraq's southern borders from the Gulf to Transjordan. This included the redrawing of the Kuwait/Saudi frontier to the latter's advantage, with Iraq gaining a portion of Saudi territory. A neutral zone in the deepest desert was established between Iraq and Saudi Arabia to reduce the potential friction between the two countries. Importantly, the Iraq border with Kuwait remained unaffected, although the distinction between red and green zones disappeared. Kuwaiti sovereignty appeared to have been consolidated and the Emir was no longer responsible for collecting dues on behalf of the now extinct Turkish Sultanate.

Progress was also made on London's relationship with Baghdad. In February 1922, the Colonial Office laid a draft treaty before the Iraqi Council, but this met with early resistance from the Shi-ite tribes led by Sheikh Mahdi al-Khalisi in Karbala. The draft had its supporters, too: Abd al-Muhsin as Sa'dun, the Sunni and pro-British minister of justice from Basra, urged the cabinet to accept it as a basis for progress towards independence. Unrest in the south delayed elections for a constituent assembly and, in the king's absence in hospital for an appendicostomy, Cox was forced to take strong measures against Shi-ite militancy. The honeymoon was over. In the north, too, flagging British troops were even compelled to withdraw from the Kurdish cities of Rawandiz and Sulaymaniyah by a revived Turkish Army under the direction of Mustafa Kamal Ataturk, who had laid claim to the old Ottoman province of Mosul. Against the background of instability at both ends of the country, a treaty between Britain and Iraq was signed on 10 October by the Council in Baghdad with the proviso that it should be ratified by a constituent assembly. Under the treaty the British role would become only advisory, a step too far for Gaylani, who was replaced by Sa'dun.

As the 1920s wore on, Britain's ability to retain control of its empire in the East began to falter. In India, the nationalist movement received an early boost from the 1922 Amritsar 'massacre', a failure in crowd control which was in itself a symptom of ailing self-confidence and a growing inability to handle local political unrest sensitively. In denigrating the officials involved, it is sometimes forgotten how so many experienced 'India hands', young and old, were lost after they had volunteered to serve in France. The damage caused by the sapping of this cadre has never been fully assessed. The Raj, as we have noted, had also to spare administrators and advisers for Mesopotamia in the immediate aftermath of the War. By 1923, the number of British advisers in Iraq had necessarily shrunk by a half. This was at a time when a resurgent Turkey under Ataturk was pressing for amendment of the Treaty of Sevres. Diplomatically, at Lausanne in July 1925, Britain was able to secure Iraq's retention of Mosul province, but was in no position on the ground to support the Kurds in their desire for independence and membership of the League. This was a major let-down, leaving yet another festering sore which has yet to be healed. Left over, too, from Cox's demarcation of the southern frontier, the border between Iraq and Kuwait was only recognised in an exchange of letters between London and Baghdad which were marked by their ambivalence and failure to define territory closely.

After a Shi-ite *fatwa* against the draft British-Iraqi treaty in June 1923 and the suppression of opposition to participation in them, elections for a constituent assembly were held later in the year. When the new body met the following March, it approved a new constitution with a ministerial council or cabinet responsible to the king. It also provided parliament with the power to bring down governments. For the next ten years, prime ministers and their ministerial teams came and went with destabilising regularity. A large part of the problem lay with the fact that the new constitution produced a tribal-dominated parliament out of sympathy with the attempts of successive governments to exert central and unifying control. With the Shi-ite areas largely in opposition to the Western concept of democracy on religious grounds and patchy Kurdish representation, attendance at the constituent assembly was unimpressive – only sixty-nine out of a hundred representatives. Only thirty-seven of those voted for the constitution, despite heavy British pressure; there were eight abstentions and twenty-four against. By no means a resounding endorsement for the first step towards establishing an independent constitutional monarchy. A month later, Abd al-Muhsin as Sa'dun, by now removed from office, actually suggested to the incoming High Commissioner, Sir Henry Dobbs (1923–29), that Iraq did not need a king. In August 1925, a gathering of leading *sadah* (land-owners) in Basra discussed the abolition of the monarchy and called for a British-protected autonomous province in the south of the country. This sort of Shi-ite particularism was later opposed ruthlessly by Sunni centralists, notably Saddam. It is, however, a tribute to behind-the-scenes British string-holding that the Iraqi constitution and monarchy lasted as long as it did – another thirty-three years.

Two factors helped to keep Iraq on an even keel. Apart from effective British-led intelligence services, a professional army of initially 7,500 was taking shape. In July 1927, the first (forty-seven) army officer cadets completed their training course successfully at Royal Military Academy, Sandhurst; thirteen others finished separate studies in the UK. By the early 1930s the Army strength had risen to 11,500. Its existence, unfortunately, raised the issue as to who should have control over it. The old-time Iraqi politician and intermittent prime minister, Sa'dun, supported the king in December 1928 against the High Commissioner in calling for the Army to come under Iraqi command. Previously favoured by the British, Sa'dun came increasingly to be at loggerheads with Dobbs and left office a month later. He returned briefly in September 1929 but on 13 November committed suicide, leaving behind a plaintiff note: "The nation expects service, but the British do not agree to our demands. The Iraqi people, who are demanding independence are, in fact, weak… yet they have been unable to appreciate advice from men of honour like myself."[100] Sa'dun was a man brought up in the British legal tradition that he admired. Sadly disillusioned, he had come to realise that it could not cure the ills of a society rooted in imperialism. Still a long way from understanding the benefits of democracy, the system was unable to deliver relief from corruption, nepotism and sufficient political progress in the face of nationalist demands. Sa'dun was also the victim of an increasingly mercurial or absent king who was not above conspiring against his prime minister.

Nevertheless, nationalism was contained, thanks largely to the arrival of oil. Until 1927, Iraq's government interest was in its possession of shares in the Turkish Petroleum Company. In March 1925, faced with Turkish aggression, the Council of Ministers had to accept a seventy-five-year agreement conceding oil rights to the company. Eighteen months later, an Anglo/Turkish/Iraqi treaty promised Turkey ten per cent of the company's oil revenues. Hiding behind its protecting power, Iraq defaulted, leaving Istanbul owed huge sums. Then, on 15 October 1927, Iraq struck oil for the first time on its own territory – at Baba Gurgur, near Kirkuk. After a fearful oil spillage that would be considered a natural disaster today, the well was capped and was soon producing 643,087 barrels of crude per day. Iraq had thus joined that small group of nations that would slake the world's increasing thirst for oil.

Despite these two elements – a professional army and oil wealth providing both employment and a potential trickle-down effect – nationalism seeped into the middle classes. Occasional British arrogance did not help. In January 1926, high school student riots erupted in Baghdad, after an English teacher at the Markaziya Central School had called his class fools and donkeys for picking up radical slogans. It was symptomatic of a long-standing superiority complex which underestimated the inherent pride of the Iraqi urban educated and officer class that had grown up during the last years of the Ottoman Empire. Exactly two years later, students were incensed again, this time at the king's insensitive invitation of Alfred Mond, the Zionist director of ICI who had arrived to discuss pipeline projects connecting the new oil wells to the Mediterranean. As a member of the economic board for Palestine, he was considered as anathema by young Arab nationalists and had to be hurriedly escorted to the British High Commission before his speedy evacuation from the country. This in a city that held in 1920 the most prosperous Jewish community in an Arab society and had provided the Iraqi minister of finance at the time. Mond's visit inspired the establishment of two nationalist clubs in Baghdad that would become centres of opposition to what would increasingly look like an *ancien regime*: Al Muthanna, named after the ninth-century Arab hero;[101] and Al Jawwal (the wanderer).

By the end of the decade, however, much had been achieved to be proud of. On the land, there were some 2031 irrigation pumps covering over 2850 square miles, a fifteen-fold rise over ten years. During 1929, the Turkish Petroleum Company was renamed the Iraqi Petroleum Company and had attracted substantial participation from Royal Dutch Shell, Standard Oil (now Exxon) and what was to become Mobil Oil. Back in London, the newly elected Labour government of June 1929 announced its support for Iraq's membership of the League of Nations. While demands were growing in Baghdad for swifter progress and the room for conciliation was lessening, a new political figure – a strongman – now stepped into the arena. Nuri (Pasha) al-Sa'id was already well-known to Sir Percy Cox on his appointment as High Commissioner. Born in 1888 in Baghdad, the son of a Sunni government accountant in imperial service, Nuri attended the Istanbul Military Academy and Staff College. During the First World War, he had defected to the Arab forces led by Sharif Hussein of Mecca, serving as an officer and advisor to Prince Faisal. Shortly after the Ottoman collapse, he was appointed deputy commander-in-chief of the newly formed Iraqi Army. A strong nationalist at heart, he believed that the best course was to support the British in what he believed to be their genuine wish to bring Iraq to full independence. Following Sa'dun's demise, he stepped into the prime ministerial seat in March 1930 and held it on and off until the fall of the monarchy.

What the middle-class intelligentsia might want in Baghdad could not solve the problem of endemic instability in the north of the country, a threat to Iraq's newly discovered oil wealth. During 1930 there were several Kurdish uprisings led by Ahmed al-Barzani[102] and Shaikh Mahmud al-Khalisi. In wild countryside, this unrest could not have been contained without the mobility and penetration of the Royal Air Force. In April, negotiations for a new British/Iraqi treaty were initiated and, just eight weeks later, agreement had been thrashed out against the background of Kurdish intransigence. The resulting instrument provided for 'a close alliance' over twenty-five years, freedom of transit for British forces and the consolidation of RAF bases at Habbaniya in central Iraq and Basra in the south. There was also a telling change in nomenclature: an ambassador replaced the high commissioner, albeit Sir Francis Humphreys was not appointed until 9 November 1933. Despite student riots, the new treaty replacing its 1922 predecessor, was signed on 30 July 1930. During the following autumn, Nuri al-Sa'id organised closely controlled elections for a new parliament and secured his re-appointment as Prime Minister. The new legislature ratified the treaty by sixty-nine votes to twelve, a substantially improved vote of confidence to that of eight years previously. Six months before he left office in October 1932, a major disappearance of imperialism took effect; the Iraqi dinar replaced the Indian rupee with an equivalent to one-pound sterling.

With a virtually independent nation beginning to take its place in the international community, it might have been judged that Britain was meeting its obligations under the mandate. At the end of 1931, indeed, King Faisal sanctioned Iraq's adherence to the Kellogg Pact,[103] the first truly international agreement in the country's experience. Then, on 6 January 1932, the League of Nations' mandate commission supported Iraq's membership and, on 13 October the same year, she was formally admitted. Iraq gained further prestige when General Yasin Pasha al-Hashimi presided over a pan-Arab conference on 30 August 1932 in Baghdad. On the agenda was discussion of a projected union of Iraq and Syria. More important for this account, the Iraq/Kuwait boundary agreed in 1913 was recognised.[104] Britain's mandate was formally terminated six weeks later on 13 October. Warts and all, a job well done.

Six

IRAQI NATIONALISM AND ITS FLIRTATION WITH NAZI GERMANY

Beneath the glitter of its emergence on to the Arab stage and away from the cosmopolitan social whirl in which some Iraqi politicians, not least King Faisal's heir, Ghazi, were all too ready to participate, there was a darker side. Shi-ite unrest was never far from the surface, the self-considered oppressed in a Sunni-dominated society. In June 1931, a strike of artisans and other middle classes in Baghdad was precipitated by a three-fold rise in municipal taxation of tradecrafts. It was a sector of the economy monopolised by the Shia and the strike soon spread throughout southern Iraq. Four months later, the capital was visited by an old enemy: cholera broke out, killing 1,203 out of 1,960 cases, despite mass inoculation. Old racial and religious rivalries also broke out. With the number of British military, police and intelligence advisers down to 260 by 1931, control of the baser instincts within the forces of law and order was much diluted. In February 1932, the Patriarch of the Nestorian Church warned both the League of Nations and London of an acute threat to Assyrian Christians after the end of the British mandate. His fears were substantiated in June the following year when his fellow Patriarch, Mar Shimun, was detained in Baghdad, against the absent king's wishes. The situation turned ugly on 11 August when the Army carried out a massacre – not the first – of three hundred Assyrians at Sumayyil in northern Iraq. The pretext was an accusation that the Assyrians had collaborated with a recent Kurdish insurrection.

There were uncomfortable precedents. During the previous decade, the Assyrians had been used by British advisers to help police Kurdish areas. In 1924, insensitive British officers had encouraged Assyrian militias to exert control over the Kurds in and around Kirkuk;[105] a series of atrocities had ensued. In a country already riddled with blood feuds, this was dangerous practice. Yet, this latest repressive action of former allies on the ground was approved by the government and, more significantly for the future, by Crown Prince Ghazi, in disregard for his absent father's wishes. Again, it was seen to stain the British hand with blood and to taint Iraqi royalty and ministers trying to establish an independent administration. In contrast to Sir Sam Hoare's romantic view of the Assyrians and Kurds, British officials were not above courting popularity by recommending a concentration of the Army in the north, at the same time luring the Assyrian leadership to Baghdad where they might be imprisoned. The action appealed to the urban streets: in the wake of the 1933 massacre, the parading Iraqi soldiers were received back in the capital with wild scenes of enthusiasm. Old scores had been settled, or so it was thought. It was left to the Royal Air Force to evacuate Mar Shimun, an act which caused British stock to fall to a new low.

The RAF had to fly another body – a corpse – a month later. King Faisal had spent the summer being feted at Buckingham Palace, the Hyde Park Hotel, in Scotland and down in Torquay. During the last visit, more of a whistle stop, the Royal Navy had put on an exercise purely for his benefit. This had all been too much for an ailing heart and he moved on to Switzerland for medical treatment. In turn, his convalescence was interrupted in the middle of the Assyrian crisis, which obliged the king to return to Baghdad. With affairs put back in some semblance of order, Faisal left again for Europe on 2 September. His much-reduced popularity was marked by only fifty people seeing him off at the airport. He died five days later, aged fifty-six, when his heart was unable to cope with Alpine altitude pressure after his driver had taken a wrong turn. His body was collected by a Royal Navy cruiser from Genoa and then taken by the RAF from Haifa back to Baghdad. A good friend of Britain was no more and the Iraqi monarchy passed to his inexperienced and unstable twenty-one-year-old son, Ghazi.

Throughout the early 1930s, governments continued to rise and, soon after, fall – five in less than five years. In the face of this political uncertainty, unrest erupted in various parts of the country: in March 1935, a tribal revolt along the Euphrates brought down a cabinet within days of its formation and forced the new king to dissolve Parliament; at the end of the same year, the Yazidis in northern Iraq, a sect following a mixture of Islamic and Christian beliefs, revolted and were brutally repressed, a distant augury for the vicious genocide carried out some eighty years later by so-called Islamic State. In face of intermittent uprisings, the Army was enlarged to 19,500 by 1936 and conscription was extended. After their two-year service, conscripts entered reserve echelons, thus creating what would become a tool in the hands of nationalism. The country had meanwhile reached self-sufficiency in the production of small arms' ammunition, achieving an annual capacity of one and a half million rounds from the first munitions factory completed at the Baghdad Citadel, also the seat of Army headquarters. Previously, the government had had to rely on supply from Britain but now began the development of an arms industry that would eventually become the predominant sector of the economy. With the young Iraqi Air Force continuing to expand, along with the intelligence services, the bulk of oil revenue was committed to fresh military expenditures rather than social improvement. The foundations of a society ripe for militarism were being laid.

Taken on their own, these military augmentations might not have augured anything particularly sinister. In civilian life, however, Iraqi social attitudes were not changing for the better. In education, the concept of *al futuwa* (chivalry and brotherhood) was being introduced into school curricula to promote nationalism. The mindless, but fervent, protestations of a ten-year-old heard in 1989 were an indirect result of this embryonic policy of inculcating mantras into young minds.[106] It was promoted by Iraqi intellectuals who modelled their educational institutions after watching the progress of the Nazi Party in Germany and Ataturk in Turkey. In some respects, Iraqi political mores began to reflect both the ideals promoted by the Hitler Youth and the emasculation of parliamentary democracy as witnessed in Mussolini's Italy. German and

British social democracy was not eclipsed altogether, since there were still an appreciable number of academics who pressed for stronger trade unions and shunned support for the introduction of dangerously authoritarian political leadership, but they were becoming a less respected minority and regarded as a privileged ivory tower. Meanwhile, largely underground, the other notorious ideology of the twentieth century began to take root, initially in Basra and Nasiriyah, where both cities had been hit by a sharp decline in Iraqi exports during the Great Depression and a consequent dramatic fall in wages and employment. Communist literature, often in manuscript, began to appear from December 1932. Fifteen months later – on 31 March 1934 – the Soviet-leaning Communist Party of Iraq was founded by 'Comrade Fahd'[107] as its leader in Baghdad. The squeeze on moderate centralism was tightening.

The mix of old-style court politicians and former Ottoman officers in successive cabinets proved increasingly ineffective in the face of intermittent rebellions and street unrest. Conversely, as it grew in strength, the Army became a nest for younger officers impatient with the perceived ineptitude of their ageing superiors. On 15 March 1935, in the middle of serious tribal unrest in the Euphrates region, the pro-British and Jewish Prime Minister Jamil Beg Midfai,[108] who had only taken office ten days before, made way for General Yasin Pasha al-Hashimi.[109] Drawn from the cadre of Ottoman military officers, Hashimi had served as Finance Minister before a first tour as head of government in 1924–25, yet he was not a British favourite. He had been arrested by the British in 1919 for recruiting Arabs to resist the arrival of the French in Syria and had opposed the Anglo-Iraqi Treaty. He had set up the National Brotherhood Party in opposition to the treaty negotiations. His takeover coincided with the appointment of a new and imaginative British ambassador, Sir Archibald Clark Kerr.[110] A man of left-leaning views, wit and a wide experience in developing countries, particularly in South America, the Whitehall choice suggested that London appreciated the need for a man of sensitivity and a contrast from old Indian and Arab hands.

For just over a year the Iraqi political scene stabilised under an ardent nationalist, intent on reducing post-independence British influence.

Rather than concentrate on making improvements at home, however, Hashimi turned his mind to foreign affairs and pan-Arab unity, including the promotion of close relations with Syria. In addition, by January 1936, he had also made progress towards a non-aggression pact with non-Arab neighbours Iran, Turkey and Afghanistan. On 16 April, he secured the ratification in the chamber of deputies of a formal treaty of alliance with Saudi Arabia. This had important inferences for the integrity of Iraq's southern border. It also began to mark Iraq out as a prominent player in Middle East politics. Nonetheless, these foreign policy successes did not improve order on the home front; anti-government demonstrations continued. Then, overnight 29/30 October, General Bakr Sidqi,[111] who had spent the previous three years putting down brutally rebellions up and down the country, mounted a coup reinforced by the Iraqi Air Force dropping leaflets and two bombs on Baghdad. The first of several Iraqi strongmen had overturned budding democratic institutions in the name of nationalism and public order. General Hashimi and other former cabinet ministers fled, mostly to Syria. King Ghazi was allowed to retain his throne, but a new leftist administration pursuing an 'Iraq first' social policy was formed. It was led by Hikmat Suleiman,[112] who had manoeuvred behind the scenes to bring down Hashimi, his former National Brotherhood Party colleague. It is evident that Clark Kerr and his staff were caught unawares by the coup, not the last ambassador to find himself in that position. He would have had mixed feelings, too, about a government intent on reducing the hitherto considered Sunni monopoly in power by the introduction of a number of unknown Shi-ites into its ranks. When General Bakr then sought arms from Britain for the Iraqi Army and Air Force, he was rebuffed by a suspicious Whitehall. As a further sign of the times, Fritz Grobba, the German head of mission in Baghdad, was all too ready to provide an alternative supply. We will come to hear more of Grobba's influence in pages to come, but his intervention marked a first major rift in the British/Iraqi alliance and encouraged a rapprochement with Hitler's Germany. As negotiated by Grobba, Iraqi Army officers travelled by train to Berlin, rather than by sea to Sandhurst, for staff training; German officers spent long spells in Iraq. Under

General Bakr and Suleiman, there was a similarity between Baghdad's pursuit of socialism laced with militarism and the National Socialist policy pursued in Berlin. Indeed, there is a parallel between Hitler's augmentation of authority through the construction of autobahns and Suleiman's inauguration of the Baiji-Mosul link in the Baghdad Railway, ever a hallmark of past German influence. A further ingredient in Iraqi/German relations was a continuing rise in anti-Semitism, epitomised by expressed support in October 1936 for the Palestinian Arabs.

The Bakr coup pointed the way to the future: force, not the ballot box, was the way to remove an unpopular regime. Democracy was not in the veins of the religious leadership either; over millennia, it had never even reached an embryonic state in Mesopotamia. And, if murder was necessary, so be it. On 11 August 1937, General Bakr Sidqi and his friend Major Mohammed Ali Jawad, commander of the Iraqi Air Force, were assassinated at Mosul airport on their way to Turkey for military manoeuvres. This followed months of unrest in the Sunni-officer-dominated Army over the way Bakr had promoted the Shia. Five days later, Sidqi's prime minister, Suleiman, was forced to resign, only to be replaced by yet another representative of the old school. With the recall to the premiership of the pro-British former Ottoman officer, Jamil al-Midfai, it appeared that normalcy had been restored, but resentment continued to fester not far below the surface. Earlier in the same year, meanwhile, there had been a most significant Iraqi birth. On 28 April, at Shawish in Tikrit, about one hundred miles north of Baghdad, Saddam (meaning 'punch' or 'strike') Hussein entered this world in obscurity. In the years to come, he would study the political failures of his childhood with growing determination that he would never repeat them.

Notwithstanding the return of a pro-British cabinet, a strong pro-Palestinian policy persisted. Nine days after General Bakr's murder, the new Iraqi government sent a note to the League's Secretary-General protesting against moves towards partition of Palestine and calling for a unitary state in which Jews might 'enjoy fruits of the Balfour Declaration', a strange mix of British-influenced good intent and Arab nationalism. In London there was relief all round that the monarchy had survived. It had been touch and go; as Clark Kerr had reported in his end-of-year despatch to Anthony Eden. This had referred to a conversation the ambassador had had with King Ghazi over General Bakr's determination to transform Iraq into a republic. The threat to the monarchy continued: in March 1939, the discovery of an alleged plot to murder the king necessitated the ambassador's intervention to save Hikmat Suleiman and his Shi-ite supporters from execution. Ironically, a month later – on 4 April – Ghazi was killed pursuing his love of fast cars; he was drunk at the wheel. The crown passed to his infant son, Faisal, and the late king's cousin, Abd ul-Illah, was appointed Prince Regent. Ghazi's death removed a latent anti-British nationalist voice and one of the first to call for Kuwait's absorption within Iraq. On his private radio station, he was wont to depict the Kuwaiti Emir as outdated and feudal. Anti-British feeling did not abate; on the very day of Ghazi's death, the British consul in Mosul, Monck-Mason, was felled by a pickaxe and his building burnt down by rioters who had just heard of their nationalist-leaning king's demise.

On the eve of the outbreak of the Second World War, nevertheless, Iraq appeared to have entered calmer political waters. A new strongman had taken over the reins of government and was largely content to pursue policies conducive to British interests. Nuri al-Sa'id,[113] Sir Percy Cox's one-time confederate, had replaced Midfai at the end of December 1938 during a dispute over the removal of over-zealous nationalist army officers. Nuri restored the balance by re-instating a number of anti-British exiles while dismissing supporters of Hikmat Suleiman within the military. He also understood that public opinion had to be more effectively represented in Parliament. He was aided in his bid to enhance stability by improving economic circumstances. Although still well under half of Iran's production, Iraq's oil revenues were now financing the five-year economic plan initiated in May 1938. During 1939, a rich new field was opened up in the north at Ayn Zulah, capable of producing 18,425 bpd. Substantial infrastructural improvements had also been achieved, perhaps the most impressive being the Kut barrage opened by King Ghazi just a week before his death. This controlled the flow of the Tigris into the Shatt al-Gharraf river and, with its fifty-six electrically operated gates installed by Balfour Beatty, brought about the irrigation and revival of a previously depressed area of southern Iraq and established the ancient city of Kut as an inland port. By the end of the year, too, Iraq was able to sell two hundred thousand tons of barley to war-beset Britain. In addition, on 17 December, the USA announced the signing in Baghdad of a treaty of commerce and navigation affording Iraq most favoured nation status.

That the government of Iraq felt able to honour its treaty obligations with Britain and cut relations with Germany on 3 September 1939 without significant opposition and could intern Germans living in the country, can be attributed to the comparatively quiet political atmosphere instilled over previous months. This was despite public knowledge and anger at Britain's crushing of the three-year-long Palestinian Revolt, sharpened by the Grand Mufti of Jerusalem Al-Hajj Amin al-Husain's resort to refuge in Baghdad. Pro-German sentiment, however, was never far from the surface and, although Iraq agreed to sever relations with Italy on 13 June 1940, there was no question of the Iraqi government actually declaring war on Mussolini, any more than doing so against Hitler. This was, in fact, against the spirit of article four of the Anglo-Iraqi Treaty, which had stated: "Should... either of the high contracting parties become engaged in war, the other high contracting party will immediately come to his aid in the capacity of an ally." Pro-British politicians led by Nuri simply did not have sufficient clout to do more; neither could they argue for Iraqi forces to be engaged outside the country to bolster strained British imperial resources in the region. With the fall of France in June 1940, moreover, important elements within the Baghdad government intensified discreet exploration of how German support might be engaged for the removal of British influence from Iraq. These initiatives came to light in the late summer and caused positions to become entrenched. Regent Abd ul-Illah adhered to the British side, while his close political mentor, Nuri, took shrewd advantage of the dire French predicament by calling for full Syrian independence from the recently declared Vichy regime. He was also able to persuade the government in July that the oil pipeline to French-held Tripoli in the Lebanon be cut, while keeping open the spur to British-occupied Haifa in Palestine.

The pro-German faction continued to devil away, conscious of swaying British fortunes in the Middle East and beleaguerment in Europe. It was led by senior army officers, most notably the commander of the 3rd division, Colonel Salah-Uddin Sabbagh,[114] whose kinsman would later become Iraq's ambassador to Saudi Arabia before the run-up to the invasion of Kuwait in 1990 and, subsequently, Saddam's minister of agriculture. Colonel Sabbagh left a posthumous autobiography – *Fursan al-Uruba fi al-Iraq* (The Knights of Arabism in Iraq); published in 1956 in Baghdad, it would inspire the young Saddam. In February 1941, Iraqi plotting got all too much for Sir Kinahan Cornwallis,[115] adviser to the Iraqi Interior Ministry. He delivered what amounted to an ultimatum to Regent Abd ul-Illah and Nuri, that they should sack the Prime Minister, Rashid Ali.[116] The latter had been a thorn in the British side throughout the 1920s and 1930s, as both an Arab and Iraqi nationalist. Since the end of March 1940, he had held the premiership in tandem with the Interior Ministry. Ever aware that the rise and success in battle of Nazi Germany provided a golden opportunity for Iraq, he had used his position to help facilitate the German intelligence services' use of Baghdad as a forward base. It was this that provoked Cornwallis to deliver his threat to treat the Iraqi government – from the Regent downwards – as the enemy. His experience as a controller of intelligence had been enriched by his spell as director of the Arab Bureau in Cairo (1916–20). He had then used what he had learnt of behind-the-scenes tactics to secure the ratification of the 1922 Anglo-Iraqi Treaty. He and Rashid Ali had sparred with one another for years. The Regent duly obliged Cornwallis and Rashid was replaced on 1 February 1941 by the Minister of War, General Taha al-Hashimi (1888–1961), the older brother of Yasin, twice a former prime minister.

Meanwhile, the German Ministry of Foreign Affairs and Abwehr had been working on plans to stir up a revolt in Iraq which might undermine Britain's already stretched position in the Middle East. They had a man who could play a crucial part in achieving such a venture's success, having for many years been active in promoting Berlin's interest in Baghdad. Fritz Grobba (1886–1973) had served in France and with the Asia

Corps, a detachment sent to assist the Ottoman Army during the latter years of the First World War. After demobilisation, he had entered the German Ministry of Foreign Affairs' legal department before transferring to Department Three, covering the Middle East. In October 1923, he was appointed Germany's first representative in Kabul where he was soon involved in semi-clandestine work and exfiltration of secret agents. By 1926, he was back in Berlin, where he was departmental head for Iran, Afghanistan and British India affairs. Then, in October 1932, he was appointed Germany's first ambassador at Baghdad, with the advantage of a fluency in both Arabic and Turkish. He spoke frequently in support of Arab nationalism and argued for the removal of British influence from the Middle East. Purchasing a Christian-owned newspaper – *al-Alam al-Arabi* (The Arab World) – he used its columns to serialise Hitler's *Mein Kampf*. He also fed in anti-British material to Radio Berlin, which had just started broadcasting in Arabic. In September 1933, he persuaded the gullible King Ghazi to send Iraqi officers to Germany, where they were accorded 'amazing' treatment. The king also accepted German 'research expeditions' in Iraq, whose members stayed on and embedded themselves, much to the consternation of British Intelligence. All the while Grobba was able to influence young anti-imperialist officers, talent-spotting them for the Abwehr. His access came to an end in 1938 in the face of accusations that his hands had been soiled by the sabotage of oil pipelines. The German MFA posted him on to Saudi Arabia as ambassador in November, where he remained in waiting until the outbreak of the Second World War.

Grobba's legacy survived. During the 1930s he had encouraged a circle of senior army officers in their resentment towards the British. They were to become known as the Golden Square; we have already come across one of them – Colonel Sabbagh. Back in Berlin from October 1939 to early 1941, Grobba plotted in the MFA for an Iraqi coup, building on the German ambassador in Turkey, Franz von Papen's meeting with Rashid Ali on 5 July 1940 in Istanbul. On that occasion, Rashid had carried a message from the ousted Mufti of Jerusalem expressing the desire for a treaty of friendship and collaboration against the British. For months thereafter, Rashid as prime minister, played a double game. He oversaw the transfer of many official posts to Iraqis while reaffirming the alliance with Britain. On 7 January 1941, he was reported in *The Times* alluding to 'the nobility and political wisdom' of the British people who, he considered, appreciated that Iraq was fit for full independence from the British Empire. At the end of the month, however, in the face of pressure from Cornwallis, he resigned after refusing to break with Italy. On 26 February, Cornwallis was appointed ambassador to help underpin the new prime minister, General Taha al-Hashimi. Excluded from power, Rashid conspired with German agents using the Italian embassy's facilities. Within weeks, on 1 April, he had brought down the government, declared himself head of a government of national defence and was threatening the lives of pro-British figures, including Regent Abd ul-Illah. The latter fled the country, thanks to the auspices of the American minister in Baghdad, who smuggled him down to Basra for his evacuation by the Royal Navy.

For Britain, the timing could hardly have been worse. She was still standing alone against the Axis powers and, in the Middle East, was coming under increasing pressure from crack German forces under Rommel, an already German-occupied Greece and mounting threats from enemy air and submarine power. A hostile regime in Baghdad controlling the head of the Gulf, oil pipelines to the Mediterranean and serving as an example to other Arab populations in the theatre would have secured a major victory for Berlin on the eve of Hitler's blitzkrieg on the Soviet Union and Crete. Backed by the Golden Square commanders of the Iraqi Air Force and the 1st and 3rd divisions of the Army together with elements of the Royal Guards, Rashid received assurances from Berlin that he could rely on German Army and air support, plus ammunition re-supply, to keep him in power and assist him in ridding Iraq of the British yoke. The coup might have been launched earlier but for a dulling of nationalist ardour in Baghdad following news of General Wavell's success against the Italians in Abyssinia during the latter half of 1940. In the event, it was launched prematurely only days after the discovery by British Intelligence of Rashid's involvement in a plan to assassinate the Regent.

British forces reacted with commendable speed, urged on by Churchill, who was quickly seized of the gravity of the situation. Ignoring Ali's protestation on 6 April that he still intended to observe the British-Iraqi treaty, the Prime Minister ordered the Viceroy in India two days later to despatch a column of ground troops to relieve beleaguered loyalists and expatriates in Iraq. Known as the Sabine force, it was made up largely of Indian Army units that embarked at Karachi and landed near Basra on 18 April, capturing the city on the 30th, before starting the long march on Baghdad. By then, Cornwallis was already surrounded in his embassy and had burnt papers and destroyed ciphers. His only contact with the outside world was by wireless – *en clair*. Meanwhile, the 1st battalion, the King's Own Royal Regiment (Lancaster) and twelve hundred Assyrian and Iraqi levies had entrenched at RAF Habbaniya, some fifty miles north-east of the capital. British civilians, including 230 women, took refuge at the base where Air Vice Marshal Smart[117] commanded on the spot; his military resources were negligible in the face of the nine thousand Iraqi troops occupying the plateau overlooking the base. Despite an order from London to the contrary, Air Marshal Arthur Longmore, about to depart from his command of the RAF in the Middle East at Cairo, sent six Gladiator fighters to Smart's aid. They would represent the only non-obsolete or non-training aircraft to hand at Habbaniya. Perceptively, however, Smart had arranged for as many available aircraft as possible to be modified with improvised fittings to carry bombs and guns. Sadly, he received scant praise from the incoming successor to Longmore, Air Marshal Arthur Tedder, for his handling of a first attack on 2 May against the Iraqis on the plateau. Tedder felt that Smart had wasted surprise and had not used what he considered more effective low-level attacks by aircraft mounting machine guns against troops exposed on the ground. He also thought that Smart had lost his nerve and cited his 'somewhat hysterical messages'.[118] The hapless Smart was replaced and evacuated on medical grounds. He received little recognition for his conduct. In the days that followed, however, RAF pilots operating out of Habbaniya in a mixed force of thirty-three aircraft, backed up by ten Wellington bombers from RAF Shaibah (near Basra), succeeded in dispersing the enemy and raising the siege. The seal was set when two German ME110s were short down by British Gladiators. Any threat to the relief column coming up from Basra was nullified.

Meanwhile, caught on the hop, it was not until 3 May that the German Foreign Minister, Von Ribbentrop, was able to persuade Hitler – with the imminent invasion of the Soviet Union uppermost on his mind – that he should support the secret despatch of Grobba to Baghdad to meet Rashid in preparation for the arrival of German land and air forces. The small special force (*Sonderstab*) did not reach Mosul, via Aleppo, until 10 May. Here, a small contingent of the Luftwaffe was to fly using Iraqi markings. It was all too little and too late to make a difference. Grobba, too, was only able to meet Rashid and senior dissident officers on 16 May, by which time the opportunity for a link-up of Iraqi forces to block the British advance had passed. Neither could Rashid keep his cabinet together since several ministers objected to the terms Grobba brought with him. These included Iraqi recognition of the original concession given to Germany by Turkey for the Baghdad Railway: Kirkuk Oil to come under Berlin's control and all aerodromes to be handed over to the Luftwaffe for the war's duration. Grobba panicked and fled back to Germany. In February 1942, he was named the MFA plenipotentiary for Arab states, little more than a protocol post for the hosting of dwindling Middle East delegations in Berlin. At the end of the war he was captured by the Russians and held until 1955. He died in 1973.

Rashid Ali fled Iraq on 29 May and, after a few months in Iran, was forced by the British-Soviet invasion there to move on to Germany. He was received by Hitler and recognised by Berlin as the leader of an Iraqi government in exile. In 1945, he fled Germany and, having been refused entry to Switzerland, took passage from Marseilles in June to Beirut disguised as a stoker on board the SS *Marrakesh*. He did not return to Iraq until 1958, after the fall of the monarchy. Still a man ready for intrigue, he was arrested for his involvement in an attempted coup against the Qassim government and was sentenced to death. Thanks to a pardon, he was allowed to go into exile again and lived out his years in Beirut, where he died in 1965.

The so-called British-Iraq War of 1941 exemplified timely and determined action in the face of a potentially game-changing threat, however much its perpetrators had bungled their opportunity. It was

British resolve, both on the ground and at the centre of Middle East command in Cairo, that restored order without muddying the water by agreeing – as some wished – to negotiate with Rashid. Nevertheless, it was a close-run thing, with the Germans using Vichy Syrian resources and facilities and over half the Iraqi Army disaffected. In the event, the Regent and Nuri al-Sa'id were able to return to Baghdad by 23 May and Iraq was secured for the rest of the war. At 0800 on 1 June an armistice came into force. All Axis prisoners were interned and the governor of Mosul, Khairallah Talfah, who had been embroiled in the revolt, was arrested. As a result, Saddam was taken from his future maternal uncle, Khairallah, and transferred to the care of his sadistic stepfather at Shawish. Despite prompt action, the British failed to prevent one atrocity: several hundred Jews were killed in riots during the revolt, egged on by disgruntled young Iraqi officers. Midfai, the new prime minister, had to declare martial law on the 3rd and Nuri was despatched to Cairo, where he could act as an immediate liaison with the British high command in the Middle East. In the midst of a world-wide conflict, the Empire had managed – just – to hold on to what it still considered its own area of influence.

Seven

THE FALL OF THE MONARCHY (1958)

With Rashid Ali humiliated and the monarchist politicians back in control, the British authorities, civil and military, could turn away from what history would judge to be a side-show. Rashid, like Netaji Subhas Chandra Bose and the Indian National Army fighting for the Japanese, had demonstrated the strength of nationalist resentment against membership of the British Empire. Whatever the constitutional freedoms achieved so far, there were many Iraqis in 1941 who still saw their country as slave to an imperialist power – and to a Zionist supporter to boot. An attempt at reconciliation with these opposing views was overturned in September when Prime Minister Midfai resigned in the face of those who believed firm measures were needed to root out the perpetrators of revolt. On 10 October, the arch-supporter of the Anglo-Iraqi treaty, Nuri al-Sa'id, took over the premiership once more, together with the Defence Ministry. He directed the process that had already seen, since August, between seven hundred and a thousand rounded up and interned, including the commanders of the Royal Bodyguard and the Air Force.

With Nuri back in power, the pace quickened. Fifty Axis agents – a measure of the German espionage effort – were arrested and seventy-five Rashid Ali partisans detained. The Iraqi government then broke with Vichy France, including its administration in Syria, on 17 November and with Japan three weeks later. In the following year, no less than 324 military officers were pensioned off as Nuri sought to purge the Army of unsound elements. Rashid was sentenced to death in absentia in January and Saddam's future maternal uncle, Khairallah Talfah, incarcerated.

A number of Iraqi prisoners-of-war previously sent to Rhodesia were brought back and executed. Retribution went back further: leaders of the 1937 Bakr coup were tried and hanged. The harshness of Nuri's action, which the British did nothing to stop,[119] sowed the seed for bloodletting over many years to come. In addition, assassination would become an extra-political tool, as presaged by the murder of the moderate anti-Zionist opponent of the Grand Mufti, Mohammed Fakhri Nashashibi, in November 1941. The Nashashibi clan had been ready to work within the system in spite of their pro-Palestinian sympathies. The moderate centre was already being eviscerated.

After further strengthening his position at the end of 1942, Nuri was able to induce his government's declaration of war on 16 January against Germany, Italy and Japan. This was the first declaration of an independent Arab state against the Axis powers. Relations with Britain at the top remained close, with Regent Abd ul-Illah visiting London in November and staying at Buckingham Palace. On his return journey he met Churchill in Cairo. Ties thickened further in June 1945 with the announcement of a UK-Iraqi financial agreement by which Iraq received a £3.5 million subsidy (£12.5 million today) in return for an Iraqi foreign exchange contribution from exports to the Sterling area. During the previous year, a British military training mission had arrived in Iraq, leading to the re-officering of the Army under UK-trained cadres. In striking contrast, other ranks were treated abysmally; at the end of the War, the Iraqi Army was deprived of food, equipment, uniform and boots, with men in the ranks being recruited from deserters.[120] Deliberate neglect, perhaps, which aimed to emasculate a once strongly nationalist force that might then be reduced to little more than a militia under imperial control. The result, however, was to build up resentment amongst old military families.

At the end of December 1945, Regent Abd ul-Illah promised social reform and the setting up of political parties. During 1946, five parties were recognised, including *Istiqlal* (Independence) formed from the remnants of the nationalist movement and calling for an end to British controls and the National Democrats, a collection of usually foreign-educated middle-class intellectuals and professionals leaning towards socialism.

The old-style politicians were combined into the *Ahrar* (Liberal) Party, led by Nuri al-Sa'id's less conservative former deputy prime minister, Tawfiq Suwaidi.[121] The left-wing consisted of the *Sha'b* (People's) Party, formed from Marxist groups, and the Moscow-leaning Communist Party (CPI). The building of political infrastructure in any society takes decades and the mere recognition of the existence of different groups of opinion and philosophy is insufficient to produce stability in a country with no democratic tradition and a parliament with limited franchise. Hence, just the acceptance of the CPI as an entity was insufficient to prevent that party from fomenting an oil strike around Kirkuk in July 1946 and what was described as a 'massacre' on the 12th by the police. Moreover, the British imperial power, seriously weakened by the War, was everywhere under severe pressure and not in a position to shore up the civil power in Iraq. Across the border in Iran, British troops were forced to withdraw to Basra because Abadan was riot-bound by Communist-inspired students. In Baghdad, the cabinet had to resign in face of rail and printing strikes; once again, Nuri, the perceived strongman, had to take over. In the months that followed, a number of Communists were arrested and sentenced to death or hard labour. Increasingly, the CPI became an underground movement. Despite all the troubles of the year, however, the British ambassador, Sir Hugh Stonehewer-Bird, still felt optimistic enough to write in the opening paragraph of his annual report: "During 1946, Iraq shone like a good deed in a naughty world, maintains peace within its frontiers, amity with its neighbours and cordiality for its ally [Britain]."[122] This late imperial tendency to cast a blind eye lingered on until the end of the Monarchy.

More fervour on the streets, however, was caused by events in Palestine as the British mandate there drew to a close. Yet another new premier, the Shi-ite Sayed Salih Jabr,[123] returned to Baghdad on 22 September 1947 from the Arab League conference at Sofar in the Lebanon; he referred to 'secret decisions' that had been taken there. Almost in the same breath he put Iraqi youth on notice 'to prepare for sacrifice in the defence of Palestine'. He then sent the USA and UK a dire warning of the consequences following any partition of Palestine. Exactly a month later, three thousand sheikhs and their followers met at Hillah near Babylon and called for *jihad* in defence of the Palestinians. Jabr was there to back up the threat. On 24 November, Iraq joined eleven other Arab states in proposing a unitary Palestine state. This was rejected by the UN Palestine committee along with the Arab demand for the Balfour Declaration and UK mandate to be referred to the International Court. Six days later, Iraq and twelve other Arab states walked out of the UN General Assembly when it agreed to partition. Despite an abstention by the British representative in New York, the Baghdad streets erupted. During December, the British Institute kindergarten was destroyed, fortunately without loss of life amongst the twenty-six British-Iraqi children, thanks to the bravery of their teacher. Elsewhere in the city, the US Information Centre was wrecked.

With the setting up of Israel on 14 May 1948, Iraqi forces were sent to support the other Arab states in their war against the new state. Some ten thousand troops, poorly led and equipped, deployed to present-day north-west Jordan, where they stood but could not engage in any fighting, principally because the Jordanian government, strongly influenced by the UK, blocked their advance to the war zone. Back in Iraq, martial law had to be declared, while the oil pipeline to Haifa, that had survived the Second World War, was abandoned. Subsequently, new pipelines with a greater capacity were laid to Tripoli in the Lebanon and Banias (completed in April 1952) in Syria. In the Iraqi chamber of deputies, where the atmosphere was one of outrage, a law was passed making Zionism punishable by death or imprisonment. In the wake of this, some 125,000 Jews migrated to Israel. On 12 October, along with Egypt, Iraq recognised the government in Gaza set up by the Palestinian Higher Committee – two or three days ahead of Syria, Lebanon and Saudi Arabia. When Israel signed an armistice the following April with Jordan, Syria and Egypt, and Arab forces withdrew from Palestine, the Iraqi signature was missing. Iraq remains at war with Israel to this day.

The Palestinian crisis was a highly disruptive background to what was to prove an abortive attempt by London and Baghdad to create a more realistic relationship between the two countries. Regent Abd ul-Illah had first proposed the renegotiation of the 1930 British-Iraqi treaty in May 1947. On 15 January 1948, Foreign Secretary Ernest Bevin and Prime Minister Jabr signed the Treaty of Portsmouth. Under this agreement Britain gave up its right to air bases in Iraq but made way for a joint military planning committee to be set up. The new treaty would have expired in 1973, but it was never to be accepted in Iraq. Jabr was forced to resign on 27 January in the face of violent demonstrations on the streets of Baghdad, during which seventy were killed and three hundred injured, having been machine-gunned down.[124] Shades of Amritsar, but contrary to myth, it was the Iraqi police – not British troops – that killed the demonstrators. A new cabinet of old-style politicians took over and was obliged to reject the draft treaty as it did not realise 'Iraq's national aims'. In response, the British government could only insist that, in the absence of a fresh arrangement between the two countries, the 1930 Treaty still remained in force. Jabr was forced to flee to London two weeks later. In the face of hostile popular feeling, the British military mission was withdrawn from Iraq and remaining servicemen had to stick closely to their bases. By the beginning of 1949, Nuri al-Sa'id was back in the chair and elections had produced a chamber of deputies no less vehement about Palestine and opposed to any attempt to produce a new treaty. The Baghdad government had to content itself with continued suppression of the Communist Party, two of whose leaders, in jail since 1946, were hanged.

Behind the post-war charges of imperialism laid by Iraqis were two further grounds for resentment. Since 1930, the country had been all but independent and was recognised successively as such by both the League and the United Nations. Nevertheless, the financial relationship was perceived as unequal and the production and marketing of Iraq's largest asset – oil – to be under the control of foreign companies. The two issues were closely related since the Iraqi dinar remained within the Sterling area. When the British Chancellor of the Exchequer, Stafford Cripps, devalued the pound in September 1949 by thirty per cent, Iraq had to follow suit. As a result, the dinar was devalued from 4.03 to 2.80 dollars, thus reducing the value of its savings and investment. More embarrassingly for the Baghdad government, it took a substantial toll of earnings from the oil industry. Ironically, it was at a time when the first field in southern Iraq – at Al-Zubair – had been discovered, producing in the years to come nearly eighty thousand bpd. Over the following years, several more major discoveries[125] raised Iraqi production to a point whereby foreign debts could be paid off and credits waived. To a large extent, sensitivities were assuaged by a series of accommodations over Iraq's drawing rights in the Sterling area and the companies' acceptance of increased royalties payable to Baghdad. The rising levels of black gold and the wealth it engendered also helped to reduce resentment, but it lingered on.

Unequal financial relations might have irked some sections of the middle and professional classes, but it was events outside the country that brought rioters repeatedly onto the streets. Within the context of the Cold War and the politico-philosophical competition between East and West, it was all too easy to overlook the growing strength of Arab feeling. Both sides went out of their way to recruit Third World states to their cause. This led to the likelihood of countries already within one sphere of influence or another being taken for granted. The rise of the Non-Aligned Movement was the reaction to this and it was many years before the Western powers in particular were able to take the views of the Arab demonstrators on the streets fully into consideration. Too often, Western politicians and officials adopted a patronising attitude, best exemplified by an American official in Kuwait who told me how he dealt with his contacts there in government. "I just shout at them," he insisted. This, of course, was no different from the statement often heard from British tourists in the 1960s and later who thought they could get over their ignorance of foreign languages by 'speaking louder – in English'. It was not an approach which engendered respect; resentment was more likely.

It was a form of arrogance which spilled over into ill-considered trade deals with developing countries. Whether it was the Soviet sale to hot countries of tractors with exhaust pipes heating the cabin, Western white elephant warships or combat aircraft and missiles from all quarters, it was all part of a competition for influence rather than serving to build creative infrastructure and produce enhancement of prosperity. In foreign policy it was much the same. Both blocks sought to persuade Third World countries to their side, not least at the United Nations. Oil-rich Iran and Iraq, placed at the centre of the world's greatest area for slaking the driver's thirst, were principal targets for London, Moscow and Washington. Baghdad became a centre for competing intelligence services. The British had a head-start from the end of the First World War onwards, if not before, but the Americans were increasingly active after 1945. The Soviet Union had its sources within the CPI long before it was able to open an embassy in July 1958. The Russians also had the services of the notorious Cambridge spy Kim Philby, who last visited Baghdad in April of that year and had potential access to the entire British network of agents.[126]

With Regent Abd ul-Illah, supported by loyalist politicians led by Nuri al-Sa'id and Tawfiq al-Suwaidi, the Iraqi government in the early 1950s was always open to influence from London. In September 1952, the Regent accompanied the young King Faisal II to the UK as guests of the British government and stayed with the new Queen Elizabeth at Balmoral, among the first overseas visitors to do so. Other senior politicians enjoyed the hospitality they received in London. Not surprisingly, therefore, in July 1950, Iraq was the first member of the Arab League to express support for the United Nations' action in Korea, albeit this was linked with a demand that resolutions in support of Palestine should be implemented. While this stance might have salved the consciences of senior Iraqi ministers, it was not enough to assuage the increasingly shrill cries on the streets. As the 1950s wore on, these cries were turned as much against what the demonstrators regarded as traitorous imperialist lackeys as they were aimed at the Western powers involved (meddling) in Middle East affairs.

Trouble was already brewing close by. On 28 April 1951, Reza Pahlavi, the Iranian Shah, was obliged to appoint the secular and radical long-serving minister in several posts, Mohammed Mossadegh, as Prime Minister.[127] The Iranian Parliament (*Majlis*) had just voted for Mossadegh by seventy-nine votes to twelve. He had protested consistently against the 1919 British/Iranian Treaty and throughout his political career had argued for the removal of foreign domination of his country's economy through control of the oil industry. Just over a year after taking office – on 1 May

1952 – Mossadegh announced the nationalisation of the Anglo-Iranian Oil Company, the cancellation of oil concessions and the expropriation of assets. What he regarded as an arm of British government was lopped off and the reaction in London was furious and harsh. Measures were taken to prevent Iran selling its oil, which the British government considered 'stolen'. Apart from substantial Royal Naval units being sent out to mount a blockade, British technicians were withdrawn and customers penalised for buying Iranian oil products. As a result, oil output was brought to a near stand-still: the number of barrels per day sank from 242 million in 1950 to 10.6 million in 1952. At the same time, Britain used its influence to secure a doubling of British Petroleum and ARAMCO production in Saudi Arabia, Kuwait and Iraq. President Truman's outgoing Secretary of State, Dean Acheson, called the British reaction 'rule or ruin', an interesting foretaste of Donald Trump's sanctions policy since then.

When Eisenhower took over from Truman in January 1953, Churchill was soon able to persuade him that Mossadegh was a dangerous man who would inevitably come under the sway of Moscow through his apparent close relations with the Tudeh (Communist) Party. Accordingly, the American President called in the head of the CIA and tasked him with the engineering of a coup to remove the Iranian Prime Minister, in close collaboration with the British Intelligence Service, SIS. Kermit Roosevelt, the grandson of Theodore, the American President (1901–09) best known for talking quietly while carrying a big stick, was sent to Tehran to direct the operation, code-named Ajax. The resulting coup attempt on 15 August 1953 was foiled but caused sufficient disruption to induce Mossadegh to resign four days later. When the Shah returned from taking temporary refuge in London, Mossadegh was arrested and his policies put sharply into reverse. Negotiation between the oil majors and the Iranian government were restarted. The fact that Anglo-American foreign intelligence services had brought about the removal of an independent government and had secured the detention of its prime minister – until his death in 1967 – was one of the worst-kept secrets of the Cold War. The Americans did not finally admit their involvement until 2013, but long before that, Mossadegh had become a rallying point for anti-Western, principally American, protest. 'Big and Little Satan', in short, with the emphasis on the 'little'. Indeed, the UK was seen as the initial protagonist, having been compelled to persuade the Americans to enter the fray since London had neither the forces on the ground, nor, if the truth be known, the willpower to mount an operation on its own.

In Baghdad, the government watched with increasing nervousness. London was clearly no longer able alone to deploy the power it had once commanded to protect its national interests or those of its friends in Iraq. In their political clubs, nationalists took note that the British lion was losing its teeth. Many Iraqis had watched with admiration Mossadegh's admittedly mixed success in throwing off the foreign yoke from the Iranian oil industry and their resentment grew over what they considered the vindictive behaviour of the British government. However much the British hand in the ousting of Mossadegh was kept under wraps, serious suspicions had been aroused and added to the incredulity of policies and statements coming out of London. Deniability of being involved in a shady operation is never enough.

Another and less successful British venture underlined the increasingly obvious fact that the UK was no longer capable of policing its former empire. On 5 November 1956, Anglo/French forces landed in Egypt. Within seven weeks, they had been forced to withdraw by a mix of political and financial pressure, plus veiled military threats from the real superpowers. The man regarded as the villain of the piece in British eyes, Gamal Abdel Nasser, remained in power, Soviet influence in the Middle East was enhanced and the Suez Canal, a vital link in Western trade, was blocked. The Suez Crisis knocked more teeth out of the British lion's jaw than any other confrontation during the Cold War and lost London many friends. And, ostensibly, it had promoted a new Arab champion, a man with whom Nuri al-Sa'id had been discussing – from September 1954 onwards – the prospects for the unification of military policies and the implementation of an Arab League collective security pact, not least to bring about a solution to the Palestine problem. In the throne room, King Faisal and Regent Abd ul-Illah might sympathise with British action and put forward potentially helpful suggestions for mediation, but this would have cut no ice with pro-Egyptian demonstrators on the streets of Baghdad. Arab nationalists would have been appalled by the way the Regent waved aside the British ambassador's embarrassed apologies for the posting to Baghdad of two SIS officers expelled by the Egyptian authorities. The writing was on the wall for the old-style politicians.

Another section of tradition was under severe pressure. Iraq's trenchant support for the Palestinian cause never abated; the same was true for the Baghdad streets' vehemence against the still unrecognised state of Israel. In the face of this hostility, by 1954, nearly all of the once prosperous and wealth-promoting Jewish community had migrated to their Biblical homeland. In March 1951, sixty-four thousand Jews had been deprived of their citizenship and their property sequestrated. Two months later, the number of Jewish emigrants in the previous twelve months had risen to eighty-one thousand. At the beginning of 1955, the total remaining was under six thousand, mostly elderly, and reducing. For most Iraqis, however, the autumn of 1956 was less about the Anglo/French operation designed to secure the Suez Canal than the injury to the Arab cause induced by Israel's rapid military success against Egypt in Gaza and the Sinai Peninsula. If it was not a matter of public knowledge at the time, the collusion between Israel, France and Britain was heavily suspected. It was a mood that lasted down to the end of the century and beyond; not for nothing were Iraqi troops led to believe that they were invading Israel in August 1990 – not Kuwait.

Post-war Iraq was not all doom and gloom. Well before the Allied victory, educational infrastructure was receiving successive boosts. An engineering college was established in Baghdad in 1942. A first college for women was set up in the capital four years later. By 1950, out of a population of well under six million, 203,127 were in elementary, 32,430 in secondary and 4,900 in higher education. The basis for an intelligentsia to complement the traditional middle class was being formed. In time, this would offer the literacy and numeracy that would bolster a dictatorship requiring the scientific and engineering skills it needed to hold on to power, even after defeats on the battlefield. During the 1950s, however, the educated classes were never strong enough to produce a viable and vocal centre ground to prevent the rise of populism and tyranny.

During the Cold War, the West had one major objective, apart from that of its self-protection. Having given up any realistic hope of pushing back Communist control of countries already within Moscow's orbit, it set up a system of regional alliances to provide unity of purpose and bolster potential waverers: in Western Europe, it was the North Atlantic Treaty Organisation (NATO); in the Far East, the South-East Asia Organisation (SEATO) and, in between, the Central Treaty Organisation (CENTO). The last was formed on 24 February 1955 in Baghdad – the 'Baghdad Pact' – where its headquarters was set up. Unlike the other two regional alliances, it was to last less than twenty-five years. Unlike the other two, also, the Americans avoided membership of CENTO and it was left to an ailing Britain to try to hold the ring of several disparate states. Like NATO and SEATO, it committed the membership to mutual cooperation and protection as well as non-intervention in each other's affairs. In British-American minds it was to prevent Soviet expansion into the oil-rich Middle East, despite the fact that only one of the five member-states – Iraq – qualified for membership of the Arab League. There was also a fundamental contradiction in that CENTO had an underlying pro-Israeli streak, certainly in Turkey and Iran, if not in the UK and, thus, was out of step with the very countries it sought to protect. Over the course of its existence, its principal enemy, the Soviet Union, was able to leap-frog over the alliance and to build strong economic and political ties with countries beyond – notably Egypt, Syria, South Yemen, Somalia and even India. By 1970, the Soviet Union would have twenty thousand troops in Egypt and enjoy naval facilities in Aden and Mogadishu. The Russians had succeeded in what they had failed to achieve throughout the nineteenth and early twentieth centuries: warm-water port facilities for the expanding Soviet Navy. The first casualty would be Iraq with the fall of the monarchy in 1958; that, in turn, would also sound the death-knell for the Shah's regime in Persia twenty years later.

The circumstances on the eve of CENTO's formation were hardly auspicious. A Soviet note to the Iraqi government in March 1954 had made it quite clear that any Arab country that joined a Middle East defence pact would be 'considered unfriendly'. A clear signal that Soviet intelligence services and propaganda would become increasingly aggressive,[128] using to the full its major asset on the ground, the local Communist Party. Local rivalry was also a distraction. The Iraqi government was already at loggerheads with its neighbour, Syria, over the power struggle in Damascus; each side's intelligence officers and diplomats were regularly declared *persona non-grata*. At the same time, Israel was constantly protesting at American military aid to Iraq, the country she considered the prime instigator of Arab attacks. The path to the Baghdad Pact was tentative. Following a military aid agreement on 21 April 1954, the USA and Iraq announced four days later in Baghdad that they had reached an understanding 'without any political obligations or commitments'. In February the following year, the path was made straighter by the signing of a Turkish/Iraqi treaty in Baghdad and the sympathy shown for it by Pakistan. Support from Iraq's neighbours was one thing, but within a few weeks of the signing of the Baghdad Pact, there was a wave of fervent nationalist opposition and vehement denunciation from Moscow. The CPI took note and weighed in too. Despite endorsement of the Pact by the Iraqi Parliament, it was to become one more anti-imperialist drum that demonstrators on the streets could beat – with the help of provocative, if often clandestine, participation by Moscow's many cells in the capital and other major population centres, including in the oil fields.

While Regent Abd ul-Illah and Nuri al-Sa'id could keep reshuffling the cabinet pack if individual ministers became too unpopular or there was a threat of serious disagreement, Parliament was becoming less manageable. Following Nasser's coup in Egypt in July 1952 and in the midst of port strikes fomented by the CPI and student riots in Baghdad, King Faisal had been forced to dissolve Parliament on 27 October. The following day, four nationalist and centre-left parties petitioned Parliament – not the king – to dissolve the cabinet, seek agrarian reform along Nasserite lines, demand disclosure of individual politician's wealth, abrogate the British-Iraqi Treaty and prevent participation in Western proposals for Middle Eastern collective defence. With many urban centres in disorder, the Regent sought the proclamation of martial law and his appointee as Prime Minister, General Nur-ud-din Mahmud,[129] dissolved all political parties.

Opposition leaders were arrested, newspapers closed down and a military governor general appointed for the capital. Assemblies of more than five people were banned. During the mass riots, the American Information Service building was burnt down, the English-language *Iraq Times* office sacked, the government's Constitutional Union Party's headquarters stoned and British-owned premises, including British Overseas Airways (BOAC), attacked. A new electoral law, based on direct voting for the first time, only produced a parliament even more out of step with successive cabinets.

There was a short period of improved harmony after September 1953 when Dr Fadhil Jamali,[130] former president of the chamber of deputies and Iraq's representative at the UN in New York, brought together a cabinet of young Western-educated progressives. Martial law was suspended. Sadly, Jamali lasted less than eight months and, once again, Nuri al-Sa'id had eventually to be brought back in as Prime Minister on 4 August 1954 – his fifth term. By royal decree, Parliament was again dissolved and ordinances were issued by the Ministry of the Interior, depriving Communists, Anarchists and Zionists of citizenship. The relatively moderate National Democratic Party was also banned. Within a month, a further ordinance abolished all political parties once more. From now on Parliament, when it sat, comprised individuals acceptable to Nuri's old Constitutional Union Party. A healthy opposition that could be seen to be able to bring to account what the government was doing did not exist. This narrowing of support for the executive destroyed what little political fabric had been achieved since the end of the Mandate. Hence, the legislature might endorse the government's foreign policy, as it did in February 1955 when negotiations were climaxing towards the conclusion of the Baghdad Pact, but its compliance did not filter down to the streets or political clubs. The political liaison between governed and government, so vital in any would-be democracy, was non-existent. This meant that however much Baghdad tried to mediate – and it did – during the Suez Crisis, or work with Western governments to check Israel's military ambitions, there was little or no appreciation of this in the mind of the ordinary Iraqi. Instead, serious demonstrations became more frequent and could only be put down with inevitable brutality which, in turn, only increased a pent-up vengeful resentment. A devil's circle. A British correspondent writing in February 1957 gave Nuri al-Sa'id's chance of survival two years at most. He was closer to the actual pulse than the British embassy, whose ambassador, Sir Michael Wright, described to the Foreign Secretary in the very same month his view of Nuri as: "like a great vintage claret, [who] conveyed the impression after nearly seventy years [that] he had much of his best years still to give."[131]

That turned out to be an optimistic prognosis. On 8 June 1957, Nuri had to resign the premiership on health grounds. Fellow conservatives replaced him, but by the end of the year, yet another reshuffle had to take place, adding to administrative discontinuity. On 3 March 1958, Nuri was back for his sixth term of office. By 15 July, he had been discovered trying to escape the capital in women's clothing and was shot dead.

Any number of elements might be cited as leading to the 1958 Iraqi Revolution or, better expressed, military coup. The long-standing anger over the persistence of foreign influence, particularly the British-Iraqi Treaty, was undoubtedly a factor, but Nuri al-Sa'id and his colleagues were not unsympathetic and had tried to negotiate it away. British soldiers had long since disappeared; the RAF had handed over its bases to the Iraqis in May 1955. Remaining British advisers were not visible. Perceived Western control of oil had also pricked sensitivities, but the problem had been diluted by sensible pricing arrangements; from November 1955, the Iraqi government's first refinery had been brought into operation. During the Mossadegh and Suez crises, order had been kept under control, admittedly with difficulty, but the regime had survived.

So, what was the catalyst that brought about the end of the monarchy and the *ancien regime* that had been in place for nearly forty years? It is self-evident that during this period neither British nor Iraqi politicians and officials had been able to create anything approaching a democratic society. After centuries of tyranny it was always going to be a tall order and, in the end, the system in place was unable to stand up to what was really only a *putsch*. Moreover, Britain as the former mandatory power was too exhausted by war to be able to provide the advice and support to establish a security infrastructure sufficiently reliable to keep the Baghdad government in power. Yet, there had to be a spark that set off the explosion – for such it was – in July 1958.

Ultimately, the combustibility was Arab-centric. In the wake of the Suez Crisis there was increased instability in all the adjacent countries. In face of this, the Middle Eastern monarchies tried to stick together. In September 1956, King Faisal met King Saud at Damman in north-east Saudi Arabia to discuss ways to prevent Suez from disrupting oil revenues. King Hussein of Jordan visited Baghdad the same month to take 'immediate measures' under the Iraqi/Jordanian Defence Treaty, in existence since the establishment of the two Hashemite kingdoms. In May 1957, King Saud visited Baghdad and agreed a joint communique that rebuked the radical and provocative propaganda coming out of Cairo. It also ended the Saudi/Hashemite feud stretching back to the early 1920s. A rather smug Nuri al-Sa'id threw in for good measure that 'the Arabs could always settle differences', in a side-swipe against potential Soviet interference. Sir Alan Munro, one of the FCO's senior Arabists, said something very similar in July 1990.[132] The following month, King Hussein spent three days in Baghdad seeking financial aid for industrial, agricultural and irrigation projects to cover the budget deficit that Egypt and Syria had previously promised to underwrite as replacement for former British subsidies. This was yet another example of the weakening British lion withdrawing support from its old friends. The monarchies closed ranks further in late October when King Faisal and the Shah issued a statement in support of the Baghdad Pact during the king's twelve-day visit to Tehran. Once again, the concern was over the increasing Soviet influence in the radicalised Arab countries, principally Egypt and Syria.

In February 1958, Egypt and Syria formed the United Arab Republic, a geographic and economic nonsense, but it was aimed at the more conservative states in the Middle East and had backing from Moscow. In response, King Faisal visited Amman the same month and on the 14th issued a joint statement with King Hussein proclaiming an 'Arab Federation' under the Hashemite flag of black, red, white and green. The intention was to form one parliament, one army and one currency.

The two kingdoms were at least contiguous. Three days later, the Iraqi Parliament ratified the new federation unanimously, apparently oblivious of what the streets or aspirant nationalist officers in the Army might think. As if to underline the distance between the legislature and real feelings in the country, the Iraqi general election on 4 May returned only twenty-seven elected representatives out of a chamber of 145. With no legally recognised political parties, only supporters of Nuri al-Sa'id, the latter became the first (and last) prime minister of the Arab Federation. Ironically, on 19 May, Nuri invited Kuwait to join the Federation. For a month, all seemed more or less normal – and then all hell let loose.

It started in Lebanon where the Maronite Christians, under the presidency of Camille Chamoun, were moving towards closer relations with Jordan and Iraq, while Muslims in the country were being courted by Nasser and the Syrians. Given a free hand, Chamoun would have joined the Baghdad Pact too, but that was always going to be anathema to Arab nationalists. Before a revolt could break out in the Lebanon, King Hussein sought the active support of Iraqi Army 20 brigade that had just been posted into his kingdom. One of the battalion commanders, Colonel Abdul Salam Aref,[133] passed through Baghdad on his way to Jordan and seized the radio station on 14 July. He announced the Iraqi revolution and, within hours, King Faisal, Regent Abd ul-Illah and many courtiers had been murdered. The British embassy was ransacked, burnt down and the assistant military attaché, Lieutenant Colonel Graham, killed in crossfire. The sheer horror of the outrages caused international revulsion. Onto the political stage stepped Brigadier Abd al-Karim Qassim,[134] commander of 19 brigade, which was based at Jawawla camp close to the capital. He ordered the withdrawal of Iraqi troops from Jordan and, under his authority, Baghdad Radio exhorted Jordanians to bring down King Hussein. Colonel Aref, now in Syria, applauded Qassim as the General Neguib[135] of Iraq and called for union with Egypt. Although Qassim insisted that his new regime was not anti-Western, within days – on 22 July – a Soviet mission had opened, headed by Grigori Titovich Zaitsev,[136] head of the Soviet MFA's Middle East department, and packed with KGB and GRU operatives. Kim Philby, who had visited Baghdad only two months before, had clearly helped pave the way. The Iraqi Army and Police were purged of 150 officers and eleven of the fourteen governors were replaced. Well over a hundred supporters of the old regime were arraigned; show trials ensued. The Baghdad Pact headquarters were closed on 23 October and transferred to Istanbul. Ten days before that, an Iraqi/Soviet trade agreement was signed in Baghdad; this was closely followed on the 26th by a similar agreement with East Germany. By the end of the year, any opponents of the Qassim regime had been executed and the new Soviet embassy was congratulating itself on the startling progress of Moscow's influence in the Arab world.

Eight

THE RISE OF SADDAM

To the man in the London street, the 1958 Iraqi Revolution would have meant little; hardly the fall of the Bastille in 1789 or the Bolshevik takeover in October 1917. It was, however, a further body blow to British post-war foreign policy and every bit as heavy as the deposition of the Persian Shah twenty years later. The writing was on the wall, too, as far as British oil interests in Iraq were concerned. Longer-term, Britain's sphere of influence through years of support for ageing political friends was at an end and could never be restored. No longer would a British ambassador or SIS head of station have automatic access to Iraqi ministers or senior intelligence officials; there would be no more discreet advisory secondments from London. Vital political and economic information was no longer obtainable. SIS station officers, now all but enemies of the Iraqi state, had constantly to have eyes in the back of their head, their hitherto trusted sources having gone to ground, often literally. Mandarins in the Foreign Office understood that the overthrow of the Monarchy was irrevocable, whilst admitting to having been taken 'completely by surprise';[137] politicians, perhaps, less so. Selwyn Lloyd, the Foreign Secretary, as much taken aback as anyone, considered that events in Baghdad on 14 July were simply the result of an undiscovered plot: "Unfortunately, the plot was not found out in time in Baghdad. I believe that the world must face up to this problem and devise a method of dealing, and dealing speedily and effectively, with this kind of effort to interfere with the integrity and independence of nations."[138] What precisely did he have in mind? Another Suez expedition every time a friendly government was overthrown? Call in the United Nations? Alas, statesmen used to cigar-smoke-filled drawing rooms and Parliamentary facilities could not easily relate to the turbulent personalities appearing in both Africa and the Middle East. Reporting to his colleagues in early 1967, after a visit to Damascus, Lord Gladwyn,[139] one of the architects of the United Nations and certainly no reactionary in Whitehall, threw up his hands in dismay at the 'crazy men' – he may actually have called them 'thugs' – he had met there. He wasn't alone in expressing this sort of sentiment. Few understood angry militants whose English was limited and who would not have been seen dead in a London club. So different from that nice Arab, now what was his name, made welcome at Buckingham Palace!

Undoubtedly, the main beneficiary of the Iraqi Revolution was the Soviet Union, behind a cluster of economic and technical agreements the new government negotiated with her Warsaw Pact satellites.[140] Much as the West might have deplored this palpable expansion of Soviet influence, these new ties brought much-needed practical support for an economy too reliant on oil. The understandable fear stemmed from what had happened in Eastern Europe: each Warsaw Pact country would pack its legations and technical delegations with intelligence officers and commissars who would report back to Moscow Centre and infiltrate vital sectors of the Iraqi state. Neither was the other leading Communist power, China, to be left out. The Sino/Iraqi trade agreement signed on 4 January 1959, before all the others, facilitated Beijing's export of machinery in return for dates, wool, cotton and animal hides. The most comprehensive agreement, however, was with the Soviet Union. It came into force on 16 April 1959 and covered 550 million roubles' worth of loans, increased by a further 180 million the following year. The sums were to fund imports of steel, electrical goods, glass, textiles, railway stock, oil exploration, technical training and support for agricultural reform. All of this was considered with a high degree of suspicion by the West, but in many ways, it was a logical shopping list for an underperforming economy. Equally worrying, the agreement was followed up in May by a similarly comprehensive cultural accord that provided for the training at Soviet universities and research institutes of Iraqi graduates, along with the whole panoply of teaching and arts exchanges, together with opportunities for learning Russian. Soviet medical specialists arrived shortly afterwards to teach at Baghdad and Mosul medical schools.

All this was observed in London with increasing misgivings. Only a few weeks previously, Britain had agreed with Iraq that the RAF base at Habbaniya should be closed; the first families of servicemen had flown out on 6 April. This was days after Brigadier Qassim had announced his country's withdrawal from CENTO. By the end of May, Baghdad had also terminated a series of military aid agreements with the United States and was accepting the delivery of some 150 Soviet tanks as well as the re-structuring of the Iraqi Air Force. Bevies of young Iraqi officers sent annually to Sandhurst or Cranwell, it seemed, were to be a thing of the past, a largely unseen loss of potential influence. To the satisfaction of no one, Britain countered with a statement from War Minister, 'Jack' Profumo, that Britain had reached an agreement with Iraq to supply a 'limited' number of aircraft and 'reasonable quantities of other arms, including tanks'.[141] A futile gesture, the first of several misperceived as retaining some degree of military influence in Baghdad. The trouble with this sort of military supply was that the equipment sent could not be anything approaching state-of-the-art and Iraq would not be the only country to recognise this. Little short of patronising.

Rather more positive was the UK/Iraq cultural agreement signed in Baghdad on 14 December 1959, which, among other things, provided a chapeau for the British Council to resume student exchanges and the employment of English teachers, interrupted eighteen months before. Under the Monarchy, the Council's buildings had always been an Aunt Sally for rioters; now it was to be hoped that the Iraqi authorities would provide adequate protection. There was, after all, still some recognition in the Iraqi capital that the teaching of the world's lingua franca was requisite and, in contrast to United States' agencies, the lesser of two evils. Yet, it paled into immediate insignificance alongside the technical cooperation agreement with Moscow reached at the end of the same month. This set up ten large Soviet-staffed centres to train four thousand Iraqis in radio communications and technological support for the oil sector, agriculture, river transport, electricity, railways, weaving, spinning, metal sheet cutting, road-building and air control. Another shopping list realised and dwarfing the library and tutorial staff at the Council.

In parallel, Baghdad was determined to loosen economic ties with the former mandatory power. On 4 June 1959, Qassim announced his country's withdrawal from the Sterling Area, affecting its $337 million holdings in gold and currency, the bulk of which was held in London. There was palliative talk of continuing friendly cooperation between respective specialists, but there was also no doubting the thrust behind the move. Even plainer was Baghdad's purpose behind the petroleum talks with British companies which had begun two months earlier. A ten-day visit at the same time by Lord Monckton,[142] chairman of the Iraqi Petroleum company and a senior member of the then Midland Bank board, was hardly likely to blunt Iraq's ambitions to control its one major asset. Churchill's friend and propaganda expert during the Second World War, however, had a secondary qualification for his appearance in Baghdad; he had been the only minister to challenge Eden over Suez, receiving the sack as Defence Minister as a result. A nicety in Whitehall, perhaps, but not a negotiation clincher. The talks wittered on until 19 December 1960 – without any positive outcome. If Iraq did not immediately press on, it was because it still needed the oil companies' expertise, technology and equipment. She was about to make up for this dependency: on 23 April 1961, the Iraqi Ministry of Industry authorised a contract with Soviet Technoexport – for the supply of oil-drilling equipment. The talks with the oil companies that had resumed on the second of the same month, not surprisingly, broke down almost immediately. It was now only a matter of time before a complete break, if not just yet.

Against the background of the East-West global struggle for influence, internal divisions plethorated shortly after the Revolution, often with horrific results that only built up a developing legacy of blood feud. The rightist Arab Nationalists took on the Soviet-inspired Communists in not such a different ideological struggle from that experienced during the Weimar Republic in the 1920s and early 1930s. The West was always going to err on the side of the nationalists with a motivation not so dissimilar from Neville Chamberlain's belief that he could do a deal with – or manage – 'Herr Hitler'. This, combined with the fear, verging on paranoia, of Moscow's inevitable success in dominating Iraq, blinded Whitehall policy-makers to what the country really felt it needed. If ever offers of technological support were made, they were decidedly half-hearted. Beyond that, the recent Suez fiasco and apparent one-sided support for Israel undermined any middle-of-the-road grouping in Baghdad still seeking for help from the old and weakened one-time mandatory power, or indeed, the relatively new presence on the block, the United States. Until the latter part of the Second World War, the Americans had no significant intelligence effort in the Middle East; the OSS (CIA predecessor) station in Cairo did not open until late 1943. Before that they had based themselves in Istanbul and, almost needless to say, they had few Arabists. Neither of the two main Western democracies, moreover, found it easy to stomach a regime that had shed so much blood when seizing power. No one could have foreseen that it was going to get a lot bloodier. Russians, on the other hand, were used to gore.

Without a real political base, apart from his immediate brother officers, Qassim, by no means a warm personality, was soon faced with serious unrest. It started with the killing of Kamil Qazanchi,[143] a senior Communist Party of Iraq (CPI) cadre, during disturbances in Mosul on 6 January 1959. Under the previous regime, trouble might have been scented more quickly and security forces, primed by a functioning intelligence service, could have been deployed in time to control events. Instead, two months later, two hundred and fifty thousand 'partisans for peace' made up of CPI cadres from all over the country mounted demonstrations in the north-western city. Within a few days, frustrated at government inaction, a full-scale Arab Nationalist revolt had broken out in Mosul led by Colonel Abdul Wahhab al-Shawaf, brother of the Minister of Health, Dr Mohammed Al-Shawaf,[144] who made no secret of his view that Qassim had been too soft on the Communists. Outside Iraq, leaders in the United Arab Republic looked on with growing concern. Damascus was accused of stirring things up.[145] When the Iraqi Army did eventually arrive, a massacre of Nationalists was already under way at the hands of the so-called 'partisans for peace'. From Cairo, Nasser accused Iraq of being controlled by Communists and alleged that Britain was making an alliance with them to suppress Arab Nationalism. Nothing could have been further from the truth, but the post-colonial power was in no position to intervene in any way. Britain could not do right, whatever position it adopted. For their part, the Communists pressed for representation in government and the legalisation of political parties. They won their first point when the first Communists joined the cabinet on 13 July.

Only a year after seizing power, Qassim was walking a tightrope. Not only did he dissatisfy Arab Nationalists at both home and abroad and was unable to keep the CPI corralled, but in mid-July, the authorities in Kirkuk could not prevent Communist Kurds from massacring the local Turkmans. The atrocities, however, opened Qassim's eyes and, from then on, he took successive measures to restrict Communist participation in government. At this distance, one cannot help but feel that the decimation of counter-intelligence following his putsch had removed a vital part of state control in a country riven by religious, racial and political strife. The Americans would repeat the mistake after their overthrow of Saddam in 2003. Qassim did not escape unscathed: on 7 October, his car was fired on when stuck in a traffic jam. Qassim's left arm was fractured and his right hand grazed; his driver and an assailant were killed. Forty-three bullets were found in the car. The outrage was the work of a relatively obscure group – Ba'athists – of whom the world knew little but would soon come to hear much more. For the moment, at least, Qassim was able to recover quickly from his injuries and many of the suspected perpetrators were jailed. It is a symptom of his feelings of insecurity that he did not press for more stringent sentences.

In the face of extremist forces closing in on all sides, Qassim tried to bring about some semblance of parliamentary government by restoring political parties. In early 1960, three parties were legalised: the National Democrats, a socialist grouping including elements from before the Revolution; the Democratic Party of Kurdistan (KDP), seeking extended rights for the northern minority but within a united Iraq; and the Titoist wing of the CPI. Shortly afterwards, he commuted death sentences and reduced severe prison terms meted out to pre-Revolutionary personalities and rivals within the Army. These measures, however, did not appease large sections of the Kurdish minority; nor could it prevent weeks of Ba'athist-provoked street demonstrations in the capital. By March 1961, these were threatening to get out of hand. This was the background, therefore, to Qassim's attempt to deflect the mob's attention away from domestic issues. On 25 June, he announced Iraq's claim to sovereignty over Kuwait, which he maintained was part of Basra *wilayah* (province) as, so he put it, it had been in Turkish times. The immediate catalyst for this act was the British/Kuwaiti agreement that gave the emirate its independence and candidacy for United Nations membership. Given the Iraqi delegation in New York's acceptance of this new status, Qassim's position was quite illogical. As a professional military officer who already faced a massive security problem in Kurdish areas, he must have known, too, that a substantial thrust to the south would be an unrealistic undertaking. Whatever the legitimacy of his arguments and the actual menace at the time, the Kuwaitis took fright, invited back their former British protectors and the events outlined in my first chapter ensued.

Qassim's subsequent paper tiger statements did not impress the Baghdad streets. Furthermore, the flower of his army was soon embroiled fruitlessly in an attempt to quell yet another Kurdish revolt which, by September, had spread across a third of the country. At the end of the year, Qassim had to admit that the Kurds were still resurgent, despite the razing of some five hundred population centres and the displacement of eighty thousand people. From now on, there was little hope of either of the KDP or its subsequent rivals accepting integration within a unitary Iraqi state.[146] The British 'Tommy' might have suffered in the desert for no good reason, but Qassim had 'not learnt his lesson'. He felt compelled to boast that Kuwait was 'under my thumb' and that he could occupy the Emirate 'in half an hour'; 'no power on earth' would be able to prevent him from doing so.[147] Such empty threats, coupled with having to give way to Kurdish demands, led directly to his overthrow and execution the same day on 9 February 1963. Before his claim on Kuwait, he might have been tipped off by the British ambassador or others of the impending threat, but he had run out of friends.

The victors in the 1963 Revolution – if only short-lived – were the Ba'athists who were able to organise the streets into support for their assumption of power. Where did they come from? The first Ba'ath Party was formed, not in Iraq but in Damascus during the early 1940s. Its leading light was Michael (Michel) Aflaq, born in 1910, the Syrian Orthodox Christian son of a grain merchant; he gave up a career in education to enter politics and was appointed Minister of Education in 1949. His close associate was Salah-ud-Din Al-Bitar, also a schoolteacher and the son of a grain merchant. A Sunni, he served as Syrian Foreign Minister for two years from 1956. The name Ba'ath means 'Party of Resurrection or Renaissance' and at the outset purported to be a secular modernising movement aiming to promote Arab spiritual rebirth through unity, liberation and socialism. Colonial powers were to be finally pushed out of the Middle East, Israel was to be eliminated and the 'Arab Nation' was to fall under the authority of a supreme decision-making body, the National Command. In reality the last was never effectively established, but Regional Commands would be set up in individual Arab states, most successfully in Iraq. Islam was not expected to occupy a central position within the ethos of the Ba'athist Movement; indeed, in the latter half of the twentieth century, its leadership paid little more than lip service to religion.

Ba'athism attracted one young Iraqi who would become its leading exponent, albeit in a way that exploited its popularism and infrastructure for his own politico-military ends. Hitler did the same with the Fascist Movement which was actually formed in Italy during the First World War and adopted by the one-time Army corporal, Benito Mussolini, when he came to power in 1922. Saddam – the name means 'punch' or 'to strike' – Hussein Al-Majid Al-Tikriti was born on 28 April 1937 in the village of Ouja, close to the small but historic town of Tikrit. Allegedly he was of the Al-Bayat tribe, a member of the Albu Nasir tribal confederation. Whether or not this was true, as Iraqi official accounts record, it allowed him in years to come to claim that he was descended from the Prophet.

Saddam lost his peasant father just before his birth or shortly afterwards. His cause of death remains a mystery and it is possible that the man abandoned his family. Saddam's mother, Subha Talfah, was able to marry again: this time to a distant paternal relative, Ibrahim Hassan, who beat his little stepson repeatedly. Saddam, true to name, is said to have stood up to this abuse and eventually outgrew Hassan. Whether or not a degree of licence was taken by sycophantic biographers, Saddam was to display all the cruelty that those abused in childhood are known to exact over the subsequent generation. Just like one of his idols, Adolf Hitler. Life in his stepfather's household was primitive: no electricity, no mains water, blistering heat in summer and mud everywhere in winter. A photo of the mud, straw and wood-built house survives. Like other political leaders who emerged from the bottom of the pile, Saddam was able, in due course, to use his early childhood experiences to relate to the common man, something Brigadier Qassim would not have been able to do.

He had some fortunate connections, however. His mother's brother, Khairallah Talfah, had joined the Army and had gained a respectable revolutionary reputation after his arrest in 1941 during the Iraqi uprising that year; he spent six years in prison and emerged as a minor hero. Khairallah's cousin, Ahmed Hassan al-Bakr, a former primary school teacher, had also joined up and later entered local politics. Left to the clutches of his stepfather, Saddam would have remained a poor, underfed lad, fit only for scraping a living off the land. His locally influential relatives, however, rescued him and enrolled him in a distant school at the age of ten. Quite why Khairallah took a shine to the boy has never been explained, but he must have seen some potential in him. Pity does not cover it. Illiterate until 1947, Saddam was encouraged to read and write by his younger cousin, Adnan Khairallah; they remained close friends until a spat over the marriage of Adnan's sister caused an irreversible split. Adnan died in a mysterious air accident in 1989. No one crossed Saddam Hussein and got away with it. Yet, without his Uncle Khairallah, he would never have entered education or have been provided with a home in Baghdad from where he could attend Kharkh High School from the age of eighteen. Sitting at Khairallah's table, he absorbed his strong pro-Nazi opinions, his ruthlessness and lack of consideration for other people, and acquired a sweet tooth.[148] Affection that he might have felt for his benefactor, however, evaporated in later life. A cold, calculating heart never had the chance to warm up.

Throughout this account I have sought to highlight historical events that had an effect on the mind of the young Saddam and were to mould his character and attitude towards others. The events that now follow reinforced those traits and helped to create the ogre that eventually took supreme power in Iraq. His arrival in Baghdad during the autumn of 1955 was timely; he was old and strong enough to play a leading part in street riots against the Monarchy. Again, encouraged by his uncle, he joined the Ba'ath Party and was very soon recognised as a useful cadre. For this and implication in the murder of an official in Tikrit, clearly a man who had crossed his path in the past, he was expelled from high school and imprisoned for six months. Not surprisingly, he was refused entry to the Baghdad Military Academy. Come the 1958 Revolution, he was back out on the streets and, on 7 October 1959, was one of the young Ba'athists who sought to assassinate Qassim. During the shoot-out, he was wounded in the leg and is said to have supervised the bullet's extraction while in hiding. A tough individual. He fled to Syria, where he was warmly received by Michel Aflaq, who, the following year, helped him on his way to Cairo.[149] There, he entered law school, graduating in 1961, and continued his rise in the Ba'ath Party by becoming a member of the local Regional Command. Short of money, he is known to have worked for the Egyptian Intelligence Services (EIS) and to have visited the American embassy. He is most unlikely to have been discussing cultural issues; rather, the CIA would have regarded him as a potential informant in need of ready funds. Whether in Cairo, or shortly after his return to Baghdad in early 1963, Saddam married his first cousin, Sajida Talfah, his uncle's daughter who had befriended him in childhood. A whole treatise could be devoted to the course of the union and Saddam's many dalliances with other women. Saddam was back in time for Qassim's overthrow and threw his support behind his old kinsman, Ahmed Hassan al-Bakr.[150]

Qassim's removal followed disgust in the officer corps at his offer, out of desperation, of autonomy to the KDP. The immediate catalyst was the sudden retirement of fifty-eight officers considered to have Ba'athist sympathies. It was always suspected that the CIA had helped mount the power grab and it would seem likely that Saddam was one of the Agency's informants and/or a channel to the Ba'ath leadership. Ahmed al-Bakr was an army officer first and the acceptable face of Ba'athism amongst a new regime which was an uncomfortable mixture of Nasserists and Ba'athists. Bakr trusted Saddam to help hold the middle ground and he was soon to be seen in command of the National Guard force based in the middle-class and cosmopolitan Karrada Miryam area of Baghdad on the banks of the Tigris. During the aftermath of the coup, the National Guard was used to root out Qassim supporters, whose property assets – many in Karrada Miryam – were then frozen. Saddam was never to be poor again. Any Communists found were executed, so many that even *Pravda* attacked 'the wave of terror' in Baghdad. Saddam revelled in this activity.

As the new Iraqi Prime Minister, Bakr sent messages of assurance to the West, particularly to the USA and major companies. Friendly relations were restored with Cairo, whose EIS would also have assisted in the coup, and with Kuwait. The new Minister of Foreign Affairs even opened negotiations for Iraq's re-entry to the UAR. At Westminster, Edward Heath, as Lord Privy Seal and thus voicing the official Foreign Office position, declared only two days after the coup[151] that 'all the evidence' indicated that the new regime had the support of the armed forces and the bulk of the population: 'it was in effective control'. Based on its 'readiness to respect international commitments and treaties', Britain was able to recognise the new government. Heath also welcomed Baghdad's 'realistic' attitude towards foreign oil interests. Clearly, Whitehall was more than happy with a government that was expected to roll back Soviet influence and allow Western companies to flourish. Indeed, the speed of the formal recognition suggests that there was enormous relief at the development with an element of pre-cooking. The Americans followed suit. The Soviet Union, too, albeit with a decided reluctance in light of the many CPI activists now dead or in prison.

Western confidence in the regime, however, was belied by continuing running battles in Baghdad between Nationalists and Communists, the rallying of anti-Ba'athist troops at Kut-al-Amara and further fighting in Karbala and Najaf. The south of the country was decidedly not content. Neither were the Kurds. A lull in operations against their positions while the new government sought a return to negotiations on extended rights came to an end on 10 June with Baghdad threats to destroy more Kurdish villages. This split the cabinet. After several months of ministerial resignations and jockeying for position between Ba'athists and moderate Nationalist members, the former were ejected from office on 18 November by the Iraqi President, Colonel Abdul Salam Mohammed al-Aref,[152] Qassim's old rival after the 1958 Revolution. Bakr was removed from the premiership and appointed as a toothless Vice-President.

The Ba'athists retired to lick their wounds. With a membership of only 2,500, the party could hardly claim mass support. The Nationalists were left to row their own course, but if Western officials hoped for a more pliant government in Baghdad, they were to be proved sadly imperceptive. From early in 1964, Soviet arms deliveries were resumed and were to include the installation of surface-to-air missiles, three (more) MIG 21 fighter-bomber squadrons and the first TU16 medium bombers. Soviet construction of Iraq's first atomic reactor was also soon completed. Persecution of Communists petered out and, instead, there was a return to imprisonment of former Monarchists. Neither were the Ba'athists spared, a factor which spurred them to abortive attempts to wrest back power. During one of these, in September 1964, three thousand party followers were arrested, including Saddam. To bolster the government's strength, five thousand Egyptian soldiers were deployed onto Iraqi soil.

Indeed, as well as mending fences with Moscow, the predominantly Nasserist atmosphere in Baghdad, created largely by President Aref, encouraged moves towards closer relations with Cairo and re-alignment within the United Arab Republic. By 20 December the UAR and Iraq had ratified agreement for a unified political authority. Internationally, Aref was able to cut a dash by mingling with Nikita Khrushchev, and Nasser as they congratulated one another at ceremonies on 13/14 May 1964 marking the damming of the Nile at Aswan. It was the sort of project many Nationalist supporters in Iraq dreamed of. Aref used the occasion to call for a union of all Arabs. At home, however, the ongoing struggle with the Kurds teetered between negotiation and scattered outbreaks of fighting. A questionable bonus for Baghdad was a growing split in the KDP, with the more militant wing under Jalal Talabani moving his newly formed PUK closer to the Persian Shah. The Kurdish threat was not weakened by this in the long run; it was simply two-headed and harder to negotiate with.

Emulating similar moves in Egypt and India, Aref's Nationalist government now introduced a series of measures aimed at a takeover of the banks, insurance, cement, flour, textiles and cigarette production. It also brought in controls on the import and distribution of pharmaceuticals, cars, tea, sugar and other commodities. On my first posting in Calcutta only a few years later, I well remember the deadening effect this attack on private enterprise had on the Indian economy and employment. Nevertheless, the CPI and their Moscow backers applauded quietly, as they did in New Delhi and Cairo. In Iraq, however, this strait-jacket approach did not, as some Western commentators predicted, damage the economy, since the production of earnings from oil continued to rise. The problem was that private enterprise was unsettled and had to shed, rather than take on, labour. More young men remained out of work and available for street demonstrations. For the moment, a sequence of Nationalist power groups – eight cabinets from the fall of the first Ba'athist government until mid-1968 – undermined continuity of purpose. This hardly stable situation could never have lasted long, but its end was hastened by two apparently unconnected events. On 13 April 1966, President Aref was killed in a helicopter crash on his way back to Basra from Al-Qurnah, where he had been indulging in his favourite activity – speech-making! At the time, there was no suggestion of foul play, but given the high incidence over the years of unexplained air accidents over Iraq, speculation has never been scotched. Aref's death brought his alcoholic elder brother, Abdul Rahman, to power, largely because other contenders felt they would be able to control him.

Abdul Rahman Aref might have proved them wrong, since he was able to demonstrate personal valour which won him the affection of the

Army. He also made peace with the Kurds at the end of 1966 and found solid support from Cairo. What goodwill he might have engendered was lost through no fault of his own. On 5 June 1967, Israel launched pre-emptive air strikes on Egypt to gain control in the sky and, within six days, a last-minute coalition of Arab states was rendered in complete disarray. The Egyptian Army, following destruction of the Air Force, was shattered in the Sinai Desert and the Syrians were driven off the Golan Heights on Israel's northern border. Jordan's West Bank was occupied by the Israeli Army. The perception in the West was that the brave little Israel, the only democracy in the Middle East, had given her surrounding Arab neighbours a bloody nose. Western popular opinion and politicians applauded alike. It was an intrepid politician in London who voiced a contrary view. Unsurprisingly, both American and British ambassadors were expelled from Baghdad, and Washington and London responded in kind. Channels for quieter counsel were closed down. Even Qassim had received tip-offs from British Intelligence, through the then ambassador, Sir Michael Wright. This discreet yet helpful support was now all but closed off. On the Arab streets, however, the blame for the disastrous defeat was placed firmly on the Iraqi government for failing to deploy its forces fast enough to come to their neighbours' aid, particularly Syria. Only six months previously, alas, Baghdad had been at daggers drawn with Damascus and had cut oil pipelines to Syria. Spats between the two countries had been intermittent since time immemorial and, in June 1967, underlying mutual differences sabotaged the unity of the UAR in the face of a determined country that had always known it could never afford to lose a fight.

In the wake of the Six-Day War, resentment against the Iraqi political leadership mounted in the Army; President Abdul Rahman's support base narrowed dangerously. Less than three months after the Arab defeat and as the mid-summer heat began to abate, the Ba'athists returned to the Baghdad streets, blaming an alleged fifth column for having betrayed the anti-Zionist cause. President Abdul Rahman had to cancel foreign visits for fear of losing control during any absence. In the face of rising turbulence, he and his perceived strongman Prime and Interior

Minister, General Taher Yahya,[153] could do little more than shuffle the political pack of Nasserist officers and an increasing number of Ba'athist sympathisers. The position worsened when the Kurds, exploiting division in Baghdad, re-started hostilities in April 1968. Yahya had previously built up relations with the KDP leadership and had argued for a deal over autonomy which might have allowed for a withdrawal of the Iraqi Army. For the Ba'athists this was one more example of weakness at the top and plotting for another coup intensified. There was little attempt to keep this secret and Yahya felt obliged to resign on 12 July after his warnings to the President had gone unheeded. During the political hiatus that followed, the Ba'athists struck two days later. At 0300 on the 14th, they assaulted the Presidential Palace; in command was Saddam Hussein. As the man on the spot, he took control of security and played a prominent part in a freshly constituted and sinister Committee for Emergencies. This was the vehicle that would be used to quash any opposition, from whatever quarter.

The 1968 Iraqi Revolution, like many before and since, was a two-stage development. First, the ousted politicians had to be dealt with; President Abdul Rahman and General Yahya were put on a plane to London and the wealth of over two dozen of their supporters was sequestrated. For a short period, calm was restored with Colonel Abdul Razzak al-Naïf[154] appointed as Prime Minister over a cabinet majority of conservative Nationalists and non-party specialists. Yet another old-style administration, perhaps. Except that the traditionally Nasserist military officers were excluded and the younger Ba'athists were activating their own administrative channels in parallel through their party's Regional Command infrastructure. Behind the scenes, the gloves were off. While orthodox politicians might try to restore a government not so different from before, Saddam and his henchmen were fabricating plots against any centres of potential resistance. Classed as 'conspirators', they were rounded up wherever they could be found: on 17 September, it was in a Basra church.[155] Nothing was sacrosanct. Before that, on 30 July, Colonel Naïf was confronted at lunch with General Bakr by a group of pistol-toting thugs. While Bakr formed a cabinet the next day, Naïf and General

Yahya were on their way to exile, the former having been forced onto a plane for Morocco at gunpoint. Two weeks later, Naïf was announced as ambassador there. His fate, however, demonstrated the ruthlessness of the men behind the new regime. In June 1969, Naïf was accused of having been a CIA agent and was condemned to death in absentia on 18 February 1970. Even in London, where he had sought refuge, he could not escape Ba'athist retribution. Twice the victim of assassination attempts, he was eventually gunned down outside the London Intercontinental Hotel on 9 July 1978. As Saddam would have ordered beforehand – 'cut the head'.

Coverage of the 1968 Revolution by the press considered that it had been 'a bloodless military coup'. In contrast to Qassim's usurpation ten years earlier it was. Most, if not all, were lulled into false optimism. Introducing the Commons debate on foreign affairs on 18 July, the Labour government's Foreign Secretary, Michael Stewart, considered 'there seems no reason to suppose that the recent change of the Government of Iraq will at all adversely affect the relations which we have recently re-established with that country'.[156] There was only one other mention of Iraq during the entire debate; the Tory back-bencher Douglas Dodds-Parker could only say of any likely outcome: "We do not yet know." The former Liberal leader, Jo Grimond, speaking generally, was closer to the truth about the immediate British assessment: "Conventional wisdom, as expounded by the Foreign Office, has nearly always been wrong." A little harsh, perhaps, since senior officials were watching events unfold in Czechoslovakia which was coming under increasing Soviet pressure to row back from the liberal reforms of the so-called Prague Spring. The United States, supported by many of its anxious NATO allies, was investing heavily in the first concrete steps towards disarmament; they were prepared to turn a blind eye or indulge in wishful thinking – about the danger of Russian tanks rolling into Czechoslovakia. By comparison, what was happening in Baghdad was very small beer. In his annual review for 1968, the Charge affairs, Trefor Evans, opened his account with the fateful words: "In this country *plus ca change, plus c'est la meme chose*."[157]

The situation on the ground was far from pleasant. Every month that followed the Ba'athist takeover witnessed show trials, public executions of

Jews, suspected CIA agents and alleged opposition conspirators. Zionism was public enemy number one, with the Kurds a close second. As much to keep the Army (another possible threat in the early days of the Revolution) occupied, the new government deployed sixty thousand troops north in January 1969 and carried out renewed air strikes on Kurdish population centres. The offensive ebbed and flowed for much of the year, and it was not long – at the end of June – before the first accusations were made of Iraqi use of horror weapons, napalm and nitric acid bombs, to blunt Kurdish counterattacks. The new dimension of brutality being used over much of Iraq induced little more than bland reproaches from the United Nations. To his credit, Adnan Pachachi, the Iraqi ambassador at the General Assembly, resigned in protest at the public executions of many personalities well-known to him. For their part, the Great Powers remained silent. More used to extremes of cruelty and suffering than most, the Soviet Union pocketed Baghdad's recognition of East Germany as a sovereign nation on 30 April 1969 – the first capital to do so – and concentrated on extending 'peace and friendship' through economic and cultural ties coupled with promotion of the CPI onto the Baghdad political stage. Meanwhile, France, that had kept its nose largely clean in Arab eyes during the Six-Day War, busied itself supplying Mirage aircraft to Iraq and maintained a discreet silence.

What then of the British government? Foreign Secretary Stewart had said it all during the 18 July foreign affairs debate already cited. Britain should and would use her influence overseas but, in what was surely the understatement of the day, was not in the position (of strength) she had enjoyed in the nineteenth century. Behind this was the reality that, since early 1968, Britain had been in the process of withdrawing from 'East of Suez' land bases; with a mixture of American connivance and encouragement, she was falling back on a string of replenishment island bases across the Indian Ocean. There was no RAF Habbaniya from which to evacuate loyal friends and agents. The new British ambassador, returning to Baghdad in early 1969 after diplomatic relations broke down in June 1967, was hardly in a good place to more than lodge a plea for clemency. Michael Stewart could only admit to the House of Commons on 30 January that 'the Iraqi government felt unable to show clemency'. In the years to come, that position would not change substantially.

Where were the Americans in all this? Increasingly mired in South Vietnam and pursuing its own agenda with the Russians over Strategic Arms Limitation,[158] the United States was content to watch a strong government being forged in Baghdad which would be compelled by its own self-pride to keep the Soviet Union at bay. The emphasis, therefore, would be on more subtle methods of achieving influence than constantly harping on about a man's abuse of man in a distant country. This was little different from Chamberlain's policy towards Nazi Germany in the 1930s. The US Secretary of State, William P Rogers, might express 'repugnance' and 'deep concern' to the Security Council,[159] but he could not even lodge a protest in Baghdad; diplomatic relations had remained broken since June 1967 and an Interests Section would not open until 1 October 1972. Full relations would not be restored until 1983. The alternative was to build up Iraq's neighbours – Iran and Saudi Arabia – which were both staunchly opposed to Soviet infiltration towards the Gulf. Given the mounting tensions of the Cold War, the American apparent lack of concern at Moscow's signing of a fifteen-year treaty of friendship and cooperation with Baghdad in April 1972 might have seemed remarkable. Since the death of Gamal Abdel Nasser on 28 September 1970, however, Washington had found a new friend in the Middle East. The succession of Anwar Sadat in Cairo and his Corrective Revolution launched on 15 May 1971 was to re-balance Egypt's relations with the superpowers. Moreover, if nothing else, the Kurds could always be relied on to keep Baghdad occupied.[160] With the CIA in the driving seat in Washington and Tehran, State Department's argument that political support for moderate Ba'athists against Saddam would reduce the likelihood of driving Baghdad further into Moscow's arms were simply dismissed. In any case, State's main objective in the 1970s was to achieve a rapprochement between Egypt and Israel; the effort was rewarded with the peace treaty signed on 26 March 1979 in Washington. What did it matter that Iraq was able to marshal sufficient support in the Arab League to have Egypt expelled unanimously? The Americans had never invested much faith in that organisation.

Much has been written about how Saddam manoeuvred himself into a position of undisputed power, less about just how quickly he reached it. Suffice it here simply to outline his methods. As we have already noted, right from the start of the Second Ba'athist Revolution he took control of the executive forces of law and order, a euphemism for coercion through thuggery. This instilled fear in most; few were bold enough to stand up to him. Those who did were tortured, often with Saddam present, to betray their associates – before execution. Those suspected were the butt of false allegations after which those around them were arrested and tried in a special prosecution court. From January 1970, this was presided over by Saddam's grimly cynical henchman, Taha Ramadan.[161] Across the political spectrum, no one was safe. The Ba'athists might have toyed with the CPI at various intervals, even inviting them to take small minority representation in the cabinet, but that did not protect their senior cadres; Ahmed Khoudari, a senior party official, was found murdered in a Baghdad street on 23 March 1970. Ba'athists, however senior or reputable, who did not conform to Saddam's wishes, were eased or forced out of office[162] and replaced by cronies. President Bakr was hardly in a position to restrain his former protégé; he suffered a heart attack on 30 August 1970. Six weeks later, Saddam obtained his blessing as his nominated deputy. From that moment on, the thirty-three-year-old Saddam was able to branch out of domestic and party security matters into all areas of government policy, not least foreign affairs. In early December, he spent seven days leading a delegation to Moscow, using his political offices of Vice-Chairman (under Bakr) of the Regional Command Council and Assistant Secretary-General of the Ba'ath Party. All the reins of power, in effect, were in his hands, in little more than two years after the Revolution.

The significance of Saddam's grip on power was largely lost in Whitehall, although there was no denying the regime's control of the intelligence agencies. While referring back to the violent intimidation of 1968–69 in this 'hapless and masochistic republic', a new ambassador considered that there were 'fewer flaming swords at every gate'. He congratulated Saddam as the architect of the peace achieved with the Kurds in 1970 which had brought a 'measure of credit to a regime badly in need of it'. Further, the

Iraqi number two's long postponed visit to Moscow in August had been a 'resounding success'. In his peroration, he contended that 'the present regime is here to stay... and we must make the best of it... [the] only likely beneficiaries of further alienation between us and the Iraqis will be the Soviet Union'.[163] At this distance, one is tempted to ask, how much further could relations have deteriorated? In response to the report, the Old Etonian and one-time Third Secretary in Kuwait, Stephen Egerton, was close to despair: "Their internal politics," he inveighed, "are so obscure (and yet, some would say, starkly simple) that no Westerner can make any worthwhile prediction on anything. Whoever pretends to be able to discern a pattern or foretell a trend is either lying or deluding himself." It was the sort of lofty statement an Assistant Under Secretary in the FCO was prone to make. It failed to grasp the obvious that Saddam was already well-anchored down and was not a man to be encouraged. He was clearly unwilling to gainsay voices 'encouraged that the regime [is] readier to do business with us'.[164] Never mind the persistent reports of human rights violations coming out of Iraq and the increasing thuggishness of its so-called diplomats on the streets of London.

During the rest of the decade, Saddam continued to play a leading part in relations with the Kurds, both causing offensives to be launched and negotiations to be reintroduced. In relations with the Oil Companies and Iraq's nationalisation of the industry, Saddam banged the drum for control of the country's assets. In the Arab League, he aligned with the most fervent anti-Israel members. In the Non-Aligned Movement, he established a rapport with a wide range of leaders, from Tito of Yugoslavia to Castro of Cuba. The 1972 Peace and Friendship Accord with the Soviet Union, not forgetting a secret codicil on intelligence cooperation negotiated with the paranoid Yuri Andropov, then head of the KGB, was very much his work, at least from the Iraqi side. In all his activities on behalf of his country, however, he remained his own man. Meetings in Moscow or Baghdad with the top Soviet leadership did not prevent him from torturing and taking out senior cadres of the CPI whom he regarded as a threat. On those occasions when things did not go the government's way, notably in the complex relationship with the Kurds, Saddam was always able to put the blame for failure on others, who were quickly removed, or he would make accusations of foreign interference. The United States was an obvious Aunt Sally, albeit the CIA could always give cause. Bakr remained head of state and retained respect within the Ba'ath Party, but Saddam was in command of decision-making and enforcement. As long as his old patron agreed with him, they could coexist.

In June 1979, the worm finally turned. That month, Saddam appeared in Amman, the first high-level visitor since 1958. The chemistry between him and King Hussein was surprisingly warm and various military, economic and political protocols were signed. Speaking years later during the aftermath of Iraq's invasion of Kuwait, the then Crown Prince Hassan conceded that Saddam had always been able to exert a certain charm on his elder brother. Whatever the physically imposing Iraqi really thought of the diminutive Jordanian, he had an intense dislike of President Assad of Syria. The latter had persecuted Saddam's one-time idol Michel Aflaq, who had found refuge in Baghdad. Over the years since the 1968 Revolution, if not well before, the Syrian and Iraqi intelligence services had been at one another's throats. Saddam regarded the General Directorate of Intelligence (DGI), formed in 1973 and better known as the Mukhabarat (*Jihaz Al-Mukhabarat Al-Amma*), as his personal fiefdom. Its establishment went back to his secret discussions with Andropov in February 1972. Next door in Syria, Assad had developed similarly collaborative relations with Moscow. Trouble began to brew, however, when only a few days after Saddam visited Jordan, Assad was received in the Iraqi capital at head-of-state level. The occasion was the third meeting of the Iraq/Syria Joint Commission which had been set up the year before with the long-term intent of unification – with the Egyptians out of the equation, another stab at achieving a united Arab Republic. At the end of three days, the two presidents declared on 19 June that their countries constituted a 'unified state with one president [Bakr], one government and one [Ba'ath] party'. There would be a joint political command structure based on a council composed of seven members from each country headed by their respective presidents. Assad, in effect, would become Bakr's deputy.

To Saddam, this was anathema. At best, he would be number three in such an arrangement. What control would he retain over the most vital organs of state, the respective intelligence services? The time had finally come for the sixty-five-year-old Iraqi president to be retired off. Well before his Jordanian visit Saddam's intelligence services were ear-marking loyalist Bakr supporters for detention and/or their families were being taken into 'protective' custody. By 11 July, he was ready for the final push. At a meeting that day of the Regional Command Council (RCC), now packed with his henchmen, Saddam 'persuaded' Bakr to retire; it was later put out that this was for health reasons. The Council immediately approved Saddam's appointment as Iraqi President, as RCC Chairman and as the designated Secretary-General of the Party; he had enjoyed access to membership records for years. He was officially installed in office five days later. The coup was not yet over. From 20 July, there were widespread arrests as Bakr supporters within the Ba'ath were purged. It all culminated on the 22nd at an extraordinary meeting of senior party cadres in the wake of widespread rumours circulated in Baghdad of a Syrian-backed plot to bring down the Iraqi leadership – Saddam. It was left to a grim-faced Taha Ramadan to announce the results of an investigation into the plot and to name those whose disloyalty had been uncovered. Many sat in the audience, perspiring for fear that they might be included in the list. One or two with tears in their eyes actually stood up to confess their involvement; they were quickly led away. At a signal from Saddam, the accused, who had all been deliberately seated unwittingly in two distinct groups, were marched out. True to Fascist form, the proceedings were captured on film for history to see but also for others to beware of the fate of any who stepped out of Saddam's line.

Six days later, a seven-man court tried the plotters: five members of the RCC, fifty military officers and one hundred party members were arraigned. By the beginning of August, five hundred senior Ba'athists had been executed and all five of the accused RCC members were condemned to death. The story soon leaked out that those in the leadership whom Saddam had spared were obliged to shoot their former colleagues so that they might be complicit and underline their loyalty to him. On 8

August, the new dictator president claimed in a speech that the plot's exposure was a great achievement of the Ba'ath Party. It was nothing of the sort; Saddam had merely used the power he had held for a long time to manipulate the party for his own ends and to bring about a clean sweep every bit as impressive as Hitler or Stalin would have organised. Closely supported by ruthless killers like Ramadan as his first Deputy President and the increasingly sinister Izzat al Duri[165] as Vice-Chairman of the RCC, Saddam now had a full grip on all affairs of state, both administrative and political. He would now continue to work on men's bodies and minds, far from Iraq itself and on his front doorstep.

Nine

THE IRAN/IRAQ WAR AND THE INVOLVEMENT OF THE MAJOR POWERS (1982-1988)

The year 1979 was a turning point in international relations on several counts. Some months before Saddam's seizure of total power in Iraq, another larger-than-life figure had assumed supreme religious authority and the ultimate say in neighbouring Iran's decision-making. Ayatollah Khomeini, who had been allowed to live in Najaf since 1965 when he was exiled from Iran, landed at Tehran's Mehrabad Airport on 1 February. Some reports claimed that as many as five million rapturous Iranians had been there to welcome him home. Within hours, even if it was not fully recognised at the time, the United States had lost its most reliable ally in the Middle East, the Sunni Gulf states were taking fright at the threat of a militant Shi-ite neighbour and many in Baghdad shuddered at the thought of the effect the Ayatollah might have on those it had always regarded with deep suspicion in southern Iraq. Indeed, under the guise of 'medical treatment', Khomeini had been obliged to remove himself from the Shi-ite shrines to Paris at the beginning of the year after his alleged involvement in a plot to bring down the government; an Air France jet brought him back to Tehran. It is questionable whether the major powers fully understood the religious implications; Saddam certainly did not, since he had connived in the Ayatollah's return to Iran and would express support for him in the early days. The Soviet Union was happy enough to see a strong anti-Communist bastion brought low, while the West's attitude towards the ailing Shah had become increasingly jaundiced over his failing grip on law and order. To see the new Iran as still part of a sphere of influence, however, was to miss the point. What had happened was much deeper than any move from one camp to another. The establishment of a theocracy in Tehran changed all the political rules, above all in Islam. The Sunni-Shia rift may have lasted almost as long as the religion itself, but both sides had tolerated one another rather more than history has recorded. A senior Kuwaiti security official, rejoicing at Khomeini's death on 3 June 1989, told me shortly afterwards that, until the Iranian Revolution, there had never been any problems between the two communities in the Emirate. He knew many Shia and they were 'good friends'.

There were few shockwaves in London. I well remember the long reporting telegrams from the embassy in Tehran detailing every reaction at the Shah's court in the months before a cancer-ridden Reza Shah fled the country two weeks before Khomeini's descent onto the tarmac. There were audible yawns in Whitehall amidst concerns at the prospect of the Shah wishing to lay his head down in the UK. With such a cataclysmic Revolution, there was little or no intelligence coming in about what was likely to follow or to replace the safe and reasonably reliable flow of the past. There was an element of relief that what had become a discredited and highly unpopular administration, accused of cruelty towards its people, had been removed. Journalists on the spot were tinged with this emotive impression and reported with sympathy towards those who preached reform. In a Whitehall now pre-occupied with membership of the European Community and the Cold War, Farsi was rated a long way down the linguistic priorities. Business with Iran had invariably been conducted in English and, if there was still a Third World language specialism in the Foreign Office, it was Arabic. In Bonn one morning, the politically astute British ambassador, Sir Oliver Wright, turned to his press counsellor, an Arabist, and asked him to brief the many uninitiated brains round the table on the great Islamic religious divide. He, at least, recognised a major shift when he saw it; for others round the table it was a small diversion from more important business. Large-scale events always blind governments – as in 1958, 1963 and 1968 – especially when eyes on the ground, many of them long-running sources, have fled, been detained or eliminated. It was going to take decades, if ever, to replace them.

The Americans were soon to be in a far worse situation. Angered by their acceptance of Reza Shah as a political refugee, a group of students broke into the United States' embassy in Tehran on 4 November 1979 and seized fifty-two staff. As dangerous, in the longer-term, they ransacked the filing cabinets and, in the years that followed, painstakingly pieced together the shreddings of secret documents. The identification of dozens of sensitive sources and compromise of the CIA's modus operandi wiped out its spy network for a very long time; its 'humint' has never been rebuilt. This and the huge resentment at their staff having to languish 444 days in captivity colours the American public view of Iran to this day. By the time of their release, Iraq had already declared war on its neighbour; it followed that both sides of the Atlantic regarded the conflict as a struggle between the mad and the bad. It was an undesirable choice to have to make, but for the most part, both Moscow and the West came down on the side of the bad – Iraq – partly because they understood a strong political leader more than a theocracy. In contrast, the voice of the Tehran taxi driver, who had always blamed Britain for everything, good or bad, that had ever happened in the world, was drowned out by clerics preaching against both 'big' and 'little' Satan. They were right, at least in one respect: Britain had lost most of its power to influence events, despite the empty claim made by many politicians in London that she continued to punch above her weight.

As noted previously, there had always been strife – racial as much as religious – between Arabs and Persians. This had largely subsided during the nineteenth century; adjacent Turkey had looked to the Balkans for expansion, with the occasional foray south into Arabia. The border with Persia, however, had remained open and fluid;[166] former British technicians working on communications in support of the developing oil industry maintained that there was no let or hindrance to their trans-border travel during the 1920s and 1930s. Nevertheless, as production stepped up to meet the mounting world demand for carbon fuels, issues concerning tanker-borne exports from the Gulf began to arise. The thorniest was who controlled the Shatt al-Arab waterway below the confluence of the Tigris and Euphrates. Some two hundred kilometres in length, it was accepted under the British mandate as the logical boundary between its charge and Persia. It was divided on the *Thalweg* (valley floor) principle; that is, along a line that followed the deepest point along the stream. All this changed in 1937 when a treaty between Iraq and Iran, brokered by Britain, settled the border as being along the low-tide mark on the eastern bank of the Shatt, except at Abadan and Khorramshahr, where the *Thalweg* principle continued to apply. With the needs of the oil-producing companies as much in mind as national interests, therefore, the treaty facilitated tanker-borne traffic from ports, Iranian and Iraqi, either side of the Shatt. More importantly, apart from giving Baghdad control of almost the entire length of the waterway, all shipping was obliged to fly the Iraqi flag and pay tolls for the privilege.

This uneven agreement could only last as long as Britain remained the dominant power in the northern Gulf. Under Reza Shah, in no small part placed on the peacock throne by London, Iran grew in military potential and influence, while Iraq suffered from successive destabilising upheavals. On 19 April 1969, while Saddam was still rounding up his opponents, both in the army and in political circles, Iran abrogated the 1937 treaty, adopted the *Thalweg* principle unilaterally and refused to pay tolls. Three days later, British-built Iranian warships were deployed as escorts for commercial traffic in the Shatt and, after lodging a protest, the militarily weaker Iraq backed down from confrontation. The issue and the deep sense of humiliation was not forgotten in Baghdad. Saddam was helpless. His response was to do what he could always do best: arrest and execute ten Iranian 'spies' in the teeth of protests from Tehran. Border incidents soon followed: on the Iraqi side, they were as much imagined as real, but it was Baghdad's way of rattling a sabre without actually having to draw a sword.[167] Closure of Iranian consulates in southern Iraq ensued and diplomats were expelled mutually. This followed the detention and torture of an Iranian second secretary in Baghdad, Abdul Khaliq Bushehri Zadeh. Saddam observed this flagrant abuse of the Geneva Convention on diplomatic privilege in person and in company with the

Iranian oppositionist General Teymour Baktiar, who had set up his anti-Shah headquarters in Baghdad. The atmosphere calmed down only after fierce threats of retaliation were made by the Iranian Foreign Minister, if the Iraqis put one step the wrong side of the picket wire. The Americans failed to take note of this precedent in July 1990.

Another potential area of conflict was brewing. Iran was also able to bruise the Iraqi Achilles' heel in Kurdistan and, increasingly, encouraged the Talibani-led PUK in Sulaymaniyah province adjacent to its north-western border. Baghdad responded in September 1971 by expelling forty thousand Kurds to Iran.[168] A month later, Iraqi pressure caused the clearing-out of eleven thousand Shia inhabitants on Abu Musa and the Tunbs Islands in the middle of the lower Gulf, just short of the Straits of Hormuz.[169] Iran's response was to claim sovereignty and to occupy the islands on 30 November. A peeved Saddam broke off diplomatic relations with Tehran, obliging the Iranians to put their affairs in the hand of the Swedish embassy. During the following year, there were sporadic skirmishes and incursions along the border and further expulsions from Iraq, mostly Shia from the south. The bilateral relationship remained most uneasy until the 1973 Yom Kippur War when Egypt surprised the Israelis in the Sinai desert. Iran accepted Iraq's overtures for the restoration of diplomatic relations and agreed not to undermine her troop deployments to the Syrian border in support of the united Arab cause.

The extended hand of friendship was only temporary. At the beginning of 1974, clashes on the Iran/Iraq border became increasingly ugly, the situation complicated by Kurdish forces receiving indirect assistance from Tehran, with or without CIA connivance. On 12 February, Iraq raised the issue in the Security Council. Subsequent UN mediation facilitated two weeks of discussion between Iranian and Iraqi diplomats in Istanbul, where Ottoman records might have assisted their researches, but these ended without agreement against the background of further clashes on the border. Faced with increasing Kurdish insurgency backed by Iran and the United States, however, Saddam sought an accommodation over the Shatt. In January the following year, he sent his newly appointed, sour-faced Minister of Foreign Affairs, Sa'dun Hammadi,[170] to Istanbul for further negotiations. As on a number of occasions, Saddam recognised when he could not win, at least for the time being, and accepted the *Thalweg* principle along the Shatt, withdrew Iraqi claims to the islands in the Lower Gulf and accepted the legality of Iran's abrogation of the 1937 treaty. With assistance from the Algerian President, Boumediene, whom he had met on 3–4 March, he clinched a deal that also procured Iran's agreement to withdraw its support for the menacing Kurds. This gave the Iraqi Army much-needed respite and room to prepare for a renewal of hostilities when the time was ripe. Respective radio broadcasts dropped invective while diplomats started a study of how the Shatt and adjacent waterways might best be shared. Iran obliged, too, by executing two Kurdish hi-jackers of an Iraqi Airways flight on 7 April.[171] Rare official cooperation, assisted by the hi-jack-prone Algerians and the Shah's mounting problems at home, paved the way for the signing in Algiers on 13 June 1975 by Foreign Ministers Hammadi and Abbas Ali Khalatbari of the Iran/Iraq Reconciliation Treaty.

Until Khomeini's arrival in Tehran, the autocratic Shah and the Baghdad dictator agreed to coexist. There was even some further rapprochement in 1978 when Iranian Intelligence (SAVAK) uncovered a Soviet-inspired plot amongst the Shia to topple the Ba'athists. This was behind the expulsion of the Ayatollah from Iraq and his 'medical treatment' in Paris. However, with mounting chaos in Tehran and the emasculation of Iran's armed forces, Saddam was not going to miss out on the opportunity to restore the balance along the Shatt in Iraq's favour. In the wake of Kurdish forces' increased use of Iranian border areas as refuges and Saddam's alarm at Khomeini's repeated calls for an Islamist uprising in Iraq, he denounced the 1975 accord on 30 October 1979, just a few days before the students' seizure of the American embassy. He also demanded that Iran withdraw from Abu Musa and the Tunbs Islands and set his mind on the annexation of Khuzestan, Iran's oil-rich, western-most and largely Arabic-speaking province. Unsurprisingly, Tehran rejected Baghdad's demands and protests.

This did nothing to dampen Saddam's increasing megalomania: as the last minutes of the decade ticked away, he claimed in a radio broadcast that Iraq was as 'great as China, USSR and the USA'. All those schooldays dreaming of the ancient wonders of Mesopotamia had not been forgotten. Two weeks before the broadcast, Iraqi artillery had already begun shelling Iranian border areas. Tensions bubbled over on 9 March 1980 when an exasperated Tehran expelled the Iraqi ambassador; Baghdad reacted in kind the next day. As more diplomats were shown the door, shells from either side continued to fall and bellicose statements rang out from both capitals. It was not, however, until early October that a state of war became apparent. On the 4th, Iran shelled the Iraqi border towns of Khanaqin and Mandali in the Diyala Governorate, predominantly Kurdish in population and close to the southern end of the Kirkuk oil fields. This, it was later considered, was the casus belli. By that time, Iraqi troops had certainly crossed the picket wire to 'liberate' two pockets near Qasr-e-Shirin, a town famous for a story of early seventh-century romance between a queen of Armenia, Shirin, and the twenty-second Sassanid king, Khosrow Parviz. What had been a haunt for archaeologists would soon be turned into a battlefield and heaps of rubble. Any hopes of peace were shattered when, on 17 October, Saddam addressed the Iraqi National Assembly and declared war formally on Iran. With this, he repeated his claim to Iraqi sovereignty over the Shatt al-Arab. From that point, neither side was going to give an inch, despite all the toothless resolutions passed in the UN Security Council.

That it took several months for periodic border clashes to erupt into all-out war might suggest an unwillingness on both sides to take up cudgels. For all its new-found religious fervour, Iran was militarily in no state to take on its neighbour. Iraq, too, could better have afforded to remain at peace, to benefit from the substantial economic and social progress achieved during the previous decade. Much of this had been made possible by the huge increase in oil production, by now worth twenty-six billion dollars annually, some five per cent of world and ten per cent of OPEC production. It amounted to fifty per cent of national income. This, and the technical assistance it was receiving from Warsaw Pact countries, had facilitated huge strides in health care and technical education; the ratio of population to the number of doctors had more than halved during the years between 1968 and the opening of 1980. Education had also benefited enormously: those receiving an elementary education had risen to well over two and a half million (less than a million in 1968); secondary school student numbers had quadrupled during the same period to nearly a million, while the universities and technical colleges catered for 122,000 (only thirty-seven thousand in 1968). This impressive advance in literacy and technical capability had injected a resilience into Iraqi society that would help it to weather the huge strains put upon it by continuous warfare and isolation. In the coming conflicts, too, the government husbanded its well-qualified professional cadres and technicians and, for the most part, did not squander them on the battlefield.

Major improvements had also been made in national infrastructure. Thanks to joint Iraqi/Jordanian enterprise, in no small part due to Saddam's influence over King Hussein, the port of Aqaba at the head of the Red Sea was being developed with oil funds to accommodate Iraqi shipping so that it would no longer have to rely on passage through the Gulf and the Straits of Hormuz. A super-highway linking Amman to Baghdad was also under construction. The route took it across safe Sunni territory, much to be preferred than the poorly maintained roads in the Shi-ite south. In the end, however, Saddam's megalomania got the better of him. Did he not have an army numbering nearly a quarter of a million, far bigger than any other Third World country and substantially larger than the British Army? It needed to be kept occupied and, given a rapprochement with the Kurds, redirected against an external enemy. And were there not many Arab brothers to 'liberate' in neighbouring Khuzestan, the Iranian province just across the Shatt? Above all, he rated the Iranians inferior in mind and body, if not in religiosity. Like Hitler before him, he did not fear what a pope or ayatollah might throw in his way.

This is not the place for an account of the war's chronological course. There were no great set battles; it more resembled the slugging match on the Western Front during the First World War. Either side launched ground offensives which usually ran quickly into the sand – or mud.

Ground forces struggled bitterly for a few hundred yards of territory. When waves of fervent Iranian troops threatened to overwhelm Iraqi forward positions, there was always the option to decimate the advancing infantry using poison gas and other chemical weapons. Iran allegedly responded in kind, although this has never been established. There was nothing glamorous about the eight years of attrition that characterised the Iran/Iraq War and killed half a million combatants and, though somewhat fewer, many civilians. Then, there was what to do with the thousands of prisoners of war – fifty to sixty thousand Iraqis – by the start of 1984. Many of these were southern Shia who would be recruited into the oppositionist Badr brigade, set up in Iranian camps, that would become a running sore for years after the conflict had been brought to an end.

At the outset, the major powers had no strong motivation to bid seriously for a cessation of hostilities. Almost without exception the onlookers were content to see an Iranian regime that flouted international law and diplomatic immunity being checked by its secular neighbour; past Ba'athist brutality was swept under the carpet in the common interest. There was another underlying factor: in one way or another, they had all earned large sums from the supply of military materiel to the theatre, to one or other of the protagonists. First in the frame was the Soviet Union that, increasingly, had poured tanks, artillery, missiles and aircraft into Iraq. As war continued, this flow increased, noticeably after secret talks in December 1982 in Moscow. After this, more sophisticated weaponry, including long-range surface-to-surface missiles for the bombardment of urban and economic targets alike, were supplied. Complicit in this was Kuwait which built a high-spec seventh-ring motorway – known as the empty road – way out in the desert for the discreet transport of heavy weapons and equipment from its port at Schuwaikh to the Iraqi border. The long snaking convoys were of obvious interest to de visu observers, but their reports did nothing to enhance attempts to curb the fighting. Heavily involved, too, in its attempt since Christmas Eve 1979 to subdue Afghanistan, the Soviet Union was in no mood to stop one of its client states from weakening a vehemently anti-Communist theocracy.

In what was soon to become a struggle for air supremacy, the French of all the Western powers were the most involved in arms supply. Franco-Iraqi relations were boosted in July 1972 when Saddam visited President Pompidou in Paris. There, he also cemented a relationship with Jacques Chirac, Pompidou's former aide and soon to become French Prime Minister (1974–76). Well before the outbreak of the Iran/Iraq War, France was supplying a large number of AMX tanks and military aircraft. In return, she could rely on preferential treatment as a customer for Iraqi oil, to meet her energy requirements. Thus, a contract for Mirage F1 fighter-bombers agreed in 1977 was honoured, the first four aircraft being delivered in February 1981 soon after the first round of heavy fighting at Susangerd, across the border from Basra. At the same time, Paris reneged on its promises to supply similar aircraft to Iran, an act of war in Tehran's eyes. It did not stop there. As part of a strong inclination to side with the Palestine cause against Tel Aviv, noticeably after the Yom Kippur War, France was quick to condemn the Israeli bombing on 7 June 1980 of the Iraqi nuclear facility at Osirak, only some twelve miles south-east of Baghdad. There had been over a hundred French technicians at the site, one of whom was killed. Paris denied that the reactor was about to become operational for military purposes and a newly elected President Mitterrand promised to rebuild the plant. In February 1982, he sent his Foreign Minister, Claude Cheysson, to Baghdad to discuss further nuclear cooperation.

Iraq's already growing air supremacy was further boosted in 1983 by the delivery of Super Etendard strike aircraft equipped with the same heat-seeking Exocet missiles and guidance systems that had been so effective against the Royal Navy in the South Atlantic the year before. The only French reservation was whether or not they would receive payment. Sophisticated Russian and French aircraft flown by increasingly skilled Iraqi pilots ensured that long before the end of the year, Saddam had achieved almost complete air superiority. Mounting Exocets in both helicopters and surface vessels, he could direct their aim at vital Iranian oil installations down the Gulf. In 1984, the aim was widened; Iraqi Etendards sank three Cypriot-registered merchant vessels and, for the first time, attacked the world's then largest crude oil terminal on Kharg Island. By the end of the war, Iran's facilities there had been almost completely destroyed. French augmentation of Iraqi Air Force capability continued until the end of hostilities, earning Paris a good deal of kudos in the Gulf Arab states, not least in Kuwait.

In comparison with the commercial or cynical policies of others, the British government sought to adopt a morally more defensive approach to arms sales. This was despite the hope on the eve of Saddam's takeover, both in the embassy and in Whitehall, that bilateral relations might improve. It was 'in the interest of the British economy', the ambassador concluded in his annual review for 1978, 'that we persevere with the regime'.[172] There had even been serious consideration of a visit by Lord Carrington, the Foreign Secretary, to Baghdad, apparently at Iraqi invitation. This was never going to happen, but it demonstrated a wishful thinking, fuelled by the Iraqi market being regarded by his ambassador as 'perhaps the most promising market in the Middle East'. When hostilities broke out, the usually more optimistic embassy was presented with a conundrum: the war 'presented the Western world with the dilemma of not knowing which side it sympathises with less... in an unnecessary war'.[173] In its response, signed off by the Minister of State, Douglas Hurd, the Foreign Office position was that, although the regime was unattractive, it was 'competent, and Saddam Hussein is a particularly effective head of government... corruption is not too rampant and the Iraqis have a reputation for honouring their bargains once they have been struck'. Such a statement might have issued from the Baldwin government in the 1930s. Yes, the war was an obstacle, especially in the area of 'defence sales', but there were ways in which the UK might 'improve her share of the market'.[174]

There were those that disagreed. An FCO Planning Staff paper, commissioned by Hurd, dismissed the bogey of increased Soviet influence and set the oil factor in context; virtually all Iraq's major neighbours were 'more important to us'. The war, in fact, had been a 'godsend' with Saddam 'humbled' on the battlefield and his ambitions to lead the Non-Aligned Movement dashed. "No major Western interests would be damaged by an indefinite prolongation of the war at its present level." The paper concluded that: "it would be a mistake to pay any great price to persuade [Iraq] to get close to us."[175] Ambassador Egerton blew a fuse when reading the paper in Baghdad: he was most unhappy at its underestimate of Iraq's importance to the UK and, characteristically, belittled the author as someone who had never served 'further than Madrid'.[176] What he and, others like him, could not grasp was the mounting revulsion being expressed by non-Arabists at the crudity of Baghdad's methods. There had always been those who were ready to defend overseas leaders, if they could be regarded as 'our thugs', but by early 1981 the evidence of mass executions and inordinate use of vicious torture in Iraq was overwhelming, for all the denials Baghdad made. On 29 April, Amnesty International published a damning indictment and vivid illustration of the methods being used in Iraqi interrogation and political oppression. Two days previously, the Iraqi embassy in London had thought it necessary to dismiss the accusations out of hand in a 1,500-word statement. This flew in the face of independent and comprehensive medical examination of survivors managing to escape abroad and confirmation that many political opponents of the regime had been poisoned. Egerton must have seen reports of these outrages – Amnesty would have copied drafts to the embassy for comment – but he chose to gloss over them and, instead, described Saddam's arch-prosecutor, Ramadan, as the 'brightest' of the regime's stars. This was rather like singling out Himmler from Hitler's bunch of cronies. Sadly, there had always been a left-over attitude from colonial days in some sections of the British foreign service. Shortly after 'Corporal' Idi Amin took over the Ugandan Presidency In 1971, a senior intelligence officer lamented that 'they won't let him stay in office'. By 'they' he meant the weak-kneed mandarins in Whitehall.

With a politician's eye for public opinion, Carrington was rather more careful. He supported the completion of defence orders made before the war, but in future, there were to be no export of lethal equipment, 'not weapons and ammunition'. Even the despatch of small quantities, he observed, would cause 'difficulties in public'. The hand-held infantry surface to air missile, Blowpipe, much desired by both sides, was smartly ruled out of court. Carrington's concern filtered down into middle ranks of the Ministry of Defence who blocked any attempt at imaginative 'procurement' for some 'deniable' intelligence ploy, long before any submission for an operation might have been countenanced. Contrary to the conspiracy theorists, it was simply not allowed to happen, however small the amount of materiel. In addition, the American hostage situation ruled out any supplies to Iran; the British government held back £18 million worth of spares for the Chieftain tank, the mainstay of Iran's armoured echelons. The issue lingers on to the present day and at least one hostage prisoner with a British passport has languished in the notorious Evin prison as a result. Carrington's moral concern was slightly dented by his admission of a personal report from Lord George-Brown, who had relayed Saddam's threat that British arms sales to Iran would jeopardise London's relations with the whole Arab world.

In the years that followed Carrington's original guidelines, two contrasting items illustrate the subtleties or contortions – whichever way you wish to look at it – of British arms sales policy towards Iraq during the war: battle tank refurbishment and the much-discussed putative delivery of a strike/trainer aircraft – the Hawk. Both, on the surface at least, risked undermining the non-lethal proviso.

In a clear indication that the British government was prepared to assist the 'bad' against the 'mad' whenever circumstances allowed, a stratagem was found for the refurbishment of up to seventy Iranian Chieftain tanks captured during the early fighting. Sir John Graham's initial objection to the scheme by which the damaged vehicles would be repaired in Jordan using British spares was overruled.[177] Furthermore, it was also agreed that Iraqi Soviet-supplied M55 tanks should be up-gunned with British 105mm weapons to replace the slightly smaller calibre Russian armament. Hardly non-lethal. What is not clear is what tactical reasons were given for these upgrades, other than a fear that the Iranians might break through.

The issue of the BAE Hawk aircraft was much more one of commercial consideration. First raised well before the war as the Iraqi Air Force looked around for replacements for its ageing fleet of British Hunter fighters, the Hawk trainer/strike aircraft would have complemented the promised

French Mirage and Etendard deliveries. Early in 1981, BAE signed a contract worth £205 million for a feasibility study to confirm whether up to 150 Hawk planes could operate successfully in extreme hot weather conditions. This was more or less in line with the Whitehall view early on during the fighting that the war could not last long and should not be allowed to prejudice long-term, highly valuable defence sales. In the case of the Hawk, this would have amounted to £1,500 million. On 23 February 1981, Minister of State Hurd agreed to the despatch of a single aircraft to Iraq – via Cyprus – for one week's testing during the stifling heat of late July/early August. In the event, the proposed sale was abandoned shortly after the war ended, partly because the Iraqis were boasting they could produce a similar aircraft themselves but also because the Foreign Office argued it would undermine efforts to re-establish relations with a defeated Iran on the back foot.

These two projects were the sum total of British government-sponsored sensitive arms sales during the Iran/Iraq War. In reality, therefore, the amount of equipment provided by the UK to Iraq during the long-drawn-out hostilities was remarkably small and, for the most part, stayed within Carrington's strictures. Unfortunately, a relatively clean pair of hands was besmirched by the Matrix Churchill scandal, first unearthed by SIS in 1987. It is a sign of Whitehall's integrity that its intelligence arm was tasked to report on Iraq's attempts to circumvent the government's arms sales policy. When direct procurement was cut off, Baghdad sought to purchase companies producing what it most needed. This was not difficult to do in an unregulated capitalist system. In early 1987, the Al-Arabi Trading Company, a subordinate of Iraq's Nasr State Enterprise for Mechanical Industries, set up a holding company office in London, from which to procure machine tools. This, in itself, broke no rules. The company – Technical Development Group – set up a firm called TMG Engineering which was then used to acquire the well-established machine tool manufacturer, Matrix-Churchill and its affiliate in the United States, Matrix-Churchill Corporation in Cleveland, Ohio. Having gained control of these companies, the Iraqis transformed them into vehicles for the production of a wide range of products for use in the manufacturing of munitions, as well as other applications in the aerospace and nuclear industries. Through a number of evasive ploys, including apparent export of goods to third countries and false end-user certificates, the company was able to bypass existing regulations. Needless to say, had SIS not alerted Whitehall, the British government would probably have been ignorant of the activity. The scandal, however, did not hit the headlines until after the armistice in 1988 had brought the war to an end, but that is altogether another story. To that point the government had kept largely to its own rules.

There was good reason to do so while the fighting raged. Thanks to Russian and French military aircraft, Iraq was able to widen the hostilities well beyond the battlefield. In what was no longer the brief conflict many had anticipated, both sides began to menace the world's oil supply. It started with the Iraqi sinking of three merchant vessels leaving the port of Bandar Khomeini in the northern Gulf on 11 January 1982. Three days later, Baghdad warned all shipping to stay away from the Western Gulf or risk the same fate. In March, Iraq increased its blockade by mining the channel connecting the neighbouring ports of Bandar Mahshahr and Bandar Khomeini to the open sea. Baghdad then ratcheted up the situation on 12 August by declaring a maritime exclusion zone (MEZ) in the northern Gulf extending up to sixty-five kilometres from Kharg Island, effectively seeking to close off Iran's premier oil terminal. Within the next four weeks, Iraqi aircraft had attacked at least four ships in the MEZ. Iran took its time before making a substantive response. On 13 October, however, the Iranian Foreign Minister, Ali Akbar Velayati, warned the UN General Assembly that, if one day of his country's oil exports were stopped, no oil would be carried from the Gulf. In other words, Iran would block the Straits of Hormuz. This was no idle threat, since, unlike the northern Gulf, she had a variety of options at her disposal for sealing off what had always been a treacherous channel.

For much of the year and most of the next, attention was fixed on heavy fighting on land interspersed with tentative moves towards peace. Saddam's announcement on 13 October 1983 of the imminent arrival of Super Etendard aircraft from France changed all that. Both the Iraqi

Air Force and Navy had already used Exocets since early in the war, but the prospect of this fresh tactical option alarmed Tehran. News of the intended loan of five aircraft to Iraq in what was little short of a barter deal to safeguard oil supply to France had first appeared in *Le Monde* on 24 June. A month later, Iran threatened 'to destroy the security of the Gulf' if the missile were used against her. It was thought at the time that deployment of the missile in the Etendard might cripple Iran's oil industry and would be Baghdad's means for bringing an abject Tehran to the negotiating table.

Alarm bells also rang in Washington and, in early October, the first American naval units arrived in the Gulf – three assault ships and a frigate. Against the background of mounting threats and counter-threats to stop oil exports from the Gulf and increasing attacks on third country tankers, an international naval flotilla was gradually assembled to protect shipping.[178] In February 1984, the USA demonstrated that it meant business: the aircraft carrier, USS *Midway*, reached the Gulf at the head of a taskforce. Both NATO and Warsaw Pact naval units were soon to be engaged to keep the tankers sailing and protected from attack. At the time, it looked like stalemate, but on 17 May 1987, Iraq did itself no favours when two Exocet missiles fired from its French-supplied Mirage aircraft struck the USS *Stark* and killed thirty-seven of her crew. Baghdad's belated apology[179] and curmudgeonly attitude towards the payment of compensation threatened a substantial cut in American assistance to the general Iraqi war effort. Not that Iran's behaviour was any better in the world's eyes: its navy was sowing mines along the Gulf, some of which drifted into Kuwaiti waters; its Revolutionary Guard Corps speedboats had also unwisely attacked the Soviet freighter *Ivan Koroteyev* earlier in the same month. Both belligerents had thoroughly antagonised both superpowers, a first in the Cold War.

There was another issue which became of increasing concern to informed world opinion as the war dragged on. With the opposing armies becoming more and more bogged down and unable to deliver a knock-out blow, their chiefs of staff looked for less conventional methods with which to outflank the other. Iraq started with chemical warfare; both sides sought to obtain materials illicitly from abroad, as well as manufacture their own obnoxious materials. With her enjoyment of increasing air superiority, however, Iraq was then able to take a major step forward in achieving the progressive destruction of Iran's ability to sustain her economy. With French and Russian assistance, she was able to direct ever more severe air attacks on oil and other vital installations. This still did not bring Iran to the negotiating table and, as international naval action began to damp down the tanker war, both belligerents came to consider even more drastic options. In March 1985, Iranian ground forces launched a successful offensive across the Tigris and, for a short while, were able to cut the main north-south highway connecting Baghdad with Basra. In the same month, an Iranian missile fell on Baghdad, the first of the war to do so. Rather like Hitler's angry response to a lone RAF raid on Berlin in 1940 that determined the Fuehrer to blitz London, Saddam unleashed his extensive, Soviet-supplied missile arsenal against Tehran and other large urban centres. Thus began what was to become known as the war of aerial bombardment of the cities. This continued for the rest of the war, apart from the occasional Iraqi pause while Baghdad waited to see whether its enemy had had enough. For its part, Iran launched several offensives towards Basra and procured Silkworm missiles from the Chinese with the potential to hit back hard against vital Iraqi installations and to threaten navigation of the Straits.

In February 1988, Iraq opened a two-month Soviet-supplied SCUD bombardment of Tehran and other Iranian cities. It followed the successful repulse of a major Iranian offensive aimed at capturing Basra. It was to be the last throw; from now on, Iraqi ground forces edged forward, recapturing the Fao peninsula and positions along the Shatt al-Arab lost earlier in the war. Iraqi air superiority might not have brought the Iranian Revolution to its knees, but its forces, including the fanatical Iranian Revolutionary Guards Corps (IRGC), were exhausted. The prospects of a military victory were now bleak. Along the northern sector of the Iran/Iraq frontier, the balance had also tipped in Baghdad's favour. Until early 1988, the alliance between Iran and the PUK operating out of Sulaymaniyah province had troubled the Iraqi Army severely. Then, on 16 March, Iraqi Soviet-supplied

SU-22 and MI-8 aircraft dropped chemical bombs on the Kurdish town of Halabja, where the Iranians were pressing home an attack against their enemy's base a few miles away. From 1100 (local) to late in the afternoon, the Iraqi Air Force pelted densely populated civilian areas with what was later confirmed to have been mustard gas and, at the time, unidentified nerve agents. Subsequently, the latter were considered to have been Tabun, Sarin and VX – biological warfare in short.[180] The murderous assault was the culmination of a deliberate campaign ordered by Saddam to eradicate Kurdish resistance. Halabja, however, was far worse than anything previously thrown at the irksome guerrillas. How many PUK combatants were actually killed has never been fully ascertained and the total number of casualties remains only a rough estimate – 3,200–5,000 killed and up to ten thousand injured. Moreover, it has been impossible to be accurate about the number of those who have since died of cancers and birth defects. Contemporary descriptions spoke gruesomely of lingering deaths from burning and blistering and the coughing up of green vomit.

The outrage shocked capitals around the world, if not the people in their streets. As with so many similar events in history and despite some coverage from the free press, it was possible for the perpetrators to lie about their involvement; in addition, Baghdad pointed the finger disingenuously at Tehran. Sadly, the world let Saddam get away with it at the time, just as the Kremlin was not brought to book over the 1940 Katyn Massacres in Poland. A briefing paper in the FCO stated: "We believe it better to maintain a dialogue with others if we want to influence their actions. Punitive actions such as unilateral sanctions would not be effective in changing Iraq's behaviour over chemical weapons and would damage British interests to no good effect." At about the same time, the left-wing Labour MP Tony Benn claimed that he was told in Parliament that 'Saddam is an ally'. So that was all right then; Saddam was one of 'our' thugs. The US State Department, informed by the CIA, also considered that the Iranians were at least partly to blame. Surely the Americans could hardly have believed Baghdad and Tehran had colluded; rather, it was still all too easy to cast aspersions against those who had incarcerated fifty-two Americans almost a decade previously.

Behind diplomatic doors, the Halabja atrocity lost Iraq a large number of political friends, but there was sufficient smoke to obscure those who were the real perpetrators. There was insufficient agreed condemnation in the United Nations to bring pressure to bear on Baghdad to end it all. Who then was going to blink first? It was, perhaps, always going to be Tehran, albeit that was not immediately obvious at the time. One defining moment may have been missed: on 3 July 1988, the USS *Vincennes*, a guided missile cruiser, shot down an Iranian airbus over the Gulf, causing the deaths of its 290 passengers and crew. The warship had been sent to the Gulf from its usual station in the Far East to help cover the withdrawal of the American frigate *Samuel B Roberts* through the Straits of Hormuz after the vessel had been damaged by an Iranian mine. It was while the *Vincennes* was on patrol in the Straits that it became involved in a confused battle with a number of IRGC-armed speedboats inside Iranian waters. During the mayhem, her commander misidentified an Iran Air A300 Airbus (flight 655) as an attacking F14 Tomcat fighter aircraft and fired two radar-guided missiles which destroyed the civilian aircraft as it climbed out of Bandar Abbas. It was a genuine, if disastrous, mistake which, naturally, Tehran considered to have been deliberate. More than this, to the paranoid minds in the Iranian capital, it represented something far more ominous. Had both the Americans and the Soviet Union finally both come down on Baghdad's side and were ready to intervene militarily? It was, for many in the Iranian leadership, the inescapable conclusion and one which meant that any hope of complete victory over Iraq and Saddam's removal – as early war aims had demanded – was quite out of the question.

After months of abortive UN mediation, backed by the two highly frustrated and no little annoyed superpowers, already feeling their way towards closer cooperation in foreign affairs, Iran was finally persuaded to agree a ceasefire on 20 August, starting the very next day. Although, at the time, this agreement was regarded as fragile, there was really no likelihood that the two now punch-drunk belligerents would start hitting each other over the head again. If the world's patience was exhausted, so too were the respective fighting forces on the ground. The result of eight years' bloodshed was a return to the border situation before the shooting had started. It looked like a Saddam victory and he certainly claimed it as such, but he lacked one vital ingredient of statecraft – moral authority. Despite all the awful losses, both on the battlefields and in the conurbations, Ayatollah Khomeini's theocracy was not seriously damaged; Tehran would live for another day.

Ten

UNFORESEEN

The end of the war with Iran left Saddam as powerful as ever, but there were undercurrents. Despite his hold on all the reins, there were still occasional voices in the administration ready to question whether the leader had bitten off more than he could chew. The story is well-known. During June 1982, in the wake of a series of Iraqi reverses around Khorramshahr and Iranian counterattacks that had penetrated over a thirty-five-kilometre stretch along the border and taken twelve thousand prisoners, Riyadh Ibrahim Husain, the Health Minister, was shot dead outside the cabinet room. After reviewing the military situation with his council of ministers, Saddam asked whether any of those present had any suggestions. One nervous hand went up. Riyadh Husain was given the floor. Haltingly, he wondered whether it was not time to seek peace. Perhaps, to attract in the Iranians, Saddam might offer to step down – only temporarily, of course – in favour of his predecessor, Ahmed Hassan Bakr. This would blunt one of Iran's war aims – regime change – and once peace was secured, Saddam could return to office. There was a hush in the room and much, if quiet, sucking of teeth. Saddam smiled and conceded that this was an interesting suggestion. He invited Riyadh to step outside so that they might discuss it further. Shortly after the door closed behind them, a shot was heard and the Health Minister's term of office was at an end.[181] Later the same month, a secret Ba'ath Congress closed after re-endorsing Saddam as Secretary-General and agreeing to a bloodless reshuffling of posts. No one wanted to be shot out of hand. The changes only concentrated power into Saddam's grasp with the Revolutionary

Command Council (RCC) being reduced to nine members, all loyalists who had been with him from the outset. Three days later, Iraq announced a withdrawal from virtually all Iranian territory it had occupied.

Saddam was undoubtedly rattled and would likely have settled for a cease-fire and negotiations while his forces recuperated. Anyone who questioned his policy or position was dealt with in the only way he knew. That same summer, he was addressing a meeting of the National Assembly when he noticed a man passing a note to another. Saddam whipped out his pistol and shot both on the assumption that they were plotting to kill him. This incident demonstrated not just the Iraqi leader's impressive skill and accuracy with a firearm; after all, he had been using live targets ever since he was handed his first weapon at the age of ten. More significantly, the incident indicated that there were still members of his own Ba'ath Party who were ready to bring him down, despite the horrors awaiting those who tried and failed. And try they did. In the second week of July 1982, Saddam's motorcade was ambushed at Dujail, some forty miles north-east of Baghdad and thus well inside Sunni country. He survived unharmed, but the village was razed to the ground and its inhabitants killed. The man who made a virtue of handing out *baksheesh* to the poor in remote areas could as easily crush them if they showed ingratitude.[182]

Almost exactly three years later, when there was near panic in Baghdad at what seemed like the prospect of an imminent Iranian military victory, Saddam acted swiftly to remove any potential falterers. One of the two token Shi-ites on the RCC, Naim Hamid Haddad, was removed.[183] He disappeared from history. As did the Mayor of Baghdad, Abdul-Wahab Mohammed Latif al-Mufti, who was accused of corruption and hanged, along with four other officials.[184] The clear-out prompted the promotion of General Ali Hassan al-Majid, Saddam's cousin, to the RCC and, ominously, his appointment as Ba'ath Secretary for the Northern Command. Only those on whom Saddam could rely to carry out his commands ruthlessly remained at the centre of power. Even so, the paranoid Saddam did not feel safe from a lone wolf. Stories of the painful plastic surgery on several look-alikes who could be paraded as his double abounded in lurid detail during the last decade or so of the century.

Still, however, there were those in his own family he was not prepared to trust. The mysterious death of Adnan Khairallah Talfah in May 1989 when his helicopter crashed has always been regarded as a murder on Saddam's orders. Adnan, it should be remembered, was the young Saddam's help-mate from earliest days and one of his five Deputy Prime Ministers appointed in July 1979 to liquidate any opposition. He was still serving as the Deputy Commander-in-Chief of the Armed Forces who had served his cousin through thick and thin when, in October 1988, he had committed a grievous sin in the eyes of the head of the family. At a party held that month in honour of the visiting Suzanne Mubarak,[185] wife of the Egyptian President, who was in Baghdad as Saddam's personal guest, the proceedings were interrupted by Uday Hussein's brutal attack on Kamal Hanna Jeijo, after a bout of drunkenness. Actually, Saddam's eldest son was furious with Jeijo, who doubled up as the Iraqi leader's food taster and go-between in a matter of the heart. For some time, Uday's father had been enamoured of Samira Shahbandar, the attractive wife of the Chairman of Iraqi Airways, and it was Jeijo who arranged discreet trysts. The affair flew in the face of Saddam's protestations that his family life was a model for Iraqi society. For Uday, it was an insult to his mother, Sajida, who was also Adnan Khairallah's sister. When Saddam had his son incarcerated and pledged to see that he was tried for murder, Adnan supported Sajida's pleading with her husband for clemency. Uday was sent out of the country to stay in Geneva with his uncle, Barzan al-Tikriti, another family member whom Saddam did not fully trust.[186] Adnan continued to blot his copybook and was blamed for having failed to detect a coup plot early in 1989. From then on, he was a marked man. His father, Khairallah, escaped his former stepson's wrath but was obliged to spend his last years in Tikrit, having lost both his legs as a consequence of his diabetes, albeit he died a very rich man in 1993.

The August 1988 armistice was welcomed widely, not least in the British embassy in Baghdad. In his review of 1988, the long-serving and well-steeped in Iraqi affairs ambassador Terry Clark[187] hailed the year as momentous and attributed the Iraqi success to their 'military superiority over a demoralised Iran'. The armistice, he considered, had been preceded by a series of well-executed operations conducted by an army that was well-trained and equipped, with the great advantage of air superiority. This had brought about the Iranian collapse. Without describing him as the victor, he conceded that Saddam, since the end of hostilities, had enjoyed 'such total domination of Iraq and the means for effecting his control that he could have continued his dictatorship unchanged'. Clark also recognised that the Iraqi dictator had chosen to take small steps in economic and political liberalisation: the privatisation of agriculture and small industries had continued with 'evident success' and mixed sector banking had been promised. The easing of import restrictions had led to a surge in the availability of consumer goods. Political prisoners had been released and there had been talk of political parties being allowed once more, possibly before the elections to the National Assembly in March 1989. In early January 1989, an Iraqi diplomat told me that this was a genuine sign that Saddam wished to gradually take his foot off the brakes. Refreshingly, Clark did not go on to recommend that the time was ripe for improved bilateral relations, as might many of his predecessors have done.

In contrast, however, he drew attention to Saddam's return to the centre of the Middle Eastern stage, aided by his special relationships with Jordan, Egypt and the Palestinian Liberation Organisation (PLO), each of which already had or was developing good relations with the West. Saddam was also throwing his weight around by intervening overtly and covertly in the Lebanon through his support for the Christian leader General Aoun against the Iraqi leader's old enemy, President Assad of Syria. Further flung, he had interfered in Eritrea, Mauretania and Chad. Looking back on this not particularly coordinated meddling in foreign affairs, it seems to have been more of an expression of Saddam's self-importance than anything else. Innately, he remained conservative and supportive of fellow strongmen in power.

As for the UK, it had been a 'year of extremes', the ambassador recorded. The outburst against Israeli military brutality voiced by Minister of State, David Mellor, had gone down particularly well in Baghdad.[188] Why would it not! Mellor's subsequent visit to Iraq shortly afterwards was a 'resounding success'. Stemming directly from it came the release of the long-incarcerated British businessman John Smith.[189] A mid-summer follow-up on a different tack by the Chancellor of the Duchy of Lancaster also went down well. Ostensibly, it was to attend the Baghdad Fair and Joint British/Iraqi Commission, the clearing house for trade projects within a highly regulated economy. Margaret Thatcher waited, however, until Mellor's fellow left-wing Conservative, Ken Clarke, had been moved before she sent the middle-of-the-road Tony Newton off to Iraq with an offer Saddam could not refuse.[190] Newton bore the gift of an extended line of credit – to £340 million – but received little in return and certainly not the release of the other captive UK national, Ian Richter. The Tories, however, were involved in a further round of trade promotion with embassies being encouraged to lean towards opportunities for improving the balance of payments. Iraq was just one of these opportunities, with exports in 1988 up seventy-five per cent over the previous year and imports down by fifty per cent, a visible surplus of £330 million. Never mind that Newton's visit came only a year after Halabja. Provided the UK watched its words over the use of chemical weapons and dealt carefully with Iraqi abuse of diplomatic immunity in London, the outlook seemed fair enough. This was little short of pussy-footing. One voice in the Foreign Office addressed the political over the commercial. Assistant Under Secretary David Gore-Booth[191] minuted perceptively on 13 August 1989: "...either he [Saddam] will be toppled or he will revert to type. In the latter case, the Iranians, Syrians, Lebanese and Gulf Arabs had better watch out since he is bound to seek external relief for his internal pain."

Who or what would topple Saddam? The impressive Iraqi armed forces that Terry Clark spoke of were one potential threat. There were those in the military who doubted the President's grasp of strategy and were unhappy about, as they saw it, Iran being let off the hook. Iraqi leaders had been deposed by the Army several times before. Now it was the generals who could bask in the glory of a job well done and they had crack divisions serving under them. The Army numbered nearly a million formed into seven corps, comprising seven armoured/mechanised divisions and no less than thirty-nine infantry divisions. At the time, the British Army could barely muster a third of that strength. Such a major sector of society had to be given something to do. It could not be left idle in its barracks. There was a wider dimension. For over a decade, Saddam had placed Iraq on a war footing; the whole country and its infrastructure were organised for the production of increasingly sophisticated weaponry. What Iraq could not produce itself, it purchased from abroad, often at inflated cost because of restrictions placed on arms exports by some countries.

War had cost the Iraqi economy dearly. Its largest income by far – from oil production – had been severely hit, with revenues down from twenty-six billion in 1980 to less than half that in 1988. Ambassador Clark considered that this had caused serious doubts about Iraq's ability to 'weather the next two to three years'. The country's earnings from the oil sector would be too little to meet all demands; payments to her many creditors were already being rescheduled. Something had to give and, Clark guessed, it would be the creditors. At the beginning of 1989 that seemed to imply merely a reneging on debt. The British answer in the following weeks was to almost triple Iraq's line of credit to £900 million. Nobody, however, in the FCO or Baghdad, saw this as anything but a means for promoting trade with a temporarily cash-strapped economy. No one considered the possibility that Saddam would do what he had done in 1980 and attempt a blitzkrieg, this time on a small but very rich neighbour, instead of a country of similar size to Iraq, and driven by religious mania and not much else. If the experts of the day harboured such thoughts, they certainly did not write them down. In short, the obvious was discounted or ignored.

When Saddam first decided to seize the Kuwaiti Emirate has never been fully established, but it was a shot that had always been in the Iraqi locker. The argument over sovereignty did not disappear with the end of the Turkish Sultanate. Indeed, the Kuwaitis themselves used it when it suited them. Admittedly apocryphal, a post-First World War anecdote illustrated this. When a British soldier was found dead just outside of the gates in the town wall,[192] the matter was raised with the Kuwaiti authorities who asked where precisely the body was discovered. When told that it was outside the gate, the Kuwaiti official sucked his teeth and replied: "Outside, you say. Ah, but that is Iraqi territory." In reality, the situation was completely different. Britain's mandated authority over Iraq saw to that during the post-war settlement; Iraq gained a slice of Kuwaiti territory, as did Najd, now Saudi Arabia, but the question of sovereignty was not an issue.[193] At the time, the British concern was to stabilise frontiers now that oil discoveries were proliferating and to set up a buffer state (Kuwait) between Iraq and Najd. Emir Ahmad Jabir Mubarak al-Sabah (1921–50) was by no means happy with the loss of territory, despite Sir Percy Cox's assurances on the border with Iraq. He asked Cox whether Britain would intervene if Kuwait became strong enough to regain its lands from Najd and was assured that the British would not stand in the Emir's way.[194] In the colonial administrator's eyes, the goal was Kuwaiti ability to reach agreements with its neighbours and advance to full statehood. During the British mandate and down to the fall of the Monarchy, therefore, sovereignty was not contested, except among Iraqi military officers who had once served in the Ottoman Army. The Emir of Kuwait was permitted to use his independence as an argument for reducing tax liability on lands he owned in Iraq.

If there was any problem at all, it was caused by the Kuwaiti love of trading freely across imprecise frontiers. Despite Emir Mubarak's adherence to the British side in 1914, his successor in 1917 turned a blind eye to cross-desert trade with Syria which benefited the Ottomans. Much later, in 1934, Iraqi revenue cutters fired on Kuwaiti dhows suspected of smuggling; there were incursions, too, across the land border, as Iraq's desert police chased gangs evading customs. The problem infuriated the one-time Ottoman officer, Nuri al-Sa'id, who threatened to mount a total blockade. An increasingly nationalist press in Baghdad was also incensed, but with an appreciable military presence, Britain could keep the lid on. Even after Kuwait discovered oil in 1938 and, come the end of hostilities in 1945, was able to exploit a rich harvest, there were few covetous eyes in Baghdad. After all, Iraq had enough black gold of its own and was more concerned to gain control of its production and wealth.

Brigadier Qassim changed all that when, in an effort to appease the crescendoing voice of nationalism, he attempted unsuccessfully in 1961 to lay claim to the Emirate. He was still arguing the case for annexation forcefully in the weeks before he lost power. The issue, however, was once again buried in October 1964 when President Aref's government conducted secret negotiations with the Kuwaitis. The resulting agreement recognised Kuwait's independence in return for a loan of thirty million dinars, worth then in the region of one billion pounds. For successive British ambassadors in Baghdad, any concern over the Iraq/Kuwait border was of minor importance. In his otherwise illuminating and balanced valedictory written on 10 January 1990, Terry Clark made no mention of Kuwait. He recognised that Iraqis were good tacticians, having watched for five years how Baghdad ran rings round visiting British politicians and businessmen alike. Nevertheless, he considered them weak strategists, a judgement that would be borne out in due course. Meanwhile, he concluded, there was a trend towards all-round and continuing improvement in bilateral relations. Clark was echoing Whitehall's hope that strong economic ties with Iraq would help lead to a more stable and culturally acceptable regime that would remain a bulwark against Iranian religious mania while veering away from Russian influence.

It was against this background that this former foreign service officer found himself in Kuwait during the period between the end of the Iran/Iraq War and Saddam's invasion of the Emirate. "You've earned a good posting," the genial head of personnel told me over a canteen lunch he had invited me to. This should have been music to the ears of someone in mid-career. Four years' hard graft closely involved with plans designed to ensure there would never be another military assault on the sovereignty of the Falklands Islands had put me in a strong position. My head of department had seen fit to recommend me for a generous performance bonus: as he put it, 'the driver of a desk also deserves a fitting reward'. What could I expect? My postings hitherto had been an eclectic mix; I was no specialist, albeit I had increasingly felt able to think in a vacuum. A few days later, I was informed. "It's not the Bois de Boulogne," the personnel officer quipped, "but it's a key post with counsellor rank, an entry in Who's Who." I was being offered the position of political officer in Kuwait, notwithstanding a complete absence of Arabist experience to my credit and almost total ignorance of the language, Gulf politics and Islamic culture. The same day, 18 April 1988, the American Navy destroyed the Iranian frigate *Sahand*, an attack which had helped bring the long struggle between Iran and Iraq stuttering towards its conclusion.[195] Understandably, I asked for twenty-four hours to think about the offer – time to consult a loyal and loving wife. It was not an easy choice for either of us: my wife's parents were both frail and my father the victim of a serious stroke, which had rendered three limbs all but useless and only his left arm intact. Both of us, however, had originally accepted foreign service out of patriotic motivation; we were not going to change this now.

That I should have been chosen for Kuwait was odd and at least one senior official raised his eyebrows in disbelief. The opportunity would certainly not have come my way had the original candidate selected not pulled out after visiting the Emirate. He had withdrawn on the grounds that it was 'a cultural desert' in which he would have found it hard to live. His was a wise decision, since he was well-qualified for the top European post to which he was subsequently posted. Despite the shaking of heads of long-in-the-tooth Arabists, therefore, the Office was stuck with me. Objections were over-ruled – who else was available at the time? – and, in early October, my wife and I, accompanied by our youngest of four daughters, aged five, flew in to Kuwait International Airport, dubbed the 'Kling-on' space-ship by irreverent British Airways cabin staff. In our hold luggage lay three or four small plastic bottles of gin, especially promoted at the time by BA in the belief that the ever-vigilant Kuwaiti customs officials were not able to discover this contraband. For some years, the Kuwaiti Emir, Jabir al-Ahmad al-Jabir al-Sabah, in remembrance of the days when his drunken father had beaten his mother, had determined his country should be dry. Even non-alcoholic beer was forbidden entry, a commodity not banned in the otherwise more conservative neighbouring Saudi Arabia. There were regular articles and photos in the Kuwaiti press showing smugglers' caches of spirits being burnt out in the desert. This did not deter the expatriate from adding yeast to red wine, importing dry kits of white wine and beer, again both undetectable, or making an acceptable local gin. The last comprised ethanol cut down to forty per cent proof, to which essence of juniper or the contents of one of those plastic bottles buried in hold luggage were added. The consumption of 'geth', as it was called, and tonic produced a dubious statistic: it was estimated that every surgical instrument in use at hospitals must have been sterilised every seven seconds to account for the high amount of ethanol used. It didn't lead to blindness, but after a year without the real thing, one noticed the difference when taking a first sip of a BA gin and tonic on the way back to the UK. It has to be admitted, too, that local alcoholic recipes were a subject of conversation at parties; many a Kuwaiti, too, had his own bootlegger who brought supplies in over the desert from non-prohibitionist Iraq. My smuggled cases of Red Label whisky – not a drink that can be cloned by enthusiastic amateurs – contained a beach bucketful of sand.

I arrived with strong pressure ringing in my ears from back home to prioritise efforts to identify the extent of Soviet influence in the Gulf in the wake of the Iran/Iraq peace. At the time, that was only to be expected; in 1988, the Warsaw Pact remained the UK's most significant threat, despite noises coming out of the Kremlin and Washington of hopes for deep cuts in the holding of nuclear warheads and missiles. There was also a new spirit awakening in Moscow as, one by one, the long-serving members of the Central Committee of the Soviet Union fell to the grim reaper. The jury, however, was still out as far as the fifty-seven-year-old Mikhail Gorbachev – appointed CPSU General Secretary in March 1985 – was concerned. He had yet to demonstrate convincingly to Western cold warriors that his reforms and general approach were more than just motivated to make the Soviet Union more efficient. Had Soviet designs really changed? Despite Gorbachev's announcement in May 1988, that he wished to pull troops out of Afghanistan, many still doubted his sincerity. Soviet intentions and activity remained important subjects to address. Within a few days of my arrival, however, I had cause to see a more immediate threat to Gulf, and world, stability – Iraq.

On my first arrival in post, there were few in Kuwaiti official or diplomatic circles who were that concerned. Rather, there was an atmosphere of relief that the mad mullahs of Iran had been rebuffed and Iranian Silkworm missiles taken off their launchpads. Had the Iran/Iraq War been allowed to continue, the next round of aerial bombardment might well have included Iranian attacks on the leading Gulf financiers of Iraq, including Kuwait City. Thankfully, two months earlier, UN observers had deployed along the Iran/Iraq border and hostilities between the two countries were at an end, to the grateful surprise of many. Both were war-weary, Iran in particular, but a peace that restored occupation to the situation pertaining before the first shots were fired in 1980 – as laid down by the 1975 Algiers Agreement – was potentially, an unpopular concession, however much Saddam had been forced to accept it. The man who glorified his country's ancient heritage and, like all dictators, relied on success to underpin his authority, had led his country nowhere for the price of at least half a million casualties. Resentment also lurked in Saddam's mind; but for international pressure, above all that of the Americans, his armies could have more than stood their ground while he unleashed a mix of terrible weapons that would have destroyed much more than Iranian morale.

Loss of face was only one side of the story. As already noted, the eight years of war had drained the financial resources of once oil-rich Iraq. Saddam, posing as protector of the Arabs, had also been obliged to raise loans from the littoral states down the Gulf and from Saudi Arabia. They had their own reasons for wanting to see Iran contained. As early as April 1981, the four richest Gulf states had undertaken to lend Iraq fourteen thousand million dollars, of which Kuwait contributed four thousand million.[196] A day or so after the anniversary of the Iran/Iraq ceasefire, Terry Clark described Iraq's contrasting attitudes towards his southern neighbours: Kuwait, Saudi Arabia and Bahrain were 'sound', but Baghdad harboured serious doubts about Shi-ite Qatar, and both the UAE and Oman, which were seen as too willing to bend to Iranian pressure.[197] Well before this assessment, however, Saddam had become genuinely irritated and, to an extent justifiably so, that his Arab neighbours, not least the hard-headed Kuwaitis (still described most unfairly as the Jews of the Northern Gulf), expected to be repaid in full – with interest. Having to consider a need to restore confidence and retain loyalties at home after what had been such an unprofitable undertaking, it is hardly surprising that he should have sought forbearance from those on whose behalf he had fought, incurring such vast casualties in the process. As the nearest and most vulnerable, Kuwait was the best prospect for debt re-scheduling or even a write-off.

Saddam's annoyance with Kuwait, however, went far deeper. There was always that age-old claim on sovereignty, but this was laced with a contempt for what he considered to be an inferior people who, when it suited them, sheltered behind the protection of a colonial power, a power that Iraq had long since shaken off. It may be that he did not think at first in terms of a full-scale invasion, rather the wielding of a Damoclean Sword to put the frights up fearful yet miserly sheikhs. An example of this caught my eye within a month of my arrival. An article in the *Frankfurter Allgemeine*,[198] date-lined Cairo, claimed that Iraqi tanks had penetrated 'seventeen kilometres' into Kuwait. Few had probably seen the article, but my American colleague certainly had; he dismissed it a day or so later as a cynical use of the present continuous tense. The fluent German speaker married to a German wife, Ambassador Clark in Baghdad, had clearly seen it too, since he referred to the alleged incursion in his 1988 annual review. The matter had been a subject for discussion in his embassy since it was reported to London on 14 December, as he was drafting his review. On a slightly different tack, the Kuwait embassy had seen reports in the local press of an interview with Saddam's right-hand man, Ramadan, in which he had criticised the British, in particular, for trying to drive a wedge between Iraq and Gulf states. This was a totally groundless aspersion, but the ambassador, Peter Hinchcliffe, raised it with the Kuwaiti Ministry of External Affairs who could throw no light on why the charge had been made. When the Foreign Secretary, Geoffrey Howe, spoke to his Kuwaiti opposite number, Sheikh Sabah al-Ahmad, on 3 January, he was met with the pedestrian response: the Iraq/Kuwait border dispute was 'a long-standing problem' which Kuwait was not too concerned about and which it hoped to solve eventually.[199] At the time, I believed that the original article had been deliberately placed so that it would be seen and replayed in the Western and Arab press. It was a piece of misinformation or ploy emanating from Tariq Aziz's Iraqi Ministry of Information signalling an indirect warning to the Kuwaitis.[200] More specifically, "We need your financial forbearance, or take the consequences." The article and its several implications remained printed on my mind.

In the absence of a service attaché at the embassy, it fell to me to liaise with the Kuwaiti Ministry of Defence on politico/military matters. My first call on the KMOD increased my early apprehensions: when I mentioned the Cairo-placed article, the young but professional officer brought out a map showing how Iraqi military engineers had built a tarmac road in the desert the full length of Kuwait's northern border; it had been constructed inside the *cordon sanitaire* negotiated years before and was thus an affront to international law. He was clearly anxious. Not that anyone, he thought, was in a position to challenge it. Shortly afterwards, I was wheeled in to meet the major general in command of Military Intelligence (DMI), essentially a courtesy call. I asked him whether he was concerned about the Iraqi roadworks. He rounded on me scornfully: it was always the same with 'you British; you are always stirring up trouble'. This outburst must have been at about the same time that Ramadan was talking to the Kuwaiti press. Perhaps the general, a junior member of the ruling Sabah family, had seen a report that very morning; his reaction was decidedly vehement and spontaneous. It struck me as being as odd as it was unprovoked. I did not bother to call on him again and I was certainly never allowed to see his junior officer for any further briefings. When I tried to do so, I was told that he had been posted; a bland and uninformative colonel was put in his place. Meanwhile, Whitehall took little or no notice of the Iraqi behaviour, let alone this line of reporting.

There was another aspect to Iraq's territorial ambitions. Little more than estuary mud flats with a small police post at their eastern extremity, the offshore islands of Bubiyan and Warba lay in the path of shipping heading for Iraq's only deep-sea port – Umm Qasr. Originally, no more than a fishing village, the Allies had built berthing facilities for the landing of supplies being sent across land to the Soviet Union. After the Second World War, these temporary wharves fell into disuse and the waterway silted up. As Iraq moved towards the control and ownership of its oil industry, the post-Monarchy regimes invested heavily in Umm Qasr. Shortly after Qassim's seizure of power in 1958, a naval base was established there. Three years later, he declared the founding of a new port that would eventually serve as an alternative to Basra, which had always been vulnerable to disputes along the adjacent Shatt al-Arab. Thanks to a consortium made up of German, Swedish and Lebanese construction companies, Umm Qasr was officially opened as a deep-sea port in 1967, together with a rail link to Basra and Baghdad. During the Iran/Iraq War, it joined Schuwaikh in Kuwait as a lifeline for the supply of essential imports of food and military materiel; Basra had been rendered unusable by enemy action. With the uncertainty surrounding the durability of the August 1988 ceasefire, still breached on occasion by skirmishes in the Gulf, Baghdad looked to the improvement of Umm Qasr's access to the sea and its expansion. Iraq's overtures to Kuwait for a change in the status of the two islands met with silence from the Emirate. This contrasted with Emir Jabir al-Ahmad III (1979–2006)'s staged visit to Bubiyan and Warba in January 1989. In the margins there was mention of building a new university at Subiya on the peninsula across from Bubiyan. Articles on the richness of the bird life on Bubiyan and the virtually unspoilt nature of the islands appeared in the Kuwaiti press. There was no prospect of the Emirate ceding them or agreeing to a long-term lease; they were not for development. The feeling in the Kuwait embassy was that the Emir might buy off the Iraqis in due course and that there was an interest on both sides in maintaining the status quo. This ignored Iraq's infrastructural ambition.

During the second week of February, the Crown Prince, Shaikh Sa'ad (1930–2006) and Foreign Minister Sabah al-Sabah visited Baghdad where they were engaged in three rounds of tough talking with Saddam's hard-bitten lieutenant Izzat Ibrahim. The latter would take the lead in relations with Kuwait down to August 1990. Details of any discussion of the border and the islands were kept tight by both sides. Having spent five days in the Iraqi capital, Shaikh Sa'ad had to say something and he fell back on the neutral diplomatic word 'useful' and released details of an agreement on exports of barley to Kuwait. Small beer, indeed, and hardly warranting Sa'ad's personal attention. The Crown Prince had also used the visit to congratulate the Iraqis on their victory the previous year, a gesture considered in Baghdad to have been long overdue and under-powered. Why had it not come from the Emir himself? Saddam was clearly miffed by this lacuna in Arab protocol.

Within a very short time, Izzat Ibrahim had visited Kuwait more than once to discuss border issues. He was quoted as urging full and comprehensive cooperation between the two states in all fields, so that 'Iraq and Kuwait become one workshop and market with each keeping its own characteristics'.[201] At the same time, the often seen as respectable image of Iraq, Saddam's new Foreign Minister Tariq Aziz, was assuring the visiting British Minister of State, William Waldegrave,[202] that Iraq had no territorial ambitions. This was the context for Waldegrave's decision to loosen the restrictions on British military sales to Iraq which was to lead to the 'arms for Iraq' scandal and the laborious Scott inquiry. Here, however, was a Tory toff with little experience outside political research, insubstantial practice in tough negotiation and a fascination for intelligence coming to a judgement of Iraqi bona fides which was little short of naïve. Aziz had lied before and he would continue to do so on his master's behalf. Thanks to politicians like Waldegrave, Westminster circles would continue to think wishfully that Iraq was worth indulging. Still, essentially, one of 'our thugs'.

The following month, there was a seemingly bread-and-butter visit by the Kuwaiti Minister for Electricity and Water, Hamoud al-Roquba to Baghdad, where he was accorded the special attention of both Saddam's top lieutenants, Taha Ramadan and Izzat Ibrahim. The subject of a rail link from Umm Qasr to Kuwait City was brought up before the Kuwaiti minister walked away with an agreement for the supply of seven hundred million gallons per day of water, against Kuwait's daily consumption of four hundred mgd. Who or what would gain from the excess over demand was never discovered. On the surface, Baghdad appeared still to be in a mood for seduction rather than cajoling, but there were already signs that Saddam's regime was seeking to bind its small neighbour into a common infrastructure. A process of osmosis.

I had much more success in conversations with the Ministry of the Interior, even though the word had been put around that officials were to keep cooperation with the British to a minimum. The catalyst for this unwelcome attitude was the decision by the Thatcher government to enforce Kuwaiti selling of BP shares to reduce their stake in the company. The man behind the crisis was the then Tory Chancellor of the Exchequer, Nigel Lawson, who, in a fit of zeal for privatisation, decided that the government's stake of 31.5% (valued at £7.5 billion) should be sold off in one issue at 330 pence per share. He launched the sale much against the advice of Sir Peter Walters.[203] Most unfortunately for Lawson, during the late evening of the launch (Thursday 15 October 1987), the Great Storm hit London, East Anglia and the Home Counties, wrecking forests and buildings, and disrupting the National Grid. As a result, markets were closed on the next day and did not re-open until Monday 19 October. Mother Nature, therefore, was largely responsible for the stock market crash which came to be known as 'Black Monday', the worst slump in shares since 1929. Again, contrary to best advice, Lawson refused to withdraw the issue and the Bank of England had to step in to buttress the price. Another rescuer was on hand: the Kuwaiti Investment Office (KIO) saw an excellent opportunity and bought up shares amounting eventually to 21.6%. Despite the view of oil experts that the KIO was only buying up 'marshmallows' and had no intention of trying to gain control of the BP operation, pursed lips appeared in the City and Whitehall.

In truth, the Kuwaitis had, in the words of one observer, 'saved the government's neck'. Lawson, however, was less than grateful. He summoned the Kuwait ambassador who appeared in the Chancellor's office with the long-serving and respected Oil Minister Ali Khalifa al-Sabah.[204] An indignant Lawson accused the KIO purchase of being 'a hostile action' and, shortly afterwards, referred the matter to the Monopolies and Mergers Commission. The latter considered the KIO stake to be too high and that it might 'operate against the public interest'; the Kuwaiti government was asked (ordered) to reduce it to below ten per cent. The sorry saga cost the British taxpayer £750 million; what the Kuwaitis lost is not in one's ken, but they smarted at the brutal way in which they had been treated. The episode put Anglo-Kuwaiti relations into a deep freeze. However light Lawson subsequently made of it, his handling of the sale from start to finish was ill-judged at best, appallingly high-handed and insensitive at worst. The Foreign Office input was limited and, of course, to a significant extent, Margaret Thatcher was her own Foreign Minister. She was also a firm supporter of a long-serving Chancellor with whose monetarist views she had great sympathy. Like Lawson, she had hoped that the BP shares would be soaked up by hosts of small private investors, thus, in theory, spreading the UK economic wealth.[205]

Nevertheless, officials in the Iraqi Ministry of Information would have been rubbing their hands with glee. As in 1961, the British would have appeared to be diluting their support for Kuwait. For his part, the hard-headed Kuwaiti resented having to sell off some £500 millions of shares at British insistence. Closing down exchange of information, often an early casualty in a spat between two countries, was an understandable if unwelcome and short-sighted way of getting back at Westminster; it undermined work against difficult targets and latent threats. Fortunately, by the time I took annual leave in August 1989, the atmosphere had improved, not least thanks to a timely visit from a senior Arabist colleague. For my part, I argued against those in London who dismissed cooperation with the Kuwaitis as hopeless and considered that progress could be made in relations if our contribution to the information exchange could be seen to be relevant and timely. Playing cards close to the chest, I felt, was not the answer. I came to regard a raised eyebrow of appreciation from my Kuwaiti interlocutors as more important than being afraid of London harrumphs at my liberal and judged naïve approach.

The downing of PAN AM flight 103 on 21 December 1988 over Lockerbie sent shockwaves round the world. If it could happen once, it could happen many times. Subsequent assessment of the bombers' motives included the probable objective of exploding the aircraft over the North Atlantic, causing any evidence to fall to extreme depths and making the discovery of clues all but impossible. Aircraft that simply disappear are a terrorist's dream. They unsettle governments, airlines and passengers alike, and repetition of such an event would go a long way to blighting one of the umbilical cords between the USA and its closest intelligence ally, the UK. With hindsight, therefore, it was not surprising that the Foreign Secretary, Sir Geoffrey Howe,[206] should descend on sleepy Kuwait just after the New Year. Whether his office had received a tip-off was not clear to me, but on arrival he was slipped a note from the Kuwait Ministry of External Affairs which offered information on the possible perpetrators. What the Kuwaitis provided was, apparently, wide of the mark, but it denoted a thaw in relations and a readiness to recognise a joint interest in preventing future disasters caused by whomsoever, including those extremists seeking the overthrow of what they considered to be oppressive regimes in the Middle East. It also brought a boost for me; the Kuwait Ministry wanted a ready contact in the embassy and it fell to me as the political officer to provide it. This was a morale-raiser for me after three months of largely barren effort. Not that the new liaison proved particularly valuable since we did not really have sufficient material to attract a meaningful exchange. The spin-off, nevertheless, was there, if not immediately recognisable as such. Other Kuwaiti authorities began to take me more seriously and the quality of my contacts improved over time.

For all that, peace in the Gulf held, despite fourteen major violations down to mid-March 1989; the circumstances behind my original posting, however, had changed considerably. The priorities concerned with the area, certainly those relating to a small if oil-rich emirate, had diminished. The inevitable economies followed, notably in a reduction of staff. It was hard, too, to produce reporting that crested the boredom threshold in London. There was some consolation, however, in the personal relationships I was building with senior Kuwaiti officials, one of whom even invited me on a day's sailing on his gin (less the gin) palace out into the Gulf for a swim off one of Kuwait's desert islets. Even the bland colonel was replaced by a more forthcoming and interested officer. Family life settled down after the sad loss of both my wife's parents; despite this, she was able to stage a well-received exhibition of British products at the embassy. In March 1989, the Emirate was visited amidst little publicity by the then Prince and Princess of Wales. They were warmly received by the Kuwaitis; in the early mornings the embassy swimming pool was off-limits so that the Princess might take a dip. The Emir was clearly charmed and his table groaned with food that none of us had any time to eat before protocol demanded that we leave the banqueting hall.

Nevertheless, fuelled by the memories of the historical events mentioned at the beginning of this account, my concern about the Iraqi threat did not ebb and, slow but sure, progress was being made in establishing sources who could give me insights into Iraqi intentions. Neither did the £900 millions' worth of export credits approved at the beginning of 1989 dull my misgivings. It was small beer, in any case, compared with Saddam's huge indebtedness. It did, however, make me more acceptable as a social contact with the Iraqi embassy. I was also conscious of Kuwait's ambivalent attitude towards the Iraqi government, not so different from that of the nineteenth-century Emirate towards the Sublime Porte. In addition to the large sums loaned to Baghdad during the war with Iran, in part in recognition of Iraq's crucial role in keeping the Shi-ite Iranians at bay, Kuwait's southern port of Schuwaikh had, after all, facilitated the import and onward transportation of vast amounts of armaments, much of it from the Soviet Union to Iraq. Beyond the sixth ring road skirting Mishref, the area in which my family and I lived, and way out in the desert lay the seventh, known as the 'empty' road. It had been built by the Kuwaiti government almost entirely for the purpose of sending sensitive materiel to reinforce Iraq's forces. Even at the end of the Iran/Iraq War, Baghdad was not at a loss for military hardware. Baghdad had much to be grateful for, but Saddam did not see it that way. He and his armed forces had saved Kuwait. They were the ones who should show gratitude and not just the spoken word.

For the remainder of my first year at post, whatever tensions existed between Iraq and Kuwait, they remained hidden beneath the surface. Mounting concern over terrorism, following Lockerbie and the Palestinian Intifada,[207] obscured Iraq/Kuwaiti bilateral relations. There were reports of threats to further British Airways flights, including in the Gulf area, which were duly passed to the airline's country manager. He was not fussed by them. More seriously, Israeli brutality against Palestinians on the West Bank and in the Gaza Strip put Western countries on the back foot and gave Saddam much to complain about to his fellow Arab leaders. Zionism was highest in his order of pet hates and with his Iranian backdoor more or less closed, he could afford to rattle a sabre or two in Tel Aviv's direction. The Kuwaiti border question seemed to go dead. Then, after speculation and rumour about a possible visit, Amir Jabir left for Baghdad on 24 September for a three-day visit at Saddam's invitation. His Foreign Minister, Sheikh Sabah, insisted that Jabir was responding out of courtesy; there would be no discussion of the border. Saddam met the Amir twice, hosted three banquets in his honour and received his congratulations on the Iraqi victory over Iran with apparent geniality. He invested Sheikh Jabir with Iraq's highest honour, the Rafidain Order first class (civilian) and received the Grand Mubarak Order, Kuwait's highest, in return. On his return to the Emirate on 27 September, Sheikh Jabir spoke of the event as a meeting between 'brotherly Arabs'; he had been appreciative of Saddam's hospitality at the presidential palace and the personal tour round his capital the Iraqi leader had afforded him. Unlike on previous occasions following a Kuwaiti visit, the Iraqi press had maintained silence; any complaints had been withheld. Official circles on both sides were unwilling to shed further details. All might have seemed sweetness and light, but for remarks to me by a senior Kuwaiti official who had accompanied his leader to Baghdad. While tucking into the Cadbury's chocolates I had presented to him on my return from leave,[208] he admitted to relief at having got back to Kuwait after what had been a grim few days. But then, he added, he always felt that way about Iraq.

For the best part of two years my posting was little more than routine, even humdrum. During the heat of the 1989 summer, when for six weeks I was on leave in the UK, the embassy underwent a makeover which transformed the tired old colonial-style building. An impressive new Consular/Commercial section was added to the walled compound's facilities. A few months later, the Anglican Church, whose chaplain (nick-named 'the jolly vicar' by my daughters) my wife and I admired, put on a 'mission' in the newly erected conference hall nestled within fresh, flower-bestrewn landscaping watered, possibly, by brackish irrigation from Iraq. I was even drafted in to sit on the interviewing panel charged with the choice of a new pastor. This afforded me a further forty-eight-hour visit to London. Otherwise, until early July 1990, life went on more or less as normal. I was then looking forward to a month or so's release from temperatures of approaching fifty degrees Celsius, admittedly only when dashing from one haven of air conditioning to another. I was also without my wife, who had gone home to open up the house for our three boarding daughters, taking with her our youngest as soon as her Kuwaiti school closed for the long summer heat. It was usual for more than half the Kuwaiti population to decamp to the shopping malls of London and Paris. With social life in the Emirate more or less at a standstill, I borrowed a computer and began to explore a new toy that would replace my electric typewriter. I also had a five thousand-piece jigsaw of the Night Watch on the go. It was, however, the nearest thing I have ever come to a fool's paradise.

Eleven

COUNTDOWN TO INVASION (1990)

There were straws in the wind. Both in Baghdad and Kuwait City, the embassies were generally aware that relations between Iraq and the Emirate were coming under increasing strain. The nub of the problem was easy to understand. Saddam had asked the Emir to forgive the US eight billion dollars' debt it owed and Sheikh Jabir had refused the request point-blank. We knew at the time that Sheikh Jabir had a stubborn streak and that he was unlikely to give in to Saddam's bullying, but what we did not know was that the Emir had not conceded an inch at a meeting face to face with Saddam and several other Arab leaders concerned at the impasse between the two men. I am indebted to Said K Aburish's revelation in his biography of Saddam[209] which appeared a decade after the events I am about to describe.

Sometime during the Arab League three-day summit convened in Baghdad at Saddam's request, if not insistence, on 28 May 1990, a meeting took place between Saddam and the Emir, in the presence of Yasser Arafat of the Palestinian Liberation Organisation (PLO), King Hussein of Jordan and King Fahd of Saudi Arabia. President Mubarak was invited but refused to attend out of annoyance at Saddam's opening words at the conference. While publicity at the time confirmed the attendance at the summit of the PLO leader and the two Arab Kings, the leader of the Kuwaiti delegation was shown to have been Foreign Minister Shaikh Sabah. Sheikh Jabir had opposed the convening of the summit in Baghdad and was thought to have sent Sabah as his stand-in out of protest. At the start of this side-show meeting, Saddam and the Emir maintained an awkward silence, while the others appealed for a 'brotherly' solution to Iraq's financial problems. They then appealed to Sheikh Jabir for Kuwait to keep to its oil production quota as agreed by OPEC and to refrain from asking for repayment of Iraq's war debt. Other issues were not mentioned. The Emir shrugged and replied haughtily: he refused to commit himself to any reduction in oil production, rejected any question of Kuwait compensating Iraq for oil sucked out of the Rumaylah oil field on the border and insisted that the Iraqi debt be paid immediately. He also spoke of the sanctity of Kuwait territory. Arafat reacted angrily to the Emir's intransigence and warned that his attitude threatened peace in the whole Middle East. Sheikh Jabir was unmoved, albeit he was reported to have observed that Iraq should accept a final border between the two countries. He also made plain that internal considerations stood between him and accepting a delay in debt repayment. The following day, apparently, the Emir approached Saddam during one of the larger meetings and asked to discuss the border issue. The Iraqi leader put his arm round the Kuwaiti leader and is purported to have said that he had a surprise for him; all would be well. Beware the embrace of a tiger, especially one stirred up and hungry.

The May 1990 Arab summit has to be set in context. The end of the Iran/Iraq War may have benefited the increasing numbers of gas-guzzlers in the UK, but the fall in oil prices as the Gulf opened up once more to unmolested shipping, told heavily against the Iraqi national income. Oil production outside the Middle East had also grown substantially. Since the founding in 1960 of the Organisation of Petroleum Exporting Countries (OPEC), its members had sought to regulate oil prices through a system of production quotas. This was generally meant to prevent gluts that would cause prices to tumble and reduce all producers' incomes. At the end of 1989, several members were honouring agreed quotas in the breach, notably the major producers, Saudi Arabia, the United Arab Emirates and Kuwait. Against its quota of 1.5 million barrels per day, Kuwait had increased production by nearly forty per cent, to 2.1 million bpd. The government claimed that it needed the additional income to rebuild and modernise installations damaged or left unused during the war. It could also point to its readiness to come to the aid of poorer non-oil producing Arab states; during May, Sheikh Jabir had agreed to pay Jordan $150 million to help subsidise the Kingdom's energy costs.

This was all very irksome to Saddam, not least since he was jealous for his relationship with King Hussein. What peeved him more, however, were reports from the oil fields that Kuwait was using improved technology to tap into 'Iraqi' oil from the Rumaylah wells that straddled the border. The story was that Kuwaiti engineers, backed by American and other Western experts, had introduced slant-head drilling techniques that could reach beyond the border. There were some local, usually well-informed, specialists who told me that this could not be done, since oil reserves lay in catchments separated by vertical rock strata. Others I knew to be involved in drilling operations admitted to me in June 1990 that for months the production impetus had been almost entirely 'in the north'. The inference was clear enough: drain as much out before any realignment of the border that placed more or all of Rumaylah under Iraq's control. Whatever the truth of the matter, Saddam was convinced that Kuwait was stealing his oil.

To the paranoid Saddam, it must have seemed at the beginning of 1990 that all were conspiring against him. It started on 13 January when Turkey declared that it was diverting the flow of the Upper Euphrates to augment supplies of fresh water in new reservoirs. The inevitable result from a reduction in the flow downstream was increased desertification and, perhaps as damaging, greater silting up of the estuaries around Basra and Umm Qasr, just as Baghdad was seeking to promote development and resuscitation of both ports. Both Iraq and Syria complained to Ankara – to no avail. To Saddam, Turkey was a non-Arab pawn of the West and a backslider where opposition to Zionism was concerned.

Saddam's paranoia was also increasing at home. His half promises at some form of limited democratisation could not appease those who had for a long time wanted to avenge their kinsfolk for the suffering they had incurred at Saddam's hands. There were many military officers, too, who felt that they had been forced to fight in vain against Iran. His fear of the assassin's bullet, the first of which in 1990 just missed him in a shoot-out in early January,[210] caused his progressive isolation from the people he claimed to protect and succour. He could no longer risk walking down the streets waving to the crowds or visit villages delivering alms. Increasingly, he felt obliged to appoint only his most trusted kinsfolk to senior positions in the administration. Indeed, he was coming to the point where he trusted no one, even his best friend from childhood. In one way or another, too, those opposed to him were, as far as he was concerned, simply under the influence of foreign agencies, notably the CIA.

In September 1988, a huge explosion had been heard in Baghdad: near the city of Hillah, some one hundred kilometres south of Baghdad and close to the ruins of Babylon. One of Saddam's presidential palaces stood in the vicinity, but not far away lay the site of a long-suspected chemical and biological warfare plant that had been mentioned in a highly critical UN report issued only the previous month. The blast destroyed the plant and killed hundreds of people. Saddam was convinced that there were 'foreign hands' at work. He ordered a complete news lockdown on the event; casualty figures were withheld. Already sensitised to Iraq's brutal use of CBW, Western press circles, not least in the UK, determined to find out more about Hillah and other suspected sites – through investigative journalism. In many undemocratic countries that amounts to unwanted interference; in Saddam's eyes it was nothing less than spying. Despite the obvious risks involved, almost a year to the day of the explosion, a freelance journalist with connections to the *Observer* in London, Farzad Bazoft,[211] used an Iraqi Ministry of Information invitation to cover the Kurdish elections to wander well south of Baghdad. He was detained briefly close to the remains of the destroyed CBW plant where he had been investigating the circumstances and nature of the Hillah explosion. A British nurse, Daphne Parish, who had driven him to the site, was detained too. A day or so later, he was arrested at Baghdad airport and was found to have photographs of the Hillah area in his luggage together with some soil samples. At the notorious Abu Ghraib prison, he was interrogated, beaten and forced to confess that he was an Israeli agent; he was put on Baghdad television to repeat his confession. Saddam wrote, however, to Margaret Thatcher to assure her that Bazoft would be given a fair trial. In the event, he was tried in a kangaroo court and hanged the next day, 15 March 1990.

For the British Embassy and Whitehall, still intent on improving commercial relations with Iraq, this was embarrassing; it was later revealed that no retribution, apart from the temporary withdrawal of the newly arrived ambassador, should be made, out of political consideration. For many Western journalists, in contrast, it was seen as a dire attack on press freedom. Not a concept that Saddam understood. If ever there were an example of an unbridgeable politico-cultural gap, this was it. The tragedy of Bazoft's execution, however, was in large part due to the insult Saddam felt at the assumption of the journalist's innocence, when he had been assured by his intelligence officials that the man was an Israeli spy. Whom should he believe? Those whom he had appointed to protect Iraq or the London press who never ceased preaching about human rights and criticised what he considered legitimate measures to render his country invulnerable to Zionists? His personal order, too, was for a swift despatch well before Ramadan to prevent pleas of clemency; he wanted to get it over with and move on. Why should the British government be so concerned, Saddam would have thought, given that Bazoft was an Iranian after all? Was the journalist also working for British Intelligence? However much London might dismiss the latter suggestion, Saddam would not.

The Bazoft saga should not be viewed in isolation. Bazoft might have survived had the Western press coverage not been so shrill, but there was an important factor in the background that was testing Saddam's patience sorely and would eventually exhaust it. At about the same time as the Hillah explosion, American customs officials were running a sting operation against Iraqi agents seeking to procure triggers for nuclear weapons. One such interception might have been tolerated, but in the months to come, American and British agencies started to bite comprehensively into Iraqi CBW and nuclear procurement efforts. Saddam could or would not understand why his ambitions were being singled out. Had he not made moves towards opening up the political system in Iraq? And had he not – in May 1989 – paid $27.3 million in compensation for the damage and loss of life on the USS *Stark*, an accident of war, not a deliberate attack on the United States? He surely deserved better understanding in Washington; indeed, from the State Department he had been led to believe that he had it. In December 1988, he lectured the visiting Assistant Under Secretary, John Kelly, on the fact that Iraq, too, had signed the Nuclear Proliferation Treaty. Kelly did not demur; the old theory that Saddam should be supported as a bastion against Communism and Muslim extremism certainly retained its strong support in American foreign policy circles.

Kelly might have pressed harder. Only the previous month, the Department of Energy startled Washington out of its complacency by announcing that Iraq was developing nuclear weapons. The State Department was further rattled by a report the following January by ABC journalist, Charles Glass, who alleged that Iraq had a biological weapons research facility at Salman Pak, close to Hillah; State had denied the plant's existence hitherto. Satellite surveillance now confirmed the essence of the Glass report; this made uncomfortable reading for George Bush Senior as he took over the Presidency in the same month. He had been surrounded by pro-Iraqi advisers during his electoral campaign.

Despite criticism from abroad, sharpened by memories of the Halabja massacre, Saddam was unmoved; he was determined to press on with his regime's military programme aimed at promoting the image of Iraq as a leading power and defender of the Arab people's future. On his birthday, 28 April 1989, a military production trade fair was launched in Baghdad. American arms manufacturers were advised to stay away, but this did not prevent the US/Iraqi Business Forum from attending. No less than 168 British corporations also exhibited, along with organisations from all over the world. The old Iraqi news hound and self-publicist Sa'ad Bazzaz[212] called it 'the biggest transfer of technology in the twentieth century'; it had been a great success for the regime. Among the exhibits were two Iraqi-constructed rockets: the Hussein and the Abbas, with respective ranges of 650 and 950 kilometres. Israel took serious note and the CIA became generally more anxious at the rate of Iraq's progress in acquiring lethal weapons and strike potential. A leaked US intelligence report on 3 April had revealed that Iraq had moved long-range missiles to H2 airfield in Western Iraq, close to the Jordanian border and nearest to Israel.[213] Even so, the State Department remained leaning towards Baghdad and the new Bush administration resisted the imposition of sanctions. On 2 October 1989, the American President signed a secret order (National Security Directive Twenty-Six) which offered Iraq political and economic incentives in return for moderating her behaviour and guaranteeing the flow of oil from the Gulf. There was even mention of the possibility of US/Iraqi military cooperation. While some American politicians continued to pull their punches afterwards, this was the high-water mark of appeasement in the expectation of an improved attitude on human rights and warmer commercial relations. At about the same time, however, a Kuwaiti memorandum to Shaikh Salim al-Sabah, the Emirate's Minister of the Interior, reported an agreement with the Americans for an increased exchange of information and for closer cooperation with Iran to undermine Saddam. During the first half of 1990, both General Norman Schwarzkopf, chief of the US Army's Central Command and CIA chief William Webster made several visits to the Emirate.[214] The Kuwaitis were looking for strong friends; even my access to both the Defence and Interior Ministries received a boost!

The gloves were coming off. On 11 February 1990, the previously benign John Kelly returned to Baghdad for a further face-to-face meeting with the Iraqi leader. He registered American concern at both Iraq's record on human rights and use of chemical weapons. This was the first time Washington had raised the issue of chemical weapons officially. Kelly's words were then followed up – at least in Saddam's eyes – by something much stronger: four days later, Voice of America, using information contained in a still-unpublished State Department report, broadcast a scathing attack on Iraq's abuses of human rights and called the regime criminal. Saddam's suspicions of a foreign conspiracy against his position were further provoked by a series of episodes connected to his nuclear weapons programme, the most damning being British Customs' seizure on 28 January at Heathrow of forty capacitators, known as Kryptons – high-speed electrical switches used in the detonation of nuclear explosions. Together with the murder of Gerald Bull in Brussels[215] on about 20 March and the suspicious death a few days later in Santiago, Chile, of Jonathan Moyle,[216] both of whom were involved in Iraqi military procurement in which Saddam had a direct interest, it was hardly surprising that he should immediately blame Israel. Further, he became convinced of 'an imperialist-Zionist conspiracy'.[217] He had already used a meeting held on 23 February in Amman to celebrate the first anniversary of the Arab Cooperation Council (ACC) with King Hussein and President Mubarak to attack the US presence in the Gulf. He had also demanded financial contributions from rich Arab states in recognition of Iraq's wartime suffering and declared his abiding purpose – to reverse the 'rape' of Palestine. "From here in Amman I see the lights of Jerusalem," he added dramatically; he was going to punish the usurpers and lead a new anti-Israel crusade.

Saddam was infuriated, too, by what he considered the continuing Israeli persecution of the Palestinians, yet for all his bluster, he on his own was powerless to intervene. This did not prevent him holding a televised press conference on 2 April at which he pulled together his various complaints against what he insisted was the West's collusion with Israel. He discounted the seizure of capacitators at Heathrow as part of a 'policy of entrapment' on the part of the British, American and Zionist Intelligence. Any country which threatened Iraq with 'atomic' weapons would be annihilated by 'binary chemical weapons'. As a peroration, he threatened to 'devour half of Israel by fire [chemical weapons implied] if it tries to attack Iraq'. It was a largely empty threat since he had neither the successfully tested weaponry, nor the resources for a war with Israel. Moreover, Iraq's finances were just about to suffer a potentially crippling blow: on 21 May, the American Congress passed legislation to suspend loans to the Baghdad regime. This was probably the catalyst for the shift in Saddam's focus in the margins of the Baghdad Arab League summit a few days later – from Israel to Kuwait. He was becoming desperate for ready cash. As he grumbled to one Western interlocutor, he did not have the money to pay veterans their war pensions. Another wider-known quotation was his determination not to 'let his people starve'.

There has been some disagreement amongst commentators as to when Saddam decided to invade Kuwait. Some have suggested that it was an almost off-the-cuff decision. In an interview with the *Middle East Quarterly* published in December 1995, Saad al-Bazzaz, who was working close to the Iraqi leadership in 1990, claimed that Saddam reacted angrily to Sheikh Jabir's reception in Kuwait of his personal envoy and Prime Minister, Sa'dun Hammadi.[218] The visit took place in June as part of an orchestrated lobby of leading oil producers in the Gulf to respect OPEC quotas. It was at that point, Bazzaz considered, that Saddam decided to opt for a military alternative to long-drawn-out negotiations over debt and the border. Bazzaz also maintained that the decision was held close to the chest, only six close associates being made aware of it down to 1 August. That fits more or less into the timing of the immediate lead-up to the invasion, but there were pointers well before Bazzaz's assessment that preparations were being made for a major operation against Kuwait.

The first inkling, admittedly confirmed by hindsight, came to me in early February 1990 with the temporary detention of two young British visitors to southern Iraq. It was odd because towards the end of the previous year, there had been increasing publicity encouraging potential tourists to visit a resuscitated Basra. This was not the sort of marketing a highly centralised state tourist authority would be engaged in if its government were planning on an invasion in the area. Kuwaiti-based expatriates had already crossed over the border for a weekend's stay at one of the recently refurbished hotels along the palm-lined corniche where wines and spirits were available. This was an alternative and cheaper option to a flight down to Bahrain. After their car had been stopped on the highway, the two detainees had to wait for an interrogator to come down from Baghdad. They were then released and allowed to return to Kuwait without further let or hindrance. There did not appear to be any connection to the Bazoft saga. Was there already some sensitivity about the approaches to the border area?

Two key changes in Iraqi official appointments might have been judged as early straws in the wind. In late 1988, the man held responsible for the Halabja massacre, General 'Chemical' Ali Hassan Majid, Saddam's cousin, was transferred from his command in Northern Iraq to become Minister of Local Government. He would become the ruthless, post-invasion Governor of Kuwait. Given Saddam's view of the Emirate as little more than a provincial extremity, was his close adviser and kinsman being prepared – or preparing – for a takeover? He would certainly have been in a position to saturate Kuwait with intelligence agents. Closer to the invasion date, during March 1990, the Iraqi ambassador to Riyadh, Abdul-Wahab Mahmud Abdullah al-Sabbagh, was brought back to Baghdad to take over the Agriculture Ministry where his former expertise in food production and irrigation could be tapped. He was not replaced, a sign that Baghdad was giving up on Saudi Arabia.

Tangible evidence of something nasty in the wind came from a string of reports I received in post. In late spring, I learnt that a British company had received a huge order from Iraq for field dressings, something I regarded as particularly odd. Was Saddam expecting an exchange of hostilities with Israel or another offensive against Iran? I reasoned that the consignment suggested prophylactic logistical preparation for ground fighting rather than an aerial or missile conflict; Iran was still on its knees. This was followed in May by the arrival in Schuwaikh of three Soviet vessels and another from East Germany laden to the gunwales with vast supplies of light weapons and ammunition. Their only destination could have been Iraq; it fitted with my growing conviction that Baghdad was preparing for a major ground offensive. Iran remained a potential victim, although Saddam was putting out peace feelers to Tehran and his negotiators continued to haggle over an exchange of prisoners. In June, the embassy received an intriguing report: Baghdad had issued orders to its intelligence agents in the Gulf that they should report at once on the dispositions of American and British political officers. An attack on Iran might have needed up-to-date information on Anglo/American naval movements but not on foreign service personnel.

In marked contrast to the lack of confirmation of any troop concentrations towards the Kuwaiti border in 1961, a clear and de visu warning of Iraqi deployment to the south was obtained on Friday 20 July by two members of the Military Attaché's staff in Baghdad. They had been on their way to pick up a vehicle from Kuwait port when they passed large columns of Iraqi armour and motorised troops. They headed straight for the embassy, where I debriefed them. The description of the units they had seen dovetailed exactly with another report I had received which indicated that large elements of Iraq's crack Republican Guard were being sent to the Kuwait border. Assessments of the actual strength varied from thirty thousand to one hundred thousand in the two weeks before the invasion. American sources suggested nearer the former; I believed the latter. London was immediately informed but seemed unconcerned. I went immediately over to see the Deputy Head of Kuwaiti Military Intelligence (D/DMI) to give him a full account. It was my first appointment with him and we would remain in close contact down to the invasion. He was immediately able to give me the positions of Iraqi armour along a line opposite the border on high ground three miles to the south of Umm Qasr. No deployment had been seen further west, but while there was nothing to indicate a general move on Kuwait, the Iraqis were within striking distance of the Rumaylah oil field. It was possible that Saddam was sabre-rattling, but the grave look on the D/DMI's face suggested a more pessimistic prognosis. I sped straight over to my American opposite number, who said that none of his sources in the oil field had seen any sign of Iraqi forces. Kuwait's 35 brigade, however, was moving up to cover the area.

The overriding question remained in my mind: why would such a large force, complete with heavy armour and the equivalent of up to six divisions, move down into the desert at the hottest time of the year? The logistical problems alone would have challenged the most dedicated of military planners, especially if they had been given only short notice. Despite this, few of my interlocutors, both inside and outside the embassy, seemed unduly disturbed. My ambassador learnt of a story from his Italian colleague that the Iraqis were mounting a large feint operation to deceive the Iranians before they veered east to renew hostilities. I dismissed this as nonsense and put it down to disinformation peddled by sources not a mile from the Iraqi embassy. Rather, I reported the intelligence I learnt from the D/DMI on 23 July when he called me at my home. Iraqi forces, he said, were some seven or eight kilometres from the border, having extended west to the other side of Wadi al-Batin. This looked to me like a wide potential pincer movement. The D/DMI considered it was now 'all a question of milliards' agreed at OPEC but confirmed that the Kuwaitis had also now deployed their six-armoured brigade. I already knew that tank transporters had been seen along the seventh ring (or 'empty') road heading north. The D/DMI had not spoken to the Americans, as I might have expected. So, later the same morning, I met an American colleague who talked of a 'Mexican stand-off' and considered his ambassador 'offhand' about the situation. He also had solid information of the amount of Iraqi armour now deployed. This amounted to 210 T72 tanks, 270 armoured personnel carriers, field and anti-aircraft artillery and FROG missile launchers at various points behind the border.

Despite this battle array, I received little understanding from my American colleague. After a farewell supper on 24 July hosted by my ambassador for the departing Anglican chaplain and his wife, I called round on him towards midnight. In response to my view that we were facing a full-blown invasion, he asked incredulously: "Why the hell should the Iraqis invade Kuwait?" I offered three reasons: the Iraqi claim on Kuwait was age-old and might have been successful in 1961 but for the strong British presence at the time; one did not move such large military formations in the middle of summer without a purpose; and Saddam knew, as we all did, that the Kuwaiti government had accumulated two or three years of supplies for their people in the event that nuclear war broke out between NATO and the Warsaw Pact. If Saddam invaded, it would be to take the whole of the Emirate, not just an oil field or two. Sitting in his lounge, the American would not commit himself and appeared not to share my concern. As I was about to leave his compound, however, he attempted to reassure me in a low voice that if Kuwait were invaded, there were American naval units offshore, including a guided missile cruiser. I judged it bootless at the time to lecture him on the vulnerability of surface warships operating without adequate air cover or how a small squadron could hardly be expected to stop a determined thrust across the desert. The ships, in fact, were not in their first bloom of youth and had been hastily deployed for observation purposes only.[219]

The American position in the previous months was ambivalent at best and dangerously confusing at worst. As already mentioned, there was a continuous conflict in Washington between those concerned about Saddam's threatening and brutal behaviour and those who thought he could be reined back while ensuring America obtained a healthy slice of exports to Iraq. Another example of 'America First'. While Washington was beginning to take a stronger line on the weapons of mass destruction (WMD) that the Iraqis were undoubtedly developing, there were still senior figures in the President's own Republican Party that were unwilling to emulate this. In early April, Senator 'Bob' Dole, Republican leader in the Senate,[220] accompanied by four other senators, met Saddam in Mosul. The Iraqi leader was on his honeymoon after marrying his third wife, Nidal al-Hamdani, manager of the Solar Department of the Ministry of Industry and Military Industrialisation. These senior politicians had been sent over by George Bush with the purpose of promoting better business and political relations between Iraq and the USA. When Saddam complained about the mid-February Voice of America broadcast, he received soothing words from Dole. Senator Alan Simpson[221] reassured Saddam that the Bush position was different; the problem was the press. This potentially high-powered delegation failed to press Saddam on human rights and chemical weapons and had to read the transcript of their conversations with him which were subsequently published in the *Baghdad Observer* on 18/19 April. Dole and Simpson, however, were echoing the State Department position: on 24 April, John Kelly appealed to the Senate Foreign Relations Sub-committee against applying sanctions on Iraq. Ironically, this was at the very same time that General Norman Schwarzkopf, the American Central Command supremo, was engaging in closer consultations with Kuwait and directing exercises in the Gulf that were now using an Iraqi scenario. Whether or not Washington's position was confusing to Saddam, it did not stop him from agreeing to the expulsion of an American diplomat during the Dole visit or from refusing to give assurances that Iraq would not pursue research into biological weapons.

Only two days after his testimony to the House Sub-committee, Kelly was expressing his appreciation of Iraq's cessation of arms deliveries to General Aoun in the Lebanon, thus weakening the Christian forces there and so starting the process of winding down the long-raging civil war. Saddam was a man America could trade with in international politics, as well as commerce. Besides, President Bush was now fully focussed on his forthcoming Washington summit with the Soviet Secretary-General, Mikhail Gorbachev. Their momentous meeting would sign a chemical weapons ban agreement and normalise commercial relations. Further, there were helpful discussions on a provisional treaty on nuclear weapons and for the unfettered emigration of Russian Jews to Israel.

My growing suspicion that Saddam was preparing to at least annex a large part of North Kuwait, thus securing oil wells on both sides of the border, was given an impetus at my meeting on 22 July with a senior official in the Ministry of the Interior. While considering that Kuwait would be prepared to accept Arab League arbitration, he anticipated some sort of Iraqi nipping operation. Such a move would not have been condoned by Washington, but the Americans would have had to accept it, as would have all the powers in the Middle East. This, for me, helped to explain the lack of concern in the American embassy. Was their mission in Kuwait preparing to accept the inevitable? It crossed my mind that there might even have been an element of collusion between Washington and Baghdad. The Kuwaitis were not favourites in the USA. As the American ambassador said when entertaining his British opposite number and me in his office on 24 July, there might have to be some action to back up Saddam's words. A full-scale conflict, however, was most unlikely since armies could not fight in 'fifty degrees centigrade'. He had clearly forgotten the Western Desert in 1941–42, not to mention eight years of Iran/Iraq ground warfare. One remark from the American stuck with me: "The T72 [tank] does not have air conditioning." Neither, I thought, might Kuwait City have any fresh water if the situation were to hot up. On return to my office, I brought my staff together, voiced my concerns and instructed my slightly bemused colleagues to fill up the many empty gin bottles with what might prove a more precious liquid. In the event, these were never used.

With several embassy staff already back in the UK on summer leave, there was almost no one left to air concern or take prophylactic measures.

London did not seem seized of events either: the Current Intelligence Group (CIG) in the Cabinet Office was already advising the Joint Intelligence Committee and ministers, including the Prime Minister, that Saddam was 'only sabre-rattling' in the lead-up to the imminent OPEC meeting in Geneva. No worthwhile guidance came out to the embassy about what to do before or during a full-scale invasion. On the contrary, the strong impression received at post was that we were over-reacting. "Shred down [sensitive papers] to three months," was the slightly patronising advice given. This still left a vast amount of paper to get rid of, come the day.

In the two weeks before the invasion, there were times when I was in danger of being lulled into a false sense of security. The month of July had opened in festive mood with the end of Ramadan, a Sunday, the Eid holiday which opened four days of feasting and celebration. As a grass widower, I had freedom to take up every invitation offered, to while away long relatively cool evenings. I was entertained to an Eid supper by my Iraqi friend who did not seem too phased by events. There was no great buzz on the expatriate circuit. The new British Airways marketing man asked my view about his idea of introducing hot towels in economy class! While the embassy closed for several days, I spent some time in my office watching specialist workmen enhancing the physical security of the premises. The sun had driven off half the Kuwaiti population to Europe together with a similar proportion of the British area wardens, appointed by the Consul, to help maintain liaison in times of crisis. The running of the country was now largely left in the hands of the Palestinian, Egyptian, Sub-continental and Philippino 'castes' that supplied middle management and servants respectively.[222]

Hotels were largely empty. One group, however, interested me after its arrival at one of the more discreet beach facilities. A twenty-man Russian military team came in and divided into two; one stayed in the hotel, the other went off to Al Riqqa in the south of the city. I never found out what the real purpose of their visit was, but it would not have taken place if Moscow had been worried about a possible conflict. I, too, was sufficiently unconcerned to take the fortnightly bag down to Bahrain on

Sunday the 8th, returning the next day. On the 10th a two-day meeting of Gulf oil ministers, including from Iraq and Kuwait, met in Jeddah. The agreement by Kuwait and the UAE to cut production by three hundred thousand and four hundred thousand bpd respectively seemed like a useful sop to the Iraqis, but it was never going to be enough for Saddam. The *Middle East Economic Digest* reported immediately afterwards that Iraq had lost 3.5 billion dollars during the current year.[223] Two days later, Saddam sent a memorandum to Kuwait demanding 2.4 billion dollars as compensation for the oil 'stolen' from Rumaylah. On the same day, Tariq Aziz sent another memorandum to the Arab League Secretary-General, Chedli Klibi, accusing Kuwait of deliberately pursuing policies during the war with Iran that undermined Iraq. She had also trespassed into Iraqi territory and built military and oil installations there. In what was a long list of grievances, he maintained both Kuwait and the UAE had grown rich on wartime proceeds but were now demanding early repayment of loans which had been taken out to defend the Gulf Arabs as a whole. Saddam repeated the charges on 17 July, the anniversary of the 1968 Ba'athist Revolution. More direct than Aziz, he threatened that 'if words fail to protect Iraqis, something effective must be done to return things to their natural course and return usurped rights to their owners'. He then pointed the finger at 'some Arab states' for undermining Arab interests and security on behalf of the USA and warned that Iraq 'will not forget the saying that cutting necks is better than cutting the means of living'.

Thanks to the President of Zambia, Kenneth Kaunda, who had also tried to intercede on Bazoft's behalf, Daphne Parish was released to fly to Lusaka on 13 July, returning to the UK five days later. Was this mere coincidence, or a sop perhaps, to wrong-foot the strident human rights lobby in London, at the same time as Saddam had resolved to punish Kuwait? Kuwait was now trembling. The Army was placed on a state of alert and all leave was cancelled. In the newly elected National Assembly, a resolution was passed denouncing the Iraqi memorandum. The Foreign Minister, Sheikh Sabah, set off on an emergency tour of Gulf Cooperation Council capitals, while other Kuwaiti ministers visited more Arab League states. King Fahd of Saudi Arabia and Ali Abdullah Saleh of Yemen, one of Saddam's admirers, buried their own hatchets and appealed jointly to Saddam and the Emir to pull back. In the embassy, we received a copy of the demarche from the Kuwait government seeking the support of all five permanent members of the UN Security Council. Shades of 1961 when the then Emir Abdullah III had made a similar appeal for British help. Now, however, Shaikh Jabir was faced with a Colossus and, in the absence of sufficient support from abroad, had started moves to buy off Baghdad. In mid-July, the cabinet agreed to pay Iraq a grant of five hundred million dollars over three years.[224] Far too little, far too late.

During the weekend of 19/20 July, as Iraqi soldiers were jumping into lorries for the long drive south, diplomatic activity in several Arab capitals intensified. As the head of Security Intelligence had just predicted, Chedli Klibi, the Secretary-General of the Arab League, arrived in Kuwait City to meet the Emir and to offer his arbitration services over disputed sections of the border. After his meeting with Shaikh Jabir, he emerged in an optimistic frame of mind. "What is between the brothers in Iraq and Kuwait is merely a summer cloud which will go away."[225] In Baghdad, the American ambassador, April Glaspie, passed a message from James Baker for Saddam: "Disputes should be settled by peaceful means, not through intimidation." This fitted in with the growing clamour for both sides to calm down. Whatever Shaikh Jabir or Chedli Klibi thought about summer weather, it hardly chimed with the Iraqi armour rumbling down towards Umm Qasr and the border.

The big Middle East guns were now fully engaged. Tariq Aziz saw Mubarak on 22 July in Cairo. King Hussein joined them in Alexandria the next day and the Egyptian President issued a subsequent statement voicing his confidence that Iraq and Kuwait would 'arrive at a comfortable and calm, quiet solution'. By now, however, Iraq's propaganda machine was in full swing with Al-Thawra in Baghdad accusing Shaikh Jabir of being a CIA agent. Nevertheless, Mubarak visited Iraq, Kuwait and Saudi Arabia on 24 July and, on his return to Egypt, told the world that he had been assured by Saddam that he had no intention of attacking Kuwait or moving his forces towards the border. At the same time, he announced that the contending parties would meet on 29 July in Jeddah, at King Fahd's invitation. Meanwhile, April Glaspie was delivering a second message from Secretary of State Baker for Saddam: "We remain committed to ensure the free flow of oil from the Gulf and support the sovereignty and integrity of the Gulf states." In other words, the USA was going to maintain its naval presence in the Gulf, for all Saddam's demand that it should withdraw. A vital word – 'defend' – was missing from the message.

Everyone now seemed to be promoting peace, even Saddam. If, however, the Iraqi leader still had any doubts about the wisdom of invading his neighbour, they were removed on 25 July. That was the day when Ambassador Glaspie met Saddam face to face and spoke in a way interpreted by him as a green light. She repeated Washington's desire for a settlement by 'peaceful means' but then uttered the fateful words: "We have no opinion on the Arab/Arab conflicts like your border disagreement with Kuwait." She added that President Bush hoped to 'broaden and deepen relations with Iraq'. Essentially, therefore, the message from the United States had not changed: Washington still valued Baghdad as a potential collaborator and important market in the Middle East, warts and all. Saddam was reported to have observed to Glaspie: "Yours is a society which cannot accept ten thousand dead in one battle."[226] After reading the ambassador's report of her meeting, Paul Wolfowitz, Under Secretary at the Pentagon, reacted vehemently: "This stinks; we've got to get a stronger presidential message." Had a tall, no-nonsense American emissary been despatched to Baghdad to deliver a 'four-eyes' warning at that point, the Iraqi leader might at least have paused for thought. In the event, Washington failed to threaten him with the serious consequences he could expect if he put one step the wrong side of the picket wire. In the absence of this, Saddam considered Kuwait was for the taking.

Nonetheless, there was still a feeling in the air, certainly in Kuwait, that the confrontation would ebb away. On the same day that Glaspie was delivering her ambivalent message, a number of British journalists were in Kuwait, went up to the border, saw nothing and left the country. When the invasion came, Fleet Street was absent, along with virtually all the Western press. A strange absence indeed, when compared with the coverage of the flash points round the world today. On 26 July, however, the Kuwaiti newspapers were reporting that the crisis was at an end. 'It's over' was one headline I could hardly forget. The sudden flush of optimism was based on reports of an agreement brokered by President Mubarak under which Kuwait would write off Iraq's debts, respect its OPEC quota and provide Saddam with ready cash to the tune of four billion dollars. The Kuwaitis may have accepted the deal, but had Saddam really done so?[227] Reports soon came in that Kuwaiti tank transporters were withdrawing south along the seventh ring road, but nothing was heard of similar movement north of the border.

The tensions had not gone away. At a meeting in Geneva of OPEC oil ministers on 26/27 July, the leader of the Iraqi delegation insulted his Kuwaiti opposite number by calling him a dog and a monkey. Fisticuffs broke out. Despite this, the meeting agreed to the aim of achieving a three-dollar rise in the price of oil per barrel to twenty-one dollars by the end of the year. Overall production would be allowed to increase slightly, but the Kuwait quota would remain frozen. Analysts at the time considered that Iraq was the force behind the agreement. Washington watched from afar and 'dithered in a funk of disbelief'; policy makers, including General Schwarzkopf at Central Command, were coming to accept that Rumaylah and Bubiyan would be taken over.[228] There was no plan to intervene if they were. In what was still 'no shot across the bows', President Bush sent a three-paragraph message to Saddam talking further about the need for differences to best be resolved by peaceful means. In Kuwait, the American embassy lamented on 29 July that their contingency measures were prejudiced by the absence of many of their wardens. The D/DMI told me the same morning that Iraqi Special Forces with amphibious equipment had been spotted off Bubiyan. This, and an independent report I received of Russian vessels having been diverted since 1 June from Shuwaiba in Kuwait to Umm Qasr, were sent immediately to London. The Russians were still delivering armaments and chemicals. Another independent report the next day informed me that Australian wheat supplies to Iraq were to be diverted from Schuwaikh port to Aqaba at the head of the Red Sea. They would be transported across Jordan to their destination.

This report was spiked in London, but later came to the attention of intelligence analysts in the MOD, who considered it would have been a key indicator. Thus, at this stage, I was far from convinced that the crisis had passed. On the contrary, early on Monday 30 July, I sent my view to London: "[I was] not happy the current crisis has passed. Still some indication that it could take a sudden and violent turn for the worse." The previous day, too, I had sent a number of sensitive items in the last bag to Bahrain in charge of the youngest member in my department.[229]

Wednesday 1 August was as hot a summer's day in Kuwait as any. The reading on the large temperature gauge overlooking the main drag into the city was stuck on 49.7 degrees centigrade, just below the legal limit for labourers working outside. The actual temperature was probably already several degrees higher. By midday, we learnt that the Jeddah talks had broken down, with Izzat Ibrahim seen on television leaving the premises with a broad grin on his face. An Iraqi friend told me some years later that this facial expression had convinced him that invasion was imminent. The Iraqi Prime Minister, Sa'dun Hammadi, blamed the collapse of the negotiations on the Kuwaitis, who had not shown any serious willingness to tackle the 'major damage inflicted on Iraq'. Kuwait's Foreign Minister, Shaikh Sabah, said that his country had been ready to write off debt and lease Warba Island to allow the Iraqis to build installations for the export of Rumaylah oil field production. The *International Herald Tribune* later thought the Iraq demands were just too high for the Kuwaitis to be able, with all self-respect, to meet them. They were, indeed, formidable: a ten-billion-dollar debt waiver, 2.4-billion compensation for 'stolen oil' and renunciation of Kuwait's sovereignty over Bubiyan and Warba. Once that Danegeld had been paid, what would Iraq demand next? Her intelligence services were already packing their agents into the Emirate and were more than capable of undermining its infrastructure and carrying out assassinations.

There was no doubt in my mind which way the wind was blowing. After a speedy dash home to Mishref, twenty kilometres from the embassy, I packed a small bag with clean underwear, socks, spare shirts, my radio, the Bible and a history of Winchester Cathedral, a gift from my late parents-in-law. I was back in the embassy by 1630 and ready to set up a camp bed in my office. The ambassador, who lived above the shop, offered me a bed upstairs. Hearing of my decision, a diplomatic colleague joined us overnight; several others were away on summer leave. During the early evening I received a surprise visit from a smart young lieutenant of the Kuwait Security Service who advised me that he had been appointed as my liaison officer. I was not to see him again. Later in the evening, I made various phone calls to officials and other contacts in case they could add to the picture. At 2000, I spoke to a senior official in the Ministry of the Interior, who said: "It's all in Bush and Thatcher's hands now." Shortly afterwards, a young colleague and I read the just-received CIG assessment that talked of 'sabre rattling' and the Baghdad embassy account of April Glaspie's last meeting with Saddam. We agreed that the situation was spine-chilling.

I turned in at about 0030 on 2 August with everything quiet outside and no further alarmist calls. At 0245 I was roused from a sleepless bed to be told by the deputy head of the Kuwaiti Security Service that Iraqi troops had surrounded the Emirate's border posts. There was, he assured me, no sign of a general move south, but 'we are watching'. Within minutes I had informed the Duty Clerk in the Foreign Office. At 0345, the same official was back on the phone; the Iraqis were deploying to the south. Again, I contacted the duty clerk. Immediately after having done so, I called in a communicator to send my traffic to London. Everything was still quiet as I was going through the laborious business of opening up access to my inner sanctum in order to prepare a 'sitrep'. It was never completed. At shortly after 0415, I heard strange noises outside; like the sound one makes when popping one's cheek with a finger. Two or three minutes later, the first tank rounds exploded and Iraqi jets began to scream overhead. The invasion, so often discounted over previous months, had reached the embassy perimeter, having been launched across the frontier just over two hours previously.[230] I confess that my immediate reaction was to freeze for some thirty seconds; then I got back to it.

Twelve

BA FLIGHT 149

I did not witness the battle for Dasman Palace which raged after Iraqi Special Forces came ashore close to the embassy in their bid to capture the Kuwaiti Emir. They missed him by an hour or so, thanks to a contingency plan agreed some days or weeks before, by which he had been whisked away by helicopter to one of the 'observer' American warships that were cruising offshore. It was later considered to have been Saddam's first reverse, as it was thought to have been his initial intention to replace Sheikh Jabir with his younger and considered more malleable brother, Sheikh Fahd,[231] who, after his overnight flight from London to the palace, was the only member of the ruling family to die resisting the invasion. That fighting was going on all around was all too evident from the many ear-splitting tank rounds being loosed off and the unsettling metallic rattle of heavy machine guns, some of which were spraying their bullets across the outside of the wall where I was tending to the shredding machine. In the midst of this cacophony – at about 0500 – the telephone rang. It was the Gurkha havildar in command of the gate guard: "Mr Paice, Mr Paice, the army want to come in." My reply was terse: "Get the ambassador to deal with it." Frankly, I did not know which army the havildar was talking about, but I assumed it was the Iraqis. After all these years, I am still not sure who it was. It was understood that the occupying forces were ordered to show respect for diplomatic premises; that changed, of course, after Baghdad withdrew its recognition of the surviving diplomats in Kuwait. Nevertheless, even if it had only been remnants of the Emiri Guard, with or without their British-supplied Ferret armoured cars, the compound would have become a battle ground. As it was, we were completely surrounded, but fortunately suffered only some scorching of the freshly white-washed walls at one far corner.

The urgency behind the phone call, however, persuaded me to set off my means for instant combustion of Her Majesty's most sensitive papers. I continued to feed the flames with other secrets, producing a bonfire in the centre of my office. A desperate measure, but with ammunition flying around outside, there was no question of me finding a wide-open space. Instead, the flames shot up from the bare concrete floor and I was soon wreathed in unpleasant smoke in a room for which there was little ventilation. Inevitably, if unexpected in the circumstances, this activated the sprinklers installed in the embassy during the refurbishment the previous year. The second phone call came in shortly afterwards – at just before 0530; it was my American colleague. He rang for no particular reason, other than to find out where I was. He was 'down to confidential and burning'. As was I, I thought, but not supported by a squad of marines.

I had just kindled a further small fire on the floor and was back at the shredder when the third call came in, shortly after 0530. It was Laurie O'Toole, the British Airways country manager, who was obviously ringing from home; he mentioned that he was seeing Iraqi tanks passing his residence in the north of the city. "We've got a plane held at the airport," he exclaimed. I expressed surprise but, beleaguered as I was, and certainly pre-occupied, there was no useful advice I could give him. My mind was concentrated on matters in hand, to clean out the office of any compromise to Her Majesty's highly classified papers, given the possibility of the Iraqi Army breaking into the embassy.

I knew the BA country manager well; we had a mutually approved confidential relationship in order to provide a discreet local channel for the passing of terrorist or hi-jack alerts; I also welcomed the contact since he was able to update me on security arrangements at the airport. Only a few weeks before, I had added airport security to my portfolio so that I could improve embassy access to means for the smooth passage of VIPs. My ambition was to procure unimpeded entry airside; my healthy relations with the Kuwait Interior Ministry would likely have achieved this. It was certainly not about preserving the integrity of British aircraft or their passengers, as was subsequently suggested in press circles.

O'Toole had started his summer leave at the end of April; I had last met him on the 23rd of that month. I had no substantial business with his office during his absence, although I met a potentially helpful new member of his staff, who clearly welcomed contact with the embassy. My summer leave was due to start on 26 July, but as soon as I heard of the largescale Iraqi troop deployment, I cancelled it. On Sunday 22 July, I called round at the BA office in the city and spoke to the stand-in manager, Amanda Ball, advising her of my change in plans and the reason why. This, of course, caused her to ask about the possible threat. I cannot remember my exact words, but they were spoken within the context of my having sufficient concern to cancel my leave and along the lines of there being 'no need to panic yet'. I doubt whether anyone in Kuwait could or would have said any more ten days before the invasion and, as a member of the embassy talking to someone with whom I did not have a confidential relationship, I had a duty not to be alarmist and to stick to what was then the embassy line. There was another reason why I did not just phone up. The new BA staff member had agreed to show me the passenger list for a flight that had recently flown out of Kuwait with individuals of interest on board. If it had been any other national airline, I would not have been concerned, but the identities of the passengers were sensitive and the embassy had not been informed.

The BA country manager returned to Kuwait after two months' absence – at the end of July. In a confusing statement he made to American lawyers in 1995, he claimed to have arrived back on a Sunday, 'the 30th of July'. That date was a Monday in fact. Over the length of my posting, O'Toole rarely if ever, rang me; if I wanted a chat, I had to call him. Despite the threatening atmosphere, he did not contact me on his return, as he might have done given the worsening Iraq/Kuwait situation. Neither did I contact him, not least since I did not know he was back. By the evening of Wednesday 1 August, however, he was *demandeur*. Shortly after the visit of the Kuwaiti Security Service lieutenant mentioned in the previous chapter, O'Toole came over to the embassy; I saw him at about

1730. We talked together outside the building and then I took him to my office. I discussed at some length what I knew of the politico-military situation. I rehearsed argumentation on both sides as to whether the Iraqis would invade. I was, after all, talking to a man who was having to catch up quickly on what had been going on for the last five or six weeks. I made it clear that the break-down in negotiations earlier in the day had compelled me to pick up my grab bag and move up to the embassy. At no point did I down-play the threat. It would have been completely out of character to have done so. Was I not the one person in the embassy, not to mention London, who took a pessimistic view of Iraqi intentions? Just before he left me to call on the ambassador, I said the following: "Whatever others may say, Laurie, if you have an aircraft going through at midnight tonight, it will probably get through." I then added that it was my view that the Iraqis would attack – if they were going to do so – in the early hours of the morning. He should, therefore, not 'bank on' getting an aircraft through 'the same time the next day'. At shortly after 1800 on the eve of an invasion that nearly everyone discounted, could I have said much more?[232]

I was not party to the others in the embassy O'Toole spoke to that evening, but I had reason to believe that some took a much less alarmist view than I had done. They may well have diluted any impression he received from me, but I have since learnt that my ambassador echoed my advice. Whatever, O'Toole went home to his own bed well aware that I would not be in mine. At the very least, I would have expected him to have consulted with his fellow international airline representatives, when he should have learnt that they were diverting their flights. No other foreign airline flew through that night. In his place, I would have camped at the airport.

What is also known now from O'Toole's testimony to the American lawyers is that he ensured that his wife and children were sent off on the Swissair flight to Geneva an hour or so after the warning he had received from me and only a day or so after their arrival. He has maintained that this was for reasons connected with the health of one of his children. One is entitled to question, however, why he returned to Kuwait with his family in the first place. In his testimony, he also spoke of his return as being brief in order to cover for his deputy who required two weeks' leave to attend a wedding. He was planning to go back on leave on 20 August. Whatever, he did not, apparently, take into account what his fellow country managers were doing; neither did he speak to London. Here, I have to confess a prime motivation in giving this part of my account; it is to clear my name that has been repeatedly and gratuitously smeared over the thirty years since August 1990. O'Toole has denied that he received my warning.

It is also now imperative to state that at no time was the embassy party to the intelligence operation that is said to have used BA149. There was no question, as has been alleged, that the Kuwait embassy was involved in calling in Special Forces.[233] Certainly, no one briefed me beforehand, or sought my advice on collecting further information on the ground down to the invasion itself. All my assiduous collection of orbat and troop positions from a variety of informants was sent back in timely fashion to London. Against this, the British media, not least the BBC, named and accused me of telling British Airways that there would be no invasion. A series of so-called 'insight' articles in the press and on television appeared over the years, without any attempt to find out what part I had actually played. Not that I would have been able to say more than 'no comment'. No one ever asked me, although many from the media were assiduous in courting crew members and passengers for their stories. Neither did they try to question my ambassador. Friends and acquaintances who saw these reports asked and were met with the bland: "You shouldn't believe all you read in the media." Those who knew me accepted that I was not the sort of chap to have done what I was accused of. Only three years ago, an acquaintance mentioned the accusations against me to a much-valued friend; at the time, it might have stopped a promising relationship in its tracks.[234] And nobody in the media stopped to consider how my personal security, or that of my family, might have been prejudiced in a time of mounting terrorist threats.

The issue over BA149 was raised several times in the House of Commons, notably by Norman Baker, the former Liberal Democrat

MP for Lewes. On 27 April 2007, he introduced an adjournment debate during which he flourished two affidavits he had received from members of a team alleging that they had been flown to Kuwait on BA149 in support of a so-called deniable operation called Iscariot.[235] The purpose of the operation was to gather intelligence on Iraq: troop strengths, positions and unit identification as well as to link up with Kuwaiti resistance. The last task was hardly credible, not least since the Americans were already busy evacuating their own intelligence assets. Baker further explained that the team was from the INC ('Increment'), a unit 'formed shortly after the Iranian embassy siege of 1980 when Margaret Thatcher authorised the set-up and operation of INC due to increased media attention being focussed on the Special Air Service...'. Members of the INC were 'drawn mainly from ex-forces and even serving forces personnel'.

The Liberal Democrat MP went on to state that the fact that the operation had taken place had been confirmed by the then US ambassador in Kuwait and, separately, by a CIA agent working alongside MI6 in Saudi Arabia at the time of the invasion. The captain of the USS *Antietam* had also provided details of the subsequent rescue of two members of the team. One of the two affidavits, Baker revealed, had claimed that 'the entire operation... was... authorised by Prime Minister Margaret Thatcher'. Over the years, however, the operation itself and Thatcher's authorisation had been repeatedly denied. Baker insisted that he was pursuing the matter for two reasons: he did not like cover-ups before Parliament and because he was doing so on behalf of 'the crew and passengers who [had] suffered weeks or months of hell under Saddam Hussein'. When I read this, I thought of Colonel Wigg and the Tory front bench in July 1961. Baker also pointed out that, while French passengers had won three million pounds' compensation and Americans had been paid off discreetly by British Airways, the British passengers had received nothing. He also repeated the gratuitous, if irrelevant and spurious, allegation of BA having been 'briefed by the person described as the MI6 head in Kuwait... that there would be no invasion'.

In contrast to Wigg in 1961, Baker was addressing a Labour front bench. Geoff Hoon, the Minister for the European Community and with no responsibility for the Ministry of Defence whatsoever, said that he had made enquiries with relevant departments and had been 'told that the government at the time did not attempt in any way to exploit the flight by any means whatsoever'. Hoon, it would appear, was being fed the same responses that I had received over the years. While the minister was ready to read the affidavits and to have the names of those involved, he considered that 'there was no new evidence before me' and was, therefore, unable 'to launch an inquiry'. In the event, Baker did not hand over the affidavits because he was not confident that their contents would be handled with discretion. Their authors had already complained of being harassed. There is some evidence that Baker's office was searched. Be that as it may, the debate did not make the newspapers the next morning and the matter was dropped.

Thirty years on, I can do rather better than the reconstruction, referred to by Baker and transmitted by BBC2 at a late hour in April 2007, in interpreting the events surrounding BA149's fate and countering the stark and totally false allegation as to my culpability and the embassy's alleged involvement. I was certainly the man on the spot at the time and my memory is very clear. I also spoke to the BA captain of the flight, sadly no longer alive. I had the privilege, too, of reading his diary. In a court of law, I would be more than willing to testify to what I now know and remember.

Captain Brunyate drove to Heathrow on 1 August 'with a sense of foreboding'. He had been on holiday but, brought up as a child in Iraq, he took the more interest in the developing Iraq/Kuwait situation. I learnt many years later that he had expressed fears for his safety in the event that he was detained by the Iraqis. He was, therefore, well aware of Iraqi troop deployment on the border and, like me, remembered the 1961 episode. It is highly unlikely that he would have agreed to fly had he been made aware of how his flight was to be used. His first officer and flight engineer were both well-known to him and, on his arrival at the airport, expressed their concern. Brunyate asked his flight engineer to make enquiries; these produced nothing of concern. Pre-departure checks, however, discovered a fault in an auxiliary power unit which supplied air conditioning for the cabin. Whether or not he was relieved to have an excuse for the necessary delay to effect a repair – as the BBC reconstruction alleged – I cannot say, but he undoubtedly used the time to gather updates from both BA Security and the FCO. Both gave him the go-ahead to fly. One account, rehearsed by the BA149 director of cabin services in 2017, has it that the FCO alluded to 'sabre-rattling', thus repeating the phrase used in the Current Intelligence Group assessment. At 1800 that evening, the captain received further assurances from the flight planners, but set up a link for updates once he was in the air. I do not know whether or what the Kuwait country manager might have reported to BA in London, but had he done so, there would have been time for airline operational security to take account of my advice. After all, 1800 Kuwait time, when I had briefed his colleague, was still only 1600 in the UK.

Shortly before BA149 was cleared for take-off – two hours late – the director of cabin services on board was shown in the reconstruction reporting to his captain that a group[236] of young, single and well-built male passengers had boarded and were sitting towards the rear of the plane. Brunyate made no mention of this in his diary, nor did he raise the matter with me when we spoke in the embassy.[237] According to the reconstruction, he thought the late passengers were 'oilies', technicians working in the oil fields. As I have every reason to believe that Captain Brunyate was kept in total ignorance of their real provenance, I can understand why their presence raised no particular concern. An interesting passage in the reconstruction had the young men smirking over whether they needed to fill in Kuwait landing cards. When they were told that it was essential, one of their number took over the completion of formalities. For all their military skill and audacity, British Special Forces do not easily lend themselves to operating under alias and acting their cover. On their arrival at Kuwait airport, however, they were seen to exit downstairs which would have allowed them to bypass immigration and go straight to the baggage hall. I have also learnt recently that they were met by a uniformed Kuwaiti officer who was concerned at the late arrival of the flight. The men collected their baggage and disappeared into the night.

This last-minute boarding of the flight at Heathrow should have produced an updated passenger manifest. Despite repeated requests for this, including as the aircraft door was about to be closed at Heathrow, this was not provided, against the usual procedure and, I am advised, against the law. The director of cabin services was advised that copies would be faxed to the aircraft during the flight and to Kuwait airport. In the event, this did not happen. On paper, at least, the so-called 'oilies' did not exist.

During the flight to Kuwait, Brunyate had kept in regular touch with BA Operations and the BBC. About an hour before reaching his destination, he passed BA148, the west-bound flight that would have departed Kuwait at midnight. This was the very flight I had told the BA country manager would probably get through. The pilot of BA148 told Brunyate that the situation at Kuwait airport was 'normal'. It was still normal when BA149 landed at 0200 local, at least as far as the captain of BA149 was concerned. He was assured by the control tower[238] that all was well but, still concerned, asked for permission to make an additional circuit for reconnaissance purposes. This would have taken him towards the border area. He saw nothing. Once landed, Brunyate checked again with BA Operations and handed the plane over to Captain Peter Clarke, who was to take it on to Madras and Kuala Lumpur. After ensuring that his crew were well catered for, he then retired to bed. He would hardly have done so if the area was resounding with shellfire. It was only at 0630 that he was roused from his slumber by a phone call from O'Toole, still at home, informing him that 'there had been an invasion of some sort'. He was assured that there was nothing to worry about and that the crew should take a day's holiday. At 0845, Brunyate rang O'Toole at his home, who said that he was unable to get to the airport because he was surrounded by Iraqi troops. Brunyate returned to bed in his hotel room and was again woken by his country manager at 1100, who said that lines to the embassy were down. According to Brunyate, O'Toole did not manage to get to the airport until 4 August. Brunyate and his crew and passengers would be prevented from returning home for four months, many of them being taken up to Baghdad as early as 8 August. They were all to suffer privations of one sort or another throughout this period, many to be treated as hostages by the Iraqi government. On their release, they began to ask questions. Why had BA149 not been diverted? Why had it been allowed to fly at all? It was only over twenty years later that I had it confirmed – not by management – what reason there had been for it to have to fly on to Kuwait. I can only agree, therefore, at this juncture that the late-boarding passengers were the cause; they had to be infiltrated into Kuwait, albeit this has never been admitted to me.

On the contrary, over thirty years I have received denial after denial of the real reason why BA149 flew that night. Only a year or so ago, officials were still talking in terms of 'if there was an operation'. To begin with, when I was able to return to London towards the end of August, I was welcomed with open arms by family and office alike. Not a word was breathed about BA149. I was congratulated in person by senior officials for my 'percipience'; records will show in due course an appreciation of my part in providing timely warnings. Many heaved a sigh of relief that I had evaded the clutches of Saddam's thugs. It was not, however, until the New Year, with the liberation of Kuwait well in hand, that the fate of the flight was brought up in Whitehall. During the spring of 1991, I was invited to attend a meeting in the Foreign Office, chaired by Minister of State Douglas Hogg.[239] Mr Hogg was anxious to know who knew what in the FCO during the hours before BA149 was detained. On hearing my account of how I had kept the duty clerk informed during the early morning of 2 August (late evening in London), he expressed concern at where this left the Foreign Office; my information should have been acted upon. There were grounds for embarrassment if the matter got out. I wrote up the meeting for my personal record; it was as well that I did, since I was never able to discover the Foreign Office official record which would normally have been written by the Minister's private secretary, who was present at the meeting. I shared my record with colleagues, who agreed that I had acted with honour. What further action was taken by the minister, if any, remained a mystery.

An article by Richard Norton-Taylor in *The Guardian* in January 1992 included a reference to an MI6 officer serving in the Middle East having judged events correctly but whose view had been 'rubbished' by his ambassador. This was seen by some as referring to me. My head of department called me in with a worried look on his face; he showed me the article – which I had not seen – and asked me whether I had spoken to the press. I had not, I assured him, and had no intention of doing so. Only the year before, the same man had given me my annual appraisal, during which he had suggested, perhaps a little unwisely, that my achievement and foresight in Kuwait would be recognised appropriately. It had already dawned on me: Whitehall could not afford for my honourable record to become the subject of press speculation that could reflect badly on many others who had got it so wrong. To my distress, my name did appear in the media, but always charging me with having misled British Airways, which was totally untrue. At best, I was accused of having a conflict of interest; at worst, of being incompetent. Meanwhile, others got off scot-free.

Over nearly two decades, whenever some new or repeated allegation over the fate of BA149 cropped up in the media, it was always coupled with the speculation, increasingly the assertion, that Special Forces had flown on the plane in order to put intelligence boots on the ground. On each occasion, I would take the matter up, since it affected both my reputation and, potentially, my family's security. An enquiry would be made with the Ministry of Defence; there was no question of the embassy having been involved, I was assured. The MOD always came back with a disclaimer, on one occasion adding that they were 'ninety-nine per cent sure' there had been no operation. I have lived long enough to suspect the one per cent. As time went on, people clearly became tired and just a little irked at my concern. I was, for example, given no warning of the 2007 BBC2 reconstruction and would not have known of it but for my late wife turning on the programme half-way through and calling me through to the lounge to watch it. The next evening my local parish priest exclaimed with others present: "Tony, you were all over the TV last night." In Whitehall, however, there were more serious pressures to worry about. If anything, I had become an embarrassment, if not a scapegoat.

Such an infiltration operation, however last-minute, could not have gone ahead without being signed off by someone in high authority.

Rules on approval for intelligence operations, however risky they may seem, will always be cleared at an appropriate official or political level. This is a system that dates back to the mid-1950s following the scandal surrounding the disappearance of Commander Crabb, the diver who had been sent to explore the hull of a Russian warship in Portsmouth Harbour.[240] The higher the risk/dividend balance, the higher the submission will go before it is signed off. Agreement to risk a British Airways plane and its complement would have been deemed high, but the value of the intelligence the operation could produce, not least to save the lives of those engaged in any future military operation, would also have been seen as potentially vital. In normal times, as political officer, I might have been consulted during the preparation of a submission; my ambassador certainly would have been. In the event, neither of us were. Had I been asked on 1 August, I could only have said what I said to the BA country manager, as would have my ambassador. It would also have been a *sine qua non* that the aircraft captain should be briefed; Captain Brunyate was not, it seems.

What follows is largely speculation based on circumstantial evidence, but it would explain why Whitehall, the Foreign Office at least, was apparently kept in the dark. On the eve of the invasion, I spoke on the phone to the head of the Kuwaiti Security Service at about 2000. We exchanged bleak appraisals about what might be coming around the corner. At one point he blurted out: "Only President Bush and Margaret Thatcher can save us now." Not OPEC, not the Arab League and not Saudi Arabia or Egypt. At that very moment, the British Prime Minister was preparing to meet George Bush Senior in Washington for the first time; there would have been many transatlantic phone calls in the run-up to this historic occasion. There would certainly have been discussion of the Iraq/Kuwait situation. It would have been quite within Thatcher's character to have volunteered the services of 'my soldiers'[241] as a means for impressing the relatively new incumbent at the White House. She also had close personal and political ties to Lord King, the Chairman of British Airways.[242] With King on board, she was in a position to approve the use of BA149 to convey 'her soldiers' to Kuwait. Were they SAS regulars, is the next question? It would certainly fit with Thatcher's close relationship with the Regiment. On the other hand, the word 'Increment' has been bandied about in the media and also raised in the House of Commons, suggesting the deployment of individuals who were retired from Special Forces service but were retained to carry out deniable operations. At least one of the six young men engaged for the operation, however, appeared to be too young for such a potentially hazardous task or to fit in with the usual profile. Whatever their provenance, their involvement should still have required very high political clearance.

Number Ten, however, would not have been able to coordinate the operational planning, selection of personnel and their briefing, and certainly not at a day or so's notice. After the Second World War, the conduct of Special Operations was made the preserve of MI6. It was a minuscule part of the Service's role and activities, which is more a commentary on how scant the resources available for a marginal activity were. As years passed, those with the experience and expertise had aged and died. In parallel, British Special Services burgeoned and had acquired many of the skills necessary for such secret operations. The whole subject became a grey area, but MI6 retained some degree of overall control of overseas operations. That did not, of course, include such publicly acclaimed use of SAS in the Iranian embassy siege of May 1980 which was indeed ordered by the Thatcher government. The men engaged were regular SAS. If the men who flew with BA149 were from the so-called 'Increment', as Norman Baker's affidavits from two of their number insisted, then MI6 should have been consulted. That no one appears to have done so is decidedly odd. And certainly, no one has enlightened me at any time before or after 2 August 1990. During my career, I had been briefed after an event, months, sometimes years, after it had taken place and, in intelligence terms at least, they were more sensitive than whatever use had been made of BA149.

Only recently, I have been able to winkle out a key pointer to the provenance of the young men who boarded BA149 late. Their group tickets for the flight were easily traced back to a military account at Hereford, the home of the Special Air Service (SAS).[243] It is surely open to question whether any self-respecting intelligence officer planning a so-called deniable operation would ever have booked travel arrangements so overtly. This points the finger straight at an SAS-directed operation, undoubtedly cleared at high political level at the last minute and clumsily unprofessional. What it actually achieved, I do not know, but I would guess very little and by no means sufficient to warrant the risk to so many lives. Those not rescued by the Americans on the coast would have hiked the thirty kilometres to the Saudi border. I understand that two of the team were flown to USS *Antietam*, from whence they were transferred to HMS *York*, commanded at the time by the senior Royal Naval officer in the Gulf. One further rider. About seven days into the invasion the embassy received a long telegram from London asking for local information that might be useful to Special Services operations. Was this an indirect cry for support to help SAS cadres still trudging through the desert? I considered it odd at the time and clearly drafted by someone who had absolutely no idea of what was actually going on in Kuwait. We were in no position to be able to help; certainly not from behind the embassy's totally surrounded premises.

Why the cover-up, for that it must certainly have been? Surely, after a certain breathing space, someone in government might have revealed the success the operation achieved in providing crucial intelligence that that might well have saved military lives. A fulsome apology might then have been given and consideration of appropriate compensation. Apart from the potential political embarrassment, however, there was one considerable financial issue. Approaching four hundred passengers and crew were understandably angry at being compromised by what, on the surface at least, looked like a failure in both government intelligence and airline duty of care. MI6, the Foreign Office and the Ministry of Defence had all got it wrong, they would have judged. Why did BA fly to Kuwait when others cancelled or diverted? There was, however, no public inquiry; a senior judge apparently advised passenger representatives that the government could not be sued! British Airways, nevertheless, were the only organisation to be put in the dock, not in London or Washington but in Paris. The case came up in 1995. Compensation was awarded to French passengers, in spite of the testimony from the airline that it had received the wrong advice from the British government. The British Airways key witness was their Kuwait country manager, who testified that he had been advised by the Kuwait embassy that it was safe to fly. BA might also have had to appear in a court at Houston in Texas. So unconvincing, however, was O'Toole's pre-hearing deposition that the airline felt obliged to pay off the plaintiffs rather than risk their evidence before the court. British Airways were still able to escape, having to pay large sums in compensation for the many British passengers on board and the substantial legal costs at a time when financially it was in a bad way. The chicken has now come home to roost, sadly at a time when all airlines are feeling the strain. Quite why the saga has been allowed to fester for so long is a mystery.

One accusation – that there had been an intelligence failure on the ground – was finally rebutted in November 2021. In a statement to the Commons on 23 November, the recently appointed Foreign Secretary, Liz Truss, apologised to Parliament that it had not been informed of the timely warning provided by the Kuwait embassy. Her admission came shortly after the release of FCO papers covering events in 1990 to the National Archive. The papers, which I have seen, feature the phone calls I made during the night of 1/2 August and mirror my account above. The Foreign Secretary confirmed that the rest of Whitehall had been given the information, but not British Airways, who have always claimed they knew nothing of the invasion. Ms Truss admitted that the failure to disclose the embassy's action was 'unacceptable'.

Thirteen

OCCUPATION AND ESCAPE

The Iraqi armoured pincers to the north and west of Kuwait City swept aside any resistance from the only two – still semi-deployed – brigades of the Emirate's forces.[244] Several days later, I saw where one brave but hopeless stand had taken place in the northern suburbs. The remains of a number of British-built and ironically named Saladin troop carriers and Saracen armoured cars, with unburied bodies still lying beneath them, betrayed the ruthlessness of the invaders. What had become of Kuwait's main battle tanks, the Chieftains and Centurions, had to be left to pessimistic imagination, but the bulk, we learnt later, had fled across the border into Saudi Arabia. By 0700 on Thursday 2 August, five hours after they had crossed the start line, Iraqi Soviet-supplied T55 tanks were rumbling into the city from the north and the Iraqi Air Force had complete control of the skies. Three hours later, the consul made it into the embassy from Mishref and reported seeing Iraqi forces on the Fahaheel motorway, the main drag into town from the west. Amir Jabir and Crown Prince Saad had already received asylum in Saudi Arabia. The one major military action took place at Jahra, some twenty miles north of the city where the Kuwaiti garrison – the Al-Magaweer brigade – sustained up to a thousand dead. By 1500, the Iraqis had seized the centre of the city and were moving on Schuwaikh port where fierce fighting continued to rage well into the evening. It has been all too easy to belittle the efforts of the Kuwaiti armed forces, but they had faced a hopeless situation alone. In the coming months, however, there would be many examples of still unrecognised bravery by small groups of resistance and individuals.

Isolated in the embassy, we could only hear what was going on, although at one point towards 1700, I went upstairs to watch Iraqi tanks in pairs, stopping and starting along the coastal road below the embassy. Television and radio broadcasting was soon under enemy control, suggesting that teams for their takeover had been infiltrated some time before the arrival of ground forces. The telephones went down within the first twenty-four hours after various reports of interruptions and cut-offs. Captain Brunyate complained that the media were also clogging the lines. I was still able early evening to ring my wife in the UK to reassure her that I was well and that, whatever alarmist pictures were being relayed by British television, we had only suffered the small fire in the compound adjacent to the tennis court. In the days that followed, one embassy line remained open, doubtless the one the Iraqi eavesdroppers were tapping. They would have taken over Kuwaiti facilities which included the early development of word recognition.[245] All this, of course, was well before the massed use of mobile, including throwaway, phones. After months of quiet build-up of Mukhabarat capability in the Emirate, Iraqi control of information channels was complete and there was no foreign, least of all Western, press to monitor, let alone contest it. The only trace of defiance was a broadcast during the first evening showing the ghost-like appearance of the Crown Prince on a fuzzy screen. What comfort Kuwaiti citizens could have taken from it is difficult to imagine; the now six of us watching the ambassador's set could only shrug shoulders and return to the BBC Overseas Service.

Kuwait's one, if remote, consolation was that the United Nations Security Council had gone into emergency session at 0900 GMT (0500 in New York) and had passed a short resolution condemning the invasion unanimously. Saddam's action had flouted all that the United Nations had stood for since its foundation. However meaningless we might have judged the resolution at the time, the Iraqi leader was never going to be let off the hook he had impaled himself on.[246] Saddam responded in the only way he could – with immediate defiance. We watched with some trepidation as he warned against foreign intervention and threatened to 'turn Kuwait into a grave'. As someone who had seen many reports of

Saddam's development and use of WMD, I felt chilled to the marrow, but then guffawed derisively on hearing him claim incongruously that his troops had been invited in by 'internal revolutionaries'. This fig leaf of an excuse was picking up on the political protest that had followed the elections two months previously for the Kuwait National Assembly. Within hours of the invasion, the Iraqis had set up a puppet self-styled Provisional Free Kuwaiti Government (PFKG) which was soon broadcasting a denunciation of the 'defunct and corrupt' al-Sabah regime and announcing that the borders were closed together with the imposition of a curfew. Refusing to blink, Saddam closed Iraqi air space and borders, notably for us, the long and still possible exit into Saudi Arabia. The implication for BA's marooned flight at the airport was obvious, if not immediately recognised as a priority. As a further demonstration that he meant business in the long-term, Saddam ordered the re-formation of fifteen infantry and armoured divisions that had been disbanded after the 1988 ceasefire and called for the creation of eleven new divisions. His actions were greeted in Baghdad by cheering mass demonstrations; it was the sort of exercise a Fascist system was easily able to stage. Less well-known was the fact that Iraqi troops were misled on the eve of the invasion into believing they were invading Israel, not the territory of a brother Arab.

As dusk fell on the first evening of the occupation, firing continued in the vicinity, accompanied by the occasional crash of a tank round. Nervous Iraqi soldiers were firing at illusory targets in the dark. I waited for a lull before venturing outside as far as an outhouse, where I burnt the last of HM's secrets. My office was now empty after ten hours of shredding which broke three machines; they don't like staples, paper clips and India tags. At least I could now rest easy that the sensitive details held in the embassy in Kuwait were no longer vulnerable to a sudden Iraqi occupation. That complacency was disturbed three days later when I found as compromising a single sheet as any, that had become lodged between two desks. Returning inside to the cool of the building's still-functioning air-conditioning, I was greeted by the ambassador's bearer with a tray of assorted drinks. That whisky soda served as a memorable pick-me-up. With Iraqi soldiers patrolling outside, a feeling little short of helplessness set in. It did not, however, induce lethargy. There was still one phone line to monitor and reports to be drafted based on the helpful calls from expatriates still working in Kuwait's key infrastructural facilities, not least those supplying electricity and water. The destruction of the embassy's voluminous classified records – political, commercial and consular – also still lay before us. As will always happen in such situations, we clung to every word being broadcast from the BBC. The fact, however, that the USA, USSR, UK and France all imposed an arms embargo on Iraq that evening did not dull our apprehensions; stable door closed only after years of bolting horses.

After a fitful sleep, interrupted by gunfire and displays of tracer bullets across the sky, the morning brought more of the same: hours of shredding in the registry, interrupted by another interlude outside, this time to burn up some strange chemicals and equipment that had been hanging around in the office for years. For what purpose, I knew not, but its neglect provided a brief fireworks display. As I fed the brazier in a small area enclosed on three sides, Iraqi snipers kept up occasional fire from the tower blocks overlooking the embassy. It was still not safe to venture beyond the compound. Nevertheless, one person had to do so later in the evening. Cajoled by the Foreign Office to find some Iraqi in authority, the ambassador rode out in his official car, protected only by his locally engaged driver and the pennant flying on the bonnet. He returned late after being driven around for hours before at last locating a senior general in Ahmadi, some thirty kilometres to the south. He received general assurances that diplomatic premises would be protected but little else about Iraqi intentions, other than Saddam's troops were now deployed along the entire length of the Saudi border and that all roads south were blocked well before the frontier.

At about the same time, the US State Department was receiving reports from reconnaissance aircraft that the Iraqis appeared to be preparing for an invasion of Saudi Arabia. Some hours later, Margaret Thatcher flew into Washington and, in what was later considered to have been one of her 'hand-bagging' episodes, convinced a still-dithering George Bush Senior that the Kingdom and a quarter of the world's oil reserves were at risk. Slow on the uptake before the invasion, his advisers in State and at the Pentagon needed little persuasion. In Moscow, too, James Baker had little difficulty in reaching an agreement with Shevardnadze to condemn the Iraqi action jointly and to call for a world arms embargo on Baghdad. Russian military intelligence, however, would have been in two minds at the prospect of much Soviet and other Warsaw Pact equipment being destroyed or, worse, captured and picked over by Western intelligence experts.

While the superpowers seemed willing enough to coordinate their reactions, Saddam's move against Kuwait threw Arab states into confusion. Several still saw Israel as a far greater threat than Iraq. Their first response, therefore, was low-key, avoiding specific mention of the invasion and criticism of Iraq. During 3 August, however, the closest affected countries, those belonging to the Gulf Cooperation Council (GCC), condemned the Iraqi 'aggression' and called for an immediate withdrawal. Late the same day, the Arab League convened a meeting of the Islamic Conference Organisation, including Iran, in Cairo; this, too, called for immediate – and unconditional – withdrawal. It also stipulated that there should be no foreign intervention. For the moment, there was still a belief that the crisis might be Arabised away. Even so, four Arab states and the PLO refused to support the resolution.[247] Seeking to exploit the different strands of Arab concern, the Revolutionary Command Council in Baghdad broadcast plans to withdraw troops as from 5 August but insisted that the forces inside Kuwait still had to secure ports and oil terminals. Despite outward appearances, moreover, there was no complete unanimity in the Iraqi capital; reports soon appeared in Cairo's *Al-Ahram* that 120 officers had been executed for refusing to support the invasion. These were subsequently confirmed by Arab diplomats from Kuwait arriving in Syria. At best, these demonstrated that the Iraqi leader's political position was not as secure as he would have wished or the rest of the world had come to think. At worst, for Saddam if he had stopped to think about it, it showed that two strong voices – Egypt and Syria – in the Arab lobby were becoming increasingly ready to oppose Iraqi expansionism.

The following day, Saturday 4 August, saw the first major international moves against Iraq. During an emergency session in Rome of the European Council of Ministers, sanctions were agreed. This cut little ice with Saddam, who ordered that the Popular Army[248] might be deployed inside Kuwait. This was ominous, since whether there were troop withdrawals or not, this thuggish organisation would remain to police a continuing occupation. Early on, those witnessing the arrival of spear-head formations had spoken of responsible and courteous officers being in full control of their men. Their replacement by coarse members of the Popular Army was a far from pleasant prospect. It would also fit in with the intentions of the PFKG which was by now revealed to be exclusively Iraqi in membership. Its so-called Prime Minister, Colonel Ala'a Hussain Ali,[249] was mistakenly identified as one of Saddam's sons-in-law. In fact, he was no more than a Quisling figurehead. At his appeal in 2000 against a death sentence for treason, he claimed to have been forced into accepting the premiership. It is difficult to be certain about his motivation. Saddam, however, expected to take over Kuwait's sovereignty and to thus change the political system in the Emirate. Ali was totally expendable after a few days.

We learnt on 5 August that some Iraqi troops were withdrawing, but these were units that had been engaged in the initial firefights. They were seen returning up the road towards the northern border in battle-worn vehicles which also carried lightly wounded. Fresh second-line formations were passing towards the city as replacements. The Kuwait embassy in Jordan described the alleged 'withdrawal' as little more than a manoeuvre to disguise the theft of the Emirate's military equipment. What was to be called 'the biggest desert raid in history' was already starting. President Bush could denounce the phoney withdrawal as much as he liked, but he remained powerless to prevent the total rape of a society. The same day, however, the curfew was partially lifted and other embassy staff began to trickle in. The night that followed was the quietest since the start of hostilities. The next morning, our ever-enterprising consul set out early on a reconnaissance of the back road to the west in order to see whether it was possible to reach the Saudi border. He came close and during the drive saw masses of Iraqi armour deployed across the desert; he passed several checkpoints without hindrance. This experience induced the ambassador to ask me to lead a small convoy of non-essential staff, as much to reduce the catering burden his domestic staff had undertaken. With annexation looming, it seemed like a last opportunity before foreigners were prevented from leaving. A number of expatriates had successfully taken their four-wheel drives over the 'thirty clicks' of rough desert to the sand berm constituting the frontier and made good their escape. Our attempt proved abortive and we were turned back at the third checkpoint, along with a stream of other cars. Kuwait was being progressively shut down and, a day or so later, Iraqi soldiers fired on a fleeing vehicle, killing one of the British occupants. No more attempts were made to go south.

Meanwhile, pressure on Iraq was being ratcheted up. On Monday 6 August, King Fahd received the American Secretary for Defence, Dick Cheney, in Riyadh. They agreed immediately to the despatch of large numbers of American troops, in the first place to provide a defensive screen against any Iraqi incursion onto Saudi territory. A three-star general arrived with Cheney to take command. The danger of a full-scale invasion remained for several weeks thereafter, but with every week that passed the threat receded. Nevertheless, there could be little doubt about Saddam's intention had international solidarity splintered. Two weeks later, in Baghdad, I learnt that newspaper shops were selling maps showing Iraqi claims to sovereignty stretching the length of the Gulf down to the Straits of Hormuz. The Iraqi leader had missed his opportunity. In New York, the Security Council agreed to impose mandatory sanctions on Iraq and Kuwait that affected the transhipment of oil and many other commodities, while exempting food and medical supplies. Resolution 661 was passed with only Cuba and Yemen abstaining. The measure might have been stronger but for Ethiopia's request that foodstuffs should be excluded. This would provide a useful loophole for Saddam in the future; Brazil, for example, one of Iraq's main suppliers, soon joined the embargo but interpreted it loosely. In any case, Saddam was not going to run out of food since he now had access to Kuwait's huge cache of provisions. On the military front, deployment speeded up impressively, demonstrating what might have been done in the two weeks before the invasion. American marines went ashore at the Saudi port of Dhahran only six days after the Iraqi advance, while major naval units, including the battleship USS *Wisconsin*, left Norfolk, Virginia. Cheney presented these deployments as the first steps in assembling an international force to counter Saddam.

Had Saddam now pulled back, taking loot with him on the excuse that it was only compensation for the oil 'stolen' by Kuwait, history would have been a lot different. That was never his intention; he had taken the ground and did not believe international resolve, least of all condemnation from his Arab brothers, would persist. Like Hitler, he did not know when or how to turn back. Instead, he pushed on with what for him was logical. His creature, the PFKG, declared Kuwait a republic on the morning of 7 August, but this was soon overtaken the next day by Baghdad's announcement that it had annexed the Emirate. It was now the nineteenth province. In Iraqi government eyes, therefore, embassies in Kuwait no longer had a diplomatic function; at best, they might become consulates, although Basra would have had precedence. The bottom line was that all communication between foreign governments would now be through Baghdad. It is a point that those much hurt in being caught up in the invasion could not grasp. For the moment, Saddam was triumphant: rather pompously, his Revolutionary Command Council declared that it had decided 'to return the part and the branch, Kuwait, to the whole and origin, Iraq, in a comprehensive and eternal merger unity'. The head of the PFKG, Colonel Ala'a, was withdrawn, along with his eight fellow puppets, who were to become advisors with exalted titles, in the presidential office. In fact, they disappeared into obscurity; Saddam did not have time for niceties.

His seizure of Kuwait was still a major violation of international law, a charge now reinforced by Security Council resolutions. The issue of diplomatic missions was not, therefore, whether they should or would be permitted to stay but whether they physically could last out. How other embassies were going to react to Saddam's claim to sovereignty was a question that needed answering, not least for the benefit of those starting to build the widest possible alliance for eventually reversing the

Iraqi invasion. At 0900 on 8 August, I started the first of a succession of morning tours of key embassies, those I judged to be bellwethers. Driven by one of our locally engaged drivers, I was closely scrutinised when leaving and entering the compound but managed to get around most of the city without being checked. From time to time, an Iraqi military half-truck would pass crammed with young, untidily uniformed men who would train their small arms on us and stared fiercely. In no particular order, the embassies I visited represented Turkey, China, India, Pakistan, Bahrain, Oman and the Soviet Union. During each visit I delivered the same message. The British were standing to. Were they? I was received everywhere with courtesy and, as the days went by, with increasing appreciation. The exchange of information was of mutual advantage, but first-hand information on how a raft of missions representing middle-of-the-road international opinion were treating the situation should have been helpful to Whitehall. One thing was clear: none of the embassies I called on were letting their staff venture outside. Just this latter-day 'Carlton-Browne of the FO' dressed appropriately in white, short-sleeved shirt and pale fawn slacks. Some years later, I learnt that one friendly Arab representative had reported me as having resembled Lawrence of Arabia in flowing white garments. The sun was clearly playing tricks on him.

There is not space to detail all the amusing incidents along the way. While my Turkish interlocutor, well-known to me on the diplomatic circuit before the crisis, was perhaps the most informative and determined, my heart went out to the Pakistani ambassador. He was a member of the old school and his career would not prosper as a result. We established an immediate rapport. On one occasion I approached his residency to find it totally surrounded by angry migrant workers, of whom there were several thousand in Kuwait, as well as no fewer Indians, Sri Lankans and Philippinos. Their employers had disappeared overnight, they had not been paid and there was no early prospect of them being repatriated. The plight of stranded Europeans paled into significance when compared with what these people faced. The ambassador emerged from the relative safety of his house carrying an impressive walking stick which he flourished at the crowd. In a loud voice, he bellowed: "Remember you are Pathans." The roaring subsided and the protests abated. With some degree of order restored, I was welcomed inside for a cup of tea and some sweet biscuits. I noted later with a degree of personal satisfaction that Pakistan was one of the first non-European countries to offer ground forces for the international army assembling in Saudi Arabia.[250]

The Chinese representatives, a young man and woman, also welcomed me and took particular note that the British would not be leaving. They appeared to hang on my every word. Of all those I visited, they were the gladdest to see me every morning. More tea, of course, and the unreality of a Chinese garden in the middle of a maelstrom. From there to the grim tower block that housed the Russian embassy. Here I was able to locate one of the sociable first secretaries whom I had entertained a few weeks before at my house. As we chatted in the entrance lobby, there was a burst of gunfire which sent a group of embassy wives screaming for cover. The presence of so many frightened people in the building became all the more incongruous with the appearance of a man whose bearing, I judged, marked him out as a senior KGB officer. Previously, I had had just the one brief and empty exchange of conversation with him at a large Kuwaiti reception. It had not taken long for news of my arrival to reach his ears. From the respectful reaction of the first secretary, I was now talking to the head of the KGB station, who quickly ushered me into a side room. Without inviting me to sit down and imposing his burly frame over me, he began to quiz me on delicate subjects. For the first and last time in my career, I looked a senior Soviet intelligence officer in the eye and riposted: "Mr Putin" – it wasn't but could easily have been – "I do not know the answer to your questions and, if I did, you could hardly expect me to answer them. But, really, you and I have to deal with what's going on out there. It is time you forgot about the Cold War." These may not have been my exact words, but my meaning was clear enough. Another burst of gunfire reinforced my point. The Russian grunted: "I have to believe you." "You do," I retorted. With that, he left the room. I reported the exchange to London, not really expecting much response. Instead, I received a typical armchair lecture about how one should be careful when talking to the KGB. Who, I wondered, was living in the late twentieth century?

On a lighter note, I was able to provide assistance to the Omani embassy, whose communicator had been out of the country when the Iraqis invaded. This afforded me a helpful exchange of views and information with the ambassador. At 1200, the muezzin began to chant the call to prayer. I insisted the ambassador break off in order to perform his oblations. He motioned me to join him and we went upstairs to his prayer room. Here he prayed to Allah and, at the right moment, I uttered the Lord's Prayer.

A few hours after the annexation, Baghdad announced that all diplomatic missions would be closed within two weeks, after which they would no longer enjoy protection and privilege. Their staff were to move up to the Iraqi capital. At the same time, if it was not already manifestly obvious, the border with Saudi Arabia was closed. Anyone wishing to leave Kuwait would have to do so through Iraq. In the wake of annexation, the Kuwaiti dinar was pegged to the Iraqi currency; it had been worth far more. Towns in the Emirate were to have their names changed: Ahmadi, named after the notable Emir Ahmad (1921–50) was immediately to become Al-Nida ('appeal'). In response, the UN Security Council declared unanimously in Resolution 662 the next day that the annexation was null and void; all states should avoid any action that implied recognition of the Iraqi claim. In terms of international law, Saddam was now totally isolated. This was reinforced on 10 August at an emergency summit of the Arab League in Cairo. The seven-point resolution agreed denounced Iraqi aggression and the annexation, called for immediate withdrawal and proposed deployment of 'Arab forces' to Saudi Arabia in order to help Saudi Arabia and other states defend the Kingdom against 'foreign aggression'. The resolution left open which countries were to send troops and how narrowly the term 'foreign' should be interpreted. In the eyes of the twelve states that supported it, there was no doubt and, within a day or so, Egypt, Syria and Morocco had offered forces; Egyptian and Moroccan troops landed in Saudi Arabia on 12 August. The debate in Cairo was rancorous, with Iraq, Libya and the PLO dissenting strongly.

In the end, President Mubarak, as chairman, ordered that, exceptionally, the resolution should be agreed by majority and that it would only be binding on those who supported it.[251] For such a gathering it was as strong a statement of purpose as might have been wished for. Meanwhile, a special session of the NATO Council in Brussels agreed that each member of the Alliance should contribute 'each in their own way' outside the integrated NATO structure. This allowed West Germany to get around its particular constitutional difficulties, rather than just sit on its hands. The other superpower helpfully dismissed Saddam's claim that he was the victim of foreign aggression; Moscow now argued for a joint military force in the Gulf under United Nations command.[252]

Saddam had one major diplomatic shot in his locker that was attractive to the Arab streets. On 12 August, in response to the Arab League, he addressed those that had called for the elimination of Israel. Those who talked of 'occupation' – he left out the word 'annexation' – failed to mention the other 'occupation' in the Middle East, Israel's hold on the Palestinians in the West Bank. Why not resolve all the problems together? The Israelis should withdraw from territory they occupied in Palestine, Syria and Lebanon; Syria should withdraw from Lebanon; Iraq and Iran should withdraw from one another's territories still occupied at the August 1988 Armistice, and less specifically, there should be a 'formulation of arrangements for the situation in Kuwait'. Further, implementation should start with the 'oldest occupation' (Israel) and end with the most recent. The initiative brought pro- and anti-Iraqi demonstration out onto the streets of several capitals. Saddam knew these would bring pressure on moderate governments, but his initiative as a whole bought time to consolidate his hold on Kuwait and reminded the Arab world that his anti-Israeli record was second to none. If he considered it at all, he would have dismissed Emir Jabir's request to James Baker for the USA to enforce UN sanctions under the self-defence Article 51 of the Charter.

For the time being, especially for those of us stuck in Kuwait, there seemed little early prospect of the situation being reversed. Saddam held the ground and the one country that might have prevented the invasion could only 'draw a line in the sand', as President Bush had put it to his television audiences on 8 August. The Iraqi leader had also made an accommodation with Iran. Risking his reputation with Iraqis as their great leader and relations with the Army, who could now see it had suffered eight years' hard fighting and losses for nothing, he agreed a peace settlement, with unseemly haste, that relinquished all territorial gains from the war.[253] Meanwhile, the fifty thousand American troops now on their way, not acclimatised to desert warfare in the summer, could hardly be expected to shift hard-bitten numbers at twice their size. Neither could the still-uncoordinated naval dribs and drabs from several NATO countries being hurriedly re-deployed to the Gulf be expected to operate without sufficient air cover against an impressively equipped and battle-hardened Iraqi Air Force. While there seemed to be unanimity that Saddam should withdraw, there were still strong voices, not least the Soviet Union, warning against any use of force without UN approval. Saddam was in Kuwait to stay and he made his intent perfectly clear when, on 10 August, he appointed 'Chemical' Ali as his viceroy in the former Emirate. From the embassy balcony, we watched as Iraqi troops dug holes in the beach for the mines that would deter any thought of rescue from the sea.

The British Airways' passengers and crews stranded at the airport and surrounding hotels was one insurmountable problem that the embassy was in no position whatsoever to solve, despite the indignation voiced at the time at what some considered as pusillanimous effort. Had they been aware of the real cause of the situation they found themselves in, their reaction would have been one of outrage. There was another group, all British, who were also hostage to fortune. Some eighty or more Army and Royal Air Force servicemen, plus wives and children, lived in an encampment near the Fahaheel oil refinery some thirty or more kilometres south of the city. They made up the military training teams advising the Kuwaiti armed forces. The Americans, French and Russians also had teams in the Emirate. The Russians, at least, had insisted on diplomatic status for their personnel, usually embraced by some cultural or friendship framework agreement. The British teams, however, had no such protection, despite the efforts of successive MOD negotiators to regularise their status. Unlike Moscow, London did not wish to risk relations with the Kuwaitis and the arms sales that might ensue. Instead, when the crisis came, it was the British officers, NCOs and their families who were left at hazard. The Russians were never detained.

The western pincer of the Iraqi advance reached the environs of the Fahaheel camp towards midday on 2 August, but its residents had been rudely awakened by Iraqi jets thundering overhead some six hours earlier. At a hurriedly convened meeting early in the morning, they were advised by their officers to sit tight. And so, they did, until about noon the next day when a unit of Saddam's elite Republican Guard marched into the camp. By then, communications with the families had all but been cut off, a last call from the UK having been received in the early hours. At just after 1800, the local Iraqi commander ordered the senior British warrant officer in charge to collect all his men together, some eighty-five all told, who were then taken to nearby Ahmadi for questioning. More alarming for the women and children left behind, was the replacement shortly afterwards of the well-behaved soldiers of the Republican Guard by second-line, and rougher, troops. The next morning, 4 August, the women learnt that their menfolk were being taken up to Baghdad. In Iraqi military eyes, they were prisoners of war. It did not take long before the occupying troops started looting and 'hot-rodding' cars on the compound. The next day, two of the British women were molested, but fortunately, an Iraqi officer intervened and had the five culprits marched away. News of this soon reached the embassy; the ambassador immediately despatched his commercial officer to the camp. He talked to the women who had been abused and then remained at the camp as sole guardian. His presence ensured that the otherwise unprotected women remained safe, albeit some looting of empty properties persisted. On 6 August, the ambassador went down to Fahaheel to meet the military wives and resolved to have them evacuated to a hotel. As Iraqi troop discipline threatened to break down once more, all of some one hundred women and children were escorted in their cars the next morning from the camp to the International Hotel close to the embassy. The ambassador led the way, accompanied by a strong contingent of Iraqi soldiers. The abruptness of the evacuation caused understandable distress and feelings of vulnerability were exacerbated by Iraqi insistence that all passports should be handed into hotel reception. Whatever the expectation, the ambassador was in no position to do more. None of the passports, in fact, were lost in Kuwait and, had they been, would have been immediately replaced. All the British military dependants were now safe, well-housed and fed, at least for the time being.[254]

Given annexation, however, this could be no more than a short-term solution. During the evening of 13 August, the military wives were briefed on outline plans to have them moved up to Baghdad; they were in general agreement with this, if only in the expectation of being re-united with their spouses. The next day, a large Iraqi delegation turned up at the International Hotel to discuss how the journey might be arranged. The British embassy would organise a convoy of cars to be accompanied by an Iraqi military escort. Some distress was caused that evening by the discovery that several of the family cars had been vandalised and had to be replaced. Further annoyance was aroused by Iraqi refusal to provide coaches for what would be a well over five hundred-kilometre drive across unknown and poorly maintained roads. Most of the drivers would have to be women. At 1800 on 15 August, embassy staff briefed the families at the hotel for the journey planned the next day. They were told to expect a twelve- to fifteen-hour drive and warned to conserve petrol by not using air-conditioning. Water and lunch boxes would be provided; no one was in a position to give assurances about refuelling. There was some elation when it was learnt that a few excitable French passengers from BA149 had been taken up to Baghdad and already released. It was by no means certain that they had been able to leave the country.

The next morning – Thursday 16 August – the families drove their vehicles round to the embassy and formed up on the rough ground in front of the compound. The previous evening, my ambassador had deputed me to assume command of the convoy. At 0800, I introduced myself to the assembled families who had been joined by the Anglican chaplain and his wife and one or two other expatriates. Several members of staff and dependants who were no longer required at post were also to come with us, bringing the total to 105 passengers in twenty-nine cars.

With the ice-cream van doing a roaring trade, including in the sale of (de-hydrating) fizzy drinks, the gathering looked more like preparation for a Sunday-school outing than what I expected to be a potentially treacherous trek across the arid wastes of southern Iraq. Nevertheless, spirits were high amongst a group of people whose lives had been turned upside down and had spent days in uncomfortable limbo. Now, at least, something was happening. The Chaplain offered a prayer; I followed up with a warning about the dangers of de-hydration. I also expressed my fear that before we reached our destination many would have come to hate me.

Spirits were soon dampened. The Iraqi escort failed to appear. My ambassador resolved, therefore, to lead the convoy round to the Iraqi embassy, where he hoped we might meet up with it. After an hour waiting outside the building in the rising morning heat, some military personnel emerged and, at 1000, a twenty-six-hour endurance test began. Things went wrong from the start. We were equipped with two short-range walky-talky radios, one for me at the head of the convoy and one for a trusted embassy colleague in the rearmost vehicle. As we moved into the northern suburbs, I lost contact with the other radio, probably because the long trail of cars exceeded the range of the sets. The last seven cars were adrift before we had left the city. I only learnt later that several had pulled over for a reason I have never been able to confirm.[255] Whatever, it left the phone contact dead and I spent an abortive hour with a helpful Russian second secretary trying to find the missing vehicles.

The long Russian and British convoys then paralleled each other along the broad Kuwaiti highway going north, our military escort assuring me the seven cars would be found. On our way to the border we were passed by dozens of lorries carrying rejoicing, guitar-playing Iraqi troops brandishing the booty they had stolen from the city. The Russians pulled ahead of us and eventually peeled off on the less circuitous western route to Baghdad. My last sighting of them was their refrigerator van belching dark smoke. Given the greater clout Moscow had with Iraq, I was hardly surprised to hear subsequently that they had been allowed to proceed out of the country without let or hindrance.

We arrived at the Safwan border post towards 1400 and were obliged to wait twenty minutes out in the burning sun with temperatures over fifty centigrade. While driving along, we could enjoy air conditioning; this was not possible with the engine turned off. I had a mother with her baby in my car and she became anxious during the periodic stops on the way that the infant would overheat without the air-conditioning running. I turned to the baby's Indian ayah for all the reassurance I needed; the words '*baba tikhai, sahib*' were all this old India hand needed to hear. As we waited, our escort melted away. At last, we were allowed into a large room with insufficient seating. By this time, I could feel the effect of the sun taking its toll after continuous exposure over the best part of eight hours. Fortunately, I was able to find the kitchen, a (hot) water tap and some salt. Anticipating yet another long wait, while the Iraqis decided whether we were to be let into their country, I lay down on the bare concrete floor to conserve energy. An Iraqi official asked me: "How is your health, Mister?" My reply was lost on him. The delay, I was then advised, was caused by Baghdad's failure to arrange hotel accommodation for so large a party. This was not to be the last lie that was sold to us while the Iraqi government decided what it was going to do with the majority of my charges. Much to the surprise of the Iraqi border officials, we launched into 'community' singing, led by the chaplain and his wife.

After nearly two hours' delay we were told to return to our cars. As I did so a smart olive-green uniformed officer introduced himself to me as our new escort's commander. We were about to move off when the missing seven cars drove into the compound. Re-united, the whole convoy was led to the Safwan petrol station, where an incident occurred that did not cover me with credit. In the parking chaos round the pumps, a huge Sudanese lorry bore down on one of the smallest cars of the convoy, threatening to bulldoze it out of the way. In some desperation, I shouted at the driver to move. Unfortunately, the poor woman was at the end of her tether and broke down. "I can't," she exclaimed; it was all too much for her. To no great personal satisfaction, her car remained undamaged and someone else took over the wheel.

All tanked up, we moved on at last and reached the outskirts of Basra at about 1800, still no more than 120 miles into our journey. Here I used up a large amount of official cash to buy bottles of water for all, at an exorbitant price. This expenditure in my account would puzzle the bean-counters a few weeks later. As dusk fell, we moved on to Kut al-Amarah, site of the calamitous British defeat during the First World War. Here, the authorities had arranged for trusted local families to issue iced water. On the way to Kut, the escort commander requested me to hand over all passports since, he contended, it would be easier to get them processed at checkpoints. I demurred, pointing out that they were the property of Her Majesty the Queen, and so I was not in a position to comply. After a short but amicable altercation, we agreed that I should collect in the documents and keep them in my official briefcase.

At 2300, after a particularly bumpy detour, we stopped for more petrol; the many gas guzzlers were taking their toll of our supply, which had included several large jerry cans. The Iraqis paid. During the halt, two of the military wives informed me that their boys were suffering from dehydration. I had earlier noticed the two lads, aged about eleven, knocking back fizzy drinks; they now looked listless. I arranged with my helpful escort commander that they should be checked out at a local hospital, albeit it concerned me that this would separate them from the convoy. I was never able to fathom why the two women smirked at one another, as if they had scored some point or other. Whatever, the boys were able to re-join the convoy later on and recovered.[256] I was also worried that the whole company needed a decent break from driving in the dark. Happily, I was able to persuade our escort of this and, at about midnight, we parked up in the extensive car park of a large hospital for two or three hours. Quite exhausted, I lay down under a statue of Saddam; I did not sleep a wink.

Within an hour or so of restarting our journey, I could hardly keep my eyes open and was in some fear of running off the road. In apparent answer to a desperate prayer, the escort stopped the convoy for a ten-minute break. Not only that, but one of the expatriates who had joined us at the embassy, volunteered to take over the wheel from me. 'Dick' then proceeded to regale me – and keep me awake – with a constant stream of mostly very funny jokes. After one further stop at, for want of a better word, I shall call a 'service' station – towards 0600 – we moved on to Baghdad, reaching the outskirts of the city at about 1000. Here, I had been told, we should have been met by embassy staff who would take over any negotiation at the checkpoint. There was no friendly face to be seen and our escort again disappeared, a look of regret on the face of the escort commander. His men were replaced by a group of thuggish-looking individuals with whom there was little point in reasoning with a rifle butt pushed into one's chest. I was told that the embassy had not sent anyone to meet us. This was a complete lie. Indeed, embassy representatives had driven out earlier to the checkpoint and had been informed that the convoy was not coming. I was then bullied into writing down the names of all in the convoy; the Iraqis took careful note of those who were still diplomatically protected. Just as we were completing these formalities, the two members of the Military Attaché's staff I had met in Kuwait in mid-July turned up, a most welcome relief. Under instruction from the hoary and scruffy Iraqi in charge, they escorted the unprotected military families to the Mansour Melia hotel.[257] I then led the Kuwait embassy migrants to the Baghdad embassy, arriving there at noon. The job done, at least for the time being. Now, it seemed most important to report what had happened and to inform those who had the access – and the diplomatic protection – to do something about it.

It was my first visit to Baghdad; I had no idea what to expect, certainly not the extensive grounds, large enough for a cricket pitch, that met my gaze as we drove through the embassy compound gates. After weeks of tension in Kuwait and the arduous previous twenty-six hours, a cold beer in an air-conditioned conservatory was both beguiling and slightly surreal. I was immediately debriefed by the Military Attaché and delivered my list of all members of the convoy and accounted for those who were now in the hotel. He complimented me on an 'impressive' performance. In wartime stress situations, people smoke. I was no exception and, almost automatically, accepted the issue of two hundred cigarettes which, despite being a non-smoker for many years, I used up during the remainder of my stay in Iraq. An hour or so later, after further debriefings and consultations as well as a tearful call to my wife and eldest daughter – so very happy after gaining 'A' levels and university entrance – the ambassador took me back to his residence. Here I was at last able to crash out until a latish supper. Even as I slept, there was a portent of bad things to come since, that evening, the embassy was refused access to the military families.[258] What was not immediately apparent was a decision taken during the day by the Revolutionary Command Council that all Westerners stranded in Kuwait should be brought up to Iraq and detained at military installations. It took a day or two before the full meaning of the word 'hostage' really sank in. Saddam's ruthlessness was still beyond most Westerners' comprehension.

For anyone enjoying the freedoms of liberal democracy, it is hard to understand how a totally Fascist dictatorship operates or to what extent it will go to achieve its ends. At the beginning of my week in Baghdad in August 1990, I was also somewhat blinded by the satisfaction of having delivered safely all those for whom I had been given responsibility, to the realisation that they, together with their spouses, were now to be incarcerated – not repatriated. Even as the ambassador drove me from his residence to the embassy on Saturday 18 August, the first working day of the Iraqi week, neither of us were fully seized of the sheer outrageousness and affront to the world that Saddam was now to visit on thousands caught up by his megalomania. As the ambassador observed while tuning his little pocket radio into Baghdad Radio's eight o'clock news, it was just not possible to understand what a complete dictatorship was like unless one had actually lived with and experienced it. I was reminded of that when later watching the red-carpet treatment accorded various world leaders in the Iraqi capital as they sought to reason with Saddam. What did Western politicians really understand? The situation at the Mansour Melia hotel certainly, remained far from clear. Glenda Lockwood had still not realised the extent of her predicament, despite the BBC World Service's early use of the word 'hostage'.[259] There was also a mixed message coming from the authorities; in the evening, a number of husbands were re-united with their wives at the hotel. This blunted the embassy's immediate concern, even though consular access was still being withheld.

It was almost as if governments could not really believe what they were seeing and hearing, or that if they did not say too much, Saddam could be persuaded to relent.

In New York, however, the Security Council was impressively abreast of events. Resolution 664 passed unanimously on 18 August stipulated that Iraq should 'permit and facilitate the departure from Kuwait and Iraq of the nationals from third countries' and that consular access to all be granted immediately. It also demanded that Iraq 'rescind its orders for the closure' of missions in Kuwait and for the withdrawal of diplomatic protection for their staff. In just over two weeks since the invasion, Saddam had stirred up a hornets' nest of international indignation which would cement the solidarity of the alliance building against him. For now, however, he seemed to think he was free to do what he liked: he had launched the round-up of Western civilians in Kuwait for their evacuation to Iraq; he had already decided on holding them indefinitely. Faced with an anticipated flood of 'distressed British subjects',[260] the Baghdad embassy was anxious to cut non-essential staff and dependants, including my small posse from Kuwait, and get them out of the country as soon as possible. The next few days, therefore, were spent preparing in reasonable order for another long desert journey, this time west to the Jordanian border. At the same time, the ambassador called repeatedly on the Iraqi Ministry of Foreign Affairs for clarification as to how we might leave the country safely. By 22 August, he had secured a vital single sheet of paper which simply stated that we had authority to leave Iraq. It did not mention names or numbers of those travelling and none of us had a great deal of confidence in how much weight this authorisation would carry with Iraqi officials on the ground. Again, responsibility for this second, if smaller, convoy would rest with me.

At 0200 on Thursday 23 August, the deputy head of mission said farewell to me through the car window. "Don't come back," were his last words. I was supported by the Arabist First Secretary from the embassy who would accompany us as far as the border with Jordan. Apart from one brief stop at a checkpoint, the journey to the immigration/emigration complex at Trebil was uneventful and we reached the vast compound towards 0600. On first arrival it was difficult to make head or tail of what channels or procedures we had to follow. Trebil was awash with people walking aimlessly about, all apparently hoping to get across to Jordan. There was also a great deal of freight traffic coming in from Jordan and clearly breaking sanctions. In this chaos, we could not be confident of being accorded any priority, especially when we heard that an American official convoy had been turned back when trying to get out through Kurdistan and, later, that the French had lost all their vehicles and possessions in a similar attempt.

My Baghdad colleague and I eventually located the office from which exit visas were issued. There, we were received by surly and disinterested officials. I made to hand over our passports in order. My attaché case was taken from me and the fifty or so documents were tipped in a heap on the table. When would they be processed, we asked? "Come back later," was the only advice. There was nothing more we could do there. So, the two of us decided to try our luck with Iraqi customs. In the centre of the complex there was a two-storey brick building, smarter than anything else surrounding it. No one prevented us from entering it and we made our way up to the top floor. At one end of the corridor we knocked on an office door and were admitted to a spacious air-conditioned suite in which the head of customs sat behind his imposing desk. Throughout the next hour or so he could not have been more courteous, given what he must have known of the state of relations between our two countries. To begin with he saw to it that our parched throats were slaked by iced water and then he asked how he might be of assistance. My Arabist colleague led off by explaining our situation; the Iraqi did not appear to speak English. When it seemed that the conversation was running into the sand, I asked my colleague to interpret for me. In English, I related how many years before one of my close kinsmen had been strung up and garrotted in Palestine by members of the Israeli Stern Gang. A photograph of the atrocity and the body of Sergeant Paice had been published in Nigel West's book on British Intelligence since the Second World War. The customs official listened intently, nodded in appreciation and, from then on, agreed to take personal charge of clearing all our possessions and seven of the eight cars in which we were travelling. The eighth car was found to have no papers, so he could hardly be faulted on that account. His bewildered subordinates remonstrated with him, but he swept their objections aside and insisted on the issue of our clearance papers. He accompanied us downstairs and we shook hands on the steps outside the building. As we did so, I said: "I will always remember you." He smiled and replied: "Inshallah." At that moment, it struck me that he had probably understood every word that I had said in his office and that he had chosen to go out on a limb for our sakes. I could only conclude that my apparent readiness to understand Iraqi sensitivities on the subject of Israel had decided him to go out of his way to help us when his colleagues at other customs posts had proved totally obstructive.

With one of two major hurdles crossed, we returned to collect our charges and called again at emigration. By now it must have been mid-afternoon, although it was all too easy to lose sense of time. The previously difficult officials seemed more positive and a smiling man produced a small canvas bag containing about a third of our passports. This seemed at first to be all the Iraqis were ready or prepared to return. The look on the official's face told me otherwise; they were playing with me, possibly baiting me. I played along. Taking each passport individually, I called out the holder's name, handed it over and motioned for him or her to move to one side. At the end of this charade, I turned to the official, who, still beaming, produced a second batch. I repeated the process, after which a third and final batch was brought out. Sure enough, when I handed out the final passport, my own document was missing. I turned, still smiling, to the official, who giggled and produced my passport complete with the vital, if smudged, exit visa stamped inside. At this, I called on my party to give three rousing cheers for the Iraqi Immigration Service. The Iraqis smiled back in appreciation. How to make friends and influence people. Not by losing one's rag or acting pompously when you don't have a leg to stand on.

Our seven drivers and their passengers were now issued with little pink tickets to show that we were permitted to approach the border fence and final checkpoint. As we drove forward we could see a hundred yards or so beyond the fence an air-conditioned bus that had been sent up by the Amman embassy to collect the long-suffering women and children. I was even able to step over the fence and go over to speak to an old colleague I recognised. When I returned back over the picket wire, I found that there were still problems. We had been pulled over to make way for a long train of articulated lorries coming from the opposite direction. The stream seemed interminable, its length obscured by clouds of dust and approaching dusk. These were supplies for a now sanctions-ridden state that had no reason whatsoever to offer us any favours. There was also the presence of an olive-green uniformed official who wanted to know our business and to see our papers. I thought I recognised the uniform. My suspicions were soon confirmed: he was from the Mukhabarat. When shown the much-thumbed authority from the Ministry of Foreign Affairs, he merely commented: "My office has not been consulted." He was about to walk away when he noticed one of the women in our party taking a photo. He shouted out angrily, snatched the camera and dashed it to the ground, spilling the film. My Arabist colleague went at him, but the Iraqi had no need or intention of listening. He turned on his heel and walked away. I followed him and put my arm around his shoulders. I apologised for the woman's stupidity and then excused my colleague, explaining that he had been a very long time in the sun and was not used to it. It had affected his behaviour. Still with my arm round the man, I said that we really needed his help since, among other problems, we had a small baby – in my car; she was dying.

My pleas were then reinforced with the timely appearance of a tall colonel in military sand-khaki who came over to see what was going on. He inspected the MFA document, spoke to olive-green and nodded to me. Olive-green walked away, disgruntled but obviously either outranked or outflanked. The colonel bent over me with an assurance that all was well. It was, however, to be another hour or more of waiting for clearance through the gate. One of my passengers sat crying over and again: "It's no use, we are never going to get out." It was becoming increasingly difficult to settle her down, as much because – as I had felt continuously since 2 August – I could not see how indeed we would be able to get out. It was getting dark; when did the border gate close? Would we be here all night? What would become of the small baby? In the end I could take it no more. I excused myself from the car and walked behind an outhouse, where I knelt down. It was a simple cry of desperation. "God help me [not us – but me]!" Pulling myself together, I returned to the car and almost at once we were waved through the gate, my vehicle the last in the queue. On my return to London, I was asked by a well-meaning personnel officer how I had managed it. "I had a lot of help from God," I answered, quite sincerely. "Ah yes," he said, "an inner strength." I did not contest this. What was the point! Good man though I knew him to be, he had not been there, so how would he know?

We crossed the border finally at 2015 and disgorged passengers onto the bus. Having wolfed down several refrigerated sandwiches – the ham was the best – the first food since the previous evening, I led the seven remaining cars on the start of the still twelve-hour journey to Amman. There were yet some two hundred or more kilometres to cover and a long wait at the Jordanian border post. We drove in pitch-black conditions, occasionally pierced at the side of the road by a Jordanian Army machine-gun nest faintly illuminated by an oil lamp. As we drove along a British camera team blinded us as they tried to film the convoy. I was rather less polite to their young presenter – still active today – than I had been towards my recent Iraqi interlocutors. The conditions, however, no longer worried me. I (we) was free after weeks when the light at the end of the tunnel was very faint, if non-existent. Indeed, until the BA flight was heading west along the Mediterranean two days later taking us back to London, my fear of somehow being intercepted remained.

Fourteen

LIBERATION AND IMMEDIATE AFTERMATH

I spent two nights with my colleague in Amman, recovering during the day but my dreams invaded by nightmares of driving along endless roadways. These flashbacks lingered for a few weeks afterwards but then evaporated. I cannot pretend that it was a serious symptom of post-traumatic stress disorder. On Sunday 26 August, British Airways off-loaded us at a closed-off area well away from Heathrow terminals. Before being allowed to alight, MOD officials checked us out; it gave me the opportunity to sound off about the plight of the British military trainers and their families, which I blamed on a lack of diplomatic status. I was indulged and let off the plane to meet my wife, who had been allowed airside, along with the loved ones of others in our party.

Back home and after a barbecue on that late summer sunny afternoon, I received a phone call from my line manager welcoming me back. Had I, he asked, escaped, or been let out? With hindsight, I might have answered that the situation had been rather more complicated than a simple either/or. Instead, I said truthfully that, ultimately, the Iraqis had let us go. A slightly bizarre call followed from a senior official who seemed more concerned about a suspected suitcase bomb that had arrived on our flight than congratulating me on my safe return. It was ticking. In the event, it was found to be a clock belonging to one of the women from the Baghdad embassy. On reflection, I could understand that his concern was symptomatic of extreme uneasiness about the possible fall-out from what was happening in the Middle East. Apart from the divisions caused by the Kuwait Crisis, deaths during the *Intifada* on the West Bank were still creating a lust for revenge. Bombs might go off anywhere at any time against soft targets. An ironic contrast to the complacency of just a month before.

I reported in to the office the next day and was debriefed in what I considered at the time in an uninformed and cursory manner. I received a number of plaudits and complimentary comments from colleagues and learnt that I had been dubbed 'percipient' at a large briefing meeting. Before the morning was out, I was sent on two weeks' gardening leave. Within a day or so, however, I was asked to return and to take over an Iraq assessments desk. Down to just after Christmas, I remained a member of a team receiving and processing reports on the crisis coming in from all over the world. In the New Year, I was reassigned to another Middle Eastern desk job. There was never any discussion as to whether I should return to Kuwait after its liberation. What follows now is a broad brush of my impressions of how the British government and its agencies handled the lead-up to the eviction of Saddam's forces from the Emirate.

Ironically, this part of my account is being written during the Covid-19 lockdown, a major threat which crept up on the British government in a not so dissimilar way to Saddam's invasion of Kuwait. Just as officials flew off for their summer leave in 1990, so the Prime Minister in early 2020 missed important COBRA meetings on the eve of a pandemic. Measures to reduce the rate of infection were too little too late, just as they had been in the weeks before Saddam sent in his troops. In both crises all the signs were evident but London – and Washington – remained at sixes and sevens: senior officials who should have known better denied that anything really serious was going to happen. The catastrophic legacy of Covid-19 has yet to be experienced; the damage that has resulted from the Kuwait invasion remains with us today.

It is perhaps surprising that there was no call for any inquiry after the Kuwait Crisis. That had certainly been the case shortly after the conclusion of the campaign to eject the Argentines from the Falkland Islands in 1982.[261] There was no such inquest in 1991, partly, I believe, because so many sections of government had failed. Lord Carrington had fallen on his sword in 1982. There was no one to do so in 1990–91; Margaret Thatcher had already gone, for completely different reasons. Yet, on the eve of the Iraqi invasion, there had been a complete failure in assessment by the Foreign and Commonwealth Office, the Cabinet Office and Ministers, not to mention Intelligence. The pointers had all been there but had been incorrectly assessed or ignored. Despite this, there was no public pressure for an inquiry and certainly not from the Fourth Estate. Why? For the simple reason that the Western press as a whole had also been totally wrong-footed and in the days before Saddam's walk-in were covering at least three other headline catchers around the world. In the West Indies, on the West Coast of Africa and in Moscow, press interest was diverted from the main event coming around the corner.

The events are hardly memorable now: an attempted coup by a militant Islamic entity in Trinidad and Tobago on 27 July grabbed the British newspapers' attention – as seedy Commonwealth matters always do – and required an immediate response from the Royal Navy. Rebels close to taking over America's client state of Liberia required the intervention of two thousand US marines and six warships over the same period. In Europe, Hungary had just withdrawn from the Warsaw Pact. This last event was a scene-changer in international relations and the balance of power. It was accompanied by Boris Yeltsin's resignation[262] from the Communist Party of the Soviet Union on 12 July; assessors everywhere were struggling to come to terms with the fact that the Soviet Union was going into meltdown, inducing major and heartening progress in superpower détente. When it came to the last flight for Kuwait – BA149 – there may have been 'squaddies' on board but no representatives from the British press. With one exception: a Middle East correspondent for the *Financial Times* played a hunch and travelled east when all his colleagues had chosen to go elsewhere. Not even the ubiquitous John Simpson joined him, which was probably just as well since, possibly because they had scanned the BA149 manifest, Iraqi intelligence were out to catch the *FT* man. Tipped off about Iraqi intentions I was able to warn him that he was being hunted and to advise him to get out over the

Saudi border double-quick. This he did. There was, therefore, no one to tell the public: "We told you so!"

During my early weeks back in London, I became increasingly frustrated at the seemingly slow pace of the preparations for the expulsion of Saddam from Kuwait. At one meeting of senior officers to which I was invited by virtue of my recent experience, my view that Iraqi forces should be ousted as early as possible, surely by mid-October, was received with mild amusement. My admittedly subjective reasoning was that the longer Saddam was able to dig in, the more difficult it would be to dislodge him. What had been missing, hitherto, had been a sharper cutting edge to the series of UN resolutions. After all, the USS *Wisconsin*, a battleship armed to the teeth with Tomahawk smart missiles, had been cruising off the Saudi coast since 24 August; she could surely put the fear of God up Iraqi troops exposed and vulnerable in the desert. American aircraft carriers were entering the Gulf and Anglo/American submarine strength, invulnerable to anything the Iraqis might have had to detect them, was lurking within easy range of many juicy targets.

There were, of course, a number of factors which were determining the pace of the Coalition build-up. The United States, in particular, had a real fear of Iraqi missiles, especially the Russian SCUD mounted on mobile and easily disguised launchers. They could fire and disappear. Both Tel Aviv and Riyadh were at hazard from them. Had not Saddam threatened to turn Kuwait into a grave? He had WMD and had demonstrated that he was not slow to use them. The fear of them was real. As troops went out to join the international army assembling in the Saudi desert, they were given a cocktail of anti-nerve-gas shots. This was very much belt and braces and, in the end, probably did far more harm than good. A former colleague of mine stationed in Riyadh told me some years later that he had never felt well since receiving the injections. Again, the United States failed to read the riot act; if Secretary of State Baker could threaten Tariq Aziz in early 1991 with a massive response to any use of WMD, why was this threat not wheeled out earlier? In the event, Saddam never used them, knowing full well that he would have been obliterated if he had. There was, however, still a lobby in Washington that believed Saddam could be saved for better days in the future and that Iraq must not be broken entirely, to Iran's advantage. Thus, British officials serving in the Middle East were issued with full suits of protective clothing and one or two of them sat in their offices wearing them, much to our irreverent amusement in London.

Saddam had one major card up his sleeve and one that military threats and tough sanctions could not out-trump. Apart from the British military personnel and the stranded BA passengers, there were steadily increasing numbers of expatriates being deported from Kuwait to Iraq to be placed in what was to become known as a human shield. Glenda Lockwood, the senior NCO's wife, was already being held at an Iraqi chemical plant on 26 August. The Iraqi leader, however, proved to be not quite so ruthless as many were coming to expect. In the wake of some highly damaging publicity worldwide, two days later, he conceded the release of all foreign women and children from Iraq and Kuwait. His big mistake was that he indulged his liking for parading himself before a crowd, in order to receive their acclamation. He thought that the detainees were ready to speak against their governments. Just as people living in a democracy are unable to understand what it is like to live under a dictatorship, so a dictator, for all that he may despise a liberal society, cannot foresee public outrage that it is impossible to suppress. Thus, when the television screens throughout the world relayed an Iraqi news item on 23 August portraying Saddam towering over a young boy held in a military camp and patting him on the head, the effect was quite the opposite of what he had intended. The release of women and children reduced the brutality of his profile and offered some prospect of undermining the growing cohesion of opinion against him.

The British families were transferred back to the Mansour Melia hotel pending their return to London on 1 September, exclusively on Iraqi Airways. Right to the end, however, they were kept on tenterhooks by Saddam's exploitation of the positive publicity he thought he could gain by attracting in world celebrities to his Baghdad palace. Jesse Jackson, the American Baptist minister, renowned Civil Rights campaigner and Democratic Party activist, had just managed to get into Kuwait under

Iraqi auspices and now arrived at Baghdad Airport to be present at the departure of the women and children. A delay in his appearance meant that they had to wait eight hours. To make a further point, the British and Americans had to go to the back of the queue. They were the last to leave on an Iraqi Airways jumbo with Jackson sitting up front in first class. One of the many dichotomies in what would become a long-running saga of negotiation for the release of all the other foreign hostages. The British families' arrival at Heathrow was not until the early hours of 2 September, timed by the Iraqis to reduce exposure to negative publicity. In the days that followed, many British women and children living in Kuwait were brought up to Baghdad for evacuation home by air. They rode in buses hired by the British embassy in Kuwait, now reduced to four male staff and, since 24 August, no longer enjoying diplomatic privilege.

The release of so many hostages in just a week since their incarceration still left Saddam with a formidable card in his hand. Besides hundreds of men he still held, there were women who had refused to leave their spouses, including our Anglican chaplain's wife. Her husband continued to minister to his imprisoned flock in the months to come, occasionally being able to officiate at St George's Church in Baghdad. Saddam could argue that he was only holding on to the able-bodied, pending a peaceful resolution of various aspects of what he considered were interrelated Middle East conflicts. On 29 August, he agreed a proposal with Yasir Arafat of the PLO that all foreign troops should be withdrawn from Kuwait and Saudi Arabia, to be replaced by 'Arab and international forces from the region'. This was aimed directly at the Arab streets[263] and had strong support from several pro-Iraq states in the Middle East. Nevertheless, it cut no ice with the two superpowers or with other major supporters of the Coalition now being masterminded by Secretary of State Baker, including both Egypt and Syria. A poorly attended meeting of Arab League foreign ministers on 31 August simply produced another resolution calling for Iraq's withdrawal. Within a few days, its Secretary-General, Chedli Klibi of Tunisia, had been forced to resign after Saudi accusations that he had not cracked the anti-Saddam whip sufficiently. Saddam had lost any prospect of winning over moderate Arab opinion.

If he believed he could divide the superpowers, Saddam underestimated the strength of the détente tide. He was expected to visit Moscow on 3 September, but Gorbachev refused to see him. Instead, the Russian leader received Tariq Aziz two days later when 'considerable differences' were acknowledged. The next day, the Russian Foreign Ministry spokesman rejected any 'linkage' between an Iraqi withdrawal and other Middle East issues. Saddam returned to the offensive, calling on the Saudi and Egyptian peoples to rise up and overthrow their governments. The fear of his influence and the extent of his reach, exercised through his agencies abroad, increased with the sudden and mysterious death in London of Colonel Salim Fakhri, the head of the oppositionist Democratic Rescue Movement. By mid-September, the Iraqi leader had reverted to defiance: he would not pull out of Kuwait 'under any circumstances' and urged the Soviet Union not to give in to American demands. His warning had already been countered by Bush and Gorbachev meeting in Helsinki at very short notice. Their joint statement on 9 September had said it all: "We are united in the belief that Iraq's aggression must not be tolerated. No peaceful international order is possible if larger states devour their smaller neighbours." The two leaders agreed to consider additional steps in line with the UN Charter, if Iraq failed to comply. If the Russians remained cautious, it was because they still had 150 military advisers in Iraq, albeit they would soon be leaving as their contracts expired. There were thousands more still at large in Iraq working on various projects.

The end could be agreed by many and, indeed, many had given or promised material support. How the end should be achieved, however, met with different shades of opinion, but there was only one country that could physically remove Saddam from Kuwait. The Iraqi leader had a point when he contended that the American people would not accept large numbers of casualties. He was, of course, harking back to their defeat in the Vietnam War and what he believed to be war weariness. In addition, he was thinking of Washington's latent isolationism. In Europe, too, there were reservations. Fortunately, James Baker appreciated that he had to play his hand with sensitivity. On 9 September, he met NATO foreign ministers in Brussels and called for 'responsible sharing' not only in the transport of troops to the theatre but in the committal of forces, however symbolic. His first concern was to create the image in the world's eyes of a grand coalition and, in Europe, he had to tread carefully. While the UK was quick to promise troops,[264] on the Continent, there was a majority reluctant to take up swords. On 12 September, the European Parliament passed a resolution by three hundred to seventy, with nineteen abstentions, stating that only a diplomatic solution could put an end to the crisis; it called for a European summit to find that solution.

Saddam should have been able to exploit this disarray; instead, he allowed his troops in Kuwait to adopt strongarm tactics against foreign missions in Kuwait. The day after the European Parliament vote, Iraqi soldiers entered the Dutch embassy and, on the 14th, compounded the felony by sacking the French ambassador's residence. Not content with that, the Canadian, Belgian and French missions were all violated, and several consuls, including the Irish, Australian and American, were detained. The Iraqis were looking for more hostages to take, but in doing so, they hardened those countries that usually took a moderate line in international relations to the stark reality of the Saddam phenomenon. From then on, France was no longer a member of the awkward squad and when the fighting stopped at the end of the following February, it was the French echelons that had advanced the furthest. On 15 September, Paris announced preparations to despatch four thousand troops with tanks, helicopters and thirty fighter aircraft.[265] No fewer than forty Iraqi diplomatic staff in Paris were shown the door. All those European countries that had suffered the abuse of Saddam's forces now threw in ground force commitments of one sort or another. Baker had achieved his first goal; any eventual campaign against Saddam would not just be an American show.

The Arabs remained split, but Saddam had yet to mobilise the streets sufficiently for the major players to be deterred from opposing him. Syrian and Egyptian troops had already tramped proudly down the ramps of C130 aircraft onto Saudi soil and, during the rest of the month, their governments added to their commitments. They constrained the influence, too, of the minority of Arab countries that still supported

Saddam. During an emergency session in Cairo on 10 September of the Arab League Council, boycotted by nine of the twenty-one members, it was agreed that its administration would be almost completely transferred from Tunisia to Cairo, thus distancing it from Arafat's PLO headquarters in Tunis. From now on, Mubarak of Egypt and, to a lesser extent, Assad of Syria, would call the Arab shots. I well remember meeting the head of Syrian Air Force Intelligence in London who, having heard of my recent experiences, protested what retribution he would make if one hair on my head were harmed by an Iraqi assassin!

On the same day that the UK committed a substantial force in support of its old ally, President Bush issued a key statement of US policy towards the crisis. Drawing on the precedent of his predecessor Roosevelt's launch of the United Nations during the middle of the Second World War, he declared a further objective that should emerge from the struggle with Saddam – 'a new world order'. This, he said, was the 'vision which I shared with President Gorbachev in Helsinki'. These were brave words for, like the situation on New Year's Day 1942, Hitler had still to be tracked to his Berlin bomb shelter.[266] Although the new American generalissimo, 'Storming' Norman Schwarzkopf,[267] now had nearly 150,000 US forces in theatre and various arrivals from several countries, he was quick to dampen speculation about an offensive into Kuwait in mid-October. As of 13 September, he was arguing for at least another two months in order to bring up to sufficient strength the force he judged necessary to remove the Iraqis. Back in the Pentagon, there were still those who considered a major ground offensive unnecessary. US Air Force General Michael Dugan was dismissed on the 17th for telling the press that, in the event of war with Iraq, his aircraft would bomb Baghdad and target Saddam specifically. He saw massive bombardment and regime decapitation as the only way to force the Iraqis out of Kuwait. This ran counter to those who still saw Saddam as a buffer to the religious madmen in Tehran.

The deployment of such a multifarious force to Saudi Arabia brought with it problems beyond purely military considerations. As the Protector of Islam's Holy Places, King Fahd was in much danger of over-extending his credit with the influential Wahhabist forces in his country that continued to dictate total abstention from alcohol, widescale limits on female freedom completely alien to the West and the banning of any non-Islamic religious observation. They viewed with increasing resentment the pouring in of hundreds of thousands of troops along with their chaplains, not only those of Christian persuasion. Much against the grain, diplomatic and military negotiators were compelled to accept that the wearing of a crucifix and dog collar had to be forbidden. This was easily understood by anyone who had smuggled a Bible into Riyadh or had taken part in a Communion service behind closed doors and, for safety's sake, preferably within diplomatic premises. This self-discipline in normal times was never going to be enough. It aroused much resentment on both sides of the religious divide, but nowhere near as much as in the mind of a young and wealthy Wahhabist, Osama bin Laden. From the autumn of 1990, the seed was sown for a bitter terrorist campaign that ultimately produced a series of devastating attacks spear-headed by his Al-Qaeda followers. These culminated in the destruction of the Twin Towers in New York and severe damage to the Pentagon in September 2001, exactly eleven years after the arrival of Coalition forces in Saudi Arabia.

The Coalition continued to suffer from intermittent strains. In the UK, the tabloid press aired reservations about the eventual command structure. A British general with only a brigade or, at most, a division could hardly act independently from an American, commanding two or more army corps at least ten times the size. Interestingly, the MOD tactic was to appoint an Air Chief Marshal, Sir Patrick Hine, as joint commander of all British forces involved in theatre, thus diluting any dispute over who should lead troops on the ground when the shooting started. The best kind of product from the old grammar school system with no latent public-school arrogance to put off Americans, 'Paddy' could hold his own with the top brass in the Pentagon and in the desert.[268] Together with Lieutenant General Sir Mike Rose, Thatcher's favourite soldier after his successful career with the SAS, they retained the respect of servicemen on the front line and desks well behind.

More difficult, perhaps, was the way in which the French would sublimate themselves to an integrated Coalition command. Here, Saddam was rather more adept at muddying the water. On 23 September, he repeated his position that the annexation of Kuwait was irreversible but added that the only basis for a peace initiative was the inclusion of an Israeli withdrawal from all occupied territories. Paris was always going to be more diffident about Israel than Washington. Saddam spoke as the French aircraft carrier *Clemenceau* unloaded five hundred troops and forty-two helicopters at the Saudi port of Yanbu. Before the UN General Assembly, the next day, President Mitterrand condemned Saddam strongly and voiced his disgust at his use of human shields. To Baghdad's delight, however, he added that the release of hostages and a promise to withdraw troops would make 'everything become possible'. In Coalition terms, the French President's four-point plan[269] was sound enough, but he had offered a chink which Saddam would seek to exploit down to the last week before hostilities began. Meanwhile, his forces continued to dig themselves in. The same day, nevertheless, Saddam riposted by demanding that President Bush be put on trial for war crimes against the Palestinians, cooperation with Zionists and for killings on his back doorstep in Panama and Grenada. The UN Security Council responded on 25 September by passing Resolution 670 – by fourteen votes to one (Cuba) – imposing an air embargo on Iraq. Better still, Shevardnadze, as current president of the Council, depicted the invasion of Kuwait as an 'act of terror against a nascent new world order'. He could support the use of force within UN auspices, if the Iraqi occupation continued.

During the following weeks, while the military build-up grew, the hostage issue was never out of the headlines. Saddam started the pot boiling in a broadcast aimed at the American people on 26 September. Claiming that two hundred million Arabs supported him, he insisted that Iraq was holding foreigners 'to give all parties concerned time to think' and for dialogue. James Baker had just received a letter from Baghdad with the threat that anyone found sheltering in the American embassy – without diplomatic protection – would be hanged. Recognising the potential power of the Arab streets and, essentially, a reluctant warrior, Foreign Secretary Douglas Hurd sketched out ideas on 4 October for an Iraqi withdrawal which would then be followed by a peace conference on the Middle East, to include the five UN Security Council permanent representatives. Meanwhile, Saddam was letting it be known to both those still in hiding or already held captive that he would release all hostages, if he were given sufficient assurances that he would not be attacked. Still holding out in the Kuwait embassy, the British ambassador received a number of phone calls, doubtless intercepted and located, from expatriates still at large and suffering increasingly from privation and uncertainty, urging him to press for just such a guarantee.

On 12 October, Saddam achieved a minor coup. That was the day that he was first able to receive the former British Prime Minister Edward Heath at his Baghdad palace. Heath was one of several prominent, yet out of office, politicians who used up capital to tread a softer line in the hope that they might influence the Iraqi leader to compromise. One or two, like Tony Wedgewood-Benn a month or so later, came close to acting as apologists for Saddam, something he would have relished. Heath, at least, was on a specific and humane mission. Working closely with FCO consular records, he visited Baghdad again on 21 October and handed Saddam a list of British hostages whose age or infirmity commended them for early repatriation. Heath's visit was also linked to medical supply flights organised by Richard Branson, who had added a plea for the release of sick hostages. Two days later, Heath was still in the Iraqi capital to observe the exit of thirty-three ailing Brits who had been on his list presented to Saddam. In a blatant attempt to drive a wedge, Saddam announced the same day that all French hostages would be released. Seven days later, 267 French hostages were flown to Paris from Baghdad. Accordingly, the seven-strong French embassy in Kuwait was closed, leaving the American and British missions the only diplomatic presence left in the Emirate.

Heath's efforts had met with mixed results. Yes, he had achieved the return to Gatwick of forty nationals all told, including two children, several women and elderly or sick men. Sadly, there were also casualties. Two teenage brothers sheltering in my Mishref residence were tragically injured, one mortally, in a car accident at a Kuwait ring road intersection where the Iraqis had plundered the traffic lights. There were strong indications that the dead boy might have been saved, had Iraqi Intelligence not been more concerned to find out where his father, a senior military officer, was still in hiding. The effect the accident and death had on Heath was evident from his countenance at the subsequent funeral at Worth Abbey he had the grace to attend.

Others, too, had been working hard to persuade Saddam to release their nationals. Moscow's special envoy, the ubiquitous Yevgeny Primakov,[270] flew from capital to capital, apparently in search of a peaceful solution, before arriving back in Baghdad on 28 October to meet Saddam. His one success was to extract a promise that the well over a thousand Russians left in Iraq should be allowed to return to the Soviet Union in the following weeks. In parallel, Gorbachev was in Paris suggesting that his emissary had discovered some flexibility in the Iraqi leader's position; it was 'not the same as before'. This gave encouragement to those – Westerners and Arabs alike – who still argued that an international peace conference on the Middle East should take place soon after an Iraqi withdrawal. They were to be immediately disappointed; Saddam had no intention of changing his position, only to spread confusion in Coalition ranks. Meanwhile, more and more British and American expatriates hiding in Kuwait were being discovered or were having to give themselves up. One can only survive so long in an air-conditioning conduit.

November opened with the resignation of Sir Geoffrey Howe as Chancellor of the Exchequer. The one-time sheep-like loyalist had finally lost patience with the Iron Lady; within days, Margaret Thatcher had been forced out of office. This would have given Saddam some encouragement, but John Major's takeover changed little in British policy towards the crisis. The following day – 2 November – there was news that all Germans and Italians were to be released, thanks to the impending visit to Baghdad of the former West German Chancellor Willi Brandt. Five days later, he secured the return of over one hundred Germans and seventy Italians. Some British hostages were suddenly given the opportunity to phone their loved ones and others were kitted out in new suits. There were signs that the Iraqi government was beginning to count the cost of poor publicity in holding so many foreigners in the face of united international outrage.

Saddam also knew the pressure individuals could bring to bear on their families back home and, in turn, anticipated how the latter would form a lobby against politicians at Westminster, especially during a leadership crisis.

The same might have been true amongst Americans. On 6 November, the mid-term US elections gave the Democrats improved majorities in both Houses of Congress. If Saddam had thought this result might reduce resolve, he was much mistaken. With the election campaign out of the way, President Bush was left free to pile on the pressure. American troop strength was now to be doubled with the inclusion of a whole armoured corps (three tank divisions) from Germany and another marine division, accompanied by three more aircraft carriers. It was at this point that an outflanking 'left hook' tactic against north-west Kuwait was being devised, rather than a frontal attack on Saddam's dug-in tanks. By early January, thirty-four per cent of the US Army's total strength, some four hundred thousand was to be deployed to Saudi Arabia.[271] In Baghdad, the Iraqi leader must have come to realise at last that Washington meant business. He looked around for other cards to play. On 14 November, he welcomed the Iranian Foreign Minister, Velayati, to his palace, the first senior government official from Tehran since the 1979 Khomeini Revolution. Apart from some progress in the prisoner-of-war exchange process, Velayati's prime purpose in making the visit, Saddam received scant reason to hope for Iranian solidarity with him against the huge international armada building in the Gulf. Tehran, too, wanted to see the back of the Iraqi leadership, however much it hated Washington.

Four days later, the Revolutionary Command Council announced Iraq's intention to release all hostages, starting on Christmas Day. All might return home over a three-month period, provided nothing happened to 'disrupt the climate of peace'. At the same time, an Iraqi Airways plane was sent to London to pick up 133 people, mostly women, so that they might visit partners and parents. This was no more than a plucking of heartstrings; any apparent Iraqi change of heart was no more than disingenuity. Three months' grace, in fact, drove timing for the onset of any Coalition campaign past the cool weather.

Nevertheless, the fact that the Iraqi leadership had mentioned a readiness to release all hostages was indicative of a degree of panic. Sanctions were clearly biting. Cereal hoarders were being hanged. Iraqi troops in Kuwait were half-starved; the supply of cart-loads of water-melons seen in the Kuwait streets in August had long since disappeared. There were strong rumours of unrest in Baghdad and elsewhere. In contrast, President Bush was visiting his troops for Thanksgiving and calling on his principal supporters in the Middle East, King Fahd and President Mubarak. There was no sign of a fault line in the Coalition thanks to his Secretary of State's constant oiling of the wheels. The day that Margaret Thatcher was pushed out of office, President Bush heard the announcement of the additional British deployment of 4 Armoured Brigade, the old 'Desert Rat' unit of Second World War fame. Seizing on this fresh reinforcement, Bush exclaimed triumphantly on television that 'the Rats' are coming out to the Saudi desert.[272] During the War, they had been assigned to 7 Armoured Division in the Western Desert and fought at Alamein.

On 28 November, the left-wing Labour Party maverick Tony Wedgewood Benn arrived in Baghdad, the last prominent British politician the Iraqi leader was to receive. Benn's visit coincided with the passing of the key UN Security Council resolution 678 which authorised the use of force 'by all necessary means'; it was unopposed. It was the first such resolution since 27 June 1950 when the Security Council had agreed to defend South Korea, on that occasion in the absence of the Soviet representative. This, rather than any eloquence from Benn, convinced Saddam that he had to make some dramatic gesture to win back at least some of his ailing international support. Even Cuba and Yemen had deserted him at the Security Council, so that the US was able to shelve the Middle East peace conference proposition. Closer to home, his governor in Kuwait and successor to 'Chemical' Ali, who was needed back in Baghdad, had just been killed by Kuwaiti Resistance. More importantly, Yasir Arafat had called on Saddam to convince him that he could only hope to defuse American intent to use force by releasing all hostages at once. After the usual glitches where Iraqi officialdom was concerned, most British nationals held in Iraq and Kuwait were back in the UK by the beginning of the second week in December, although doubts remained over the fate of about one thousand foreigners who had chosen to stay in the Emirate for one reason or another. Whatever, Saddam had thrown away his last trump card.[273] There is no way that the Coalition could have initiated hostilities with well over five thousand hostages still in Saddam's grasp.

The Iraqi leader's gambit gained him little time; it was followed by President Bush's refusal to see Tariq Aziz in Washington on 18 December. The increasingly isolated Iraqi Foreign Minister was receiving the same kind of diplomatic medicine his colleagues had meted out to Western missions the previous August. In the end, Aziz was only seen by James Baker on 9 January when the message he received was grim, with no concessions whatsoever. General Schwarzkopf had already announced – on 29 December – that H-hour (170300) would commence only twenty-four hours after the expiry of the ultimatum for Iraqi withdrawal from Kuwait. The delay in the date set – 15 January – was the price the Americans had had to pay to obtain Cuban and Yemen agreement not to insist on a Palestine peace conference before Saddam's expulsion. Apart from getting through the Christmas break, it afforded Western governments the opportunity to pull out their remaining diplomatic representatives in Baghdad, among them my host in August, Hooky Walker, who was able to get back to the UK in time to give away his daughter at her wedding after all. Iraq broke diplomatic relations with the US and UK on 9 January. Even at this late stage, however, James Baker was assuring Tariq Aziz that Washington had no wish to remove Saddam from power. There was still support for the 'bad' versus the 'mad'.

There were several last-minute attempts to persuade the Iraqi leader to withdraw, in return for imprecise promises of international peace negotiations. Arafat declared the day before the ultimatum expired that 'Palestine and Iraq are standing in the same trench to regain Arab rights'. If Saddam thought the streets would finally rise up, he was once again seriously deluded; Arafat's words were never backed by any substantive action. Moreover, despite much Iraqi provocation through indiscriminate firing of missiles towards Israel, Baker was able to keep that particular red flag from being waved in the ensuing conflict. It is not my intention, or within my competence, to provide a detailed assessment of the campaign that sent Iraqi troops scuttling back over the border. I must, however, admit to delighted relief at seeing on television from about 2200 on 16 January (0300 Saudi time) the spectacular fireworks display that was the Coalition's opening air salvo on Iraqi ministries, vital installations, bridges and the elite Republican Guard. The air campaign continued until 24 February, when, at 0400 local time, two American marine divisions stormed across the frontier sand berm and headed for Kuwait City. They met little determined resistance from the second-line, mostly Shia, troops Saddam had deliberately placed in the front line while pulling back his Sunni Republican Guard into Iraq. The one area of intense fighting was around Kuwait International Airport, where a wrecked BA149 still stood.

Little over three days after the onset of the Coalition offensive, Saddam issued a general order to retreat, but not before he called on certain units to set the oil fields ablaze in North Kuwait. Television pictures caught the sight of a disgusted tank officer blasting at a large hoarding near Basra displaying his leader's face. Schwarzkopf ensured that Kuwait and other Arab troops headed the entry into Kuwait City, the vanguard arriving at 0900. In the short and unequal struggle, the Coalition suffered about eleven hundred casualties, while the Iraqi Army lost anything between thirty thousand and 150,000 dead and wounded, along with thousands of military vehicles. Given the ease and speed of the victory, one is entitled to question why an earlier assault had not been launched. The belt and braces policy, however, proved a complete success.

What followed was not. It is said that President Bush wanted to wind up the military campaign within one hundred hours. And so, he did on 28 February. A year or so later, Douglas Hurd wrote that the fighting could not have been continued since the Royal Air Force did not feel it morally right to continue strafing defenceless Iraqi convoys of every type of military vehicle struggling up the Mutla Ridge towards the border. Hurd could not have read Clausewitz, one of whose main maxims was that victory must be followed through by routing a defeated enemy. Clearly, too, his statement was that of a politician who did not understand the temperament of pilots who had spent weeks hazarding their lives in the face of tough anti-aircraft resistance, had taken losses and watched the ill-treatment of captured comrades. Squeamishness ill becomes senior politicians who then have to get armistice terms right and, equally important, ensure they are enforced against the threat of a return to hostilities, if they are not. In the event, Coalition negotiators did neither.

There were, however, considerations, other than a president's simple reputation. During the middle of the afternoon on 27 February, President Bush held a meeting in the Oval Office to discuss the situation on the ground. It was shortly after the last effective Iraqi unit, a brigade of the Republican Guard Medinah division, had been destroyed in a forty-minute tank battle in which old generation Soviet T-55s were knocked out in droves by superior American technology. Informed by the latest almost too optimistic reports from Schwarzkopf, the Chairman of the Joint Chiefs of Staff, General Colin Powell argued that all Iraqi military formations were no longer operational. This was incorrect: three Republican Guard divisions – the Adnan, Nebuchadnezzar and Al-Faw – had escaped intact, along with two other armoured divisions. Many other units were still combat effective and were ready to fight again. The bulk of Iraqi losses had been suffered by second-line troops. The American ground forces commander, General Yeosock, asked for at least one more day to complete the task. The head of the US Air Force, General Tony McPeak, pleaded for two or three more days of air strikes. Despite this, in the Oval Office, Bush called for a cessation of all operations. This came into effect from 0800 on Thursday 28 February, Saudi time. Word had meanwhile been received at the United Nations that Iraq was suing for peace and was ready to agree to Coalition demands. Saddam was immediately relieved to learn that these did not include his removal from power, or any retribution against his person. Fighting did not stop immediately. The next day, the ceasefire collapsed for seven hours as the Hammurabi Republican Guard attempted to escape; it lost six hundred vehicles in the attempt.

Armistice negotiations opened almost immediately: on 3 March, at the Safwan Iraqi air base close to the border crossing where we had been obliged to wait on the invaders' pleasure the previous August. There, Schwarzkopf, leading for the Coalition, and Saudi General Khalid bin Sultan, met two Iraqi generals: Staff General Sultan Hashim Ahmad al-Jibouri, Chief of Staff at the Iraqi Ministry of Defence,[274] and General Salah Abid Mohammed. Saddam's second sigh of relief was that he had not been compelled to come down to negotiate and sign anything himself. He could not have survived if the victors had insisted, as they had had every right to do. His first public response should have been a warning to all. In a radio message to the Iraqi people on 28 February, he claimed that the cessation of hostilities was the result of 'the glorious Iraqi victory'. In a sickening perversion of the truth, he went on to assert that Iraq had 'demolished the aura of the United States', had 'rubbed [the Americans] nose in the dust' and that 'the [Republican] Guards had broken the backbone of their aggressors and thrown them beyond their border'. Unlike Hitler in May 1945, Saddam was still alive and still controlled the Iraqi media, despite the actual military situation. Amazingly, for all their overwhelming strength, the Coalition leadership let him get away with it. The reason why has never really been explained, but the failure was to cause years of conflict and tens of thousands of deaths.

Unlike Eisenhower and his team in May 1945, Schwarzkopf allowed himself to be beguiled right from the start. After what was described as a congenial conclusion to the 3 March ceasefire agreement at Safwan, he declared that: "We are well on our way to a lasting peace."[275] The burly American general, reputed for his negotiating abilities, was fooled by what he took to be 'a positive attitude' on the part of the Iraqi side. Instead of treating the Iraqi generals as fully paid-up cronies of a vicious dictator and subscribers to a cruel Fascist society, he took them at face value. Towards the end of what he saw as affable discussion, he accepted their request that they be allowed to continue the independent use of helicopters for the evacuation of casualties. This was to have tragic consequences.

At the same time, Tariq Aziz was crying for mercy and assuring the president of the UN Security Council that Iraq would abide by the latest resolution (686) which called, among other things, for Iraq's renunciation of its annexation of Kuwait, but not specifically of its claims on sovereignty. With his country's army on its knees, he could have hardly done anything else. He also promised the Council that Iraq would accept the principle of legal liability for any loss, damage or injury caused during its occupation of the Emirate, would return plundered Kuwaiti assets and release all captured civilians and prisoners of war.

Both the Coalition High Command and their political masters were hoodwinked. Instead of using helicopters for the wounded, the Iraqi generals employed their gunships to savagely quell the spontaneous rising of the Shia in the south of the country. These were the very people President Bush had repeatedly encouraged during the Desert Storm campaign. Whether it was recognised at the time or not, Saddam was able to cling on to power thanks to this military loophole and had no intention of keeping other commitments made to the Security Council by his oily Foreign Minister. Back in Washington, ambivalence towards the Iraqi leader remained. As late as 15 February, Bush had called upon Iraqis 'to take matters into their own hands and to force Saddam Hussein the dictator to step aside'.[276] By 8 March, however, the White House spokesman Marlin Fitzwater had all but reverted to a pre-invasion tack. In a statement that might have emulated April Glaspie's approach the previous August, he declared: "We don't intend to get involved in Iraqi internal affairs." He added: "We have these reports of fighting in Basra and other cities, but it is not clear to us what the purpose or the extent of the fighting is."

It was becoming clear that, however brilliant the planning for the liberation of Kuwait might have been, no one had considered how the immediate aftermath should be handled. There had been little or no consideration of the extreme likelihood that the Iraqi people would seize the opportunity to throw off the fearful oppression they had had to suffer increasingly from 1968. Indeed, instead of standing aside, as Fitzwater seemed to be suggesting they should, American forces colluded with Iraqi units seeking to suppress the rebels. Worse, commanders in the field allowed helicopter gunships to strafe and terrorise Iraqi citizens as well as cause widespread damage to holy places in Najaf and Karbala. This was completely against the spirit, if not the letter also, of the Safwan ceasefire agreement and was a totally missed opportunity to rein back tyranny.

This negligence did not stop there. While all Coalition prisoners of war had already left Iraq by 6 March, Tariq Aziz's solemn promises as far as Kuwaitis were concerned were not kept. Happy to see their bruised and battered – but very much alive – pilots back on their television screens describing privations and interrogations in grim Iraqi cells, the free world chose to ignore those who had suffered far worse and would continue to do so. In mid-December 1990, the *International Herald Tribune*, quoting Kuwaiti sources, suggested that, in addition to the seven thousand Kuwaiti subjects killed since 2 August, some twenty-five thousand had been detained. The director of US Middle East Watch had demurred at these figures: there had more likely been only a thousand deaths and five thousand arrests. He did not wish to overstate the abuses committed and risk being accused of 'whipping up war fever'. Two days later – 17 December – the UN General Assembly passed a resolution by 144 votes to one (Iraq) condemning Iraq for serious violations of human rights, torture, detention, summary executions and disappearances. This was backed up by Amnesty International's report published at the same time claiming, apart from the many incidents of torture, rape and murder, that six or seven thousand Kuwaiti troops had been transferred to Iraq. Further, there were thousands, including children as young as thirteen, in Iraqi and Kuwaiti prisons. Most of the abuses were said to have occurred in the first three months of the occupation, but Amnesty could hardly have had many sources during the latter drear days of November onwards.[277] There was certainly no Fourth Estate to apply methods of investigative journalism.

Throughout the occupation, however, the Kuwaitis had maintained a brave effort to resist, despite the severe retributions the Iraqis under 'Chemical' Ali were all too ready to mete out. Expatriate diaries and personal accounts attest to the many explosions heard by those in hiding, indicative of continuing acts of sabotage. During November, indeed, I learnt of one brave group that was rounded up as they were eating a frugal meal in what they thought to be a safe house. It is not clear whether they had somehow compromised themselves or been betrayed. The Iraqis had total control of the phones, almost exclusively landlines in an age before the all-pervasive mobile phone. They were all taken up to Iraq for interrogation and were never seen again. One of the group had been a regular and helpful contact in the Kuwait Security Service. He could have fled the country like many others, but he chose to stay behind. My abiding memory of him was his delight at receiving tickets in London for a football match in which his beloved Liverpool were playing. Whether or not he survived to be among the six hundred or so Kuwaiti citizens who were believed to have been held by Saddam after the 1991 Armistice had been signed, we may never know. The fact remains that no government or international organisation lifted a finger to insist on their release as the Armistice terms demanded. It was not until the invasion of Iraq in 2003 and deposition of Saddam that their corpses were discovered. One account said that the detainees had been starved to death, a latter-day Buchenwald. No inquiry was ever held. Nor did any authority consider that this heinous breach of the armistice terms was, in fact, casus belli and, in legal terms, cut and dried. As the years went by, however, the lawyers, including in the Foreign and Commonwealth Office, considered that the time for action was past. A complete betrayal of both moral and judicial principles.

Fifteen

TAKEN AND MISSED OPPORTUNITIES

There is no such thing as an epilogue in international relations. Watersheds, perhaps, but one major event will always lead to another, often unexpectedly. There are, however, clear phases: if the West's failure to stop Saddam from walking into Kuwait in 1990 was the opening of a phase, the fall of Kabul in 2021 was the end of it. Stunning military success in 1991 led inexorably to abject military defeat thirty years later, made all the more inevitable by repeated mistakes and misjudgements piled up on one another. Take, for example, the West's expectations of its creature government in Afghanistan and consider the words of the former British Secretary of State Dominic Raab.[278] He told the House of Commons Select Committee on Foreign Affairs on 1 September 2021 that 'the central assessment that we were operating on – and it was certainly backed up by both the Joint Intelligence Committee and the military – is that the most likely and central proposition was that, given the troop withdrawal by the end of August, you would see a steady deterioration by that point and it was unlikely that Kabul would fall this year'. Perhaps, while sunning himself on a Greek beach, he did not fully ingest the less sanguine despatch from Britain's ambassador in Kabul of 2 August. "For now," he reported, "Kabul remains insulated from the intense fighting occurring elsewhere in the country." In strong words for a British head of mission, he considered this was 'very unlikely to last indefinitely' since 'the Taliban are positioning to put the capital under intense security and economic pressure when they see fit'. They saw fit on 15 August, less than two weeks later, when their forces entered the Afghan capital with few shots being fired, except in jubilation. The new regime immediately set about the removal of all the social and political improvements achieved in the previous twenty years at enormous financial and human cost to the West. Afghanistan was returned to the Middle Ages.

Plus ça change, at least as far as the optimism about how long the Taliban might be kept at bay is concerned. It was the story of 1990 all over again when British and American official forecasts and working assumptions considered that Saddam's forces would be held up for several days by the Kuwaitis, thus offering a margin for last-minute political, even military action. Quite rightly, and in stark contrast with his predecessor in 1990, Raab was obliged to resign; a week or so later, the American special envoy for Afghanistan, Zalmay Khalizad, offered his resignation after more than three years in post, serving both Presidents Trump and Biden. The rather more prescient Ambassador Bristow simply lost his job. Many other heads in both the Pentagon and in Whitehall should have fallen for the catalogue of assurances over many years that the Afghan government could become viable, even after the removal of Western steel that had propped it up for so long.

Officials, however senior, still have to serve political masters; it should not be forgotten that the man who pulled the rug out from under the NATO operation in Afghanistan was Donald Trump. Like several decisions Trump took during his time in office, his abandoning of the Afghan people was all but arbitrary and left lesser partners in the Atlantic Alliance, who had come to rely on American infrastructure and logistics, with no other recourse but to go along with it. So much for the Atlantic Alliance and the so-called 'twin-pillar' structure of NATO. In Trump's eyes, the European pillar had all but crumbled and was expecting Washington to continue paying more than the lion's share. At a time, too, when menaces in the Far East, military and economic, were growing. By the time the last NATO troops were being evacuated from their toehold at Kabul Airport, Western naval forces had already sailed for the South China Sea, among them Britain's only operational aircraft carrier, HMS *Queen Elizabeth*. Poodle-like, Britain's flagship sailed without sufficient escorts, as several Royal Naval destroyers and frigates had to limp back to port for repair. With China rattling sabres over Taiwan, Washington wanted to involve as many Western military assets in the area as possible. In the same breath, Beijing was welcoming the new regime in Kabul.

How did we find ourselves in this ridiculous position? For what reason were so many Coalition and NATO lives lost and resources expended in Afghanistan from 2001 and in Iraq from 2003? As with Vietnam on 30 April 1975 when many tried to clamber up to the roof of the American embassy in Saigon to get on the helicopter parked precariously there, a lot of people need and deserve explanation, if not closure. What led to the precipitate destruction of democracy in Afghanistan by the Taliban with its vile attitude towards women and cruel approach to justice. Who should atone for the shame this must surely have provoked?

We have to go back to the first half of 1991 to find out where the rot set in. I have already described the unsatisfactory truce, not a peace settlement, reached with Saddam's generals and the US/UK failure to bring him to book immediately over severe breaches on the Iraqi side. For more than twenty years, Saddam was allowed to get away with murder – literally – and during which the West had to face a new and intangible threat that it had helped in no small measure to create through its handling of the expulsion of the Iraqis from Kuwait. I cannot go along with the thesis that the Americans persuaded the Saudis on false military intelligence in September 1990 to accept large numbers of troops in the land protecting the Holy Places of Islam,[279] but the fact remains that Osama bin Laden's motivation to attack Western emanations traces back to that occasion. Ever since, the West has had to deal with an asymmetrical warfare from mushrooming fanatics that oppose fundamentally the political philosophy of 'demos', introduced by the Ancient Greeks, and are determined to reverse the liberalism of Western society. For all that politicians in Washington and London may assert that acts of terrorism will not win what is essentially a battle of diametrically opposed philosophies, Islamic thugs are making solid progress. However substantial the resources thrown at the problem, fanatical minds are not being cleansed by either persuasion or detection; the threats from lone wolves through to a particularly nasty item left on a Metro seat have not receded. Indeed, following the Taliban triumph they have become more likely.

Back in 1991, there was one small victory for common sense in the defence of the largely secular Kurds. For decades it had been in the accepted common interests of the American, British, Iranian, Iraqi, Syrian and Turkish governments to keep the lid on moves towards the formation of a Kurdish state. Littoral governments were afraid of losing territory within their borders occupied by Kurdish minorities and the big powers were afraid of upsetting those countries and their territorial integrity. Even now, after years of horrific Iraqi persecution, Kurds are obliged to accept some form of autonomy within Iraq. This has been hard-won despite a clear national identity, language and viable economy. In the wake of the Coalition victory over Saddam, they might have expected better. Operation Desert Storm, after all, was a UN-authorised campaign to restore international values laid down at the end of the Second World War. They were based on the widely accepted view that evil promoted by monsters like Hitler should not be tolerated. In 1990, however, things were not so straightforward. As the late doyen of military history, Sir Michael Howard pointed out on the eve of the land war against Saddam, although the Americans wanted a campaign fought on Clausewitzian terms – total war sufficient to destroy Iraq's evil influence in the Middle East – this was a goal that was not universally shared.[280] It was not until the world's media crowded television screens with thousands of fleeing Kurds taking to the freezing conditions in the mountains of northern Iraq that steps were taken to deter an Iraqi advance north of Kirkuk and from driving local Kurdish populations away from their homes. Reports of thousands of men being rounded up by Iraqi forces were pouring into the Western press by the last week of March. Early the following month, banner headlines spoke of a 'Kurdish Exodus'.[281] At one point it was estimated that four hundred thousand had fled to the Turkish border region. A cartoon the same day said it all: it showed Saddam standing over a carcass with a large meat cleaver and answering a comment from a much smaller figure of President Bush. "Well, I can only hope Desert Storm taught you a good lesson." "It certainly did," the Iraqi dictator replies, "in future I'll be a butcher you can live with." And Washington did for well over a decade or more.

Washington was not alone in tolerating Saddam. It did so, in part, on the advice of Arab leaders; the White House admitted as much at the time.[282] The one redeeming feature was that, with UN backing, US/UK forces were able to establish effective security zones, at least in northern Iraq, where Kurds might take refuge. Several hundred American troops and the bulk of a British commando brigade were swiftly deployed and, by the end of the month, had established a line that Iraqi soldiers dared not cross. As a result, Kurdish refugees were able to descend from the mountains to tented shelter hastily constructed by Coalition troops where they were fed and watered. It was a largely unsung operation but a highly successful one. It also allowed the Kurdish political leadership to re-start their efforts to obtain a measure of autonomy within Iraq. Back in New York, diplomats sought to put an international stamp on the rescue operation: a scratch UN police force recruited from 'glorified doormen' at Geneva, Vienna and New York was put together to take over from skilled professional soldiers well-versed about conditions on the ground. It is to Prime Minister John Major's credit that he insisted on 24 June that British soldiers should remain until the safety of the Kurds was assured. Although this determined action could not stop Saddam from abusing his own people, it was a respectable move towards fencing him in without offending fellow Arab countries.

There were still those in both the American and British air forces who felt that the military campaign on land had not gone on long enough after Kuwait's liberation. From mid-April 1991 onwards, their jets were in the skies over Iraq enforcing a no-fly zone. This did not please everyone. Alastair Cooke's *Letter from America* broadcast in late April[283] bewailed as 'unannounced' the continuing US/UK air forces' activities; politicians and commanders alike were sensitive to the toes of Arabs – and others – that should not be trodden on. Nevertheless, aerial policing of the no-fly zone continued. In May, the newspapers were covering F6 Falcon raids on northern Iraq from Incilik in Turkey. Not all in Ankara liked that. On 12 May, American planes bombed radar and anti-aircraft sites near Mosul. It was not long before Iraqi propaganda countered with tales of shepherds and two hundred sheep being hit. Air strikes are always liable to cause collateral damage. Very soon, the Ministry of Information in Baghdad started to develop another bleat: it complained that 'Western' sanctions were affecting the health of the Iraqi people; worse, it was causing a high death rate amongst infants. This theme was taken up by anti-war circles in the UK and other European countries, some of whom had shown sympathy for the Kurds only a few weeks before.

Saddam realised that he could use a cat and mouse campaign to further his aims of consolidation at home and for the gradual restitution of his position amongst fellow Arabs. He might lose the odd defence installation after one of his planes had 'locked on' to an American aircraft, but twentieth-century warfare had taught him that control of the skies was not the be all and end all. He needed to be seen at home as a tough leader ready to defend his country with whatever means he had at his disposal. Besides, the military situation was beginning to tip in his favour. While air supremacy might be vital for an invading army, control of territory could only be secured by forces on the ground and the Coalition had all but removed its forces – with what now seems like indecent haste. The broad base of the Coalition had quickly shrunk with the early departure of Egyptian, Syrian and French forces, causing the remaining credible units to look like – and become – overwhelmingly American with a sprinkling of British units. Saddam judged correctly that there would be insufficient public support in all Western countries, not to mention amongst the handful of supporters of the Coalition in the Middle East, to send troops back to the desert. Moreover, President Bush had already passed the midway point in the American electoral calendar and had lost the popular edge he had won by achieving so rapid a victory. Facing him was a Democrat party that had little stomach for further military action and sought another tack for restraining the Iraqi dictator.

There were several explanations offered why Saddam was allowed to save the flower of his army. They ranged from Douglas Hurd's claim that RAF pilots would have jibbed at bombing fleeing Iraqi forces to repeated assertions that Arab countries had insisted on a halt. As mentioned previously, Hurd's point was ill-informed, while there were many in the Arab leadership who would have been quietly relieved to see Iraqi forces reduced and Saddam forced into exile; he gave them a bad name. Deprived of his security apparatus, the dictator would not have lasted long; there were more than enough with personal scores to settle for atrocities visited on their families. Many awaited American leadership, but this reverted to the ambivalence pursued before the invasion of Kuwait. Despite a rattling of the sabre or two and the retention of assorted armour in Kuwait where it was actually more felicitous to park than back in Europe, President Bush felt unable to satisfy his latent instinct that the Middle East could never be stable if Saddam was left in power. Thus, the failure to follow Clausewitzian principles, as had happened in 1945, left the ogre dining at whatever domestic feast he chose. Not without justification, he could claim to his people that the 'mother of battles' had yet to be fought and there were many on the streets of Baghdad and Jerusalem who believed him. Besides, his scientists and engineers – mostly trained in the Soviet Union and Eastern Europe during the Cold War, not to mention English universities – had for a decade or more been developing carefully guarded nuclear, chemical and biological facilities for the creation and delivery of weapons of mass destruction. Saddam was still in a position to turn Kuwait into a mass grave.

Sixteen

WMD - A UN RESPONSIBILITY

Despite appearances over the years since 1990, it is necessary to remind ourselves that the liberation of Kuwait was a UN-authorised operation. Although it was undeniably down to the Americans to provide the iron in the fist, Washington took pains to present a velvet glove to keep the Security Council onside. It continued to do so after the March 1991 truce, especially when it came to the thorny issue of Saddam's possession of WMD. In pursuing a campaign for their destruction, there was a refreshing sympathy coming from Moscow, at least in the first few years. In addition to a readiness to halt the export of sensitive materials to Iraq and its adherence to sanctions, the new Russian leadership also held to the principle that any continuing action against Saddam should remain within the authorisation given by Security Council resolutions. The issue of WMD, however, would remain contentious since it was far more intangible than the invasion of a member country. The longer the matter remained unresolved, the more it would become possible to argue whether Iraq was still in breach. If that line could no longer be held, what price the continuation of sanctions against Baghdad.

That Saddam still held WMD after his troops had been thrown out of Kuwait and would probably have used them but for the fierce threats from Washington has never been in doubt. His setting fire to Kuwaiti oil fields was not a final military resort; rather, a fit of pique inflicted on the neighbour he despised. Knowledge once obtained, moreover, can never be destroyed. With the advantage of Western expertise, the UN tried valiantly for ten years to identify Iraq's existing WMD assets, to rid the world of them and to prevent their renewal and reconstruction. It was an honest endeavour against the background of constant Iraqi harassment and disingenuous behaviour. At the end of the period, there were still questions to be answered about Iraqi WMD, but these did not prevent ridicule from Vladimir Putin, a man who has shown himself more than ready to lean towards autocracy and to use methods no different than those used by Saddam in his pomp. With Saddam still in power, there was always the prospect of his use of noxious methods – if he thought he could get away with it.

With one or two exceptions, international commitment to remove the dangerous nuisance and return Iraq to legality under the conventions on WMD it had signed up to, was firm. Spearheaded by British diplomacy in the Security Council,[284] the American delegation presented a draft peace plan by which Iraq would adhere to a strict schedule concerning her possession of WMD – and their destruction – before a permanent cessation of hostilities might be put into effect. Originally, it was envisaged that Baghdad would provide information on types of weaponry still held and their location within fifteen days. Their destruction should then follow within forty-five days of the UN Secretary-General's signing off of a plan for supervision of the operation. The schedule was inserted at British insistence in the teeth of Russian and Chinese opposition; both permanent members wanted an early end to hostilities. Arguments were intense. It was even reported that the British delegation was threatening to use the veto against any draft resolution that excluded satisfactory mention of Iraqi WMD abolition. Security Council resolution 687 was finally adopted on 3 April 1991 by twelve votes to one, with two abstentions;[285] all five permanent members supported it.

The measure authorised an inspection regime under which Iraq was to declare all its holdings of WMD as well as facilities and programmes for their manufacture. A special commission (UNSCOM) was set up to cover biological and chemical weapons, together with missiles with a range of over 150 kilometres that might be used to deliver them. The task of identifying and taking action against Saddam's nuclear arsenal and potential was handed to the International Atomic Energy Authority in Vienna, the organisation policing the observance of conventions on nuclear power. While hostilities were now to cease and sanctions against non-military supplies lifted, the resolution also directed that no country should import Iraqi oil until all prohibited items and programmes had been eliminated. A bold enough plan but one still vulnerable to evasion where political will was lacking, honour in the breach and a gradual falling off of commitment to its implementation.

From the outset, there were disputes over who should carry out the inspections, however unlimited their access. The Americans, drawing on their experience of IAEA failure to home in on undeclared Iraqi nuclear installations before the Israeli attack on the Osirak plant in 1981, wanted an inspection regime that probed well beyond anything Baghdad might admit to. To a large extent, Washington got its way, but as years passed, it became too easy for accusations of a Western, even US/UK monopoly, to be made. As head of UNSCOM Hans Blix lamented that 'this seriously reduced the Commission's intended UN legitimacy'.[286] Baghdad propagandists were soon able to exploit this serious vulnerability. Neither did it take long for the Iraqis to start blocking access to their sites. As someone familiar with the ease with which those in complete control of the ground can limit freedom of movement using the most ludicrous excuses, I would have had sympathy with the inspectors who were repeatedly baulked in their efforts to meet the clear terms of Resolution 687. In the circumstances, their record of achievement should stand as honourable, daring and imaginative.

Saddam did not take long to demonstrate his incorrigibility. The first inspection teams entered Iraq on Thursday 15 May, the start of the Islamic weekend. On arriving at Tarmiya, some fifty miles north of Baghdad on the Tigris, already firmly identified as a nuclear site, they found everything in ruins. One can imagine the remarks made by their Iraqi minders. Subsequent analysis in Vienna of the team's findings, however, confirmed that, contrary to Iraqi protestations, the site had been used for enrichment of plutonium. It was hardly surprising then that a second team sent to look at another suspected site north of Baghdad was turned away. In the months and years that followed, obfuscation followed obfuscation. When inspectors managed to outwit the Iraqis and tracked down their trucks clearly moving sensitive materials away from the site, they were fired on. As a result, the UNSCOM chairman Rolf Ekeus went to Baghdad to protest, taking with him photo evidence of the shoot-out. This was accompanied by US naval and army air force preparations to carry out retaliatory strikes. Baghdad was forced to back down and to admit it had been enriching nuclear materials using several different methods. Early IAEA success was capped by its chief inspector David Kay finding a paper on 23 September which described the planned Iraqi nuclear weapons programme. Even then, Iraqi officials tried to stop the paper being taken away; it was only the close media coverage that ensured that they were retrieved and despatched back to Vienna. 'In recognition of his outstanding leadership, determination and courage', Kay was given the IAEA's distinguished award. A committed CIA intelligence source, Kay was always going to cross swords with international bureaucrats like Blix, who admitted that his first priority was the search for weapons, not documents.

This false distinction only sowed division in the search for the real truth about Iraq's actual knowledge and holding of WMD. It did not help that Kay, nicknamed in the CIA as 'ramrod', resigned from UNSCOM in February 1992 to become Secretary-General of the Uranium Institute. Nevertheless, Baghdad's early obstruction tactics irked Washington: the Pentagon rattled sabres and threatened to step up military action and slow down troop withdrawal. More seriously, President Bush refused to shed his vital demand and condition for the removal of trade sanctions – the ousting of Saddam from power.

Public opinion in the USA was changing as election year approached. Long before the end of 1991, other presidential contenders began to jostle in the Republican Party as more exigent domestic issues crowded in. Many, in a country where the vast majority had never considered the need to hold a passport, were more concerned about a failing economy and rising unemployment. An early critic of the president's record against Saddam, Mario Cuomo, Governor of New York and father of Donald Trump's lawyer, told *The London Times* in July: "Saddam Husayn has wound up a winner after we beat him… I'm not sure we did do better than he did."[287] Bush was in a position whereby he was both damned if he did and damned if he didn't. To re-open a land campaign would have aroused cries of 'not another Vietnam' and would have had much-reduced international support. To leave Saddam with his hideous weapons, however, was unthinkable, but the only apparent military option was the use of surgical air strikes against a cancer that could pop up anywhere. None of those would kill Saddam. American policy towards Iraq was bankrupt.

In November 1992, Bill Clinton was elected president by a landslide. He faced the same problems with Iraq as his predecessor but began to promote diplomacy above increasingly empty threats of military action. Meanwhile, the Iraqi Foreign Office was gradually rebuilding its relations overseas. In March 1993, Hans Blix's own Swiss government permitted the re-establishment of the Iraqi consulate-general in Geneva headed by Saddam's ruthless half-brother, Barzan al-Tikriti.[288] As a result, darker Iraqi forces began to demonstrate their muscle once more; on 12 April the following year, Lebanon severed diplomatic relations with Baghdad after the assassination of the Iraqi dissident Talib Suhayl al-Tamimi. Saddam, who had early on learnt all about dirty tricks from the KGB in Moscow, was extending the reach of his secret agencies into his near neighbours once more. Only four days later, two members of the Iraqi embassy staff, almost certainly DGI officers working under diplomatic cover, confessed to the murder. While the matter was largely ignored in the Western media, a new Iraqi ambassador arrived in Moscow, where diplomatic relations with the new Russian Federation had been agreed over two years previously.

Apart from one American air strike in June 1994 which, the Iraqis contended, had hit the Saddam Arts Centre, killing its director, instead of the targeted headquarters of the DGI, the mid-1990s were relatively quiet and for the IAEA inspectors largely trouble-free. All fissionable material was being removed to Russia, where Western experts were already helping to dispose of dangerous substances left over from the Soviet period. Under supervision, many large installations were dismantled, while back in Vienna, a full understanding of the Iraqi nuclear programme had been achieved. In its report to the Security Council on 8 October 1997, the IAEA was able to give assurances that there were no significant 'disarmament' matters to clear up. This was grist to the mill, as far as those now supporting a complete end to both hostilities and trade sanctions were concerned. It did not, however, address the fact that Iraqi scientists could not forget what they had learnt and developed, or that some were already finding opportunity to continue their research in Syria, another nuclear renegade. In addition, even though the inspection regime had been able to eliminate the nuclear threat, Blix was unable to exclude the existence of undeclared missiles and chemical and biological weapons.

Neither was Blix in a position to give assurances about acceptance in Saddam's mind, or in those of his closest henchmen, that Iraq should be forced to abandon its long-held ambition of leading the Arab destruction of the 'Zionist regime' in Tel Aviv. The Iraqi leader could bide his time while reconstructing elements of the state damaged by the Coalition and moving personnel and facilities for WMD development beyond the UN's gaze. He had also not come to accept the outcome of a war which had restored Kuwait's territorial integrity. In October 1994, he tested Western resolve. On the 7th, two Republican Guard divisions with some 350 tanks were detected heading for the Kuwait border. This was a clear repetition of what had happened in July 1990. Clinton's response was decisive; the United States was not going to make the same mistake twice. Firm words accompanied by the immediate despatch from the Adriatic of the aircraft carrier USS *George Washington*, complete with fifty strike aircraft that would have pulverised any Iraqi armour not dug-in, stopped whatever the Iraqi leader's intentions really were. Such determination in July 1990 would have saved a lot of subsequent heartache. If Saddam's intention was to add merit to his charm offensive in previous months to procure support for an end to sanctions, it was not, in the words of one American official, 'very charming'. As American troops were rushed out to Kuwait to sit in the desert and an amphibious task force moved up to the Northern Gulf, Saddam suddenly relented and withdrew.

The Iraqi leader had made a point that was not lost on an American president who could rebuke a commentator with the words: "It's the economy, stupid." Clinton and his advisers realised that Saddam could periodically carry out manoeuvres of his now reformed and re-equipped armed forces at very little additional expense. The fuel came from Iraq's own resources and movement of forces kept the military occupied when, back in their barracks, they might have time to plot against the government. Every time Saddam feinted, he could do so at vast cost to the American Treasury. The only winner, perhaps, was the Russian Federation, whose Foreign Minister, Andrei Kozyrev, offered his services to broker a negotiated settlement of the crisis. At the same time, after a visit to Moscow on 18 October, Iraqi Oil Minister Safa Hadi Jawad was able to preen that 'constructive talks' with Russian officials had achieved the launching of technical studies aimed at implementing 'economic projects and developing oil resources'. One might as well have been back in 1958 after the collapse of the monarchy opened the door for a major advance in Soviet influence in Iraq. Moreover, Saddam's manoeuvres also caused intermittent and unhelpful spikes in the price of crude and made would-be investors in the Gulf tremble.

A rating on HMS *Cornwall*, anchored off Kuwait at the time, aired the sentiments of many in the armed forces. "If anything happens militarily this time, the feeling of all the lads on board is that we shall go all the way to Baghdad and finish the job. It is too costly for Kuwait and the world to let this sort of behaviour go unchecked."[289] The Marsh Arabs at the foot of the Tigris/Euphrates delta, the southern Shia, the many Iraqis in exile, all Kuwait and, surreptitiously, several Arab leaders would have echoed the sentiments of the Royal Naval seaman. Even Tehran would have sat on its hands. Saddam, however, was left to fight another day while continuing to murder and torture to his heart's content. Back in the UK, Britain's senior commander during Desert Storm, General Sir Peter de Billiere, came close to admitting that the Coalition had got it wrong. "I do not think," he told a journalist, "you can sit back and assume that Saddam Hussein is just going to pack up and go home, any more than we thought he would pack up and leave when he came into Kuwait in 1990."[290]

During the otherwise relatively quiet first five years of the Clinton presidency, there was one event that set many hearts fluttering in Washington and London. In July 1995, Staff General Husayn Kamal Hassan al-Majid, Saddam's cousin and still serving as Minister of Military Industrialisation, visited Jordan. There, he had opportunity to talk discreetly with American officials. It would not have been the first time: in July 1990, he had told the American ambassador, April Glaspie, that Iraq would not use violence to solve its oil dispute with Kuwait. Since then, however, a worm had turned in Husayn Kamal's stomach. Having previously been dismissed by Saddam as Minister of Defence in November 1991, he learnt during his absence in Amman that he was to be replaced again. On 9 August, he fled back to Jordan, taking with him his wife, Raghad, Saddam's favourite daughter, and the children. He defected to the Americans and for many weeks thereafter was debriefed by the CIA and other Western agencies about Iraq's WMD programme.

Husayn Kamal was not a nice man. Aged about forty-five and a Tikriti by birth, he came from coarse stock; he was also cousin of 'Chemical' Ali Hassan al-Majid, a man ruthless without giving any quarter. Husayn had commanded Saddam's bodyguard in 1983 but had then been put in charge of boosting military production. By late 1987, he was head of Iraq's rocket programme before, on 3 April 1988, being made Minister of the all-important Military Industrial complex. He was a major thug and was thought to have placed the bomb on the helicopter that killed Saddam's former favourite, Adnan Khairallah Talfah. He was known as 'the whip' for his brutality. He was a completely different type of man from the head of Iraqi Military Intelligence during the Gulf War, General Wafiq Jasim al-Samarrai. He had defected to the Americans after his dismissal in 1991 and brought with him credible information concerning Iraq's stock of some two hundred anthrax bombs hidden in Salah al-Din province, not far from Saddam's ancestral home. Ten years older than Husayn and a professional soldier, his explanation about the bombs' existence was as objective as it was frightening. They were, he said, a putative last throw of the dice should Saddam ever face absolute defeat, not unlike the setting ablaze of the Kuwaiti oil fields. Oddly, that atrocity which destroyed huge reserves and damaged vast habitat, was submerged by a number of other issues at the time.

On the surface, Husayn's defection looked like an intelligence coup, but when he was lured back to Iraq in February 1996 by a presidential pardon, he was promptly killed and doubts began to accrue about the value of his information. He had peddled disinformation before. As the minister who had been in overall charge of WMD programmes, he was certainly in a position to know, but there were other major personalities who had recently been given tasks in the same field independently. Notably, these included Saddam's two evil sons, Uday and Qusay. Further, for all Husayn's protestations that Iraqi chemical and biological weapons had been destroyed on his orders in 1991, there was no collateral to verify that this had been carried out. There was no telling what Saddam's sons, with a father's blessing and limitless resources, might have been promoting in a remote laboratory yet to be discovered. The irony was that neither side could be sure of the accuracy of what Husayn had reported. Baghdad, however, appeared to be so lacking in confidence about what Husayn had actually revealed that it placed the blame firmly on him for any undisclosed WMD activity. It followed up by handing over a welter of information which had allegedly come from Husayn's farm – the so-called 'chicken farm' dossier. As Hans Blix has recorded,[291] this new stream of information actually confirmed that Iraq had not only developed nasty biological substances but had weaponised them. Saddam's threat to turn Kuwait into a mass grave was all the more realistic; Halabja in 1988 had demonstrated that he had the will to perpetrate such horrors.

The Kamal Husayn episode interrupted a period of apparent progress in Washington's dealings with Baghdad. Only a month after Saddam's October 1994 manoeuvres and dicing with what IAEA inspectors might or might not discover, President Clinton chose to relax the remaining grip the Coalition retained in the Gulf. On the eve of Congressional mid-term elections in November, he announced that all American ground forces would be withdrawn by Christmas. While it was undoubtedly a blatant attempt to placate the electorate, it received a positive response from Baghdad. On 10 November, three days after Clinton's announcement,

Washington was gratified by Saddam's signature to Iraq's recognition of Kuwait as a sovereign state and territorial integrity. Britain fell in line by withdrawing its last forces, some one thousand marines, a precursor for the future. Behind these moves was the implication that the removal of Saddam was no longer a key objective. In the UK, Prime Minister Major signalled his opposition to any further British engagement in pursuit of such an objective. Within two months, the French had broken ranks and had recognised the Baghdad regime, re-opening its embassy the following March. On the fourth anniversary of the Coalition's first military action to liberate Kuwait, Saddam was able to trumpet that 'the number of enemies is decreasing and these enemies [remaining] have become desperate'.[292] A day later, his Minister of Oil, Jawad, was claiming that production had hit pre-1991 levels.

Well before Husayn Kamal's brief appearance on the international scene, the world was becoming tired of the Iraqi question. Russia was continuing to press for an end to trade sanctions, egged on by the Baghdad propaganda machine pumping out tales of children suffering from lack of medicaments. Despite Ambassador Madeleine Albright's diplomatic counterattacks at the UN pointing out that the Iraqi leader was still building more 'pleasure palaces' in the face of sanctions, the will for their retention was weakening. In February 1995, Mrs Albright, born a Czech and knowing all there was to know about dictatorships, travelled to London, other European capitals and to Riyadh to drum up support. The FCO responded positively on the 24th: "There is no case for a relaxation of sanctions." At the same time, the Russian Nationalist politician Vladimir Zhirinovsky arrived in Baghdad with a fifty-strong delegation, including twenty members of the Duma. He called on Saddam to join an anti-West coalition, praised Saddam and promised to work for the lifting of all sanctions. The Russians continued to intensify their talks with the Iraqi oil, agriculture, trade, finance, education and even defence ministries. It was shades of what had happened during the Cold War in the 1960s. In the face of growing pressure from Russia, China and now France, the six-monthly UNSCOM report to the Security Council submitted on 10 April 1995 was still able to kill off any hopes for an early lifting of UN sanctions. The Commission stated: "Iraq has now provided a full and comprehensive disclosure of it past biological programme [and] the only conclusion that can be drawn is that there is a high risk that items and materials have been purchased for a proscribed purpose – acquisition of biological warfare agents." A stalemate had been reached, a situation that had placed Saddam more than marginally at an advantage.

Seventeen

THE ROAD TO CHAOS IN IRAQ

The year before my retirement from foreign service in 1997, I found myself bobbing up and down in company with a number of colleagues on a dhow off the coast of Oman. We were all meant to be considering the issues that would trouble the Middle East in the coming years. I was in a minority in that I was more concerned about the danger Iran represented than other countries in the region. The UK, the West in general, had few who understood Farsi or the theocracy that reigned from Tehran. I would have been at one with a crossword solver in Tehran faced with the anagram clue that appeared in *The London Times* on 11 May 1992: 'one ran over the first person, an Arab'. I leave it to the reader to come up with the answer, but the one inference I could draw was that, even among those whiling away their time on a commuter run up to Waterloo, many could not distinguish between the long-established and totally distinct civilisations either side of the Persian – or do I mean Arabian – Gulf. Certainly, on that balmy evening, I felt quite adamant on the point and expressed my view forcefully. A senior colleague turned to shut down my argument: "Tony," he said, "it is not Iran, or the Middle East – it is all about Europe." I could not then have imagined that the same individual, in retirement, would broadcast his strongly pro-Brexit views repeatedly, including in *The Times*.

To a certain extent his comment on the dhow was right. The festering sores of the Middle East – Palestine, Iraq and Islamic Revolutionary Iran, to name but the most obvious – had already claimed too much attention in international affairs, not to mention many lives, habitat destruction and population upheaval. For those paid to conduct external relations through diplomacy, constant engagement in insoluble disputes that only led to warfare was a waste of effort and resources. Popular opinion in America had always tended to think that – hence the reluctance to enter either of the two world wars – and much of Europe remained lukewarm in joining any so-called Western Alliance attempts to solve Third World problems by military intervention. The European Community, too, was now fully absorbed with the building of the third largest economic bloc on the planet. It had achieved a great deal: traditional rivalries between long-standing enemies had been eliminated; there was a healthy cordon sanitaire along its border with the Russian Federation and it was in the process of smothering local yet extremely bitter divisions, of which Northern Ireland, Gibraltar and provincial nationalism in Spain were the most sensitive.

There was, however, a reverse side to the coin. Given this Eurocentric view of the world and a desire to build internal cohesion and economic muscle, Brussels was hardly likely to spend as much time worrying about Iraq. The Community were the more likely to believe that the problem of WMD had been satisfactorily dealt. It was also less attentive to Saddam's internal terror policy laced with 'mystical nonsense' in which he compared himself with ancient heroes of Babylon. Instead, oil-rich Iraq posed an attractive market for European exports and a relatively cheap source of hydrocarbons. The stability produced by a strong leadership, however vile his methods, promised lucrative trading prospects. What price, therefore, the continuation of sanctions, especially when the Russian Federation and China were already offering their wares. Never mind the systematic draining of the southern Iraqi wetlands which was ruining the livelihood of Marsh Arabs, or continuing missile attacks on Kurdish militias. In both cases, they were acts of a vengeful Saddam who loathed the Shia for having rebelled against him in 1991, and he had always acted brutally against the Kurds, not least for their readiness to collude with Iran. Like the awful plight of the many Kuwaitis taken to Iraq before their country was liberated, these issues caused concern in New York but never attracted sufficient support in either the Security Council or the General Assembly to bring about effective action and resolute action. Understandably, there were other serious international issues – the plight of Bosnia for one – which pre-occupied international civil servants and NATO planners, but there was also an attitude of mind, not so different from the sigh of resignation that accompanied the often-heard sentiment: "That's what they do."

Nevertheless, Security Council resolution 687 remained set in stone; the issue of Iraqi WMD remained to be honoured and (mostly) Western scientific boots were still on the ground. Furthermore, the daily cooperation between ministries and agencies had developed a bonding, both amongst the inspectors visiting Iraq and the experts back home analysing their findings. New departments had been established and, once a bureaucratic structure is built, it is not easy to pull down. Moreover, resolute UN action could still defeat Iraqi recalcitrance. When UNSCOM's executive chairman Rolf Ekeus was sent to Baghdad in June 1996 to complain to Tariq Aziz about continuing denial of access, the oily Iraqi deputy prime minister promised 'immediate, unconditional and unrestricted access to all sites which the Commission and the IAEA may wish to inspect'. There was, however, the important face-saving rider that UNSCOM would 'operate with full regard for the legitimate security concerns of Iraq'. Why would it not! The trouble was that in a society riddled with paranoid secret agencies, intelligence and counter-intelligence networks, it was second nature to accuse others of espionage. UNSCOM had, also, been vulnerable to criticism that it was too close to Western intelligence, having employed experts who could be seen as probable former CIA assets.

In the wake of the Ekeus/Aziz agreement, the Iraqis still edged towards a toughening of their position. They were encouraged by a number of instances whereby inspectors turned up at an intelligence-identified suspected – and sensitive – site, only to find nothing but Iraqi smiling faces. The deduction in UNSCOM, strongly supported by Washington, was that the Iraqis had developed an ever more sophisticated means for hiding their secrets, documents and materials. A new 'ramrod' appeared on the scene. A former US marine major with eight years' service as a military intelligence officer, including in the Soviet Union and on Schwarzkopf's staff, Scott Ritter was given his head to investigate how the Iraqis concealed materials and paper they were thought to be holding back on. Ritter's experience had inured him to the lies and obfuscations both Russian and Iraqi agencies were capable of. Had not one taught the other? For some, Ritter was sent in to prove a negative; for others, the Iraqis had been caught out too many times burning documents, while inspectors were kept waiting at the gate. Ritter was not pre-supposed to trust anyone and his bordering on the arrogant manner was never going to win any Iraqi friends. In the end, Baghdad bit back. In late October 1997, the Iraqi government informed the Security Council, among other things, that it would no longer allow UNSCOM officials with American nationality to work in Iraq. They were all suspected of spying and, even if they were not paid agents of the CIA, they showed no respect for Iraq's legitimate interests. Oddly, this proscription was not extended to American inspectors working for the IAEA; as it happened, there were fewer American nationals working for the IAEA. Moreover, with Vienna all but satisfied that Iraq no longer possessed nuclear weapons or fissile materials, there was little point in putting IAEA noses out of joint.

A stand had to be taken against Baghdad's arbitrary decision; both UNSCOM and IAEA inspections were suspended. This situation could not be left unresolved. What would the Iraqis get up to if their activity were no longer monitored? American sabres were rattled in parallel with intense diplomatic activity, in which Moscow played no small part. The UK closed ranks with the Americans, as demonstrated by the despatch to the Middle East of the Royal Navy's flagship, HMS *Invincible*; the Falklands' veteran aircraft carrier had passed through the Suez Canal by mid-January with her escorts.[293] The absence of any military support from other European countries was a source of comfort to Iraq which she pocketed; the Coalition was well and truly split. After his first visit to Baghdad in December, the new UNSCOM chairman, the Australian Richard Butler,[294] had come away with renewed promises of cooperation but also in the knowledge that Baghdad would be insisting on a further condition: there were to be no inspections of so-called 'presidential sites', essentially those large areas surrounding Saddam's several luxury palaces. This move only increased suspicions that there were still nasty substances waiting to be discovered. Meanwhile, Baghdad was using every ruse to weaken the case against the continuation of sanctions: when Butler arrived in the Iraqi capital on 19 January, he was greeted by sixty taxis carrying coffins, allegedly containing the corpses of dead children. It did not help either that the crisis played out against the background of President Clinton's dalliance with Monica Lewinski. Who held the high moral ground, the Baghdad taxi driver might have asked. Clinton's State of the Union speech, for all its tough rhetoric, could not answer that question.

Action on the ground might. By the end of the month, Sea Harriers from HMS *Invincible* were flying over southern Iraq for the first time since 1991. The Americans had three hundred strike aircraft and up to twenty-four thousand military personnel in the Gulf, only 1,500 of whom were actually in Kuwait. Although there was much ill-informed speculation in the media that a military solution was inevitable, Baghdad knew that threats from Washington were no longer credible; both Moscow and Paris had the handbrake on, too. Diplomacy and face-saving were the only option. After UNSCOM had been permitted to survey the sites the Iraqis had listed and much debate in the Security Council, the UN Secretary-General, Kofi Annan, was invited to Baghdad on 14 February, on the same day that a large anti-war demonstration was held in front of 10 Downing Street. On the 20th, he flew in to the Iraqi capital, where he was received by Tariq Aziz. After intense and virtually non-stop negotiations, Annan finally met Saddam for four hours on the 22nd. The next day, the Iraqi leader signed a memorandum of understanding which agreed that, from now on, all suspected sites were to be open to inspection. An ebullient Annan claimed that the agreement was a major step forward since it had Saddam's signature, but his optimistic take was belied by his reluctance to reveal the small print. He had been obliged to concede that UNSCOM officials should be required to not only respect previous Iraqi concerns about sovereignty and security but also should do nothing that could be construed as offending the country's dignity. In order to ensure the latter, a chaperone system was to be introduced whereby a number of senior diplomats accepted by both sides would accompany inspection teams. This had the effect of loosening ties round Iraq further and opening the debate to more sceptics about the continuation of sanctions until the unprovable had been proved. With a tough talking Australian in charge of UNSCOM and Iraqi disingenuity, however, the new regimen was never going to work. For a start, the agreement did not put a stop to immediate demands from Tariq Aziz that US/UK forces leave the Gulf or that the Security Council should end sanctions.

For a short while, there was calm, but in March, a group of independent biological warfare experts meeting in Vienna with UN officials asserted that Iraq's declaration of its plans and holdings was still incomplete. Further, there were persistent fears that Baghdad continued to work on nerve agents such as VX and had hidden stocks of it along with other noxious substances such as anthrax. Scott Ritter was certainly convinced of Iraq's duplicity and, in resigning from UNSCOM on 27 August, blamed American and British weakness for allowing Baghdad to get away with it.[295] Much to Iraqi annoyance, the Security Council voted on 9 September not to review its sanctions policy while Baghdad remained in breach over freedom of UNSCOM inspections. Three days later, the Iraqi rubber stamp Parliament voted against further cooperation with UNSCOM. Impasse had been reached. In Washington, it did not help that the Starr Report investigating the Lewinski 'affair' and delivered to Congress the same day, cleared the way for impeachment of the leader of the Western world. Any disdain in Baghdad, however, was capped by mounting anger at the Security Council's refusal to lift sanctions, despite the IAEA's report on 8 October that there were no significant 'disarmament' matters to clear up. With continuing concern over Iraq's suspected holding of VX and Sarin nerve agents, this cut no ice with the US and UK delegations.[296]

In an attempt to move the debate on, the Security Council offered a review of sanctions on 30 October which might have helped suggest where some easing in Baghdad's favour might take place. To the surprise of many, Saddam's Revolutionary Command Council dismissed this out of hand and confirmed that, as far as the Iraqi government was concerned, cooperation with UNSCOM was at an end until sanctions were lifted entirely. In response, and not without some difficulty, the Council finally produced a tough resolution on 6 November accusing Baghdad of flagrant violations and demanding compliance. While Washington and London were now claiming there to be sufficient cause for military action, however, Paris, Moscow and Beijing dragged their feet. As American and British spokesmen became increasingly bellicose, UNSCOM prepared to pull out of Iraq; on 11 November, nearly all staff were seen evacuating by road to Jordan. Despite his personal domestic concerns,[297] President Clinton warned the same day at Arlington Cemetery that 'time has all but run out'. US/UK tough talking was fuelled by renewed reports of Iraqi possession of nerve agents. In the absence of inspections on the ground, there would have to be punitive air strikes on any remaining suspected sites.

By now, Washington was pouring aircraft, cruise missile-carrying naval vessels and troops into the Gulf. In the UK, Prime Minister Tony Blair claimed that there would be disaster if Saddam were allowed to get away with non-compliance. American air and naval forces were now poised for attack and reports reached British television that the Iraqi Ministry of Information was at panic stations. The real threat of heavy attack from the air produced an appeal from Baghdad to Kofi Annan and his special envoy, the Indian diplomat, Prakash Shah, to use their best offices for peace. In parallel Iraqi diplomats lobbied sympathetic Arab governments and the three permanent members of the Council, pressing for further attempts at negotiation. American cruise missiles had already been primed and aircraft were within minutes of releasing their bombs when President Clinton called a halt to attacks he had ordered; he did so in response to a last-ditch appeal from Annan.[298] The Security Council remained hopelessly divided; another opportunity for pinning down the Iraqi leader had been missed. Although the inspectors were allowed to return to Iraq, they faced an intensification of cat-and-mouse tactics, along with protests that UNSCOM activities were 'provocative and unprofessional'. Richard Butler was singled out for his rude and arrogant behaviour. Ignoring pleas from Paris, Moscow and Beijing, Clinton felt compelled to use American muscle after all. London supported him. In response to a further refusal to allow the UNSCOM inspectors to do their job, Operation Desert Fox, largely an air offensive, was launched on 17 December. At the time, the pasting of targets in Baghdad and over much of the rest of Iraq looked impressive and was given saturation coverage in the Western press. Despite the ferocious firepower loosed off, the attacks only pointed up the limitations to which the West was prepared to go to. Crucially, there was still no willingness to commit ground troops. Saddam and his henchmen could simply take to their bunkers, while any hidden stocks of nerve agents remained untouched. When the Iraqi leader re-emerged unscathed, he was able to talk up civilian casualties, including many children to touch Western consciences, and to hammer away at the alleged injustices sanctions posed for the Iraqi people.

Timing of the 'escalation', as Paris called it, was hardly fortuitous. The Islamic Holy month of Ramadan started on the night of 18/19 December; this was a time of peace, not war. Any surviving support on the Arab streets melted away and even the Egyptians sucked their teeth; Syria promised support for Baghdad by threatening Israel. The attacks were called off on 20 December with American and British claims that much had been achieved. Much, however, had been sacrificed. Air strikes could not verify what WMD Saddam still held. They had not crippled his military infrastructure. And UNSCOM's surveillance was at an end. As Taha Ramadan, Saddam's surly lieutenant, remarked: "UNSCOM's regime of spies was finished." The Security Council was more divided than ever with the Russians emphasising the serious strain that had been put on their relations with the United States. The halcyon days of East-West détente were over, with a vodka-swilling Boris Yeltsin in his last days as President of Russia and the more sinister ex-KGB officer Vladimir Putin waiting in the wings to take over the Kremlin. At the Vatican, Pope John Paul II, no push-over where dictatorships were concerned, weighed in with a condemnation of the bombings, only two weeks before Clinton was due to call on him. Early in the New Year there were damaging reports of the influence and 'penetration' within UNSCOM that the CIA had enjoyed for too long. In the minds of many the ogre Saddam had become the offended party and the ordinary Iraqi had been made to suffer for far too long. Western policy towards Saddam's regime had reached a dead end.

If the Ba'athist government in Baghdad could not be safely contained, it had to be changed and that could only happen with the removal of Saddam and his apparatus. This represented a major departure from policy pursued in the immediate aftermath of Kuwait's liberation. Saddam was no longer to be regarded as a necessary evil to be tolerated in order to preserve Iraq's stability and the balance of power at the head of the Gulf. Thinktanks on both sides of the Atlantic had been considering the issue for some time, but the political will was missing. Besides, other international crises, predominantly those stemming from the break-up of Tito's Yugoslavia, did not augur well for the removal of a strongman. The idea of removing Saddam from the outside was hopeless from the outset. Had the world not removed Hitler until after Soviet forces menaced his Berlin bunker? Inside Iraq, Saddam's popularity remained surprisingly buoyant, especially in the northern and western Sunni areas. With every moral victory chalked up against Washington, his approval ratings went up; the converse happened in America and Europe. Saddam and his people had become the victims.

Only in the southern (Shi-ite) areas was there smouldering resentment, but this was age-old and Saddam's intelligence agencies knew how to deal with it. For those enjoying a system in which civil rights are largely protected, it is difficult to understand how a total dictatorship can easily choke protest and prevent the formation of any viable opposition. And Saddam's dictatorship was as brutal as it was total: punishment and retribution meted out to dissidents ranged from peremptory executions – on occasion carried out personally by Saddam – through excruciating torture – sometimes with Saddam present – to the humiliation inflicted by his son, Qusay, on the Iraqi national side for losing a football match. Oppositionists arrested did not last long enough to be sent off to a concentration camp.

The only alternative, it seemed, was to encourage Iraqis in exile overseas to band together and consider their options for bringing about an end to a monstrous regime. Increasingly, both Washington and, to a lesser extent, London provided funds to the various opposition groups that had formed in the West. For decades, the UK had sheltered Iraqis escaping abroad, but even in London, individuals were not completely safe from the assassin's bullet or a savage axe attack. In any case, the many different groups might be united in their wish to see Saddam removed, but they had seriously divergent views about what should be set in his place. The political dimensions stretched from old monarchists to those who wanted to re-found an Islamic Caliphate. Encouragement of Iraqi oppositionists abroad provided much work for American and British intelligence agencies, but on the whole, this achieved very little. It was never going to oust Saddam.

Aerial activity did not cease after Desert Fox, but it underwent a substantial change in emphasis. Two new Iraqi threats were becoming apparent which, to a degree, put the issue of WMD on the backburner. Emboldened by growing support from Moscow, epitomised by Yevgeny Primakov's announcement at the end of December that Russia would not tolerate further bombing, a still largely intact Iraqi air force became increasingly aggressive along the edge of the two no-fly zones protecting the Kurds and southern Shia respectively. Two or four Iraqi fighters would fly tantalisingly along and briefly into the zones in the hope that policing aircraft might be lured within easy range of mobile air defences on the ground. It soon became clear that Baghdad was hoping to shoot down an RAF Tornado or USAAF F16 and score a further propaganda victory aimed at the Arab streets. Better still, the pilot might be captured, paraded before intimidating crowds and then used as a bargaining chip. The US/UK response was to attack missile and radar sites, particularly those locking on to their patrolling aircraft. More cat and mouse, but potentially deadly. More significantly for the future, however, were Iraqi diplomatic efforts in Ankara to persuade the Turkish government to suspend American usage of Incilik air base. At first, as a fellow NATO member, Turkey refused Iraqi overtures, but in the following months and years, the repeated drip of cheap Iraqi oil into thirsty Turkish tanks gradually weakened Ankara's stance. Inevitably, in February 1999, an

American bomb severed the oil pipeline into Turkey; President Demirel immediately declared this incident to be 'unacceptable'. Alastair Cooke went further: he called it 'imbecilic'.

Iraq had also regained its self-confidence when dealing with its southern neighbours, Kuwait and Saudi Arabia, both in solid support of US/UK policies. Very soon after Desert Fox, Washington had withdrawn its naval task force, led by USS *Enterprise,* its nuclear-powered and longest aircraft carrier, from the Gulf, together with substantial ground forces, thus reducing the strength of the border trip-wire. At about the same time, on 10 January 1999, the Iraqi Parliament voted not only to end cooperation with the United Nations but to de-recognise the border with Kuwait, a highly retrograde move which was played down. It also called for compensation for losses incurred during Desert Fox. Two weeks later, Tariq Aziz held out an expansive olive branch to Iraq's Arab neighbours: Iraq would apologise for its past mistakes, if other Arab states apologised for all theirs. Kuwait turned down the initiative forthwith but must have been concerned by Iraq's renewed denunciation of the border and threats of retaliation if US/UK air attacks, now without an aircraft carrier, continued to take off from its soil. A further limitation on US air power deployment was the American decision to suspend the northern no-fly zone protecting the Kurds in order to build up forces for the impending offensive in the Balkans against Serbia. HMS *Invincible,* too, was diverted to the Adriatic in April.

In the two years that followed Desert Fox, the problem of what to do about Iraq took a back seat. Both sides had gone to the cliff edge, had looked over and had pulled back. Hostilities in the air continued intermittently, with Baghdad making accusations about the 'evil American and British' killing and wounding many civilians in the southern no-fly zone. It was propaganda as much for domestic consumption as any other. Inspections were all but moribund, but IAEA personnel were allowed in to carry out routine duties under the terms of the 1968 Non-Proliferation Treaty. In December 1999, Tariq Aziz turned down as 'trickery' the Security Council offer of a reduction of sanctions in return for the resumption of UNSCOM inspections. Baghdad had by now learnt how to live with sanctions; they really had no further hold on the country. The ten-year anniversary of their imposition (6 August 1990) was marked by French condemnation of them as 'cruel'. A UNICEF report published the same day claimed that the mortality rate for children had doubled in the decade since the invasion of Kuwait. Demonstrations against sanctions were held all around the world. During the autumn of 2000, French and Russian transport planes landed at the recently opened Saddam International Airport laden with doctors and medical supplies. Shortly after, the Germans appointed a chargé d'affaires in Baghdad. At the beginning of 2001, Tariq Aziz could crow at a rally on 17 January in the Iraqi capital that Iraq was 'stronger and more united than before the Gulf War'. The occasion, of course, was the tenth anniversary of the start of the Coalition's bombardment prior to Desert Storm. Worse still, at the beginning of February, the Iraqi government revived its claim on Kuwait. In diplomatic terms, nothing had been gained since March 1991.

The atmospheric deterioration coincided with Clinton's replacement at the White House by George W Bush in January 2001. As the imposition and effect of sanctions continued to crumble and even the British military began to doubt the policing of the no-fly zones to be a realistic long-term policy, Washington appeared to be ready to take a stronger line with Saddam. President Bush had chosen his father's former Defence Secretary, Dick Cheney, to be his Vice-President and Donald Rumsfeld to be Defence Secretary, both considered to be hawks where Saddam was concerned. Although less so, former chairman of the Joint Chiefs of Staff Colin Powell, the incoming president's Secretary of State, was quick to confirm that sanctions 'in some form' must remain in place until Iraq complied with Security Council resolutions; he also acknowledged the need to 're-energise' allies. Powell's preference was for an overhaul of the sanctions regime which would have the effect of liberalising all trade except military materials. So-called 'smart sanctions' received rebuffs from both Baghdad and Moscow and the idea ran into the sand. Instead, 'regime change' began to be spoken of more loudly. Shortly after the new administration took over, US Congress authorised four million dollars to be made available to the Iraqi National Congress, the main umbrella opposition group. The President made it known that the INC might use the funds for operations both inside and outside Iraq. As noted before, this was never likely to remove the Iraq dictator, certainly not on its own.

An early visitor to Camp David was the British Labour Prime Minister, Tony Blair; he was received by the Republican Bush on 22 February – only a month after the presidential inauguration – and, despite their apparent differing political journeys hitherto, immediately hit it off. From then on, the two men grew ever closer together on what had to be done to rid the world of Saddam. If the truth be told, Blair recognised early on that Bush was intent on completing the task his father had failed to achieve in 1991. They stuck together as US/UK bombardments, including of Baghdad, continued and despite the still crescendoing calls for an end to sanctions. There matters might have rested for years but for the cataclysmic events of 11 September 2001. Neither man, not to mention nearly everyone else, could have expected that terrorists operating under the flag of Al-Qaeda would hit the United States right in the solar plexus – central New York and the Pentagon in Washington – even though their leader, Osama bin Laden, had been threatening to do so for years. During the days that followed, security experts in the West were slow to believe that a terrorist group could carry out such an act on its own. Fingers, instead, were quick to point to the likelihood that the attacks had been mounted with Saddam's sponsorship; he had the motivation. There was some evidence to support the hypothesis, as, sadly, it always was. Had not Baghdad offered bin Laden asylum in February 1999?[299] More recently, the leader of the suicide attacks, Mohammed Atta, was reported to have met a senior Iraqi intelligence officer somewhere in Europe several months previously. There was even the story of a meeting between bin Laden and Tariq Aziz at the Rashid Hotel in Baghdad.[300] From now on, the hunt was on to confirm the Iraqi connection, while US/UK forces began a slow but inexorable build-up in the Gulf.

The attacks on America, however, caused a substantial change in threat assessments. They had demonstrated that few places in the world were invulnerable to fanatical attack and intensified concerns that Saddam's possession of WMD, in whatever form, had to be demolished once and for all. From now on the two capitals worked closely to achieve this. Whatever differences there might have been between officials in Washington and London, as soon as the two heads of government came together, these disappeared. Determined to emulate his father, Bush was the more emphatic: on 11 December 2001, he warned that 'rogue states' with weapons of mass destruction would be his next priority in the 'war' against terrorism. He repeated this objective in his first State of the Union address on 29 January 2002.

The Pentagon was immediately set to work on a plan to topple Saddam and over the next two years ambitions grew; it was not just to be about how to remove an ogre but to bring about a transformation of Iraq itself along Western lines. All that was missing was some casus belli that was sufficiently persuasive to convince a respectable majority amongst hitherto doubting electorates on both sides of the Atlantic. Even so, there were many, accepting of the desirability to remove Saddam, who argued that this could only be done within the bounds of international law. Washington and London still faced long, discordant sessions in the Security Council where the other three permanent members were substantially less amenable than they had been in 1990/1.

On 3 February 2003, Prime Minister Blair's Director of Communications and Strategy, Alastair Campbell, issued a briefing document, now more commonly known as the 'dodgy dossier'. Entitled 'Iraq – Its Infrastructure of Concealment, Deception and Intimidation', it was based on a wide range of sources which were not spelled out for security reasons. When these were later put under the microscope, they were found to be less impressive than the authors of the document claimed them to be. Perhaps the most striking claim in the document was the allegation that Iraq's biological weapons could be deployed within forty-five minutes of an order from the Iraqi leader. The strong suggestion was that even London might be threatened. Campbell's paper was based on an earlier document, now known as the 'September dossier', which was published by the British government on 24 September 2002. It was thought important enough for Parliament to be recalled to discuss its contents. They included the assertion that Saddam still held or was working on all three forms of mass terror – nuclear, chemical and biological. It was unclear just how far the Iraqis had been able to weaponise the substances available to them, but there were still questions to be asked of Baghdad about the missiles Iraq still held. The material upon which the document was based came from reports produced for and by Whitehall's Joint Intelligence Committee. The same body that had got Saddam's intentions so wrong in 1990. Nevertheless, it impressed or fooled even those highly sceptical of military action to eradicate a regime alleged to have been involved in state terrorism. The leader of the Liberal Democrat Party, Menzies Campbell, was certainly taken in: "We can also agree that [Saddam] most certainly has chemical and biological weapons and is working towards a nuclear capability. The dossier contains confirmation of information that we either knew or most certainly should have been willing to assume."[301]

Whatever the truth behind the report, it hardly merited the headline in *The Sun*: 'Brits 45 mins from doom'.[302] It did, however, sway public opinion in the UK and bolstered Colin Powell's position in the Security Council when advancing arguments for military action. His address to the Council on 5 February 2003 contained the words: "…the facts and Iraq's behaviour show that Saddam Hussein and his regime are concealing their efforts to produce more weapons of mass destruction… every statement I make is backed up by sources, solid sources." Powell, an internationalist rather than unilateralist, later regretted his words and felt that he had been led by the nose.

This writer has little doubt that Saddam and his henchmen still held the know-how for all three forms of WMD terror. If he had ever meant to use them, Tel Aviv would have been a more realistic target than London, something Washington appreciated all too well. As far as actual materials were concerned, it is hardly surprising that nothing was found, despite exhaustive searching after Iraq's defeat: Baghdad's nuclear scientists had found refuge in Syria, where they continued their research. Given the long lead-in to the invasion of Iraq, there was plenty of time for nasty substances to be literally 'flushed down the Tigris'. Whether this was true or not, the debate over the existence of Iraqi WMD missed the point, as it always had. The case against Saddam was more firmly based on his repeated flouting of the armistice agreement he had allowed his senior generals to sign in March 1991. Unilaterally, he had rescinded Iraq's recognition of Kuwait and had reclaimed sovereignty over her territory. He had not released the many Kuwaitis he had taken hostage; they would be found murdered in 2003 after his removal from power. Unfortunately for them, they found few champions at the United Nations or in legal departments of State or the FCO. For them, the issue had become too dated to even try, not even in the international courts.

The invasion of Iraq by a US-led Coalition began with air strikes on 19 March 2003. Unlike in 1991, the ground offensive started the very next day, since there were no questions about air superiority. Unlike 1991, too, the Coalition was narrowly based, only Americans, British, Australians and a token Polish contingent taking part. The governments of France, Germany, Canada and New Zealand were strongly opposed to the action. United agreement in the Security Council for a new mandate was totally impossible. Throughout the world, people demonstrated against the invasion, including in Rome, where over three million constituted the largest ever anti-war rally recorded in the *Guinness Book of Records*. The campaign followed months of debate in the United Nations which solved nothing by way of legitimising the bid to remove Saddam and any terror weapons he might still hold. The process, seen as necessary to exhaust all avenues for a diplomatic solution, achieved one thing. It pushed military action into the heat of the long Iraqi summer. The battles were over quickly enough: Baghdad was taken on 9 April and Saddam's home city, Tikrit, on the 15th.

That, however, proved to be only the beginning of military engagement that has failed to prevent chaos and instability in Iraq. Coalition forces were unable to capture Saddam until 13 December, nine months after troops crossed into Iraq. His senior lieutenant, Izzat Ibrahim al-Duri, who brought peace negotiations to a precipitous end on 1 August 1990, has never been caught. The number of troops deployed to occupy a country of Iraq's size and geographical contrasts was woefully inadequate. At the last minute, Turkish intransigence prompted by several years of advantageous oil trading with Baghdad and a hatred towards the Kurds, forced Washington to divert to the south a division that should have overwhelmed Iraqi forces in the north. Through a combination of the absurdity in American insistence that all forces of law and order, including the Ba'ath Party, should be disbanded and the vicious heat, what demonstrable joy there had been amongst the Iraqi people that they had been freed from tyranny soon evaporated.[303] Communications were soon seriously disrupted by the theft of copper wire only just installed by Coalition engineers and long power cuts left swathes of the country devoid of air conditioning, the only comfort available in temperatures now soaring into the late forties centigrade. Very soon the average Baghdadi was complaining that life had been better under Saddam. Neither was the Coalition capable of controlling the extremer elements, both Sunni and Shia, let loose by the disarming of every means that had restrained them hitherto. Few in the Coalition ranks understood Islam or Arabic. Unsurprisingly, when outrages occurred against them, the best guidelines for military conduct were not adhered to. The locals became seen as 'unfriendly'.

The hopes for the creation of a civilian government, democratically elected, faded quickly as the real and deep divides within pre-invasion opposition groups came to the surface. Elections to a constitutional assembly could not take place until January 2005. Nearly a year elapsed before parliamentary elections could be held on 15 December. The new Parliament divided not along political lines recognisable at Westminster or in Congress but religiously and racially – a toxic mixture. The populous (Shi-ite) south took 128 seats, the Sunni north-west won only forty-four sets and the Kurds fifty-three. Under Saddam, it had been the Sunni who had been allowed to rule the roost; they now resented being under-represented. In the new order, the majority was riven by factions wanting a more Islamic society, so simple arithmetic did not add up to political stability. All the old prejudices remained and the Coalition was powerless to damp them down. As was always on the cards, a bloodbath replaced Saddam's cruelties, as deep-seated feuds erupted in a country still awash with small arms and no veneer of law and order. Had Washington simply been able to remove Saddam and appoint a tough general to take his place, the Coalition might have withdrawn in six months. As it happened, the Americans set themselves the impossible task of reconstituting and training new forces of government and law and order along Western democratic lines in a country that for thousands of years had never really experienced democracy. In the end, it was too much for America's most loyal ally; the bulk of the British occupying contingent was withdrawn, tail between its legs, on 30 April 2009. Down to 2010, the cost to the British taxpayer has been assessed at £9.24 billion.[304] The real cost to the United States is incalculable, as is the often-hidden damage done to many of those who took part. Beyond that, the credibility of the USA as a world leader and champion of freedom has been shattered, just at a time when it had embarked on a fresh – and impossible-to-win venture – its 'war' on terrorism.

Eighteen

KABUL IGNOMINY (2021)

The lunch hour had just finished. The corridor should have emptied with officers back at their desks, but this day – 11 September 2001 – a large group was gathered round the monitor displaying BBC World News and uttering gasps of dismay. The horrible spectacle of hi-jacked airliners crashing into the centre of New York was as riveting as it was appalling. At the time, no one could have known who the perpetrators were, but there was muttered speculation: "Al-Qaeda." The Americans were quick to point a finger; Colin Powell reacted almost immediately, naming Osama bin Laden, the leader of Al-Qaeda, two days later, as the prime suspect for sponsorship of the attacks. American troops in the Gulf were put on high alert; on security advice, President Bush took to Air Force One to control the response from the skies and promised to hunt down those who were responsible for the atrocities. Perversely, certainly unwisely, Baghdad media supported the attacks as 'the fruit of American crime against humanity'. Anticipating where the seat of the blame would lie, the United Nations started to withdraw its eighty staff from Afghanistan. Exceptionally, NATO and Russia issued a joint statement calling for international efforts to combat global terrorism. Moscow, after all, had its own problems with bomb attacks and other outrages launched by Muslim opposition activists against Russian rule in Chechnya. The Russian Federation had in the past appealed for intelligence help from the West, an appeal that was not easy to respond to; this made Moscow's move all the more welcome. Even the ageing Palestinian leader Yasser Arafat was urging all Arab states to declare their readiness to join a coalition against terrorism. The world, bar one or two notable exceptions, was united in its support of the United States.

Asymmetrical warfare by those with deep grievances against an overbearing authority was not new. A terrorist might be a freedom fighter. Ireland, the Balkans and Palestine, to name but the most obvious, had witnessed horrific bloodshed in the previous hundred years or more, created by individuals and small groups. A terrorist assassination opened the road to world war in 1914. In the wake of Israel's annexation of the West Bank in 1967, Arab groups, Islamic and secular, had mushroomed and were well-known to Western intelligence agencies, if not always fully understood by them. Al-Qaeda ('the base') was little more than a decade old and its motivation was still being analysed, albeit the more perceptive had recognised that bin Laden's anger was directed at the Americans for stationing troops in Saudi Arabia whose king had been given responsibility for protection of the Holy places. Before 1990, the rich, young Wahhabi had been a potential bedfellow in the struggle to prevent the Soviet Union from taking over Afghanistan.[305] Al-Qaeda sprang from the Kuwait operation; by 2001, it was said to have the aim of spreading 'Islamic fundamentalism and the destruction of American interests in the Middle East'. In fact, its activities were far wider: in December 1992, it carried out three bombings against US troops in Yemen; in 1993, it claimed to have shot down US helicopters in Somalia; in 1995, it tried to organise the mid-air bombing of no less than twelve US airliners; and, in August 1998, had conducted bombings of US embassies in Nairobi and Dar as Salaam, killing over three hundred people and wounding five thousand others. In February 1998, it had called on all Muslims to kill American citizens and their allies. Because of this, bin Laden had become an internationally hunted criminal; he had sought and found refuge in Afghanistan with the Taliban,[306] where he was given space to attract in recruits for training in a wide variety of terrorist techniques, including explosives, poison and biological warfare substances. Many of those answering his call were from the UK.

Before examining the American response to the 'nine-eleven' atrocities, there is a general point to be made by way of understanding the motivation of those attracted to Al-Qaeda. For centuries, a huge swathe of the Earth's surface – stretching from the Maghreb through the Middle East and Central Asia into South and South-East Asia and beyond to the Philippines – had been controlled by rich rulers or by their colonial masters. The former were cowed by the strength of the mostly European great powers and, in order to maintain their positions, sucked up to them. Some still do at Ascot and other horse-racing venues. Two world wars, the rise of nationalism and the Western thirst for oil changed the balance, while not always changing the system. Resentment was keenest in the Middle East. Just as Christianity's early championship of the poor had helped to undermine the Roman Empire, so Islam gave a strong edge to those who no longer accepted the mores handed out by the industrial world. By the post-war period, there were many – particularly in former areas of the Turkish Empire – who no longer respected the British as the former dominant colonial or protecting power; they had never respected the Americans, except for their economic and military muscle. Long association creating experience and savoir faire counted for less and less as the respect for Western values dwindled. Lurking since the second half of the nineteenth century when Muslim theologians like Rashid Rida[307] first produced the principles of a modern Islamic state, it has produced 'an intractable confrontation between a theistic, land-based and traditional culture in places little different from the Europe of the Middle Ages and the secular material values of the Enlightenment.'[308]

The lack of respect for Western values and often extreme animosity towards the Christian ethical base of the so-called civilised world, even democracy itself, became increasingly evident in the second half of the twentieth century. It was obvious to anyone involved in discussion with Muslims on the fringes of extreme Islam. It could produce amusing juxtapositions. On one occasion, a young British Muslim and would-be recruit to Al-Qaeda exploded at my questioning because he thought I was trying to convert him. Then he suddenly relented: "I should not speak to you like that," he said, "I should respect you as an old man." Tradition in conflict with a new emotive doctrine. In a contrasting dialogue, an older and much more sophisticated Islamist who apparently shunned violence had no doubt that the UK, along with the rest of the world, would eventually be Islamic and adopt the ethics laid down in the God-given and Prophet Mohammed-received Qur'an. It might take two hundred years, in his estimation, but it would happen. A new self-confidence was replacing the old subservience; it was fuelling fanatical extremism and, alas, it was God-based. One only has to consider the failure of long prison sentences and the small return from large resources ploughed into campaigns to persuade young Muslims to abandon their fanaticism, to see the effect of this assuredness. Christians waiting to be mauled by lions in the Parthenon displayed the same mettle.

In the days that followed the destruction of the Twin Towers, President Bush exchanged his father's underkill in confronting Saddam for overkill. On the day after the Taliban leader Mullah Mohammed Omar defended him against American accusations, the President – on 15 September 2001 – declared war on bin Laden as the prime suspect. Prime Minister Blair joined Bush five days later at a memorial service in New York and attended Congress in Washington. When the American chips were down, the US/UK 'special relationship' was seemingly alive and well. With Washington less willing to undertake the task, the British Foreign Secretary, Jack Straw, was sent to Tehran on the 25th to persuade the Iranians of Al-Qaeda's shocking deeds. Ayatollah Khamenei's response was to declare that Iran would not support any attack on Afghanistan. Pakistan, territorially closest to Afghanistan and a long-term ally of the Taliban and other forces that had defeated the Soviet Union, retained diplomatic relations with Kabul. This situation has never changed and, on occasion, has been useful as a channel for message-passing. Pakistan, too, refused to support any attack on its northern neighbour.

With Interpol issuing arrest warrants for bin Laden and his associate Ayman Zawahiri, leader of Egyptian Islamic Jihad, the world appeared to be girding itself up for concerted action to bring sponsors of 'nine-eleven' to trial. The FBI was able to release names and photos of the nineteen accused hi-jackers on the 27th. As a corollary, a group of Pakistani religious scholars returned home the day after, having sought to persuade the Taliban to hand over bin Laden. In response, the Taliban let it be known that they were keeping the Al-Qaeda leader 'safe', a possible euphemism. Indeed, on 5 October, Muller Zaeef,[309] the Taliban ambassador in Istanbul, declared that the Taliban were prepared to put bin Laden on trial provided the United States presented sufficient evidence of his complicity. International pressure, the commitment by NATO to stand full square with its leading member and the widespread freezing of Afghan assets had been sufficient to bring those who held the real power in Afghanistan to a point where bin Laden could be arraigned. The sticking point was where he should be tried and here, Washington insisted that this be the United States. This was refused by the Taliban, although some have argued that there was still room for negotiation.

Thus, the huge military force of the world's leading superpower was unleashed at a pigmy.[310] In addition, the coalition forming in support of American action offered enormous resources and facilities: the UK (nuclear-powered submarines, refuelling tankers, reconnaissance aircraft and special forces), France (armed and supply vessels in the Indian Ocean and special forces), Russia (airspace), Australia (1,550 troops from its Special Air Service regiment, refuelling and reconnaissance aircraft and three frigates), New Zealand (special forces), Canada (several naval vessels), Pakistan (the use of two air bases), Italy (troops 'if necessary') and Uzbekistan/Tajikistan (use of bases for US forces). Not everyone was by any means convinced that the Americans should descend on Afghanistan. When it became evident invasion was on the cards, my line manager let out a strangled cry from behind his desk: "Oh God, I hope not." Perhaps a more telling reaction came from the eminent military historian Sir Michael Howard[311] when, on 30 October 2001, he delivered an indictment of Colin Powell's 'very natural, but terrible and irrevocable error' in declaring that America was 'at war'. In deploying his arguments against the use of force against an elusive enemy, however unequal, he pointed out that in a serious campaign against terrorists what was really needed – and would now be overridden – was 'secrecy, intelligence, political sagacity, quiet ruthlessness, covert actions that remain covert, above all infinite patience'. None of those requirements ever really applied in the essentially American war on the Taliban. Sir Michael accepted that a police operation conducted under the auspices of the United Nations was unrealistic and applauded President Bush for securing a UN mandate for military action and the support of an 'amazingly wide-ranging coalition'.

He considered that bin Laden had 'taken the first and all-important trick' and could only counsel that, once the military operation had begun, it should be pressed to a successful conclusion, 'successful enough for us to be able to disengage with a reasonable amount of honour and, for the benefit of the tabloid headlines, to claim victory'. That, however in his judgement, was only the beginning of a long struggle in which there would be no spectacular battles and no clear victory. Twenty years later, his words stand totally vindicated.

The USAAF commenced night bombing of Afghan targets in Kabul, Kandahar and Jalalabad on Sunday 7 October. The first strikes included fifty Tomahawk cruise missiles, some fired from three Royal Naval nuclear submarines patrolling in the Indian Ocean. Two days later, with the benefit of total air supremacy, daylight bombing started. The Taliban claimed a relatively moderate loss of seventy-six civilians killed under such a heavy bombardment; they also lifted restrictions on bin Laden. Donald Rumsfeld crowed on 11 October that he would be 'amazed if there is a Taliban government in Kabul after this is over'. The American Defence Secretary had no real grasp of asymmetrical warfare. While the anti-Taliban and anti-Pashtun groups forming the Northern Alliance were able to seize power in three north-eastern provinces, the air offensive continued unremittingly. That did not stop bin Laden issuing a threat of suicide attacks in the UK or scares of anthrax letter bombs in the USA. Cracks in Security Council unanimity soon appeared, with Moscow and Beijing calling for a cessation of military action and the setting up by the United Nations of a new Afghan government in Kabul. Meddlesome and unrealistic. By mid-November, Northern Alliance forces, supported by American Special Forces, had entered the Afghan capital. The British Special Boat Service landed at Kabul's Bagram airport to secure the facilities for the arrival of approaching four thousand Coalition marines and paratroopers. The military battle had been won overwhelmingly in just over a month; the long political and security battles had yet to begin, not to mention the need to win over hearts and minds. At the centre of it all, bin Laden was able to slope away to an unknown hideout. He was eventually assassinated in Abbottabad, Pakistan, in 2011, where he had been left untroubled by a sympathetic intelligence service. Many criticised what they considered to be an arbitrary American killing.

This is not the place for an account of the twists and turns in twenty years of attempts to establish a democratically elected and accepted government of Afghanistan, together with security for the population. In the end, neither of those goals was achieved; there are several salient reasons why. In the first place, Washington – backed by London – embarked on a crusade, not only to get rid of the Taliban and the terrorist groups it was protecting but to persuade a people away from a traditional way of life they had been locked in for centuries. At the end, few Afghans were prepared to defend changes that many simply did not want. Western leaders, however, forgot or refused to recognise the graphic lessons of history: neither Britain's loss of a whole army – 4,500 troops and twelve thousand followers – in their retreat from Kabul in 1842, nor the Soviet Union's abject failure in the 1980s served as warnings to, principally, American politicians bent on avenging the casualties of 'nine-eleven'. Taken in isolation, the defeat of Afghan conventional forces was a walk-over with minimal risk; to hold down the seventh largest country in the world with its many formidable and inaccessible mountain refuges, however, was never going to be a realistic proposition. Yes, in the colonial era, the British had been able to establish the Raj over a far greater area with arguably greater cultural contrasts, but the age and circumstances were entirely different. A usually single-minded government in London, with a long-serving specialist ministry – the India Office – was able to delegate to a competent administration on the ground, the Indian Civil Service. The latter deployed a veneer of dedicated and experienced colonial officers. Districts with a population of twenty million or more were controlled by just four officials who left day-to-day affairs in the hands of Indian subordinates.[312] Most importantly, these imperial civil servants learnt the vernacular and could talk to Indians without interpreters. That did not happen in Afghanistan.

In India, too, the military power, for the most part, remained out of sight and was comprised, in any case, of many more Indian regiments than British. The former were drawn from a wide variety of provincial and tribal areas and great care was taken in their deployment where particularistic sentiments might be hurt. Its uniforms were deliberately designed to impress the people; colourful parades and durbars were held regularly to emphasise the attractions and power behind serving the authority of the great white queen-empress. No British officer appointed to an Indian regiment, one of the better options when leaving Sandhurst, was allowed to command troops until he could speak to them in their own language. And, even if Calcutta or Delhi had to license ruthless or secret methods, they could expect to do so without a wave of media protest if things went wrong. Back in Britain, people were proud of the Empire, at least until after two world wars had sapped the country's strength and reduced enthusiasm for overseas ventures.

None of this applied in Afghanistan. There was never any great support on the home front. The media, at best, were neutral, often sceptical and rightly so. The rapidity of modern communications brought bad news to the breakfast table daily and highlighted any misconduct by troops acting under severe pressure There had been no long lead-in during which detailed plans might be drawn up for establishing a caretaker administration pending constitutional and democratic election of an Afghan government – as had happened at the end of the Second World War. There had been no time for the acquisition of the several languages and dialects spoken and there were insufficient trained military forces to take on a vast guerrilla campaign waged in the most difficult of terrains. The problem was then compounded by the Americans and British taking on a second occupation – of Iraq – less than two years later, again without the essential tools or plans to do the job.

The result was inevitable. In the face of continuing failures to produce peace and stability, Washington's commitment faded. President Trump, more used to executive, often arbitrary, decisions in the boardroom than statecraft, started the rot by indulging those who wanted a quick if negotiated get-out. He set impossible deadlines which a movement like the Taliban, with infinite patience, was never going to respect. Kabul fell to them in days, not the months or more that Pentagon and Whitehall experts were expecting. With that, all the advances in social and political welfare tentatively achieved over twenty years were lost. The worst affected were women, who were returned overnight to total domination by males; they lost their rights to education and employment and were returned to imprisonment in their own homes. In Kabul, the Taliban have set up a government ruled by narrow religious principles that originated from desert life in the sixth century. It remains to be seen whether they will return to the days when they were perfectly willing to allow fanatics to train for the mounting of outrages throughout the world. However moderate they try to present themselves, it is doubtful whether they can prevent violence being planned in remote mountain fastnesses and then unleashed on many of the soft targets in the West. We should shudder at the prospect and prepare for losses that may well outnumber the 3,502 Coalition deaths (at 18 May 2020) since the ill-considered Operation Enduring Freedom commenced in 2001.[313] There should also be a sense of shame for the victims who will continue to suffer – the Afghan people. What they have lost since the Soviet invasion in 1979 – over forty years ago – is incalculable in terms of lives, destruction of habitat, hunger, disease and disruption of households. Anything the West, Russia and any other countries involved have had to face pales into insignificance. All the signs are that Afghanistan's future will be even darker than it is at present.

There is a passage in the Bible about a man who was cleansed of an evil spirit. Matthew's Gospel 12:45 reads as follows:

> *"Then goeth he, and taketh with himself seven other spirits more wicked than himself and they enter in and dwell there; and the last state is worse than the first. Even so shall it be unto this wicked generation."*

This, on top of pandemics, global warming and insidious pollution! As with all these, government leaders could and should have acted well before they threatened to get out of hand. In the case of Afghanistan, too, it all started because those who could failed to face down a fearful bully who then went on to create mayhem in the Middle East.

ENDNOTES

1 Brigadier (later Major General) Derek Gordon Thomond Horsford CBE DSO (1917–2007): a distinguished veteran Gurkha commanding officer during the battle of Kohima (Nagaland, India) in 1944, he was known for his ability to launch successful and swift infiltrative operations. Like 1961, he had been rushed in, from Arakan, to take over 4th/1st Gurkhas after their commanding officer had been killed. A 'tall, dark, imposing man', he was the right man for an emergency. His remarks were reported in *The Times* on 4 July 1961.

2 Kuwait was considered a British-protected state, a loose form of British suzerainty, under which the ruler retained complete control of internal affairs, while Britain had control over defence and external affairs. Compare, however, the Chapter Two conclusion, which suggests that the status was not quite as simple as that.

3 The last civilian minister, Mustafa Ali (Justice), had resigned from the government on 15 May.

4 George Blake (born 1922): after working for the Soviet KGB since his detention in Korea by the Communists in 1950, he was finally arrested in London on 10 April 1961. He had been a member of the British Secret Intelligence Service from 1944. Judging by the prestige of the awards he received from the Soviet Union, the damage he did to British intelligence networks was far greater than that done by the so-called Cambridge spies, headed by Kim Philby. Before his arrest, he already had access to knowledge of intelligence in the Middle East; coming under suspicion, he was summoned back from Beirut, where he had been attending the Middle East Centre for Arabic Studies (MECAS), before being taken into custody. Pending a damage assessment, SIS would have suspended contact with many sensitive sources.

5 Marshal of the Royal Air Force Sir Samuel Charles Elworthy KG GCB CBE DSO LVO DFC AFC (1911–93): after distinguished service

during the Second World War, including as the Deputy Supreme Allied Commander Marshal of the Royal Air Force Lord Tedder's close aide on bombing strategy, he was appointed to various staff posts, before becoming Air Officer commanding Middle East in March 1961. He was later appointed as Chief of Air Staff in 1963 and Chief of Defence Staff in 1967. He retired in 1971.

6 Air Commodore Sir Arthur Vere-Harvey CBE (1906–94): after war service, he entered Parliament as Conservative member for Macclesfield, a seat he retained until his resignation in 1971. He was sent to the Lords as Baron Harvey of Prestbury in the County Palatine of Chester. A much-respected back-bencher, he took over the chair of the Conservative 1922 Committee in the mid-1960s.

7 Radio Baghdad on 8 July. The Iraqi Military Attaché in London, Brigadier Muhammad Falk, just returned from Baghdad, denied on 13 July that there had been any concentration of troops against Kuwait.

8 George Edward Cecil Wigg (1900–83): Labour MP for Dudley (1945–67) who enjoyed close relations with the veteran front-bencher and former Minister of Defence, 'Manny' Shinwell (1894–1969). Harold Wilson, as leader of the Labour Party and Prime Minister, used Wigg as his private eye and appointed him to the sinecure post of Paymaster General, so that he could establish a closer link between the Intelligence Services and Number Ten. Wigg was sent to the Lords in 1967. Towards the end of his life, the 'establishment' had the last laugh when Wigg was arrested for kerb-crawling.

9 Alan Waller Woodruff (1916–92): Honorary Consultant in Tropical Medicine to the Army and British Airways; Wellcome Professor of Clinical Tropical Medicine at the London School of Hygiene and Tropical Medicine (1952–81). Sir David Paton Cuthbertson (1900–89): Director of the Rowett Research Institute (1945–65), during which time it became one of the world's leading centres for animal nutrition research. He was recognised as a world expert on metabolism; appointed to the Medical Research Council in 1943, he was knighted in 1965 on retirement. Professor Brian Gilmore Maegraith (1907–89): an Australian Rhodes Scholar, he served as a pathologist for the Royal Army Medical Corps in France and Sierra Leone; held the Chair of Tropical Medicine at Liverpool School of Tropical Medicine from 1944. His work in Kuwait was published in the *Lancet* in 1958.

10 Harold Watkinson (1910–95): after active wartime service in the RNVR, he was elected MP for Woking in 1950; he held the seat until 1964. Following his time as Minister for Transport and Civil Aviation under Eden, he was promoted by Macmillan to the Ministry of Defence in 1959. He, too, was sacked in the 1962 Night of the Long Knives but found his business niche as Chairman of Cadbury Schweppes (1969–74).

11 Lieutenant Colonel John Kyme Cordeaux (1902–82): Conservative MP for Nottingham (1955–64) who had a natural interest in military matters but also campaigned for pensioners.

12 John Yudkin FRSC (1910–95): founding professor of the Department of Nutrition at Queen Elizabeth College, London.

13 There was the embarrassment of three Royal Engineers being detained at the Safwan border post after losing their way. With Iraqi suspicion that they were spies, it took some months before they were returned to the UK.

14 John Lewis (1912–69): Labour MP for Bolton 1945–51 who lost his seat to the Liberal Arthur Holt, the one bright spark in the party's otherwise dismal performance in the General Election which brought Churchill back to power.

15 The mention of the Secretary of State for War was deliberate. The Commonwealth Relations Secretary at the time was Duncan Sandys (1908–87), who was married to Churchill's daughter, Diana. They had divorced in 1960, but Sandys married a second time. Wigg was also showing up Profumo as a bully, in contrast to Sandys, a much-respected war hero.

16 Clive Irving: *Anatomy of a Scandal: A Study of the Profumo Affair* (1963) p109.

17 Alfred Thompson ('Tom') Denning, Baron Denning OM PC DL (1899–1999): appointed as Master of the Rolls in 1960, a position he held for twenty years, he took just forty-nine days to complete his report after having interviewed 160 witnesses. The best-selling report was published on 26 September 1963.

18 Kuwait was admitted to UN membership on 14 May 1963.

19 See Karsten Niebuhr: *Reisebescreibung nach Arabian und andern Laendern* – 2 Vols (1774–78) vol II pp231–36. Born (1733) in Luedingworth near Cuxhaven on the Lower Saxony coast, Niebuhr was educated at the avant garde university of Goettingen. He is given credit for discovering how to determine longitude for marine (and desert) navigation; that is, without visual fixed points at ocean or ground level.

20 Francis Warden: *Historical Sketch of the Uttoobee tribe of Arabs (Bahrain) from the Year 1716 to the Year 1817* – published in selections from the records of the Bombay Government (Bombay Selections) No XXIV Bombay (1856) pp361–425.

21 Ahmad Mustafa Abu-Hakima: *The Modern History of Kuwait 1750–1965* – McGill University (1982) p1.

22 The Bible makes no mention of Adnan: see Genesis 16:11–12 and 25:12–18, later verified in 1 Chronicles 1:28–33.

23 Al-Hasa (al-Ahsa), watered by artesian springs, lies some forty miles west of the Gulf coast, bounded by Kuwait in the north, the desert of Rub'al-Khali (empty quarter) in the south and the Dahna sand belt to the west. It was probably the furthest south into Arabia that the Turks penetrated. The kingdom of Saudi Arabia had absorbed it before the First World War. Niebuhr passed through the oasis in 1765.

24 Ottoman silver piastres minted in Istanbul during the reign of Sultan Mustafa III (1757–74) measured 36.8mm in diameter and weighed 18.27gms.

25 Dr Edward Ives: *A Journey from Persia to England by an Unusual Route*, London (1773) p222.

26 ibid Niebuhr p296.

27 Factory Records, Persian and the Persian Gulf Vol 17 dispatch no. 1152.

28 ibid Abu-Hakima p9.

29 ibid Abu-Hakima p48.

30 bid Abu-Hakima pp60–1: Captain John Wainwright (died 1819) commanded the French-built frigate HMS *Chiffone* from 1806 and later distinguished himself as captain of Admiral Cochrane's flagship, HMS *Tonnant*, during the War of 1812, in helping to worst an American flotilla in Chesaspeake Bay. During his time in the Gulf, he suppressed piracy operating from the Ras al-Khaimah islands and destroyed their coastal bases in Persia.

31 Muhammad Ali Pasha al-Masud ibn Agha was born in Macedonia on 4 March 1769, the son of a tobacco and shipping merchant who also served as an Ottoman official. Without breaking with the Sultan, he established himself as governor of Egypt and Sudan during the 1820s, proclaiming himself as *Wali* or Khedive. The terms are more or less equivalent to viceroy, but in practice, he was rather more than that in the pursuit of his expansionist policies. Increasingly senile towards the end of his life, he died in post on 2 August 1849.

32 Abu Shahr (Bushire): a former Dutch trading post that was granted in 1763 to the British East India Company and became a principal naval base and factory on the Persian south-west coast in the northern Gulf.

33 ibid Abu-Hakima p68 citing a letter from Khalid Pasha in Kuwait to Mehmet Ali in Cairo.

34 John Silk Buckingham (1786–1855): born Flushing, near Plymouth, he evinced strong anti-slavery views as a naval officer before entering journalism in Calcutta. He was deported by the reactionary viceroy John Adam in 1831, but on return to England was exonerated, compensated and won a seat for the Whigs at the 1834 General Election; he sat as a radical. His account is contained in *Travels in Assyria, Media and Persia* – London (1829).

35 The Arab-built *baghlah* was a two-masted, deep-sea dhow with three lateen sails, one hundred feet in length and of about 250 tons. It sailed with a thirty- to forty-man crew as far as East Africa, the Bay of Bengal and the Spice Islands. Stocqueler (1800–85) went out to Calcutta in 1821 and was on his return journey ten years later. He wrote his account in 1832: *Fifteen Months' Pilgrimage through Khuzistan and Persia* – 2 Vols London. His Kuwaiti descriptions are contained in volume one.

36 Colonel later Lieutenant General Lewis Pelly (1825–92): *Report on the Tribes around the shores of the Persian Gulf* – Calcutta (1874) pp30–34. Unlike Buckingham and Stocqueler before him, Pelly was a long-serving Company man since 1840 and politically conservative. None-the-less adventurous, he was the first Englishman to visit Riyadh (in 1865) since George Sadler in 1819. He was part of the team that set up Britain's control of Bahrain in the 1860s. He first visited Kuwait in March 1863.

37 A Francophile sympathy persisted. Many Kuwaitis were in Paris for the summer when the Iraqis invaded in August 1990.

38 Little had changed by the late twentieth century. When Prince Charles and Princess Diana visited the Emirate in 1987, the tables groaned with food which was barely touched by the vast number of VIP guests. The leavings went to the many servants.

39 The Kuwaiti intervention was not exceptional. The Turks had prevailed upon their naval support during military expeditions in 1787 and 1798.

40 The building pre-dated the Seif Palace which Shaikh Mubarak started to build in 1904. It stood next to the Central Mosque, which raises the question whether Sabah and his fellow worshippers heard the shots.

41 Alan Rush: *Al-Sabah – History and Genealogy of Kuwait's Ruling Family (1752–1987)* – Ithaca 1987 p120 based on Jabir's personal account given to Yusuf bin Isa al-Qinai in *Safahat* p21.

42 FO minute quoted in Busch: *British Policy in the Persian Gulf 1894–1914*.

43 Memo from Stavrides sent to Lord Salisbury on 6 July 1896 (FO 539/98). The same memo reported Mubarak's 1895 visit to Colonel Wilson, then the Gulf Political Resident.

44 ibid 2 April 1897.

45 ibid FO 307 to Constantinople of 17 July 1897.

46 ibid Meade to GOI of 25 September 1897.

47 ibid TH Sanderson to India Office of 25 November 1697.

48 Thomas Henry Sanderson, 1st Baron Sanderson GCB KCMG ISO (1841–1923). Career Foreign Office and PUS (1894–1923). He was known as 'Lamps' Sanderson for his strong-lensed glasses. See Sanderson's telegram of 5 December and Hamilton's of 24 December 1898. Lord George Francis Hamilton GCSI PC JP (1845–1927) was a Conservative MP (1868–1906), 1st Lord of the Admiralty (1885–86) and Secretary of State for India (1895–1906).

49 ibid No 35.

50 Rear Admiral, later Sir Archibald Lucius Douglas (1842–1913), C-in-C East Indies (1898–99). His command included the Persian Gulf.

51 ibid Meade's telegram to the India Office of 30 January 1899. For full text of the bond and Meade's note to Mubarak, see Abu-Hakima pp184–6.

52 Sir Nicholas Roderick O'Connor GCB GCMG PC (1843–1908): British ambassador at Constantinople from 1898 until his death. Previously ambassador at St Petersburg from 1895 to 1898.

53 Al-Sarif is near Ha'il in present-day north-western Saudi Arabia.

54 ibid al-Hakima p113.

55 HMS *Lapwing*, one of nine Redbreast class gunboats built around 1890. Her commanding officer during the action was Lieutenant Commander, later Rear Admiral, John Garnet Armstrong, who was credited euphemistically with 'clever capture of a pair of pirate dhows'.

56 For full text see al-Hakima pp188–91.

57 ibid al-Hakima p195.

58 ibid al-Hakima p196–7.

59 Admiral Sir Edmond John Warre Slade KCIE KCVO (1859–1928): after an active career, he was appointed Director of Naval Intelligence in 1907

before assuming the post of C-in-C East Indies station two years later. Winston Churchill recognised his singular qualities and also sent him in 1913 to investigate the possibility of purchasing a fifty-one per cent stake in the Anglo-Persian Oil company. The purchase was completed just before the outbreak of the First World War, as timely an investment as any.

60 ibid al-Hakima p197.

61 Sir Harold Berners Walker (born 1932): career diplomat since 1956 and British ambassador to Iraq 1990–91.

62 The term applied from the late eighteenth century to the offspring of the eldest son of Noah, Shem.

63 Genesis 11:31. Ur was excavated between 1922–34 by Sir Leonard Woolley and is famous for the Ziggurat of Ur-Nammu, governor of the city (approximately BC 2113–2095), and dedicated to the moon god, Nanna.

64 The Hittites came from central and eastern Asia Minor; their capital was at Hattusha, close to present-day Bogazkale, about a hundred miles east of Ankara. Their empire flourished for some four hundred years from BC 1600 and stretched down into the Levant and the northern Tigris-Euphrates basin.

65 The Assyrians were originally based on Assur in northern Iraq and one of the original thirteen city states of early Mesopotamia.

66 A city today of some 160,000 and lying on the Tigris about 140 kilometres north-west of Baghdad. Originally an Akkadian fort, it was probably identical or adjacent to Birtha, a base set up by Alexander the Great, another of Saddam's heroes.

67 Assyrian ruler BC 1243–07 and the first known to have used the title 'king of kings'. His name means 'my trust is in the warrior god, Ninurta'. He vanquished the Hittites at the battle of Nihriya early in his reign and subsequently captured Babylon. Before his death, he had established sway over all Mesopotamia.

68 The united kingdom of Israel lasted until the reign of Solomon's successor, Rehoboam, when the ten northern tribes revolted over the heavy tax burden his father had exerted. From 930 BC, the kingdom was divided into Israel in the north and Judah to the south with its capital at Jerusalem.

69 Simon Henderson: *Instant Empire* – Mercury House (1991) p3.

70 Acts 9:10–18.

71 Full text to be found in *Ante-Nicene Fathers*: edit Roberts and Donaldson Vol 8 – Hendrickson (1995) pp535–8.

72 Gondophoros is historical. He founded an Indo-Parthian dynasty and ruled from 19–46AD. He is, therefore, a contemporary of St Thomas.

73 The contributor concerned misquoted Isaiah 34:6 which reads: "for the Lord hath a sacrifice in Bozrah and a great slaughter in the land of Idumea." The latter is synonymous with Edom, the land of the ancient Moabites, now lying within the borders of Jordan and Israel and not in any way connected with Iraq or the Garden of Eden.

74 Shi'iy (*singular*); Shia (*plural*).

75 Synagogues were destroyed in Baghdad in 1333.

76 Timur Gurkani (1370–1406): born Kesh near Samarkand, he was the last of the nomadic conquerors from central Asia. His ambition was to restore a vast empire, similar to that established by Genghis Khan a century before. He exercised power over an area stretching from Russia to India and was infamous for his cruelty. Sometimes referred to as Timur the Lame, probably descriptive of a wounding suffered in battle.

77 Ralph Fitch (1550–1611): born in Derbyshire, he became a gentleman merchant explorer from the City of London and an invaluable consultant for the fledgling British East India Company.

78 Suleiman is considered the most outstanding of the Mamluk Sultans and is best remembered for his judicial reforms. He abolished the death penalty, except where sharia courts had decreed otherwise, outlawed land confiscations and generally raised the level of administrative justice. That he recognised the value of an understanding with the British is symptomatic of his enlightened pragmatism.

79 Claudius James Rich (1787–1821): see JS Buckingham – *Travels in Mesopotamia* Vol 2 p200 (1928). An officer of the East India Company from 1803, Rich learnt his Arabic in Alexandria and his Turkish in Constantinople and Smyrna before taking up his residency in Baghdad in 1808. He initiated archaeological exploration of Babylon and provided valued insights of the areas in which he served. See also CJ Rich: *Nature of a Residence in Koordistan and on the site of Ancient Babylon* – posthumously published in London (1836). He died of cholera when visiting Shiraz in Persia.

80 Only two years after Waterloo, Daoud Pasha invited French officers to train his twenty thousand-strong army and allowed French mission schools to open. There has always been a certain even-handedness in bringing in outside influences. In the 1980s, many senior Kuwaiti officials professed to

being Francophile and preferred to spend the hot summers in Paris rather than in London.

81 Within three years of starting its operations, the River Steam Navigation (Oman/Ottoman) service had been taken over by the British Lynch Company.

82 Suleiman Faiq, the Baghdad historian writing in 1861.

83 Charles Townshend: *When God Made Hell* – Faber and Faber (2010) p4.

84 *The Waters of Babylon*: diary of WC Spackman – Imperial War Museum 74/70/1. The Bengali unit suffered worse when it was captured in entirety at the surrender of the Kut garrison on 29 April 1916 and many died when it was force marched to Aleppo.

85 ibid Townshend p8.

86 Extracts from the Keary papers cited by Townsend p300.

87 A number of soldiers on their voyage out to the Gulf claimed to have lost their false teeth when vomiting over the side with bouts of sea-sickness – real or alleged.

88 Churchill is recorded as saying that if Britain lost Abadan, she could simply 'buy our oil from elsewhere'.

89 General Sir Edmund Barrow GCB, KCMG (1852–1934): he joined the Indian Army in 1877 and took part in a series of colonial engagements, mostly on the North-West Frontier but also in Hong Kong and China (Boxer Rebellion in 1900). He became Military Secretary to the India Office in 1914.

90 Yitzhak Nakash: *The Shi'is of Iraq* – Princeton University Press (1994) pp60–1.

91 Gertrude Bell (1868–1926): the Arab Bureau in Cairo's representative sent to Basra in March 1916. She was more at home in the deserts of Syria and was less than flattering about Mesopotamia: 'the very soil of Mesopotamia exhaled emanations fatal to virility' (ibid Townsend p273).

92 General Staff War Memo 6/10/15 British Library 1OR L/MIL/5/752.

93 Major General Sir Charles Vere Ferrers Townshend KCB, DSO (1861–1924): from his long service on the North-West Frontier, notably as garrison commander of the besieged Chitral Fort in 1895, he was acclaimed an imperial hero by the London press and awarded the CB for his conduct. He was invited to dinner by Queen Victoria. He fought at Omdurman in 1898, but away from campaigning, he found time to study the works of Clausewitz and other military luminaries. After a long and sometimes

chequered career, he was appointed in 1914 to command the 6th (Poona) Division in Mesopotamia with the original task of protecting British oil assets. He is known, however, to have speculated that he might become governor of Mesopotamia.

94 Site of the AD530 victory of the Emperor Belisarius over the Persians. Saddam Hussein chose Salman Pak as a major centre for the production of biological weapons.

95 ibid Townshend p163.

96 The agreement was the product of long-drawn-out negotiations between the diplomats Francois Georges-Picot and Mark Sykes from 23 November 1915 onwards. It had the assent of the Russian Empire.

97 Lieutenant General Sir Frederick Stanley Maude KCB, CMG, DSO (1864–1917): he was not an Indian Army officer, unlike many of his colleagues in theatre, having served in Egypt, South Africa during the Second Boer War and as Military Secretary to the Governor-General of Canada. He went to France with the BEF and was wounded as a brigadier in April 1915.

98 Gaylani came from a family that claimed descent from the Prophet Muhammad and practised Islam as a moderate Sufi.

99 Batatu: p190.

100 Phebe Marr: p50.

101 Al-Muthanna ibn Haritha led the Muslim Arab army that defeated the Persians at the battle of Buwaib in 634. He was a member of the Bakr tribe centred on the Upper Euphrates around al-Jazirah, of whom Saddam Hussein's uncle was a scion.

102 Ahmed al-Barzani (1896–1969): he led the first Kurdish Revolt in 1931 against the newly independent Iraq.

103 The Kellogg Pact of 1928 was the last, but abortive, attempt to create a new order in international relations before the rise of Fascism. Signatories agreed to shun force in the resolution of disputes, but there were no means provided for enforcement.

104 Karsh and Rautsi p65.

105 Khalili: *The Tragedy of the Assyrians* – p174.

106 At an *Iftar* family supper during *Ramadan*, the elder son of the household was asked by an avuncular Western diplomat how school had gone that day. The innocent question was met by a stream of fierce nationalist protestation unworthy of the lad's gentle father.

107 Yusuf Salman Yusuf, born 19 July 1901 in Baghdad, was of Assyrian parentage. He became the first secretary of the Iraqi Communist Party in 1941 but was executed eight years later.

108 Jamil Beg Midfai (1890–1968): born Mosul, a former Ottoman Army officer who deserted to the nationalist Arab Revolt in 1916, after which he became an aide to Prince Faisal. Exiled from Iraq 1920–23 for anti-British activities but later reached cabinet level and served as President of the Chamber of Deputies in 1933. He was Prime Minister from 9 November 1933 to 27 August 1934 and on four further occasions

109 Yasin al-Hashimi, born 1884 in Baghdad, son of headman of Barudiyya quarter claiming descent from the Prophet Muhammad. A late defector from the Turkish Army, he was suspected by the British even after he had won King Faisal's confidence.

110 Sir Archibald Clark Kerr, later Lord Inverchapel, was born on 17 March 1882 in Australia; his family migrated to Britain when he was nine. Not afraid to stand up for what he considered right, he fell out with the Foreign Office (entered 1906) over its Egyptian policy and was rusticated to less important posts. His service in Iraq, however, impressed Whitehall and he was advanced to the increasingly important Chinese ambassadorship (1938–42). Subsequent heads of mission posts in Moscow (1942–46) and Washington (1946–48) testified further to his competence. Sadly, he was much affected by the defections of Burgess and MacLean and died in 1951.

111 General Bakr al-Sidqi (1890–37): born of Kurdish parentage in Kirkuk, he had watched the British in the early 1920s using the Assyrians to police rebellious areas in northern Iraq. His forces were subsequently deployed, massacring countless Assyrians in the Dahuk and Mosul districts and, in the months before he took over government, he oversaw the killing and hanging of thousands of Shi-ites in the Euphrates region. Taken together, the infamous 1913 Turkish atrocities against the Armenians and the 1935–36 persecutions in Iraq caused the coinage of the term 'genocide'.

112 Hikmat Suleiman (1889–1964), an Arab Iraqi of possible Chechen or Circassian extraction. He was a founder member and subsequent leader of the National Brotherhood Party and diverged from Hashimi's pan-Arab agenda. He signed off papers authorising Bakr Sidqi to take extensive reprisals against Assyrians and Shi-ites.

113 Nuri Pasha al-Sa'id (1888–1958): of middle-class Sunni parentage, graduate of Istanbul Staff College (1906) and spent early career fighting

against the Italians in Tripolitania. Captured by the British in Libya in 1915, he was persuaded to the Arab cause against the Turks led by Prince Faisal; he was famously photographed at Versailles in 1919 with the Prince and TE Lawrence as part of the Arab delegation to the post-war peace talks. He had led Arab forces in the capture of Damascus in late 1918. Thanks to his close relationship with Faisal, he was able to establish important political credentials in Iraq and from 1930, when he played a leading part in the acceptance of the Anglo-Iraqi Treaty, he acted as Prime Minister at the head of no less than eight administrations between then and 1958.

114 Colonel Salah-Uddin Sabbagh (1889–1945): an Ottoman officer who joined the Arab Revolution against the Turks in 1916 and was taken to Iraq by Prince Faisal. He was known to have admired the Grand Mufti of Jerusalem and became one of the four senior Iraqi Army officers who formed the *Golden Square*. He played a leading part in the 1941 Iraqi Revolt and fled to Iran and Turkey after it had been put down. In 1945, he was extradited and executed.

115 Sir Kinahan Cornwallis GCMG CBE DSO (1883–1959): born in the USA but educated at Haileybury and University College, Oxford, his early career had been spent in the Sudan Civil Service (1907–15).

116 Rashid Ali al-Gaylani (1892–1965): of parentage claiming descent from the Prophet, he trained as a lawyer but entered politics, becoming Minister of Justice in 1924 under Yasin Hashimi. They formed the National Brotherhood Party, campaigning as Arab nationalists for complete independence from Britain and opposing the Anglo-Iraq treaty. He was prime minister for eight months in 1933. After the Second World War he remained in exile until 1958 but then plotted against the Qassim government. Sentenced to death but pardoned, he went into exile again, this time to Beirut, where he died.

117 Air Vice Marshal Harry George Smart CBE DFC AFC (1891–1963): transferred from the Army to the Royal Flying Corps in 1916 and appointed commander of British forces in Iraq in 1939. He retired in September 1945.

118 Marshal of the Royal Air Force Lord Tedder: *With Prejudice* – Cassell (1966) pp86–88. Tedder claimed the credit for deploying RAF Number One Armoured Car Company (used for perimeter defence) via Amman and Rutbah as a ground force to cement the success already being achieved by the Habbaniya aircraft.

119 In 1942, the British could deploy five divisions (three Indian) in Iraq and had sufficient political influence to intervene as Cornwallis had done before the Iraqi Revolt.

120 Colonel Gerald de Gaury: *Three Kings in Baghdad 1921–58* (1961) p146.

121 Tawfiq al-Suwaidi (1892–1968): graduated in 1912 from Istanbul College of Law and also attended the Sorbonne in Paris; he taught law in Damascus during the First World War and practised in Baghdad during the 1920s. He became Iraq's youngest Prime Minister in 1928 and in 1932 was appointed the country's first permanent representative at the League of Nations.

122 National Archives: FO 481/23 – Sir H Stonehewer-Bird's annual report for 1946 to Foreign Secretary Bevin (6 January 1947).

123 Sayed Salih Jabr (1896–1967): the first Shi-ite and sixteenth Prime Minister since 1919 who took office on 30 March 1947. He had been a tough Minister of the Interion and of Defence and was disliked by nationalists. His son, Sa'ad, was to set up the first Iraqi opposition newspaper in London in 1984 and continued to publish until the fall of Saddam in 2003.

124 Figures quoted are from contemporary press reports (Keesings), but Henderson suggested that these were underestimates.

125 The Basra Petroleum field at Zubair was opened by Nuri Sa'id on 10 January 1952. Further major discoveries were made at Butmah (northern Iraq) in the same year and at Bay Hasan and at Rumaylah in the south. The last was expected to produce 172,648 bpd and was just north of the border with Kuwait. It would be one of the contentious issues in 1990.

126 Philby had also visited Iraq for ten days in 1957.

127 Mirza Mohammed-Khan Mossadegh (1882–1967): born in Tehran to prominent official-class parents and educated in law at the Paris Institute for Political Studies and at Neuchatel University. The first Iranian to obtain a PhD in law at a European university, he was successively minister of Justice (1920), Finance (1921) and Foreign Affairs (1923). Thereafter, he was governor of Azerbaijan province and remained an independent (1919–49) until he joined the National Front Party.

128 The first USSR legation opened in Baghdad after establishment of diplomatic relations on 9 September 1944. Baghdad broke with Moscow in January 1955 after the latter criticised Iraq's membership of CENTO.

129 General Nur-ud-din Mahmud: born 1897 in Irbil, a Sunni Arabised

Kurd and son of an Ottoman Army colonel – educated at Istanbul Military Academy and Baghdad Staff College – one-time military attaché in London and chief of general staff. He acted as prime minister from November 1952 to January 1953.

130 Dr Fadhil Jamali: born 1907 Kadhimiyyah of pious Shia middle-class sheikh and sanctuary guide (*muzawwer*) – PhD in Education from Colombia University New York – one-time Director of Education and Minister of Foreign Affairs – Prime Minister September 1953 to March 1954 and March to April 1954.

131 National Archives: FO 481/23 Iraq Annual Report for 1956 of 8 February 1957.

132 Sir Alan Munro KCMG: born 1935 – served as British ambassador in Algeria 1984–87 and in Saudi Arabia 1989–93 – author of *An Arab Storm*, an account of his role during the Kuwait Crisis. He is credited before the Iraqi invasion with having uttered the words 'Arab does not invade Arab'

133 Colonel Abdul Salam Aref: born 1916 in Baghdad and attended military academy 1936–37 – CO Faisal Armoured Car Regiment (6 bde 4 div) at Washshash camp west of Baghdad in 1958 – later CO 6 Armoured Bde and then military governor of Baghdad under Qassim – after short retirement returned to the Army and elected Iraqi President 17 April 1966 – ousted by Ba'athists 17 July 1968.

134 Brigadier Abd al-Karim Qassim: born 1914 Baghdad, son of Sunni Arab carpenter and small landowner/grain merchant (mother, of Kurdish Shiite stock). He was educated at primary school in the south where his uncle lived and, subsequently, in Baghdad. A schoolteacher before he entered the Baghdad Military, graduating in 1936, he was considered to have served creditably during the 1948 Israeli War of Independence. He spent six months at Camberley Staff College before becoming a brigade commander in 1955. As chairman of the Supreme Committee of Free Officers, he was a strong nationalist with active sympathy for poor and devout Sunnis.

135 General Mohammed Neguib (1901–84): he was first president of Egypt, serving from the declaration of the Republic on 18 June 1953 to 14 November 1954. With Nasser, he led the 1952 Egyptian Revolution that ended the rule of King Farouk over both Egypt and Sudan (1936–52), himself a descendant of Muhammad Ali Pasha, the mid-nineteenth-century founder of modern Egypt (op cit).

136 Grigori Titovich Zaitsev: a career diplomat, he was appointed Soviet ambassador to Iraq after the Qassim coup and had arrived in Baghdad by August 1958 before his staff joined him. He flew in via Mehrabad Airport in Tehran. He was replaced in October 1961 by Mikhail D Yakovlev, a senior CPSU official who was able to engage Moscow more closely with the Qassim regime and benefited from his natural links to the CPI.

137 National Archives: FO 481/23 – Sir Humphrey Trevelyan's annual review for 1958 submitted to Selwyn Lloyd.

138 Hansard 15 February 1958 column 1246.

139 Hubert Miles Gladwyn Jebb 1st Baron Gladwyn GCMG GCVO CB PC (1900–96): acting UN Secretary-General 24 October 1945 to 2 February 1946, deputy leader of the Liberal peers (1965–88) and spokesman on foreign affairs and defence.

140 January 1959: technical agreement with Poland; March 1959: economic and technical agreement with the USSR; April 1959: cultural and scientific agreement with East Germany; October 1960: economic cooperation agreement with Czechoslovakia.

141 Hansard: 11 May 1959 column 837.

142 Walter Turner Monckton, 1st Viscount Monckton of Brenchley GCVO KCMG MC PC QC (1891–1965). Like Churchill, an Harrovian, who graduated from Balliol, Oxford. He was used to ticklish situations, having advised Edward VIII during the Abdication Crisis and the last Nizam of Hyderabad during the run-up to Indian independence. Having served as a Tory MP for Bristol West since 1951, he was pushed up to the House of Lords in 1957. A realist, he is probably best remembered for his recommendation that the Federation of Nyasaland and Northern Rhodesia should be broken up.

143 Kamil Qazanchi was a local CPI hero in Mosul having led demonstrations there as a law student in 1947 against the Treaty of Portsmouth. He had been deprived of Iraqi nationality in October 1955, was deported to Turkey and moved on to Bulgaria (Reuters 31 October 1959). He was clearly influenced by Moscow and encouraged to return to Iraq after the Revolution.

144 Dr Mohammed Abd al-Malik al-Shawaf: an independent who was appointed Minister of Health in Qassim's first cabinet and retained his position in July 1959, when Qassim was obliged to appoint a more left-wing administration.

145 On 9 March, Baghdad radio alleged that radio broadcasts from Aleppo were backing the Mosul insurrection.

146 The Kurdistan Democratic Party (KDP), calling for autonomy and democracy in Iraq, was founded in 1946 and led originally by Mullah Mustafa Barzani, father of Masoud (born 1946) and from 2005 to 2017 was President of Kurdistan. The party split in June 1975 when the Patriotic Union of Kurdistan (PUK) was formed under Jalal Talabani (1933–2017), largely from elements in the north-eastern governorate of Sulaymaniyyah. He became President of Iraq from 2005 to 2014 and was succeeded by Abdul Aziz al-Hakim. Originally Marxist, its geographical orientation has caused it to entertain close links to Iran, not least through the passing of intelligence to Tehran's Ministry of Intelligence and Security (MOIS).

147 According to Egyptian sources, Qassim had been warned in December 1959 by Sir Michael Wright, the British ambassador in Baghdad, of a plot against the government by Rashid Ali al-Gaylani and a small group of young intellectuals.

148 Khairallah Talfah (1919–93): born in Tikrit and considered a devout Muslim, he became an ardent nationalist, participating in the 1941 Army revolt in support of Ali Rashid al-Gaylani. He took on various offices under successive Ba'athist governments and acquired huge personal wealth. His weakness for candy caused his diabetes and, before his death, his two legs had to be amputated.

149 Aflaq was one of the few people for whom Saddam retained a soft spot. When he died in 1989, Saddam ensured that he was buried with every pomp and circumstance in Baghdad.

150 Major-General Ahmed Hassan al-Bakr (1914–82): a Tikriti Sunni from the petty land-owning class but with good tribal connections, he started out as a primary school teacher before entering the Baghdad Military Academy (1938–42). He joined the Free Officers' Movement and, as a result, was involved in the anti-Communist abortive attempt to remove Qassim in September 1958. He was also present at the Mosul Nationalist Revolt in March 1959, leading to his arrest and imprisonment. He did not join the Ba'ath Party until 1960, but by September 1962, he was a member of the Regional Command for Iraq. Shortly afterwards, he was promoted to the National Command.

151 Hansard: 11 February 1963 column 941.

152 Colonel Abdul Salam Mohammed al-Aref al-Jumaily (1921–66): appointed Deputy PM and Minister of the Interior from 14 July 1958, he soon fell out with Qassim and was arrested on 5 November the same year. Qassim caused the sentence of death to be commuted to life a month later, something Aref refused to do when Qassim appealed to him for similar clemency. A staunch and conservative Sunni, Aref was known for his open manner and approachability. His death in 1966 was caused by another mysterious air accident.

153 Major-General Taher Yahya (1914 or 1916–86): another Sunni teacher from Tikrit who chose a military career and became a leading light in the Free Officers' Movement, he was appointed Prime Minister in November 1963 and led a succession of cabinets until his resignation a week before the Second Ba'athist Revolution.

154 Colonel Abdul Razzak al-Naïf (1934–79): a tribal kinsman of the Aref brothers, he had acted as Director of Military Intelligence. As such, he would have been in liaison with the Americans before the Ba'athist seized power.

155 Karch and Rautsi p41.

156 Hansard 18 July 1968 cols 1679–1805.

157 National Archives: FO 481/23.

158 Negotiations for an Anti-Ballistic Missile limitation opened formally in November 1969 in Finland and eventually produced the 1972 SALT I Treaty. The impetus for this real step towards détente came from President Richard Nixon within a week of his taking office in January 1969 (see David E Hoffman: *Dead Hand* – Anchor Books 2009 p21).

159 Rogers' note to the Security Council, rather than a personal intervention in New York. Throughout this period, State Department was largely blind to what was really going on in Iraq and had much higher priorities elsewhere in the world.

160 From October 1972 to March 1975, the CIA provided the Kurds with some twenty million dollars in aid, including 250 tons of non-attributable weaponry (see Bryan R Gibson: *Sold Out? US Foreign Policy, Iraq, the Kurds and the Cold War* – Palgrave Macmillan 2015 pp144–5).

161 Taha Yassin Ramadan al-Jazrawi (1938–2007): born at Cizre, Turkey, of a peasant family from the Mosul hinterland, he graduated from the Baghdad Military Academy and then deserted. He soon found his way into the Ba'ath Party's Military Affairs Bureau where he soon came under Saddam's

influence. From the fall of Qassim, he was a member of Hanin, a secret organisation devoted to the 'Motherland' which Saddam used for torture and assassination. At the 1968 Revolution he was appointed chairman of the Military Officers' Posting Board to increase the party's control of the Army. He joined the Regional Command Council in November 1969. As President of the Special Court set up to try those alleged to have been behind the 21 January 1970 plot, he sentenced forty-six to be hanged. He remained loyal to Saddam to the end and was buried close to him in Tikrit after his execution for his part in massacres under the Ba'athist regime.

162 The most prominent were Lieutenant General Salih Mahdi Ammash and Major-General Hardan Abdul Ghaffur al-Tikriti (both born in 1925) who were put out of office in 1970. Ammash, a Bakr loyalist, was removed from his post as Minister of the Interior, held since the Revolution, and appointed as a toothless Vice-President. He was subsequently ambassador in Moscow from September 1971 and died in obscurity in 1985. Hardan al-Tikriti was less fortunate: having lost the Deputy Premiership in November 1969 and then also made a Vice-President, he heard of his dismissal as Minister of Defence in October 1970 whilst heading a delegation to Madrid. He was assassinated in Kuwait by Iraqi agents on 30 March 1971. He had been too close to the Aref brothers.

163 National Archives FO17/1532: DF Hawley's 1970 Annual Review of 4 January 1971.

164 Ibid: Egerton m/s comment and RM Evans response from the Iraqi desk of 26 January 1971.

165 Staff General Izzat Ibrahim al-Duri (born 1932 – not 1942 as in his official biography – and not yet reported to have died): a Sunni from Samarra of low-born but mixed-race parents and easily picked out by his gaunt features and auburn hair colouring, he was an early Ba'ath recruit and was one of those members of the Hanin used for 'dirty' jobs, including the disarming of Colonel Naïf in 1968. From 1974, he was Minister of the Interior and enjoyed close relations with Moscow. After Saddam's takeover of the presidency in 1979, he was usually the one chosen to carry out sensitive missions to ensure that they achieved his leader's purpose. Named as the King of Clubs in the American list of targets for arrest and trial post-2003, he was still at large leading pro-Saddam insurgents in late 2006 (*Times* 23 November 2006). As late as April 2018, he is believed to have released a video commemorating the seventy-first anniversary of the Ba'ath party.

166 Lord Palmerston's remark in 1851 said it all: "The boundary between Turkey and Persia can never be finally settled except by an arbitrary decision on the part of Great Britain and Russia." No such agreement was ever reached and by the end of the First World War, when the Turkish Empire was carved up, Russia was out of the running.

167 On 13 September 1969, Baghdad Radio claimed that thirty Iranian soldiers had been killed after they had stepped over the border; Tehran denied the incident.

168 Karsh and Rautsi p73.

169 The catalyst for this mini crisis over strategically important islets was Britain's withdrawal of forces East of Suez. The Royal Navy had policed the Straits of Hormuz since the turn of the eighteenth/nineteenth centuries, largely to clear the area of pirates. No Pax Britannica meant that Arabs and Persians were left facing each other across an increasingly crowded seaway. As Saddam saw it, Britain was not honouring its 'obligations' to protect Arab interests.

170 Dr Sa'dun Hammadi (1930–2007: a Shi-ite from Karbala, he obtained a PhD in agricultural economics from Wisconsin University and returned to Iraq in time to be appointed an anti-Nasserist Minister of Agricultural Reform in the first Ba'athist administration (1963). As Minister of Oil, he negotiated with the Russians over the development of the rich North Rumaylah oil field on the border with Kuwait and piloted nationalisation of the industry in 1972. He was appointed Foreign Minister on 11 November 1974. He became Speaker of the Iraqi National Assembly from 1983–90 and 1996–2003. He was released by the Americans in February 2004 and resettled in Shi-ite Qatar, where he died.

171 Three Iraqi Kurd hi-jackers had caused the Iraqi Airways flight to crash-land at Mehrabad on 1 March 1975. The Iranians refused their demands for the release of eighty-five Kurdish prisoners in Iraq and a ransom of $4,500,000. One hi-jacker and three passengers were killed.

172 National Archives FCO 160/99: AJD Stirling's report of 14 January 1979 to the FCO.

173 ibid FCO 8/4126: Egerton's annual review of 31 December 1980 to the FCO.

174 ibid: Sir John Graham minute of 30 January 1981.

175 ibid: FCO 8/4373 paper commissioned on 19 November 1981.

176 ibid: Egerton of 6 December 1981 to the FCO.

177 ibid: FCO 8/4165 Richards (Carrington's PS) to Defence Minister John Nott's PS of 11 December 1981.

178 Fifty-six ships were hit in 1984 and a further forty-six the following year.

179 The Iraqi government under Saddam lied in its teeth over even the most obvious outrage, in the same way that the Soviet – and still the Russian – government has done. The two regimes shared the same philosophy – lie absolutely.

180 Following the deposition of Saddam in 2003, the freshly constituted Iraqi High Court eventually recognised the Halabja massacre as an act of genocide on 1 March 2010. Before this, Saddam's crony and cousin, Staff General Ali Hassan al-Majid ('Chemical Ali' and nicknamed the King of Spades from the Americans' deck of cards listing war criminals) had been found guilty of ordering the attack, sentenced to death and executed on 17 January.

181 It was not a story that could be easily covered up; neither would it have been in Saddam's style to do so. See *Wall Street Journal* (New York) of 27 August 1990 cited in Karsh and Rautshi's biography of Saddam – Futura (1991) p166.

182 Ali Hussein Mohammed al-Haidari, the son of one of the organisers of the failed assassination attempt, was an eyewitness to the Dujail massacre and gave his testimony at Saddam's trial on 21 December 2005.

183 Naim Hamid Haddad: a member of the RCC before 1969, he had served as Youth Minister from November 1974 and, as one of his five Deputy Prime Ministers appointed by Saddam when he took power in July 1979, played a leading part on the subsequent Special Tribunal that rooted out opponents in the Ba'ath Party. He was probably one of those Saddam ordered to carry out executions personally.

184 Saddam's personal confirmation of the executions was reported in the *Los Angeles Times* on 17 February 1987.

185 Suzanne Mubarak (born 1941): daughter of an Egyptian paediatrician and Welsh nurse from Pontypridd, she met her future husband and President of Egypt (1981–2011) at the age of sixteen. By 1988, she was well embarked on her philanthropic activities in opposition to human trafficking, but she would also have brought messages of support from President Hosni Mubarak, who had also supported Saddam during the Iran/Iraq War.

186 Barzan Ibrahim Hassan al-Tikriti (1951–2007): Saddam's half-brother and close to him during early political career. He served in various

intelligence roles and acted as a personal messenger between Saddam and Ba'athist activists abroad, notably in London. From 1983, he was under a cloud, having opposed Saddam's daughter Raghad's marriage to 'Chemical' Ali Hassan al-Majid's cousin, Husayn Kamal al-Majid. He was re-habilitated as Iraq's permanent representative to the UN at Geneva with ministerial rank in January 1989, as much to look after the wayward Uday as to head up Iraqi intelligence and procurement networks in Europe.

187 ibid FCO 8/7490 report written in early January 1989. Sir Terence Joseph Clark (born 1934): long-experienced in Gulf posts and in Jordan, he served as ambassador in Baghdad (1985–89). He illustrated his erudition in a letter to *The Times* of 10 March 2003 tracing Anglo/Iraqi relations back to 1645.

188 David John Mellor QC (born 1949): a non-practising barrister after entering the Commons in 1979, he became Margaret Thatcher's youngest minister in 1981. After serving as a junior minister in the Home Office, he was promoted as Minister of State in the Foreign Office. Never afraid to express a view, he protested in front of the world press to an Israeli Army colonel about the use of'excessive' brutality in the treatment of Palestinians. His remarks produced uproar, but he refused to withdraw them. Despite a reprimand from Thatcher, she made him her Minister of Health.

189 John Smith (born 1942): as managing director of the specialist non-military vehicle manufacturer Hestair Dennis, he was arrested in 1979 when talking with an Iraqi official in a Baghdad park. He was convicted of seeking to bribe officials and sentenced to life imprisonment. Mellor delivered a special plea from Thatcher to Saddam, who pardoned Smith in late February 1988. Another British businessman, Ian Richter, who had been caught up in the 1986/7 accusations against the former Mayor of Baghdad, Abdul-Wahhab Mohammed al-Mufti, was not released until November 1991 and only after the UK had agreed to unfreeze Iraqi assets.

190 Antony Harold Newton, Baron Newton of Braintree (1937–2012): a Conservative MP from February 1974, he served as a Party Whip and as Minister for Social Security and the Elderly, before becoming Minister of Health in 1986. He replaced the more emotive Ken Clarke on 25 July 1988.

191 Sir David Alwyn Gore-Booth KCMG KCVO (1943–2004): son of the distinguished diplomat Paul Henry, Baron Gore-Booth, and head of the Diplomatic Service (1968–69). David Gore-Booth was a colourful figure

who spoke his mind. Having fallen out with the Foreign Secretary, Robin Cook, he resigned from the FCO in early 1999.

192 The semi-circular wall around Kuwait City was erected in two months at the end of the First World War on the orders of Emir Salim Mubarak al-Sabah (1917–21). It replaced a mostly mud wall and was pulled down in 1956 to make way for urban expansion. The old gates have been preserved for historic interest.

193 Very much under the coordination of the British High Commissioner in Baghdad, Sir Percy Cox, an agreement signed at al-Uqair on 2 December 1922 by the representatives of Iraq (Cox), Kuwait (Major More, the Political Resident) and Najd (Abdal-Aziz al-Su'ud). It sought to stabilise the ever-porous Kuwaiti-Najd border while guaranteeing the integrity of the Emirate's northern border with Iraq.

194 Ahmad Mustafa Abu-Hakima: *The Modern History of Kuwait (1750–1965)* – McGill University, Montreal (1982) pp154–5.

195 The American Operation Praying Mantis was the response to Iranian mining of the Gulf which had caused the disabling of the USS *Samuel B Roberts*. The Iranian vessel was a British-built Vosper Mark V frigate, commissioned into the Shah's navy in 1972.

196 On 16 April 1981, the Kuwait daily *Al Rai al-Amm* listed the creditor states as Saudi Arabia ($6,000 million), Kuwait ($4,000 million), UAE ($3,000 million) and Qatar ($1,000 million).

197 ibid FCO 8/7490: Clark writing on 27 August 1989.

198 The cutting is long since lost, but I am sure it was during mid-November 1988.

199 ibid: Baird to MOD of 10 January 1989.

200 I experienced a less serious parallel much later in my posting. I had the honour to become a member of a high-ranking Kuwaiti official's *diwaniya* (private house group of friends and advisers) where the main activity of the evening was a merry game of Hearts. When I won a round, my host would cry out, "Tony, you are killing me!"

201 ibid FCO 8/7501: Baghdad telegram of 13 February 1989 to the FCO.

202 William Arthur Waldegrave Baron Waldegrave of North Hill (born 1946): educated at Eton and Corpus Christi, Oxford, he was soon recruited into the Conservative Party Research Department in 1971 and remained in political research circles until elected as an MP in 1979. In July 1988, he was appointed Minister of State at the FCO and was immediately involved

in policy concerning military sales to Iraq after the end of the Iran/Iraq War. He was severely criticised in the 1996 Scott Report for having changed British policy on arms sales in February 1989 and lying about this to MPs. He lost his seat in 1997 and was sent to the Lords.

203 Sir Peter Ingram Walters born 11 March 1931, by strange coincidence the same date as that of Lord Lawson, who is one year younger. Sir Peter was chairman of British Petroleum from 1981 to 1990 and, in all, clocked up thirty-five years with the company. He was much respected in the oil industry and went on to be chairman of the Midland Bank (1994–2000).

204 Shaikh Ali Khalifa Adhbi Muhammad (I) al-Sabah (born 1946). He was Shaikh Jabir's personal choice for the Oil Ministry only six weeks after his accession as Emir. Shaikh Ali was educated at Victoria College, Cairo, San Francisco (BSc) and LSE (MA). He is credited with having re-constructed his ministry within two years of taking office and was much respected in OPEC circles. He resigned honourably in June 1990 after explosions at three oil refineries had killed five workers but was then appointed Minister of Finance during the Kuwait government-in-exile (1990–91).

205 Nigel, later Lord Lawson, served as Chancellor from June 1983 to October 1989 when he resigned, largely over differences with Sir Alan Walters, who had just been re-appointed as Thatcher's personal economic adviser. His departure removed a lynchpin from Thatcher's position as Prime Minister. The KIO investment saga is not the only example of Lawson's questionable judgement. He is known for his membership of the climate warming denial circle – see his *An Appeal to Reason: A Cool Look at Global Warming* published by Overlook Press in 2008. He is also an ardent Brexiteer.

206 Richard Edward Geoffrey Howe, Baron Howe of Aberavon (1926–2015): a Wykehamist, gifted classicist and graduate of Trinity Hall, Cambridge, he was called to the Bar in 1952 (Middle Temple). First elected to the Commons in 1964 before losing his seat in the Labour landslide of 1966, he later sat as an MP from 1970 to 1982. He was considered as being on the left-wing of the Conservative party and was first promoted by Edward Heath. After serving as Margaret Thatcher's Chancellor from 1979 to 1983, he was transferred as Secretary of State for Foreign Affairs, a post he held until 24 July 1989. He was widely respected in both the FCO and the Intelligence Services; his red ink annotations were usually apposite.

207 The First Palestinian Intifada broke out on 9 December 1987 after an Israeli tank-transporter had collided with cars the previous day, killing

four Palestinians. During violent demonstrations, stone- and Molotov cocktail-throwing and deliberate attempts to kill Israelis, over three hundred Palestinians (at least fifty under the age of seventeen) and twelve Israelis were killed in the Gaza Strip and on the West Bank. It had run out of steam by later 1993 but was the subject of much outrage expressed throughout the Middle East, not least by Saddam.

208 Cadbury products were banned in Kuwait because of the company's trading with Israel. My Kuwaiti friend appreciated that their quality was superior to rival brands allowed into the country.

209 Said K Aburish: *Saddam Hussein, the Politics of Revenge* – Bloomsbury (2000) p278–9. Aburish revealed as his sub-source an unnamed member of the PLO delegation whose account was largely confirmed by the distinguished American military historian Pierre Salinger in 1992.

210 The assailant, a disgruntled military officer, was killed. The next day, 6 January, the cancellation of Iraqi Army Day sparked rumours of a failed coup, either organised by Saddam's brother-in-law, Adnan Khairallah, or negligently, perhaps wilfully, undetected by him.

211 Farzad Bazoft (1958–90): born in Iran but settled in the UK during 1975. He was sentenced to eighteen months for robbery in 1981 and issued with a deportation order, which he successfully challenged two years later. He was then able to establish himself as a freelance journalist and contributed articles to the *Observer* and BBC on the Middle East, particularly the Iran/Iraq War. With several other journalists, his visit to Iraq in 1990 was at the invitation of the Ministry of Information, but it was so that they could cover elections in the Kurdish north of the country.

212 Sa'ad Bazzaz (born 1952): and head of both the Iraqi News and Radio and Television organisations under Saddam until he fled Iraq in October 1992. See his account – *The Gulf War and the One After* p137.

213 ibid Henderson p221.

214 ibid Aburish p276.

215 Gerald Bull (1928–90): Canadian engineer specialising in long-range artillery and its possible use in sending objects into space. Some of his work was decidedly suspect and in 1977 he was arrested by the Americans for involvement in illegal arms dealing. He moved to Brussels in the early 1980s, where he worked for European Poudreries Renuies de Belgique, a subsidiary of his former employer in Canada, Space Research Corporation. Here he found both Chinese and Iraqi interest in his research and was able

to persuade Saddam to finance Project Babylon, the development of a long-range cannon, ostensibly for space launch operations. He also assisted with the upgrading of Soviet-supplied SCUD missiles. It is generally believed that his assassination was the work of Mossad on the orders of highest Israeli authority. Supergun parts connected with Babylon were seized in November 1990, thus bringing the project to its end.

216 Jonathan Moyle (1961–90): former RAF helicopter pilot and editor of the magazine *Defence Helicopter World*. He was found dead in a Santiago hotel on 31 March 1990. A UK inquest in 1998 considered his death not to have been suspect. At the time Moyle had been involved in advising the Chilean company Industrias Cardoen on modification for Third World usage of a Bell Helicopter produced by the American company, Textron. Iraq was considered to be one of several potential customers. *Lobster* magazine speculated that Moyle worked for MI6.

217 ibid Aburishi p272.

218 Daniel Pipes and Tonya Buzby of Saad al-Bazzaz on 5 October 1995 in the *Middle East Quarterly* office.

219 The two units cruising off the Kuwaiti coast were the USS *England*, a Leahy-class cruiser commissioned in 1963 with a main armament of dated Terrier surface-to-air missiles, and the USS *David Ray*, a Spruance-class destroyer commissioned in 1975. Both ships had been redeployed from the Far East.

220 Robert Dole (born 1923): Senator for Kansas and Leader of the Senate 1985–96.

221 Alan Kooi Simpson (born 1931): represented Wyoming in the Senate from 1978 and was Republican Whip there (1985–95).

222 There was a clearly defined caste system in Kuwait before the invasion. Only the true-bred Kuwaiti could own property and was head and shoulders above everyone else. Next in order came the Americans, British and other 'white' nationals. Then came Egyptians and Palestinians and, lastly, the large number of Indian, Pakistani and Philippino migrant workers. Many of the last were treated as little more than slaves. One Philippino woman who had wanted time off to attend her church on a Sunday evening was told by her employer that she was in Kuwait to work, not to be a Christian.

223 The article appeared on 13 July 1990; it estimated that Iraq had lost $1 billion with every fall of the oil price by one dollar.

224 *Financial Times* 18 August 1990.

225 Others, including President Mubarak, were also reported using the expression at the time.

226 I have based this account on two secondary sources (Atkinson p52 and Henderson p230), together with a briefing given to the British embassy in Baghdad by the Americans which was only forwarded to us in Kuwait on 1 August.

227 I knew that my senior-most intelligence contacts had been called to a high-level meeting on 25 July, but the D/DMI, whom I met the same day, was still as worried as ever.

228 ibid: Atkinson.

229 On 1 August, I told her to stay in Bahrain.

230 In comparison with the instant digital communication of today, the means for getting swift messages back to London were primitive and laborious. Despite eight or nine years of Iran/Iraq conflict, there had been no substantial upgrade of embassy systems, in contrast to posts elsewhere in less sensitive areas.

231 Shaikh Fahd al-Ahmad al-Jabir al-Sabah (10 August 1945–2 August 1990): youngest brother of Amir Jabir and, having served as an officer in the Kuwaiti Army, had been appointed to several posts in the national sports sector. According to several contemporary accounts, he was killed on the steps of Dasman Palace as Iraqi troops stormed in. The previous evening, he had remained on board Kuwait-bound flight BA149 when others in the royal party had alighted before take-off from Heathrow.

232 I know of only one other foreign service officer who felt the same as I did. He expressed his view to a liaison service in the Maghreb. A man of singular ability and with old knowledge of Iraq. Sadly, this veteran Arabist is no longer with us. There was no one in the Foreign Office, at home or abroad, who thought as we did; if they did, they did not say it at the time.

233 See Steve Davis: *The Secret of Flight 149*.

234 I have been able to trace the source. In 2017 Clive Earthy, the cabin services director on board BA149, gave a talk in Alresford (Hants) during which he described his experiences and spoke of the lack of warning from the FCO. I know the country town well. Small world.

235 Hansard: 27 April 2007.

236 According to Clive Earthy in his Alresford talk in 2017, there were eight. The affidavits listed only six names, all former serving soldiers.

237 Both Captain Brunyates and Captain Peter Clarke attended a meeting

of concerned expatriates for an ambassador's briefing a few days after the invasion. Oddly, the BA country manager did not attend.

238 Hereby hangs another important detail. Some weeks before the invasion, the Iraqis posted in a new Iraqi Airways country manager, a DGI officer who had been expelled from London months earlier when his involvement in the export of prohibited goods from Heathrow had been discovered. On the night of 1/2 August the usual flight controller was replaced.

239 The Rt Hon Douglas Hogg (born 1945): educated at Eton and Christ Church, Oxford, and an MP from 1979 to 2010. He served as Minister of State in the FCO from 2 November 1990 to 9 July 1995.

240 Lieutenant Commander CL 'Buster' Crabbe was a retired naval diver recruited by MI6 to carry out a discreet reconnaissance of the hulls of two Soviet warships that had brought Nikita Khrushchev and Marshal Nikolai Bulgarin to the UK for a first summit meeting with the British Prime Minister Anthony Eden in April 1956. His body was found the following year off Chichester Harbour. The failure of the operation exposed both operational clearance and political approval inadequacies. These were subsequently addressed in full.

241 An eyewitness in the Cabinet Room relayed the story in 1979 of how Margaret Thatcher tore a strip off a candidate for the Northern Ireland Office. She had offered the post over the phone in the hearing of others present. There was a silence while the other end responded. Then, angrily, the new Prime Minister exploded: "Yes, and some of my soldiers have wives and children, too."

242 John King, Baron King of Warnaby (1917–2005): he was dubbed 'Mrs Thatcher's favourite businessman'. Having joined British Airways in 1981, he turned the airline round from a loss of over £140 million annually to a profit in 1989 of £268 million. He stepped down from the chairmanship in 1993. On Captain Brunyates' return to the UK in December 1990, he was welcomed home by King with the words: "What have you done with my aircraft?"

243 ibid: Earthy during his Alresford talk, during which he also lamented the official clamp-down on the BA149 story.

244 IISS: Military Balance 1988–89.

245 I knew of this from an elderly telecommunications worker who had been advising the Kuwaitis for decades. Such technology in the hands of less than bilingual interceptors was dangerous; given the many nuances of the

English language, words could easily be misinterpreted by assiduous and paranoid listeners.

246 Apart from the five permanent members of the UNSC, the other representatives were Canada, Colombia, Cuba, Ethiopia, Finland, Ivory Coast, Malaysia, Romania and Zaire; one of Saddam's sympathisers, Yemen, was diplomatically absent.

247 Mauretania, Sudan, Yemen and Jordan. Libya refused to attend.

248 The Iraqi Popular Army was set up in 1970 as the military arm of the Ba'athist Party and had an important role in imposing doctrinal belief within its ranks. By 1977, it had fifty thousand members, but its ranks mushroomed during the Iran/Iraq War. During that conflict, it was sent in to support regular forces, but poor discipline and training rendered it ineffective in the fighting. As a Fascist entity, however, it was more than useful in keeping control of regime opponents. It was commanded from 1974 by Saddam's senior lieutenant, Taha Ramadan.

249 Ala'a Hussein Ali Al-Khafaji Al-Jabir (born circa 1948): he grew up in Kuwait but studied in Baghdad where he became a Ba'athist. He joined the Kuwaiti Army some time before the invasion and held the rank of lieutenant. This background suggests that he was infiltrated into the Kuwait armed forces against the day when he could act as a double agent. He was promoted immediately on the invasion and appointed head of the PFKG and, shortly afterwards, as an Iraqi deputy prime minister. Contrary to some reports he was not executed by Saddam to keep him from revealing secrets about the invasion but remained in Iraq under a false name before escaping to Norway via Turkey in 1998. He was sentenced to death for treason in 1993 in absentia, but in January 2000, he appealed against the sentence. His guilt was confirmed but sentence was commuted to life in prison, where he still languishes (see BBC News report of his trial of 3 May 2000).

250 The Pakistani decision to send troops was announced on 13 August, only eleven days after the invasion.

251 Saddam was still able to muster support from the strongest elements of the anti-Israel lobby, the PLO and Libya, while Jordan, Sudan and Mauretania continued to harbour reservations. Algeria and Yemen abstained; Tunisia was absent.

252 At Soviet request, the five permanent representatives met in New York on 14 August to discuss the proposal, which was soon kicked into the sand.

253 According to Egyptian reports, there was an attempted coup in Baghdad at the time.

254 I have used Glenda Lockwood's published account for confirmation of dates and timings.

255 See Glenda Lockwood's account p58 in which she mentions some confusion between a halt for 'rations' or for the 'Russians'.

256 In Mrs Lockwood's understandably subjective account, she maintained that members of the convoy had spotted the petrol station first.

257 ibid p63: Mrs Lockwood maintained that no one from the embassy went with them to the hotel. This, I believe, was incorrect.

258 ibid p66.

259 ibid p68.

260 The term 'DBS' stood originally for 'distressed British sailor'. The Foreign Office had always accepted a degree of responsibility for British mariners but has never recognised a duty to repatriate those who choose to travel abroad.

261 Lord Franks' Falkland Islands Review was published by the House of Commons on 18 January 1983 (HMSO).

262 Boris Nikolayevich Yeltsin (1931–2007): a member of the Soviet Communist Party since 1961 and elected as a full member of the Central Committee of the Communist Party of the Soviet Union in March 1981, he was appointed by Mikhail Gorbachev as, effectively, Mayor of Moscow. His resignation on 12 July 1990 was made before stunned party members attending the 28th Congress of the Communist Party of the USSR. The following June he would win the democratic presidential elections for the Russian Republic.

263 The British Foreign Secretary, Douglas Hurd, was greeted by hostile demonstrations against British policy when he visited Amman on 31 August.

264 7 Armoured Brigade and its 120 Challenger tanks were to be deployed from the Rhine Army.

265 With an eventual total commitment of over thirteen thousand troops, fourteen warships, one hundred helicopters, plus the very aircraft types she had given Iraq only a few years before, it was the largest French deployment since the Algerian War in the 1950s.

266 Date of the UN Declaration signed by the USA, UK, USSR and China.

267 Herbert Norman Schwarzkopf Jnr (1934–2012): he was named as

commander US Central Command (CENTCOM) in November 1988, as much for his diplomatic as military experience. Like many, he thought that Iraq would simply take the Rumaylah oil fields across the border and was surprised by the fall of Kuwait City. His nickname 'Storming' belied his less than bellicose nature; in the early seventies he had told staff colleges that a major war would soon go nuclear and was thus unthinkable. This fundamental approach helps to explain his anything but gung-ho attitude in the run-up to the liberation of Kuwait.

268 Air Chief Marshal Sir Patrick Bardon Hine GCB GBE was educated at my old alma mater, Peter Symonds, Winchester (1942–49). He was promoted Air Chief Marshall in July 1985 after a distinguished flying and staff career. We are both former presidents of the Symondians' Association. As was the late Admiral Sir Brian Brown who served as Second Sea Lord during the Kuwait crisis.

269 The four points were: compliance with UNSC resolutions, international guarantee behind a withdrawal, restoration of Kuwait sovereignty and respect for the will of the Kuwaiti people.

270 Yevgeny Maksimovich Primakov (1929–2015): a man who used senior Soviet Ministry of Foreign Affairs cover to mask his intelligence collection activities, he travelled constantly between Moscow, Baghdad, Western, Non-Aligned and Arab capitals seeking ways out of the Kuwait crisis impasse. He was rewarded in 1991 by his appointment as director of the newly formed Russian Foreign Intelligence Service (SFU). He was subsequently Foreign (1996–98), then Prime Minister (1998–99). He opposed American advances towards hegemony and considered quiet and well-informed diplomacy to be the best way to do so.

271 The US Marine strength doubled to ninety thousand. Additional Tomahawk power would arrive on the battleship USS *Missouri* and reserves were called up in anticipation of war.

272 A typically American half-grasp of British nomenclature. In fact, the 'Black Rats', to give them their full title, take their name from the jerboa insignia they wear, still the device used by their successor echelon, 4 Mechanised Brigade.

273 According to the *Washington Post*, quoting State Department, 1,175 British nationals, about 900 Americans, 197 Japanese, 180 Italians and 3,232 Russians were repatriated. A number of Australians, Canadians, Danish, Dutch, Irish and South Koreans were also released.

274 General Sultan al-Jibouri was one of Saddam's trusted commanders. He became Minister of Defence in 1995 and was still in office when captured in Mosul in 2003. He was sentenced to death and opted to be buried in a Tikrit cemetery close to Saddam.

275 *The Guardian* 4 March 1991.

276 *The Times* 16 February 1991.

277 See Amnesty International report (MDE 14/16/90) released on 19 December 1990 but completed by the end of November. Section three deals with the number of Kuwaiti civilians detained. By the time the report was written, AI had been given 875 names of Kuwaiti nationals held in Basra, Mosul and Baghdad prisons, including eleven diplomats who were serving in Iraq before 2 August. It also had the names of 152 men aged between nineteen and fifty whose fate and whereabouts were unknown. The figure of about six hundred still held by Saddam after the 1991 Armistice is a conservative approximation.

278 Dominic Rennie Raab (born 1974 in Buckinghamshire, UK): after undergraduate and graduate studies at Oxford and Cambridge respectively, he qualified as a solicitor and joined the Foreign and Commonwealth Office in 2000. He was elected to the House of Commons in 2010 and has held the seat of Esher and Walton for the Conservatives ever since but with a much-reduced majority. An ardent Brexiteer, he rose swiftly through the ministerial ranks and, on Boris Johnson's election as Tory leader and succession as Prime Minister, was appointed Foreign Secretary and First Secretary of State. In a cabinet reshuffle on 15 September 2021, he was demoted to Secretary of State for Justice but was given the title of Deputy Prime Minister.

279 See Stephen Davis: *Operation Trojan Horse* – Bonnier (2021) p82. With senior Americans in Riyadh to put pressure on King Fahd, Osama bin Laden's offer of one hundred thousand ardent Islamic fighters to face down Saddam was dismissed out of hand by the king's brother and Defence Minister, Prince Sultan.

280 See Sir Michael's article in *The Times* of 19 February 1991.

281 *The Sunday Times* 7 April 1991.

282 ibid.

283 BBC Radio 4 23 April 1991.

284 *The Times* 14 April 1991. The value of English as a mother tongue for British diplomacy should never be underestimated. Many is the time the author

has witnessed difficult issues being drafted away by British ambassadors with a superior grasp of the English language. It is a major argument in the UK's defence against any attempt to oust her as a permanent member of the UNSC.

285 Cuba opposed and Yemen and Ecuador abstained.

286 Hans Blix: *Disarming Iraq* – Bloomsbury (2004) p21.

287 ibid 16 July 1991.

288 Barzan Ibrahim Hassan al-Tikriti (born 1951 Tikrit, executed 2007): a former head of the feared Iraqi Mukhabarat (DGI) who had first been appointed to Geneva in 1989. There he ran a large portion of Saddam's European intelligence network and managed the accounts of the Iraqi leader's overseas fortune.

289 ibid 12 October 1994.

290 ibid 17 October 1994.

291 ibid p30.

292 *The Times* 18 January 1995.

293 A second similarly aged aircraft carrier, HMS *Illustrious*, left Portsmouth on 19 January 1998, bound for Gibraltar. While steaming through the Mediterranean, she was hurriedly supplied with thermal imagers and laser-guided bombs. All last-minute.

294 Richard William Butler (born 1942): entered the Australian Department of External Affairs in 1965 and resigned in 1975 to become Principal Private Secretary to the leader of the opposition, the feisty Gough Whitlam. He returned to the DEA in 1983 when he was appointed Australia's Permanent Representative on Disarmament at Geneva. Following postings in South-East Asia, principally concerned with a peace settlement in Cambodia, he served as ambassador to the UN from 1992 to 1997. His appointment to UNSCOM was after his Foreign Minister, Alexander Downer, had fired him for failing to win his country a seat on the Security Council. After the invasion of Iraq, he returned to Australia to become Governor of Tasmania in October 2003. In less than a year, his strong republican views and repeated spats with the Tasmanian premier forced his resignation.

295 On 29 September 1998 Ritter told the BBC that the US/UK governments only wanted the 'illusion of disarmament' to persist.

296 *London Times* 27 October 1998.

297 On 3 November, Clinton had to pay off Paula Jones with a cheque for

$850,000.

298 The *London Times* cartoon of 17 November captured the absurdity of the situation: Colonel Clinton and Sergeant Blair were depicted riding with sabres waving and back-to-front on horses galloping away from Iraq.

299 *The Guardian* 6 February 1999.

300 *Sunday Times* 30 September 2001.

301 Hansard 24 September 2002.

302 *The Sun* 19 September 2002.

303 The author received a call on 9 April from one of his Iraqi interlocutors thanking him profusely for having 'freed my country'.

304 BBC: 25 March 2009.

305 The Soviet Union invaded northern Afghanistan on Christmas Eve 1979 and fought a nine-year guerrilla war against several Islamic groups, collectively known as the *mujahedeen*. The latter outfought the might of the Soviet forces arrayed against them and forced Moscow to abandon its campaign. US and UK intelligence and weapons supply had played no small part in the Soviet defeat. The last Russian troops left Afghanistan on 15 February 1989.

306 The Taliban (*students* or *seekers*) is an Islamic fundamentalist movement which formed a totalitarian government, known as the Islamic Emirate of Afghanistan, in 1996. Centred on Pashtun areas of southern and eastern Afghanistan around Kandahar, it moved the capital there and, by 2001, held about three-quarters of the country. In areas it controlled it enforced a strict interpretation of Islamic law (*Sharia*). Its leader and co-founder was Mohammed Omar Mujahid (born 1960) until his death on 23 April 2013 from tuberculosis.

307 Sayyid Rashid Rida (1865–1935), born in Turkish Lebanon and died in Cairo. Best known for his work *Tafsir al-Manar* in which he described the Caliphate or Grand Imamate organised on his interpretation of the principles ordained in the Qur'an and Sharia law. An early follower of the Salafi School of Islamic thought which argued for a return to the practices of the first three generations of Islam in the sixth century.

308 Sir Michael Howard in his address to the Royal United Services Institute on 30 October 2001. He added that, "for most Americans, it must be said that Islam remains one vast terra incognita – and one, like all such blank areas on medieval maps, inhabited very largely by dragons."

309 Mullah Abdul Salam Zaheef (born 1968 in Kandahar): he was Afghan

ambassador to Pakistan until he was detained there in 2001 and handed over to the Americans, who held him first at Bagram and then took him to Guantanamo Bay, from where he was released in 2005. He was deleted from the UN's list of terrorists and was probably never actively engaged in violent activities. He is thought to have been on the moderate wing of the Taliban and was early to call for negotiation and the withdrawal of US forces.

310 Out of a population of sixteen million, Afghanistan had an army of fifty thousand, mostly conscripts equipped with ageing Soviet military vehicles and an air force of five thousand, again with out-of-date aircraft. Any resistance to an invasion and its aftermath was always going to come from far more numerous mujahedin, armed mostly by the West or from captured Soviet equipment. In 1986, external military aid from the West and allied Islamic states amounted to $500 million.

311 Sir Michael Eliot Howard OM CH CBE MC FBA FRHistS (1922–2019): formerly Chichele Professor of the History of War, Oxford; Honorary Fellow of All Souls College; Regius Professor of Modern History; and founder of King's College, London, Department of War Studies. He co-founded the International Institute of Strategic Studies in 1958 with Alastair Buchan. The author was most fortunate to come under his tutorial supervision (1962–64) at King's.

312 The four were usually the district commissioner, judge, police chief and head of forestry. They did not see one another from one end of the year to the next since they were itinerant. Between Christmas and the New Year, they would meet up and discuss policy for the next twelve months. Many were in love with the country they served – India.

313 Individual states lost the following fatalities: USA 2,355; UK 456; Canada 157; France 88; Germany 62; Italy 53; Poland 44; Denmark 43; Australia 41; Spain 35; Georgia 32; Romania 26; Netherlands 25; Turkey 15; Czech Republic 14; New Zealand 10; Norway 10; Estonia 9; Hungary 7; Sweden 5; Latvia 4; Slovakia 3; Finland, Portugal and South Korea 2 each; and Albania, Belgium, Bulgaria, Croatia, Lithuania and Montenegro 1 each. These figures do not include the large number of seriously wounded, the many mental health problems or casualties sustained during transportation to and from theatre.

INDEX

The suffix 'n' refers to an endnote.